The Life Of St. Francis Xavier : Evangelist, Explorer, Mystic

Stewart, Edith Anne, Macdonald, David

THE LIFE OF ST. FRANCIS XAVIER

By the same Author

————

PILGRIMAGE AND BATTLE

A Volume of Poems

Crown 8vo, gilt
3s. 6d. net

————

HEADLEY BROS.
PUBLISHERS, LTD.
Kingsway House, W.C.

P. Franciscus Xauerius, qui primus ex Societate
Iesu fidem in Indiam inuexit. Obijt an! 1552. Decemb. 2.
Hieronymus Wierx fecit et exc.

CHRISTE sat est, clamas: exundant vbere casti
  Pectora: nec tantum mens capit arcta Deum.
Pande sinus, FRANCISCE Pater, totum accipe
  numen.
  In quos effundas, quod superabit, erunt.

PORTRAIT OF ST. FRANCIS XAVIER

(From the first Latin edition of Tursellinus' Life)

THE LIFE OF
ST. FRANCIS XAVIER
Evangelist, Explorer, Mystic

BY

EDITH ANNE STEWART

With Translations from his Letters by

DAVID MACDONALD, B.D.

HEADLEY BROS. PUBLISHERS, LTD.
KINGSWAY HOUSE, KINGSWAY, W.C.
MCMXVII

FENECIDOS los trabaios y acabados de pasar los peligros, no sabe el hombre contar ny escreuir lo que por él passó al tiempo que estaua en ellos, quedando una memoria imprimida de lo pasado, para no cansar de seruir á tan buen Señor, así en lo presente como en lo porvenir, esperando en el Señor, cuyas misericordias no tienen fin, que le dará fuerças para lo seruir —FRANCISCO DE XAVIER

Mementote præpositorum vestrorum, qui vobis locuti sunt verbum Dei : quorum intuentes exitum conversationis, imitamini fidem. Jesus Christus heri, et hodie : ipse et in secula —HEB XIII 7-8.

TO
MY FATHER
AND
MOTHER

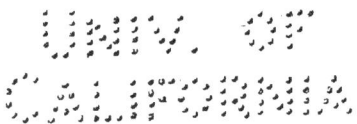
PREFACE

THE *Lives* of St. Francis Xavier fall into three main classes—the erudite, the popular, and the pious. An addition to the first or third of these groups would have been beyond the capacity of the present writer, even had they not already had abundant attention from the devout and the scholarly. But since the original Letters and documents have been printed no popular Life of the Saint has appeared in England. The present work is an attempt to fill that blank.

In studying the life of Xavier we turn first of all to his Letters. Until a few years ago these were only accessible in MS. or in very poor Latin versions, or in translations based on these Latin versions. But between 1899 and 1914 the Society of Jesus in Madrid published all the existing Letters and writings in their original forms, together with numerous other relative letters and documents, and the two oldest and most valuable *Lives*, Teixeira's and Valignano's, until then only available in MS. This great collection, covering about 2,000 pages, is called the *Monumenta Xaveriana*, and is a part of the *Monumenta Historica Societatis Jesu*.

A list of subsidiary sources will be found in the Bibliography on p. 345.

In an age that for all but the very wise and the very foolish is an age of moral and mental bewilderment, it is possible to understand why so many men and women are scanning the faces of the saints for help and comfort and light. There every disease of faith finds, by universal consent, some gift of restoration and healing. For in all these sicknesses there is present a blindness to the moral beauty and grandeur of man, and the contemplation of the lives of the saints, and the inevitable sense of communion with them which follows, restore again to the lonely mind and heart the far-off morning hours when it was no startling thing to catch a glimpse of some passing angel's face. And more than that, this contemplative communion recalls us to the very Holy of Holies itself: " For both He that sanctifieth and they that are sanctified are all of one."

How often, in this age of ecclesiastical division and so-called "religious" strife, have we found comfort in the knowledge that the Church Invisible is greater than the churches which are seen, and that we have sat at the table of the Lord, if not with the Archbishop of Canterbury, yet with Ignatius of Antioch; if not with the Pope at Rome, yet with Francis of Assisi; if not in the City Temple, yet in the Temple of a lovelier city, not made with hands, eternal in the heavens! There we have drunk of the fruit of the vine in a company which our own love and reverence are sufficient for ever to unite in our hearts.

And both the homeliness and the wonder of this feast are enhanced by every fragment of our knowledge of how those saints and prophets and heroes spent their days and nights when they lived upon this planet. We wish to know the simple and small details of their everyday life, just as lovers, when they meet again, ask each other how they spent each moment of the time of absence.

This is a healthy and a helpful curiosity, and certainly its satisfaction does not lead to pride. The lives of the saints are strangely disconcerting; their gifts were so like our own. Our failure lies, we learn, in a lack of receptiveness rather than in a lack of opportunity. A man's greatness does not depend on his circumstances, but on the way in which he reacts to circumstance.

In mediæval times the glory of the Church was ingathered in the aureoles of her saints; in the fourteenth and fifteenth centuries it flamed from the swords of her reformers. In those days, outside Italy at least, to be a great man and to be a reformer were almost synonymous terms. The sickness of religion and morals was so widespread that in every department of life the specialist could trace a mischief and prescribe a cure.

Philosophers blamed scholasticism, and cried out for a return to the Early Fathers, or for a frank acceptance of the New Learning.

Lawyers, fresh from the perusal of Theodosius and Justinian, preached the separation of ecclesiastical and civil law.

Statesmen saw that the modern ideal of national unity and independence could never exist alongside of the despotism of a degenerate Papacy. Some of them, such as Cranmer and a number of the German princes, not only refused to tolerate a State controlled by the Church, but established a Church in subordination to the State.

Ecclesiastics provided councils and inquisitions, re-established monastic discipline, and founded schools of theology.

But Francis Xavier was next-of-kin to none of these : the name of reformer sits ill on him. To find his fellows we must look southwards across the Alps, to the painters of the Italian Renascence. In this, indeed, he was one with the reformers—his permanent contribution is one of character rather than of thought, but he has a still deeper affinity with the artists. For his genius, like theirs, was a happy and positive one. He was intoxicated with the beauty of holiness. There is a colour, a tender grace, a naïve childlikeness about his life that we associate with the angels of Fra Angelico or the bright figures of Botticelli. It was not his to pull down and destroy ; he found it difficult even to reprimand. We cannot picture him chasing the money-changers out of the Temple with a knotted cord.

Had he been confronted by all the knaves of Europe in a body, he would, with that glowing and smiling countenance which the old biographers delight to speak of, have rendered thanks for so great an opportunity, and instantly have begun preaching to them "the Law of Christ our Lord." One feels that he simply took for granted that every man was a desperate sinner like himself, and as willing as himself to find and to serve God. To him the only renascence was that of the individual soul. He was therefore peculiarly aloof from the circumstances of his time. Had Ignatius Loyola never come to Paris, it is likely that the "heretics" from whom, Xavier afterwards wrote, he had been "delivered" would have annexed him to Protestantism. They, like Loyola, had appealed to him by a great enthusiasm. But Xavier as a Protestant would not have been very different from Xavier of the Company of the Name of Jesus. The greatest of Loyola's disciples was the least of the Jesuits. At home or abroad, within the visible Church or without it, Francis, after his conversion, knew nothing but Christ and Him crucified, and could do nothing but preach Him to the Gentiles.

He had in him the makings of an arch-dilettante, versatile, brilliant, so much all things to all men that what for other people would have been acting was to him the only sincerity ; he was interested in life, in men, and in things to an extent that would have absorbed all the energies of a lesser man. But he—and this sets the seal on his genius—directed all this versatility and wealth of self-giving to one single goal ; there seems hardly a moment of his experience or an iota of his knowledge that is not used, in his favourite phrases, " to increase our holy faith " or " to gain much fruit of souls."

The life of Francis was dominated by the greatest of all passions, the passion for human souls ; in him we see that ardour burning with a splendour rare even among the saints. This is his greatest claim to Christliness, that he spent his life in seeking to save those that were lost.

The name of the translator of the Letters is on the title-page. But that is not enough : I blush to think what the rest of the book would have been without his patient and continual aid. He has come to the rescue in every chapter, almost, I might say, on every page. To him, and to the Rev. Hugh Watt, B.D., of Bearsden, who has read the proofs and given much valuable help and advice, I am quite hopelessly indebted.

E. A. S.

CONTENTS

CHAPTER I

MAKERS OF SPAIN

Spanish independence of Rome—reasons for this independence—Santiago—
Dominic—Raymond Lull—opposing influences in the Spanish renascence—
Spanish Inquisition—the scope of the Catholic Reaction—work of Cardinal
Ximenes—Spanish religious genius focussed in the Society of Jesus

CHAPTER II

CHILDHOOD AND BOYHOOD
(1506-1525)

Traditions of Christian family life upheld during the Renascence, both in Italy
and in Spain—history of the family of Xavier—the castle of Xavier—birth
of Francis—the troubles of Navarre—death of Francis' father—early
surroundings of the Saint—demolishment of the keep—poverty of the
family—siege of Pampeluna—Loyola and the brothers of Francis—he
prepares for Paris

CHAPTER III

AT THE COLLEGE OF STE. BARBE
(1525-1529)

Decline of the university far advanced in 1525—Fabrian Protestantism pre-
cedes Lutheranism and Calvinism in Paris—Jacques Le Fèvre d'Etaples
—a letter to Calvin—early days of Francis in Paris—the college of Ste.
Barbe—Francis enrols as a student in arts—value of university degrees
at that time—Principal Gouvea—fellow-students and professors—Peter
Faber—Mathurin Cordier—George Buchanan—Erasmus—Calvin—Noel
Beda—letter from a priest at Meliapor about the student days—friendship with the Lutherans—love of dress—extravagance—protests from
home—letter from Xavier's sister Madeline—death of his mother—his
brothers marry

CHAPTER IV

THE FOUNDATION OF THE ORDER
(1528-1534)

Ignatius Loyola comes to Paris—his earlier life—he shares a room in Ste. Barbe
with Peter Faber and Xavier—religious strife increases—Loyola and *La
Salle*—Xavier takes his arts degree—appointed Professor at Beauvais
college—death of his sister Madeline—critical months—Faber becomes
Loyola's first disciple—Xavier his second—the Company begins to take
shape—the dedication at Montmartre—Francis receives the Spiritual
Exercises

CONTENTS

LIST OF ILLUSTRATIONS

CHAPTER I

MAKERS OF SPAIN

GRADUALLY, as they began to recover from the Moorish invasions of the eighth century, the feudal lords of Spain re-emerged from their northern fastnesses, and pressed their old conquerors ever farther and farther south, each leader establishing himself as petty king over the particular area which he had captured. In 1481 all Spain, except Navarre and Granada, was united by the marriage of Ferdinand and Isabella, but nothing seemed so much to cement the national unity and establish the monarchy as the successful culmination of the seven hundred years' war against the Moors by the seizure of Granada in 1492 and their final ejection from Spain. From that hour she leapt swiftly forward to her short-lived but dazzling European supremacy.

The ground had indeed been well prepared, for she had kept herself clean and strong throughout the " dark ages " by her unwavering crusade against the infidels, and by a united and national Catholicism which, although loyal in attachment to Rome, was never subservient. From very early times she had resented any over-interference on the part of the Roman Curia. And long before the German Reformation had begun to take shape the Spanish Cortes had been asserting in every way within their power their own legal independence of Rome, and the obligation of the clergy to submit to civil law.

The ordinances of their Kings were used, time after time, to counteract the influence of harmful papal Bulls, and to prevent the interference of Italian ecclesiastics in the affairs of the Spanish church. In the end of the fifteenth century the Spanish Bishops had been reduced to a state of dependence on the Crown; all exercise of ecclesiastical authority was carefully watched; the extent of ecclesiastical jurisdiction was specifically limited, and clerical courts were made to feel their dependence on the secular tribunals. The Crown wrung from the Papacy the right to see that piety and a zeal for religion were to be indispensable qualifications for clerical promotion.*

* T. M. Lindsay, *Hist. of the Reformation*, vol. ii. p. 489.

B

This national attitude of independence towards the Papacy was also nourished in another very different way. There was no other European people in which certain forms of mysticism played such a great part in religious life as in Spain. Spain was, indeed, the main channel through which Oriental mysticism penetrated into the Church. And to a mystic a priest is always more or less superfluous.

But if the Spanish independence had here something akin to Protestantism, the strain was only marked enough to lend colour and vitality, when the time came, to a movement which was essentially Catholic. The Spanish champions of the Church in distress did all the better service to her because they served her with their eyes open to her weakness and her need. Loyola begged his followers always to show great respect to the established Church, and the deliberate and anxious expression of this advice betrays his knowledge of the Church's shortcomings and his determination to be faithful to her in spite of them. This union of aloofness and chivalry is a strong trait both of Loyola's character and of the national religious genius.

The independence of the Spanish Catholics really sprang from their profound faithfulness to Catholic principles. For while between Rome and other European nations there had existed, throughout the Middle Ages, much of the relationship of servant to master, the Spaniards, because of their piety and the good services which they had rendered Christendom in their warfare against the Moors, enjoyed many of the rights and privileges of children in their father's house.

One cannot look back upon the mediæval history of Spain without being struck by the important place in it which was held by the national hero and saint, Santiago (Saint James), the Son of Thunder.

The legend runs that the disciples of the earliest of the Apostolic martyrs removed his body from its tomb in Jerusalem and bore it to Isia Flavia in north-west Spain. It was discovered there in the ninth century and removed to Compostela.* And throughout his unending wars against the infidels the military imagination of the Spaniard saw in Santiago no gentle intercessory saint, but an heroic, titanic

* The name Compostela is apparently a corruption of Giacomo Postolo = ad Jacobum Apostolum.

figure, riding upon the thunder clouds which hang over the fields of battle, on his white horse, bringing victory to the hosts underneath who called upon his name.

There is probably no other saint or hero in Europe who has been so identified in the minds of the people with national and spiritual ideals, nor has there been any shrine in Europe, except St. Peter's, so popular as the shrine of Santiago at Compostela. And the pilgrims to this western shrine were exempt, so runs the legend, from all perils by land or water, for the son of Zebedee had power from God to keep them.

Had it not been for the roads which run from every part of the continent to Compostela, the Peninsula would for centuries have been almost isolated from western Europe. Even as it was, Spain was far more in touch with North Africa, throughout the Middle Ages, than with Europe, and for every man that crossed the Pyrenees a hundred must have crossed the Straits.

Like all the great mythical or semi-mythical figures, Santiago is probably rather the poetic vehicle and explanation of certain national beliefs and ideals than the originator of them. Round the shrine of this saint the Spaniards gradually planted all their worthiest dreams and aims. Spanish pride, for example, was in a very true sense a high virtue. And the Spaniard gave as a gracious reason for this the fact that the legendary founder of the Spanish Church and the hero of the race was no less a personage than one of the twelve Apostles of Christ and the first of the martyrs. There was often fear in Rome that this cult of Santiago should lead its votaries away from their first love. Pope Gregory VII. thought it his duty to cut St. James rather severely, and to remind the Spaniards that it was St. Paul who had first brought them the Gospel, and that this fact ought to bind them more strongly to Rome than to Compostela. But his warning fell on heedless ears. The greatest religious poet of Spain, Luis Ponce de Leon, sings of St. James as the very author and inspirer of all Spanish greatness. And he only expressed what others believed. This pride, moreover, took for granted the reverence and devotion of all Europe towards the Saint, and looked upon every offer of service from foreign countries in the wars against the Moors as natural tributes, at the same time regarding outside help as superfluous, and ignoring the part

B2

which crusaders from the North and East often took in conquering the enemy. Beneath the banner of Santiago Spain could never fail, and it was a kindly condescension rather than an acknowledgment of weakness which allowed the knights of France and Italy and Germany, and even of England and Scotland, to share in those indubitable victories.

Besides those elements of pride and of religious enthusiasm the Spanish character is full of traits, or of something far stronger than mere traits, which it acquired through its long association with Jews and Moors. For though these two races kept very much apart from the Spanish people and from one another, especially among the preponderating middle and lower classes, they could not fail in the course of centuries to leave their indelible mark. "The whole development of Spanish culture in the Middle Ages, its originality, its influence on other nations, is based upon this inter-relationship between East and West." *

These qualities of military pride, of religious enthusiasm, of half-Oriental passion and mysticism, developing along their highest lines and among the highest spirits, contributed more than anything else in Europe to all that was best in the Catholic Revival. Long before the Reformation even, they had found expression in men like St. Dominic and Raymond Lull.

Of Dominic less is known than historians tell us, but even that little clearly illustrates the difference between Spanish and Italian saintship, and in many points his character is far more like that of St. Francis Xavier than that of his great contemporary, St. Francis of Assisi. Like Xavier, Dominic combined intense sensitiveness of character and tenderness towards individuals with a fiery ardour for the Faith which sometimes tolerated, or even countenanced, "religious" cruelty, while holding aloof from any personal share in it. For Dominic did not, as is often imagined, found the Inquisition; nor does it appear that he persecuted the Albigenses, though he spared no pains in trying to convert them—a very different matter. Yet his intimate friend, Folco of Marseilles, the Bishop of Toulouse (1205–1231), treated them with notorious cruelty.

Like Xavier again, and unlike most of the Italian saints,

* E. Gothein, *Ignatius von Loyola und die Gegenreformation*, p. 23.

Dominic was a man of learning and intellectual power. Like Xavier, he was a lover of poverty,* but that was not for either of them the central passion of life. That passion, for them both, was to teach and to convert.

In his early thirties—always critical and significant years for a man of genius—Dominic went to France with his bishop to arrange a royal marriage, and he saw Languedoc. On the return journey, Rome and Montpellier had further tales to tell. He had seen the Church as a bride torn from her husband, and her children naked, and starved, and desolate. To the good bishop, too, the journey had been a revelation, and at Montpellier he dismissed all his train excepting only Dominic, and resolved henceforth to live in simplicity. In his early childhood, Dante tells us, the little Dominic had often been found by his nurse, escaped from his cot, and upon his knees in prayer. "And soon," the poet goes on, leaping lightly over those three decades, "he became a mighty teacher." He was entirely disinterested, not seeking to gain wealth or position for himself, but only to give light to others. Cold and fierce, we have been told, he was; but the few most reliable fragments of his biography which remain tell another tale. All men desire most that which lies deepest in their own hearts, and Dominic's chief prayer was for the gift of love. Once, seeing a captive in distress, he offered his own body in exchange to free him; again, seeing those around him hungry, he went and sold his precious books that they might have bread. Dante places him along with Francis of Assisi as one of the two champions chosen by God for His soldiery in peril, a soldiery "laggard, fearsome, and thin-ranked," and it was at their doing and saying that the "straggling squadron gathered itself together again."†

Of Raymond Lull far too little is popularly known. And although he lived more than two hundred and fifty years earlier than Francis Xavier, there are many points of resemblance between the two. For this reason, and also because in Lull we have the apotheosis of the half-Eastern Spanish genius of the Middle Ages, and the very greatest precursor of the religious revival of the fifteenth and sixteenth

* Well did he show himself a messenger and a familiar of Christ,
For the first love made manifest in him
Was to the first counsel that Christ gave.
Paradiso, xii. 73.

† *Paradiso*, xii. 38 *seq.*

centuries, we shall devote a few pages to the story of his life.

Raymond Lull was born at Palma, in Majorca, about 1235. In his boyhood he refused a scholastic education, and at the age of thirty he was a gay and licentious officer ("*gransenescal*") at the court of Aragon. His conversion, like that of so many of the saints, was sudden and dramatic. He is said to have seen a vision of Christ upon the Cross, and heard the words " O Raymond Lull, from henceforth follow thou Me," and from that hour his whole life was given up to God.*

He resolved to devote himself to the conversion of the Moslems. He was ill-educated, had no powers of argument and no knowledge of the Arabic tongues. But conversion expressed itself in him, as in Loyola after him, by a colossal reinforcement of will power. He resolved to write a book which would convince the infidels of the truth of Christianity. He made a solemn vow to God, dedicating to Him not only himself, but his wife and children, and all his earthly goods except a small piece of land upon which they could live, and to which he could retire for periods of study and writing. Then, after visiting Compostela and praying at the shrine of Santiago, he went to the university of Palma, where, in absolute poverty, he began a course of study which extended over nine or ten years. He learned Arabic from a Saracen slave, who, after nine years' friendship, awakened to the fact that he was serving his own religion ill by teaching this man. He attacked Lull suddenly, and almost had him murdered.

We see him next in his hermitage on Mount Randa, directly inspired, he believed, by God, writing the books which he hoped would convert the infidels. It is difficult for us to grasp how profoundly original this missionary was. Hitherto the Cross had always been held before the Saracens with the sword close behind it; and if Lull put too much faith in the power of logic, he was at least far ahead of those who armed their faith, or rather their unfaith, with a sword. Raymond Lull—and here he resembles Dominic—could not conceive of converting a man's heart to Christ without

---

* His own account of his conversion in *De Miraculis Mundi* is of such a vision five times repeated in a very short space of time. But the passage is one which has been controverted.

first gaining his intellectual assent to Christian principles. God, he reminds his readers, commands us to love Him with all our *mind*. He wanted to reconcile theology and philosophy, and have the resulting system grasped by each individual who accepted the Christian faith. The fact that an Arab held a twofold standard of truth disturbed Lull more than the fact that this Arab was a Mohammedan. This identification of theology with philosophy went beyond the bounds of scholastic propriety, and he was therefore never canonised. For him there was no distinction between faith and reason, nor between natural and supernatural truth. " Relying on the grace of God," he says, " I intend to prove the Articles of Faith by convincing reasons." Thus he gets his title, the Illuminated Doctor. But he was no mere writer of books ; and though he published over three hundred separate writings, his other activities would have filled a score of normally industrious lives.

In 1276 he founded a school of Oriental languages in Majorca. There, and in Paris, he lectured and taught, and in the midst of all this work he tried again and again, by many ways and means, to found chairs of Oriental languages at the various European universities. He was baffled in this endeavour again and again, and at last resolved himself to go and preach the Gospel in Africa. When he was about to sail from Genoa his imagination painted the terrors of the unknown to him in such vivid colours that he allowed the ship to sail without him. He was immediately overcome with remorse, and soon found his way on board another ship. But his friends began to fear for him, and came and dragged him back. His shame now made him very ill. He could not move, and his friends thought him dying, and when he expressed a desire to go to Africa they consented with indifference, for they thought his days, in any case, were numbered. But no sooner had he set sail than health and strength came back. He entered Tunis, not as an evangelist, but as a wandering scholar, eager to talk with the Arabs, and expressing himself as ready to be converted to their faith if he could but be persuaded of its truth. But he could not keep the light within him hid, and he was soon put into prison and condemned to die. Ultimately he was banished with a warning that if he ever came back he would be stoned to death. He returned to the writing of books, to his lectures, and, above all, to the attempt to awaken some sort of missionary interest in the Moors. He was continually met by failure, and once more he determined to spend his own time in preaching the Gospel to the infidels, and for this purpose he withdrew to his native Majorca, and there " brought innumerable Saracens into the way of salvation." Later he went to Cyprus, to " Armenia," and possibly to England, and then he returned to Africa, but once more, after being stoned and imprisoned for six months in a foul dungeon, he was banished. The vessel upon which he was sent away was wrecked off the coast of Pisa, and he escaped with one companion, naked and exhausted. He was by this time seventy years old. The next ten years of his life were largely occupied in combating the heresies of Averroism.

At last, at the Council of Vienne in 1311–12, he succeeded in getting an edict passed which ordained that there should be schools of Hebrew and Greek, and Arabic and Chaldean, in various universities throughout Europe, including Oxford. Had he done nothing else but this, Lull would have been entitled to enduring fame. Finally, in his eightieth year, the veteran returned to Africa to make his last " sweet and reasonable " appeal for Christ, and there, outside the walls of Bugia, on the shore of that sea he had so often crossed in his apostolic missions, he was stoned and battered to death.

Helfferich calls him the most remarkable figure of the Middle Ages.* He certainly was one of the most remarkable men that Spain ever produced.

The story of his outward life is that of a hero and a martyr. His writings reveal the spirit which lay at the source of all he did:

" He who loves not lives not. He who lives by the Life cannot die."

" He who gives God can give nothing more."

" The image of the crucified Christ is found much rather in men who imitate Him in their daily walk than in the crucifix made of wood."

" Elevate thy knowledge and thy love will be elevated. Heaven is not so lofty as the love of a holy man. The more thou wilt labour to rise upward, the more thou wilt rise upward."

* H. Helfferich, *Raymon Lull und die Anfänge der Catalonischer Literatur*, 1858.

" He who would find Thee, O Lord, let him go forth to seek Thee in love, loyalty, devotion, faith, hope, justice, mercy, and truth ; for in every place where these are, there art Thou." *

But the same qualities which went to the formation of such a great character as Raymond Lull showed themselves capable of development along more sinister lines. And a century or two later, while Cardinal Ximenes, under the guidance and inspiration of Isabella the Catholic, was doing the great work which we shall presently study in more detail; while Santa Teresa was preparing to cleanse the nunneries, and Ignatius Loyola was founding the Order of Jesus, hordes of vicious and unscrupulous pirates and adventurers were coming and going from Spain and Portugal to the newly discovered lands, drunk all the time with the lust of gold and of pleasure ; the terrific machinery of the Inquisition was being set in order, and the boys were at school who were to turn the devout and high-minded little Company of Jesus into a pack of unscrupulous Jesuits.

Thus at the very time when Spain was the greatest power in the world we can detect the ominous auguries of her downfall. For, however immediately successful Spanish enterprise abroad might appear, and however effective the weapons of the Inquisition proved at the moment to be, no national greatness could survive the state of affairs which these activities revealed.

Spain had been accustomed to a religious outlook upon life. All she ever did was in the name of religion ; but what she began by doing sincerely she ended by doing mechanically. She began by giving up everything in order to vindicate the cause of the Cross against that of the Crescent. She ended by holding the Cross in the van of her own causes, and deluding herself into believing that the presence of the sacred symbol made all things holy. About 1455 we read that

the Iffante licensed an expedition consisting of six caravels, the command being given to Lanzarote, receiver of the royal customs at Lagos, and presented each with a banner emblazoned with the cross of the Order of Christ to be hoisted as its flag. Lanzarote and his companions raided the coast as far as Cape Branco, shouting " Santiago ! San Jorge ! Portugal ! " as their war-cry, and ruthlessly slaying all who resisted, whether

* See *Raymond Lull*, by W. T. A. Barber.

men, women, or children.   They brought back to Lagos no fewer than 235 captives; the receiver of customs was raised by the Iffante to the rank of knight, and the wretched captives were sold and dispersed throughout the kingdom.   Large tracts, both of Portugal and of Spain, remained waste or half-cultivated as a result of the Moorish wars: and the grantees of these lands eagerly purchased the human chattels now imported in increasing numbers.*   .

And the same age which produced these blasphemous pirates produced the Spanish Inquisition.   This, as distinct from the earlier mediæval Episcopal and Papal Inquisitions, did not emerge till towards the end of the fifteenth century, during the reign of the Catholic sovereigns Ferdinand and Isabella.

And in the Inquisition, as in the early voyages of discovery and adventure, we find the Spaniards taking the name of religion in vain.   While on the African coast the slave-raiders were holding the Cross before them as they ravaged the native villages, the same symbol was affixed by the Holy Office to the weapons of torture and death which made the Castilian throne secure and popular, and brought, through fines and confiscations, a continual stream of gold into the royal treasuries. For the Inquisition in Spain was, strange as it may appear, a tremendously popular affair.   "Since it was established," says the Italian historian Caraccioli, "Ferdinand reigned more peacefully, though whether it helped the country or not remains an open question." †   It was popular chiefly because it spelt ruin and confusion to the Jewish population. These were at that time far more deeply hated than the Moors, who were but little affected by the Inquisition.

The aristocracy and the poorer people were curiously divided against one another at this time by their relations to the New Christians.   While the former freely intermarried with those converted Jews, and used their influence to have their Jewish friends put into high ecclesiastical and political positions, the latter disdained all intermarriage; and while on the one hand a famous Jewish bishop was acclaimed as a collateral descendant of the Holy Virgin, on the other hand the popular preachers, with no uncertain voice, were giving

* *Cambridge Mod Hist* , vol. i., " The Renaissance," p. 14.
† Tr. Caraccioli, *De inquisitione Neapolitana Muratori S S. rerr. Ital. XX.*, quoted by Gothein, *op. cit.*, p. 34.

expression to the indignation of the people at the appointment of these Semitic shepherds and rulers.

Torquemada was the first and one of the most notorious of the Spanish Inquisitors-General. He had been the confessor of Isabella, and it was he who instigated the Catholic* sovereigns to apply for the Papal authority which by 1483 gave to the Spanish Inquisition such a unique power. It is impossible to explain Torquemada's devilries on any other ground than that of madness, and in some mysterious way, of which this outburst of ferocity is not the only example, this kind of madness seems to infect weaker characters who come under the influence of the leader. Although statistics of the burnings and imprisonments are various and contradictory, and modern investigation has been unable as yet to produce an unchallengeable estimate, it is manifest from every source that the number of those who suffered reaches a simply appalling figure.†

The inquisitors . . . travelled from town to town, attended by guards and notaries public. Their expenses were defrayed by taxes laid on the towns and districts through which they passed. Spies and informers, guaranteed State protection, brought forward their information. The Court was opened: witnesses were examined, and the accused were acquitted or found guilty. The sentence was pronounced; the secular assessor gave a formal assent; and the accused was handed over to the civil authority for punishment. When Torquemada reorganised the Spanish Inquisition, a series of rules were framed for its procedure which enforced secrecy to the extent of depriving the accused of any rational means of defence; which elaborated the judicial method so as to leave no loophole even for those who expressed a wish to recant, and which multiplied the charges under which suspected heretics, even after death, might be treated as impenitent and their property confiscated. The Spanish Inquisition differed from the papal in its close relationship to the civil authorities, its secrecy, its relentlessness, and its exclusion of Bishops from even a nominal participation in its work. Thus organised it became a terrible curse to unhappy Spain.‡

But let us turn now to the brighter side of the Catholic Revival in the Peninsula, and see how the spirit of the age

* The title of " Catholic " was not conferred on the sovereigns till 1494-5.
† See H. C. Lea, *History of the Inquisition in Spain*, 1906, vol. iv. p. 525.
‡ T. M. Lindsay, *op. cit.*, vol. ii. p. 599.

manifested itself in the loftiest Spanish minds. The Spanish Reformation under Cardinal Ximenes, because it was contemporaneous with the German Reformation rather than a reply to it, really preceded the Counter-Reformation. For in considering this movement we must recognise its limits. The Counter-Reformation was a movement within the Establishment, and only included those who were first and last loyal to Rome, those who looked for a reformation not of dogma, but of discipline and practice. The term Counter-Reformation cannot, however, include the many movements towards reform, arising from *within* the Church, which had preceded the appearance of Luther. The two main lines of its activity were interdependent. While it aimed at destroying the constructive work of the Protestant reformers, it at the same time aimed at destroying the morbid growths which had sucked away all strength and dignity from the body of the mediæval Church. The Counter-Reformers were reactionaries. They admitted no new revelation, no possibility of having outgrown the teaching of the Fathers. Their task was to lead priests and people back to the uncorrupted ideals of mediæval Christendom. Thus the term Catholic Revival, or Catholic Reaction, is more accurate than Counter-Reformation. It is impossible, in any real sense, to have a reformation within the Roman Church. To say this is in no way to deny the enormous significance of the Revival. "The Catholicism of to-day rests upon the Counter-Reformation of the sixteenth century. None of the changes which it has since then undergone have penetrated below the surface of things ; or if they have had any significance, it has been because they have been a carrying out of the programme then laid down."*

The programme had in it a healthy democratic element. For this Cardinal Mendoza must get some credit. One of his earliest dicta was that if the religious life of the country were to be quickened, the grandees must be kept from episcopal power. Mendoza, aristocrat though he was, knew and trusted the power of the people. It was he, probably more than anyone, who made a great career possible for Cardinal Ximenes ; and Ximenes was before all things a man of the people. "Das wusste und sah man," says Gothein, " dass er ein Mann aus einem Gusse war."

* E. Gothein, *Ignatius von Loyola und die Gegenreformation*, p. 1.

Ximenes' youth was a stormy one. When he was studying in Rome, Sixtus IV. promised him the first vacant benefice in his native province of New Castile. So when, in 1473, Useda fell vacant he produced an " expective " letter from the Pope, which he had long treasured, and claimed the benefice. The affair is a typical illustration of the relations between Spain and the Vatican, for the Archbishop of Toledo, annoyed with the Pope for assuming control over a Spanish benefice, put Ximenes in prison, and there he remained for six years. Four years after his release he resigned his position as grand vicar to Cardinal Gonzalez, and became a Franciscan of the Friary of St. John at Toledo. He accepted the post of confessor to Queen Isabella—a post offered to him through the influence of Mendoza—on the condition that he might continue to live in the Friary. When he was called to be Archbishop of Toledo he refused for six months to take office, and only gave in at last at the Pope's urgent command. As Archbishop he continued to live the simple life of an ideal Franciscan friar. Alexander VI. reprimanded him for neglecting the exterior pomp demanded by his position. But he would never wholly conceal the friar's garb beneath the arch-episcopal robes.

One of his earliest reforms was that of the Franciscan order. His reinforcement of the original rules was so strict that hundreds of the brothers left Spain rather than obey him. Nor did he confine his reform to his own order. In his capacity of Regent he took advantage of the liberty given to the Spanish Crown to confer benefices or to dismiss churchmen from their offices. He visited monasteries and convents, and purified the Church with such vigour and effect that the accusations poured out by the Protestant Reformers against the clergy, and against monastic life in general, hardly applied to Spain at all.

In all his work he was guided and inspired by Queen Isabella, whose motives were far less tinged with political guile than those of her husband.

Besides restoring discipline and virtue within the Church, Ximenes gave great attention to education. It was he who, in 1504, founded the university of Alcalá. About the same time he undertook the publication of the first polyglot Bible, at a cost of £25,000. This version is known as the Complutensian Bible, Complutum being the Latin form of

Alcalá. The Complutensian New Testament was printed, though not published, before Erasmus' edition. Erasmus rushed through his publication to get before Ximenes; his haste may account for the bad text in some places. Ximenes also founded the universities of Toledo and Seville.

Under Ximenes, who was later made Grand Inquisitor, the severity of the Inquisition was modified, and its procedure, to a certain extent at least, made less brutal. He also made his humanitarian influence felt with regard to the slave trade, and in all places under his control he discountenanced the possession of those African captives who were being brought into the country at that time.

Nothing, perhaps, did more to make a union of the German and the Spanish reformers seem at least within the bounds of possibility than the work of this great Cardinal. Before the Diet of Worms (1521) some such union was seriously contemplated, but that Diet revealed a gulf between the two religious parties that could not be crossed—to the Spaniards a General Council was an infallible authority, to Luther it was not, and soon, in Spain at least, every other reform, and all other reformers, were either merged into or overshadowed by the supreme influence of the Society of Jesus. Of this we will speak more fully in later chapters. It is enough at present to remind ourselves that here were ingathered all the most salient features of the Spanish genius—enthusiasm, ardour, a military spirit, Oriental mysticism, astuteness, unsparing devotion. It was this society which, in its unspoiled days, cherished the awakening spirit of Francis Xavier, and which, after he had gone eastward, was to regain a great part of Europe for the Catholic Church.

The long-mustering forces of the Counter-Reformation really took their place and began their great battle under the banner of Pius V., but it is not too much to say that the battle would never have been fought, nor the lost lands recovered, had it not been for the Company of Jesus.

CHAPTER II

CHILDHOOD AND BOYHOOD

(1506—1525)

AMID the dark records of social life in Europe during the
Renascence one lights again and again upon the histories
of men and women in places of honour and position who
upheld the traditions of Christian family life. Even in
Italy such folk existed side by side with those families whose
scandalous histories have given them a perpetual notoriety.
Books such as Domenichi's treatise on household government, and the diary of Landucci and the letters of Ales-
sandro degli Strozzi, to name but a few, may not be such
exciting reading as the histories of the Cenci or the Medici,
but they reveal a side of Renascence life which is apt to be
forgotten.

And in Spain such households were even more common
than in Italy. For there family honour and patriotism,
soldiery and religion, had become inextricably intertwined;
there, if anywhere, the sense of faith had been nourished
on the fields of battle, and the sense of unity strengthened
through generations of isolated warfare against an enemy of
an alien religion.

The great Spanish families—and to one of these Francis
Xavier belonged—had no time to relapse into an effete and
luxurious leisure. The fathers had hardly come home from
doing battle with the Moors before the sons had gone forth to
the ends of the earth on voyages of discovery and exploration.

It is important that we should recognise that the normal
channel for the expression of Spanish piety was the sword,
and the normal sphere of Spanish wit the Church. Many of
Xavier's biographers detect the aureole round his brow as
soon as he chooses not to follow, like his brothers, the profession of arms, but to become a scholar and a churchman.
Surely the balance of piety, though not of enterprise and
courage, in these choosings fell, if anywhere, on the side of the
brothers. Francis' choice was more of the brain, less of the

heart; and it was tinged, we gather from his later letters, with personal ambition.

The history of the family of Francis de Xavier y de Jasso trails far back into the mediæval records of Navarre. At the end of the fourteenth century his father's people quitted their original home in Jasso, and settled in a little village of some fifteen fires which lay in the midst of the vast forests on the southern slopes of the western Pyrenees. As the century wore on the family of Jasso—for they had adopted the name of the place from which they came—grew in importance, and the road to the village of San Juan became worn with the hoofs of couriers' horses as the king's messengers came to and from the Court of Navarre with papers of state. It was because of these long generations of faithful and intelligent service to their kings that at the time when Francis Xavier was born his father's people were recognised as noble.

About 1445 the grandfather of the Saint was made auditor of the royal accounts. He earned popularity at court and married into an old Navarrese family. In 1471 he is spoken of as the king's counsellor, and he has become wealthy and important. The father of Francis was sent to the university of Bologna, and there he took the degree of Doctor of Laws. Immediately afterwards he was employed at the court, and quickly won both respect and affection, as we may see from the following extract from a document in the possession of the Duke of Granada :

June 10th, 1478.

Don Johan (*i.e.*, King John of Navarre) . . . bears in mind the good, continual, and kind services which our illustrious, faithful and well-beloved counsellor and treasurer Don Juan de Jasso has up to the present time rendered, in many ways, to us and to the Crown of Navarre, and continues each day to render with great and intense faithfulness. Estimating that in the future he will do no less, desiring to remunerate and recompense him in some manner, and seeing that we recognise him as worthy of every recompense and favour, we give to him and his heirs for all time the civil jurisdiction of Ydocin, which lies in the valley of Ybargoiti, with all the homicides,* demi-homicides, sixantenas, calonyas,† and civil rights which obtain in the said district of

---

* "*Homicide* was the ancient tribute paid by localities when they refused to give up a murderer" (Lopez and Recalde, *Diccionario*).
† Fines for libel.

HOUSE OF JASSO
ST. JEAN-PIED-DE-PORT

Ydocin which belonged to us. He and his successors shall have the right to create mayors, judges, bailiffs, and other officials in the above jurisdiction, and we desire that the auditors of the royal accounts shall deduct from the amount due to our treasurers and receivers those sums. . . . *

During the childhood of Francis, Ydocin was probably a second home ; to-day there is nothing left of it but a ruined tower.

The Saint's mother came of an older and more aristocratic strain than did his father. The ancestors of Maria de Azpilcueta y Xavier had been for many generations lords of the manor and patrons of the Church, and, above all, distinguished soldiers.† Francis' uncle, the Doctor of Navarre, a noted Spanish authority on Canon Law, says :

Francis' ancestor, Martin de Azpilcueta, was a man whose personal qualities outshone even the glory acquired by his house. These personal qualities, indeed, were his only possession. The family was poor, and he remained almost the sole representative of bygone generations. It was then that Providence united him to the heiress of another house, of equal nobility but greater wealth, the house of Xavier.‡

Such was the stock from which Francis Xavier sprang, but mingled with this brave blood was a yet older and prouder strain. On more than one occasion Xavier declared himself a Basque, as a child he spoke in Basque, and when he lay dying on the island of Sancian all the other tongues that he had acquired were forgotten, and he is said to have murmured his last words in the language of his earliest days.

This aboriginal people were the last race to accept the Roman yoke, and they alone of all the peoples of the South kept their language pure from the romantic influence. It was this invincible tribe which originally held the kingdoms of Navarre and Aragon separate from the rest of Spain.§

* Cros, *Documents Nouveaux*, p. 50.
† Among the forbears of the Azpilcueta was the Duke of Eridon Aznar, who was also the common ancestor of the kings of Navarre and Aragon.
‡ Cros, *Documents Nouveaux*, p. 71.
§ " Let us note then, before going further, that the Apostle of the Indies, although he bore the name of Xavier, is more Jasso and Azpilcueta than he is Xavier or Aznar. The genealogy of the Aznars shows us that they were already supplanted at Xavier by the Artieda, a century before Francis came into the world, a grandson of the Azpilcueta, and himself a supplanter of the

c

Xavier stands far from the beaten track, high up among the rocky moorland passes which lie around the source of the Ebro.   Behind it rise the Pyrenean mountains, beneath its walls the young river Aragon sings, and to the south and east and west lie vineyards and olive gardens and wide pasture lands.   A few miles off is the town of Sanguessa. Half a league from Xavier there still stand the ruins of the ancient monastery of San Salvador de Leyre, and there the bones of the kings of old Navarre are gathered to the dust.

At the beginning of the sixteenth century the castle of Xavier must have been an imposing edifice.   It was surrounded by a moat and by a wall with turrets and battlements.   Outside the drawbridge stood a *castelet*.   The main building was flanked by four towers.   The entrance door, over which the arms of Xavier were blazoned, was guarded by a portcullis, and within this door was another tower. The place was a donjon rather than a home.   Instead of windows there were loopholes, and the inhabitants had to climb from storey to storey by dark and tortuous passages. In the thirteenth century the king of Navarre had presented this fortress to the maternal ancestors of Francis, and the boy, after an old Spanish custom, inherited his mother's name as well as that of his father.

Francis' mother, Maria de Azpilcueta, had married when she was at most fifteen, and probably not more than twelve years old.   She brought to her husband, Doctor Juan de Jasso, the castle of Xavier as part of her dowry, and they made this place their home.

Artieda.   The blood of the Jassos, or of the Echeberria, united to the blood of the Azpilcueta, is then that which flowed in the veins of Francis ; what he inherited from the Aznarez is rather a reflexion of earthly glory, an illustrious connection : and as the Jasso and the Azpilcueta were both pure Basques, the Jasso-Echeberria French-Basque, and the Azpilcueta Basques from the Navarrese side of the Pyrenees, one is not able, it would seem, better to answer the question so often raised as to the nationality of Francis Xavier than by saying he was a Basque.   At the time of the birth of Francis, Jasso and Azpilcueta belonged to the kingdom of Navarre, as did Xavier; the last word then on the nationality of the Saint might run he was *Basque-Navarrese*.   The Doctor Navarro, himself on both sides a Basque, writes : ' They reproach me because I am a Basque. . . . I confess it is for me a subject of rejoicing, and I hold it to be a great honour to be a Navarrese and a Basque ' The two roots of the doctor's joy and noble enthusiasm must have been shared by Francis also—' Navarrese and Basque,' wrote Navarro, ' two peoples famous for their faithfulness to their kings . . . thus, too, they have been faithful to God and to the Church ' " (Cros, *Vie de S. François Xavier*, vol. i. p. 23).   See also *Mon. Xav.*, vol. i. p. 279.

Francis was born on Thursday of Holy Week in the year 1506. At the hour of his birth the priests in the chapel adjoining his mother's room were chanting the sacred offices of the Passion of Christ. Therefore, when the time of his baptism came, his parents resolved to call him after St. Francis of Assisi, who had borne on his hands and his feet the marks of his crucified Lord. When the ceremony was over the baptismal robe was taken off and hung up in the chapel beside the five little robes of his elder brothers and sisters—Juan's and Miguel's still white and fair, the others beginning to grow dusty and grey and blending with those of the children of bygone centuries.

The old biographies are singularly devoid of any but vague and pietistic details of Francis' boyhood. Yet, by reconstructing his environment from the numerous available documents and histories, we can at least gain some knowledge of the background of his early days.

The year of the Saint's birth was one of the most troubled of all those troubled years.

Since Ferdinand and Isabella, the Catholic sovereigns, had by their marriage in 1469 joined the kingdoms of Castile and Aragon the days of the independence of Navarre had been numbered. In 1492 they conquered Granada, and their dream of a united Spain seemed then nearer than ever to fulfilment. But when, in 1504, Isabella died, a period of anarchy began which only ended with the establishment of the Emperor Charles V. in 1523. Isabella's son-in-law, Philip of Austria, the husband of Juana, whom Isabella had named as her successor, tried, and with a strong following, to drive Ferdinand from the throne. But in 1506 Philip died suddenly, and all Spain was left in confusion. Juana, who for long had been subject to fits of madness, wandered from village to village at the head of a procession which bore her dead husband's body. She would take no interest in the affairs of State. Ferdinand became dominant once more. It was a fatal hour for Navarre when he gained control of the eastern passes of the Pyrenees. From then until the final annexation in 1515 the little kingdom struggled in its death agonies, and Francis' father, the Doctor Juan, spent body and soul in the attempt to maintain a lost cause. The crisis came when the Emperor, the Venetians, the Pope, and Henry VIII. of England joined in the Holy League against

c2

France, and King John of Navarre, across whose lands troops had to pass on their way from Spain into France, allied himself to Louis XII. The Duke of Alva marched on Navarre, probably bearing with him the General Papal Bull against all the opponents of the Holy League. John fled to Bayonne and Pampeluna surrendered. France gave no help to her ally, and in 1515 Navarre was formally annexed to Castile.

Till near the end the optimism of Doctor Juan had been unshaken. But the failure of all his hopes, added to the effects of the toil and anxiety of those last six years, proved too much for this ardent patriot, and a few months after Ferdinand had annexed Navarre Francis became fatherless. He can never have known his father well, and the event must have meant to the nine-year-old boy chiefly the sorrow of his mother, a strange hush, the subdued rustle of the funeral arrangements, a tolling bell, slow music, mystery.

Although the castle stood alone on the hillside, it held within its gates a large and varied community. From his mother's tapestried chamber, or the wide rooms where his married sister's boys and girls played when they came to visit the uncle who was younger than themselves, Francis could stray through galleries hung with the helmets and breastplates of his ancestors, till he came to the chapel where the priests were chanting the holy offices of the day. Or if the altar were deserted, he could go and look at the mysterious crucifix which had been found in the thirteenth century in a crevice of the castle wall. Before his intellect was disturbed by the problems of sin and pain his imagination had become stored with the symbols of war and suffering and death.

Nor was it only in silent gallery or chapel that he learned of these things. In the dungeon beneath the great tower lay the civil prisoners of the locality. Francis could stand on the outer wall of the moat and see their faces peering through the bars, while he shouted innocent greetings to them, or chanted to them fragments of his nursery rhymes.

But there were more sinister figures lurking beneath the walls than these. From time immemorial the place had been a sanctuary for all hunted and persecuted sinners. Unlike the old Hebrew cities of refuge to which only those who had killed any person unwittingly might flee, these mediæval asylums opened their gates even to those " who thrust their enemies out of hatred, or hurled at them, or lay in wait for them, or in enmity smote them."

And it is surely hardly fanciful to trace at least some of the young mountain sources of the ultimate great river of the pity and compassion of Francis Xavier to the hours which followed his boyish conversations with those robbers and murderers, when, looking deep, he saw "the thorns which grow upon this rose of life"—hours when he learned that there were wild worlds on the yon side of those sheltering hills of Xavier, and wild sins whose names had never even crossed his mother's lips.

But the pervading atmosphere of the castle was not a sombre one. There were long, sunny afternoons when the old fortress rang with children's voices, and gay winter nights when soldier cousins and uncles and brothers came home from the wars unhurt, and raised the sounds of revelry among the rafters of the banqueting hall. Francis himself was a notable athlete; this passion was to cost him somewhat in later years, when, drunk with the elation produced by the Spiritual Exercises of Loyola, he tied cords round his calves and spoiled his powers of jumping for ever, because he had gloried too much in the legs of a man. Tennis was a favourite game—*pelota*, or *jeu de paume*, they called it, because, instead of using a racquet, they wore heavy gloves and hit the ball with the palms of their hands. To-day the Basques still play in this way. The French and Spanish soon took to stretching cords across their great gloves, and from that the transition to a racquet was natural.

Many a day of wild sport and adventure must the boy have passed among his native mountains, bracing his nerves and hardening his frame for the labours of his manhood, climbing the cliffs to find the eagle's nest, tracking the wolf by torchlight over the blood-stained snow, fishing for his Lenten fare in the dark lakes that lie in the heart of the hills, or rambling on some long summer day by pine forest and winding stream, even to where the rocky ramparts of France are cleft as with Titan sword at the far-famed Brêche de Rolande, or scaled by the sacred pass of Roncesvalles.*

The freedom of this out-of-door life was complemented by a routine within the family of unwavering piety and devo-

* *Francis Xavier*, by M. H. MacLean, 1895, p. 2.

tion towards the Church. We know nothing of the personal
religious life of any member of that household, but we know
that outwardly, at least, the people were good and devout.
The year immediately before the birth of Francis had seen
the reconstruction and enlargement of the private chapel,
the foundation of a clergy house, and the presentation of
numerous lands and increments for the upkeep of the clergy
and of the services. Pious biographers, indeed, are prone
to regard the gift of the future Apostle of the Indies as a
reward for this generosity on the part of his parents.

Every day, in this chapel enlarged and restored by the chate-
laines, one of the priests from the clergy house chanted the grand
mass.   On Saturday it was in honour of our Lady, and on
Monday for the dead. Every day vespers were sung. On
special feast days *tierce* was added before mass, on Saturdays
and Sundays, and on solemn feasts and vigils, compline, and a
dozen times a year matins.   Every evening the Salve Regina
was sung.

When he had learned to read Francis would be able to turn
over the pretty little volume, bound in leather, with a clasp,
where on nineteen pages of vellum the ordinances of Santa
Maria of Xavier were inscribed.

Here his parents had vowed never at any time to break these
rules, enjoining their sons and successors, under pain of disobedience and of losing their blessing, to praise and approve of the
present donation, and never in any way to go against it, because
it was made for the service of God and of the said church, for the
help and support of those who are buried there, for the discharge
of the souls of their ancestors, lords of this place, and of their
successors, and in order that the divine service might be held in
the church in such a manner that God should be better served
there than He had been hitherto.

. . . it, the *abbadia*, was almost more of a monastery than a
clergy house.   At every mass there was confession; women under
sixty years of age were not allowed within the walls; at table
there was silence, and books were read ; for recreation there were
gardening and fishing, but no games or hunting.   "All the
advantages of the Apostolic life are offered to you," they said.
"You have a safeguard against the perils of the world in the
church and *abbadia* of *Santa Maria de Xavier*, and you lack
nothing which is necessary in order to traverse the present life
and gain life eternal."   Such were the singularly ascetic ideas
which were held at the castle of Xavier.   If all these prescriptions
were observed, the young Francis must have always had before

him the spectacle of priestly lives which were reserved, austere, and edifying.*

All round him were good and gentle people. He had to travel far before he got beyond the neighbourhood of one or other of his virtuous relatives.

If he went into the church of San Nicolas at Pampeluna, he would see there the tombs of his maternal ancestors; he would see altar-cloths embroidered by women of the kindred house of Atonda, and arches and mosaics renewed through the generosity of the same family, and the priests who stood before the altar chanted prayers for the peace of their souls.

Francis' uncle, Pedro, lived in Pampeluna, too; but a mysterious shadow had fallen over that household. All that the boy knew was that it was something to do with his cousin Juan's affection for the beautiful Maria Periz de Herice. Francis probably thought her wonderfully lovely when he saw her on fête days in her low-bodiced dress, her long sleeves flying behind her; and doted, as young boys do, on her embroidered ruff and the bands of jewelled velvet round her hair She was the prettiest lady in Pampeluna. It was not surprising that his cousin Juan loved her so well. But his parents told him that both Juan and Maria were very wicked, and so was Juan's brother, Cousin Esteban, who had had to run away in order to escape being put into prison. These three, and the prisoners in the castle dungeon at home, were the only people he knew who were not good.

Francis' elder brother Miguel was his senior by eleven years, and Juan was two years younger than Miguel. All the three sisters were much older. Before Francis was born Madeline was a lady-in-waiting at the court of Isabella the Catholic. She was noted for her beauty and her virtue and her charm, but while still young she retired to a convent. The present Duke of Feria traces his parentage back in the direct line to another sister, Maria Periz. The remaining sister died a grandmother in 1535, while Francis was just about to leave the university of Paris.

In the nursery, in the kitchen, in the hall, the talk was always of battles and campaigns. As Francis grew older he used to sit out in the garden, under the shadow of the olives, with his book on his knees, and often he must have

* Brou, *Vie de S. François Xavier*, vol. i. pp. 10, 11.

lifted his eyes from some favourite tale—perhaps that of the brave knight Amadis of Gaul—to scan the long white road for messengers bringing tidings of his brothers and uncles and cousins who were out at the wars. One spring day, when he was ten years old, a horseman galloped up the hill with the news that Ferdinand was dead; that Navarre, in the desperate hope of regaining her independence, had risen again; that the troops of Jean d'Albret had been surprised in the Val de Roncal; and that, among others, four soldiers of the house of Jasso had been taken prisoner. His brothers were safe, but any day might bring tidings of fresh disaster.

And while the household at Xavier waited for the news of life or death, there clattered one day into the courtyard a troop of horsemen, bearing orders from the Governor of Spain to demolish the fortifications of the castle. From their high window Francis and his mother watched them day after day as they smashed the outer walls, and the watch-towers, and the drawbridge, and destroyed the battlements. Then they entered the interior and broke open the loopholes. There were no gateways left, and all the great doorways of wood were burned, and the outer stairways and the tower of San Miguel entirely demolished. The well-ordered garden was a desert of broken stones and charred beams and trampled flowers.

The glory of Xavier was departed, but Maria de Azpilcueta still lived there with her youngest son. We know nothing of his schooling, but he most likely had as a tutor one of the priests from the *abbadia* or clergy house, which adjoined the private chapel. If he went at all to school at Sanguessa or Pampeluna, it was only for a year or two before going to the university. His mother's cousin, Martin de Azpilcueta, who came to live at Xavier after the death of Doctor Juan, may have been his teacher. He appears to have been a man of great intelligence. He had, we read, " a faithful heart, a beautiful character, a pliant humour : one always loved him after having learned to know him, and to see him again was a *fête*." * The description has a special interest for us when we remember that this man was Francis' guardian from his tenth till his nineteenth year.

The family at Xavier was no longer wealthy. The fortune as well as the life of Doctor Juan had been spent for his

* Cros, *Vie de S. François Xavier*, vol. i. p. 68.

king. In 1519 his widow asked the King of Castile for an indemnity for the damage done to the castle, and at the same time she asked for the payment of moneys which had been due to her husband from the treasury of Navarre at his death. She was promised certain sums, but the money was never given to her. The collection of the numerous dues and taxes, which formed a great part of the family income, had been neglected during the last arduous years of Doctor Juan's life, and many who had ceased to pay refused to begin again. The following is one typical little story out of many in existence that treat of these troubles, and it gives us a fleeting glimpse of Francis himself:

About 1519 the chatelaine of Xavier was Doña Maria de Azpilcueta, and with her was her sister Doña Violante, and the three sons of Doña Maria—Miguel, Juan and Francisco. I was keeper, and I gathered in the dues on the flocks which traversed our lands. Now one day several herds of cattle came up, and the shepherd, instead of sending them to the place where they should be counted and the dues taken, drove them on without saying anything; but I and the three sons of the Señora of Xavier, and other companions, ran after them, and brought back all the herd to Xavier. We turned the cattle into the court of the clergy house. I took the dues from the shepherd. There was three hundred head of cattle for the Señora, but then Pedro de Tudela, the proprietor of the cattle, and old Miguel, who did the bargaining for him, made some negotiations and transactions with the lady, and I do not know what arrangement they came to.*

It was when Francis was fifteen years old that Ignatius Loyola had his leg smashed by a cannon ball at the siege of Pampeluna.

It is possible that Francis' brothers may have shot the ball, which did a bigger stroke of business for the Roman Church that day than many a Pope did in a lifetime. Loyola, lieutenant and a faithful subject of the Emperor Charles, was defending the town against the insurgents, who, under the inspiration of Henri d'Albret, the son of Jean d'Albret, late king of Navarre, had again taken to the field. Francis I. of France encouraged them; but although they took Pampeluna, their victory was short-lived.

While Loyola lay suffering agonies in the attempt to have his leg elegantly set—for these were the days of his vanity—

* Cros, *Vie de S. François Xavier*, vol. i. p. 80.

the insurgents were defeated at Noain, but even then the patriotism of some of them was unquenched. Francis' brothers were among those who refused to surrender, and in the general pardon of 1523 their names were in the list of those who were excepted from grace, and they were condemned to forfeiture of all their possessions and to death; but they were not caught. For two years, helped by the French, they held out in the garrison town of Fuenterrabia. At last both sides became weary, and the patriots were given permission to return to homes and lands with honour, if they would take the oath of allegiance to the Emperor. This they did.

When Miguel and Juan came back to Xavier, they found that their little brother Francisco had grown into a tall lad of eighteen years, of that sunburnt, bookish, athletic type of youth which is so familiar to us to-day. He had no hankerings after a soldier's life, but he was full of eager talk of Paris and the students and professors there, and of the fine positions that were open to well-educated young ecclesiastics of good family.

CHAPTER III

(1525—1529)

IN October, 1525, Francis Xavier found himself in Paris. The university of Paris had been organised since the beginning of the thirteenth century, and not many years after that she had been " the brightest glory of mediæval France."

But that was in the far-off days of Abelard, of Albertus Magnus, of St. Thomas Aquinas, of St. Bonaventura.

Abelard used to lecture to great crowds of students in the open meadows which lay upon the slopes of Mont Ste. Geneviève.

There was in those days no mediæval sage who had not studied or taught in Paris—subtle doctors, seraphic doctors, angels of the schools, Italians, Spaniards, Germans. At one moment the souls of the students would be prisoned in the hard armour of scholastic argument, and the next caught up into the third heaven of mysticism.*

But as long ago as the days of our Edward III., Richard of Bury had written: " The zeal of that illustrious school has become lukewarm—nay, even frozen—whose rays once illumined every corner of the earth." This decline synchronises with the gradual growth of despotism within the university, and with the refusal on the part of the dominant faculty to progress, to change, to be born again.

By the sixteenth century Paris, as a centre of learning, deserved all the ridicule which was flung at her from writers such as Montaigne and Rabelais and Erasmus. In the sixteenth chapter of the second book of *Pantagruel* there is a picture of student life so appalling in its utter folly and soddenness that most people feel it to be beyond the limits of caricature. But a study of contemporary letters and writings proves the picture to be almost photographic in its accuracy. A depraved moral tone among the students was the inevitable fruit of the depraved intellectuality among the

---

* Doumergue, *Vie de Jean Calvin*, vol. i. p. 50.

masters and doctors. To the doctors, scholasticism seemed bound up with their very existence. It was the foundation upon which the whole academic structure rested, and they dreaded and fought against the influence of the New Learning because they knew that a force lay there which would undermine their authority. To this day Roman Catholic historians boast that the theological faculty in Paris was the first to detect the link between heresy and humanism.

The earliest taint of " heresy " appeared in Paris before either Lutheranism or Calvinism had taken to the field. Doumergue gives it the name of Fabrian Protestantism, after Le Fèvre (Faber Stapulensis).

Jacques Le Fèvre d'Etaples was born about 1455, and he was finally driven from the university in the same year that Francis Xavier entered it. He was the first man in Paris to criticise the versions of Aristotle then in use.[*] His criticism, founded on his study of the MSS. in Italy, could not be expected to please the theologians who gloried in Albertus Magnus and Thomas Aquinas. " By liberal and intelligent handling of Scripture," says Hume Brown, " he did more than any other Frenchman, except Calvin himself, to induce a critical attitude towards the traditions of the Church."[†] Unfortunately, he still more quickly induced a critical attitude towards himself. His commentary on the Epistles of St. Paul has been called the first Protestant book. In it is found the principle of the sovereign authority of the Word of God. And elsewhere he enunciated most clearly the doctrine of justification by faith. But the theological faculty was determined to keep Scriptural truth in its naked simplicity from the people. In that same year (1525) " the books of the Holy Scripture," the Sorbonne announced, " are approved in the Latin language, and ought thus to remain." [‡] During his later years Etaples began, in exile, the translation of the Bible which became the foundation of the later French versions.[§]

There is a letter written in 1519 by Olivetan to his young cousin, John Calvin, then a schoolboy of ten years old, which gives us not only a delightful description of Le Fèvre himself,

* Graf, *La Vie et les écrits de Jacques Le Fèvre d'Etaples*, 1842.
† P. Hume Brown, *Life of George Buchanan*, 1890, p. 18.
‡ J. M. Cros, *Documents Nouveaux*, p. 277.
§ See Ranke, " Französische Geschichte " (*Werke*, Band 8), p. 111.

but also a simple yet vivid impression of the dawn of the religious renascence in Paris:

> . . . They [the doctors of the Sorbonne] so hate all new ideas that they prefer the old wrong way to the new right way. What is strange is that the priests hate good grammar more than they do bad lives. . . . I must tell you of a dear old man who is one of our teachers. His name is Doctor James Le Fèvre. I am proud of him because he is a Picard. He was once a poor boy in the village of Étaples, where he was born about 65 years ago. Perhaps there is some hope for us Noyon lads if we will be as studious and pious as he has been. He is a small man of a mean appearance, but his great soul, his vast learning, his deep piety, and his powerful eloquence make him the most charming man in the university . . . we all know that he reads and talks about the Holy Scriptures as few others do in our day. A child can understand him when he preaches. Some of the students are beginning to make an uproar about the Gospel that he preaches. They think he is fighting against the Church. But I am sure that he tells us more about Jesus Christ than we ever heard before. . . . I want your father to be ready to study a book which I will soon send him. It was written by Le Fèvre. I do not yet know whether the lovely old man is right or not, but he says if we become as little children and simply believe in Jesus, we will be saved.*

It was in the same year that this letter was written that the Sorbonne clearly showed its front with regard to the doctrines of Martin Luther. Thenceforward the official attitude towards the German reformer was one of fierce opposition. Yet all the time, especially in quarters like Ste. Barbe, where Humanism had made some advance, the followers of Luther were becoming more numerous. But they lacked a leader.† So from the noise and tumult of

---

* Quoted by W. M. Blackburn in *The College Days of Calvin*, p. 8.

† "For the absence of such a movement [*i.e.*, of religious reform] no reason can perhaps be given but the non-appearance of the men to lead it. However the fact be accounted for, the university of Paris never did see within its college walls the growth of a really religious movement at all comparable to the Wycliffite movement at Oxford, to the movement of which Hus was the product rather than the author at Prague, or even to the quieter religious revival inaugurated in the sixteenth century by men like our Oxford Tyndale and the Cambridge reformers. The complete isolation of the intellectual life of Paris from contact with the stronger currents of popular religious feeling outside is one of the strangest facts of her history" (Hastings Rashdall, *The Universities of Mediæval Europe*, vol. i. p. 557). The omission in this passage of any reference to the movement which resulted in the formation of the Society of Jesus strikes one as remarkable.

Navarre at war Francis had escaped, only to find himself
engulfed in this maelstrom of religious and intellectual strife.

The lad was now nineteen—dark, athletic, and very
pleasing to look upon. We can well imagine with what
eagerness the young freshman flung off his Spanish cloak,
donned the long black cape and pointed hat of the Parisian
student, and set out to explore the place which for the next
eleven years was to be his Alma Mater.

> I was the Dreamer, they the Dream ; I roamed
> Delighted through the motley spectacle ;
> Gowns grave, or gaudy, doctors, students, streets,
> Courts, cloisters, flocks of churches, gateways, towers :
> Migration strange for a stripling of the hills. . . .*

During his earliest days in Paris Francis doubtless found
himself besieged by such companions as were always ready
to befriend the *béjaunes*.† Eagerly they would show him
the sights of the town, and assist him to spend his full purse.
One of the chief expeditions was to the towers of the
church of Notre-Dame, whence—lacking a Baedeker—the
newcomer could gain the best idea of his surroundings. Let
us ascend those narrow spiral stairs with Francis and his
fellows, and look down upon sixteenth-century Paris. The
great trefoil, city, university, town, lies before us, inter-
penetrating yet distinct. On the old shields of the Cité
there is blazoned a ship. Sauval explains the origin of the
device in these words : " The island of the city is made like a
great ship, stuck in the mud and run aground in the current,
near the centre of the Seine." Near the prow stand the
delicately poised spires of the Sainte Chapelle, and close by,
from the water's edge, where the laundresses wash and beat
their linen and laugh and sing, rise the towers of the Palace
of Justice. The river is hardly visible, for every bridge is
laden with houses. We can picture Francis' companions
showing him the boundaries of the city ; within its walls he
could distinguish more than twenty churches. " There,"
says Victor Hugo, " on the right and the left to east and west,
within the walls of the city, which was yet so contracted,
rose the bell-towers of its one and twenty churches, of every
date, of every form, of every size, from the low and worm-

---

* Wordsworth, *Prelude*, book iii. line 30.
† *Béjaune, bec-jaune :* yellow bill : freshman.

eaten belfry of *St. Denis du Pas* to the slender needles of *St. Pierre aux Bueufs* and *Saint Landry*."

And there, to the west, the autumn foliage reddens in the king's gardens, and the falling leaves begin to reveal the *Ile du Passeur*. The king is a prisoner in Madrid, but the gardens are not quite deserted. His mother, the Queen Regent, at this time more devoted to the Pope than to the reformers, takes her pleasure there, after anxious days and weeks. The trial against the Lutherans has been so far successful ; the worst of the heretics are in prison. With the preachers of Meaux she and her friends had been less fortunate. Briçonnet certainly had accepted defeat, and forfeited for ever a place either at the right hand or the left of Luther ; but the more fervent members of the group has escaped, and were at this moment hiding in Capito's house in Strasburg.* Le Fèvre's New Testament—which she and her daughter, Margaret of Angoulême, had, in another mood, urged him to undertake—was safely in the fire. But it would be on the university, and not on the king's gardens, that the gaze of the young Navarrese would rest longest. Did he look down on that unbroken mass of houses and colleges with a feeling of ownership, of boyish pride ? Did wistful ambition surge through heart and mind as he stood there, a little apart from his gay companions ? Down among the colleges he could see the abbeys of the Mathurins, the Bernardins, the Augustins. There rose the square tower of Ste. Geneviève, and yonder stood the Sorbonne itself. The old dreams of ecclesiastical honours, which, realised, must justify him in the eyes of his house for having renounced a life of soldiery, surely seemed nearer fulfilment now. There lay the abbeys. What if up here, on the pinnacle of the

* Briçonnet, Bishop of Meaux, and his more worthy followers are known as the " group of Meaux." Among them were Le Fèvre d'Etaples, the bishop's old tutor ; Vatable, the Hebrew scholar ; Facel ; Roussel. They were separate from the Lutheran party, and although d'Etaples had anticipated, in his commentary on 1 Corinthians, Luther's teaching on faith and works, and had, in his commentary on Hebrews, denied the doctrine of Transubstantiation —while admitting the Real Presence—yet the group were more independent of doctrine than the German reformers, and expended their energy chiefly on " preaching Christ from the sources." For some years they preached undisturbed, and then, most naturally, but apparently somewhat to the chagrin of the Bishop, the theological faculty at Paris began to identify their religion with Luther's. Meaux issued a decree against Lutheranism, while continuing his work of reform, but in 1525 he gave up the difficult struggle.—(See Ranke, *Werke*, Band 8, p. 111.)

temple, one should be standing now—hush, you boisterous boys—we will go down presently to the *cabaret* and drink at my expense—one, Francis Xavier, who will in time be abbot, cardinal, Pope ? . . .

"What is that ? " he cries, as his impatient guides drag him towards the staircase. He has seen a strange white cliff, so high, so wrapped in the October mists, that it seems almost to be hung, like a drifting cloud, in the sky—a mass of turrets and windmills—but so soft, so dreamlike, that he fears it will be gone before they answer him.

"That is *Mons Martyrum*. There, in the crypt of the church of Our Lady, lie the bones of good Saint Denis. Come away down to the tavern, señor."

Yes, Francis, that is *Mons Martyrum*. And there, at the close of your student life, you will take the cup of salvation and pay your vows unto the Lord.

If the afternoon on the towers of Notre-Dame was a delight to eye and mind, the hours in the college class-rooms must, on the contrary, have been a hard trial to one whom we know to have been fastidious in his manners and tastes. The college itself was dark and ill-ventilated, and bounded by narrow streets that reeked with offal. The lectures began at 5 a.m. In 1452 benches had been prohibited, and scholars bidden to sit on the floor—for humility's sake,* the authorities said, being too proud to confess that they were short of money. So on the floor Francis sat, on straw in winter, and on mown grass in summer, while the regent, rod in hand, lectured from his solitary chair. Here and there a lamp reeked, and round it clustered a knot of students who took notes, or wrote letters to their mothers or their sweethearts. In 1491 an order had been issued advising that one of the morning lectures each day should be devoted to dictation. Each student was to be given an allowance of three sheets of paper per week.† Some of the students were not half-way through their teens; others were middle-aged men. Some were there to learn, many to rest, to write, to read, or to fool. From time to time the professor

* " They shall sit in the presence of the masters on the ground, not on benches or seats raised above the ground as in time past, when the study of the said faculty was more flourishing." (Bulaeus, vol. iv. p. 390, and vol. v. p. 573. " Bulaeus was perhaps the stupidest man that ever wrote a valuable book," says Rashdall.)

† Quicherat, *Histoire de Ste. Barbe*, p. 87.

would rise, thread his way through the black cloaked figures, and single out a special offender for punishment. Montaigne, with good reason, pitied these poor young students :

It is a verie prison of captivated youth, and proves dissolute, in punishing before it be so. Come upon them when they are going to their lesson, and you heare nothing but whipping and brawling, both of children tormented, and masters besotted with anger and chafing. How wide are they, which go about to allure a child's mind to go to his booke, being yet but tender and fearfull, with a stearne—frowning countenance, and with handsfull of rods.*

Vives, the great educationist, has very severe things to say about the education in the university of Paris in those days. " One discusses before dinner, during dinner, after dinner, in public, in private, in all places, at all times. One ends by discussing as to whether the pig is led to market by the man who is taking it, or by the string he holds." In his *Dialogus qui Sapiens inscribitur* he portrays a scene which is supposed to have occurred in one of the class-rooms in Ste. Barbe :

MASTER : Boy, tell me in what month Virgil died ?
PUPIL : September, sir.
MASTER : In what place ?
PUPIL : At Brindisi.
MASTER : On what day of the month ?
PUPIL : Ninth of the month.
MASTER : Idiot, do you wish to make a fool of me before these gentlemen ? Reach me my rod, pull back your sleeve and hold out your hand for having said the ninth instead of the tenth. Try to pay more attention. You all see, gentlemen, that this is a boy who knows a lot. Did Sallust at the beginning of his *Catilina* write *omnies homines* or *omnis homines* ?
PUPIL : The general opinion is that he wrote *omnis*, but I think he wrote *omnies*, and that so it was necessary for the printer to break the customary rule, and spell it with an " ie " and not with a simple " i."
MASTER : What was the brother of Remus called, and how did he wear his beard ?
PUPIL : Some, my master, say that he was called Romulus, others Romus, whence the name of Rome, and, as a term of affection, the diminutive Romulus. When he went to the war he

* Montaigne's *Essays*, book i. chap. xxv. (Florio's translation).

D

had no beard, but he had a long one in times of peace. It is thus that he is represented in colour in the Livy printed in Venice.

MASTER : How did Alexander raise himself when he fell on the earth in touching for the first time Asiatic soil ?

PUPIL : By leaning on his hands and raising his head.*

Surely Francis was recalling such hours when, years afterwards, he wrote from India that he often had a mind to come to Europe, to Paris, above all to the university, and " shout aloud like a madman who had lost his senses " to the students, reminding them of the things that really mattered.†

Ribadeneira, Loyola's contemporary biographer, has given us a succinct account of a normal day at college :

Rise at four, at five lecture, followed by mass, and breakfast composed of a roll. From eight to ten lecture ; at eleven masters and pupils dine together, while parts of the Bible or the Lives of the Saints were read aloud. Then, for recreation, the reading of poetry and questions on the preceding lesson. Another class from three to five ; at six supper, repetition, *salut du Sainct-Sacrement*, and to bed.‡

This probably gives a fairly accurate description of the tenor of Xavier's first four years at the university. He was enrolled as a *cameriste-portioniste*—that is, he paid both for food and for lodging, and boarded with the principal, who was required " diligently to hear the lessons of the scholars studying in the Faculty of Arts, and faithfully to instruct them alike in life and in doctrine." § There were various other kinds of students. *Bursars* were taught, lodged, and fed free of charge. *Cameristes* fed themselves, but were provided with lodging under charge of certain regents known as pedagogues. Besides all these, there was a large body of outside students known as *martinets*,‖ who attended the classes if they had time or inclination, or any special mischief in hand. These men formed the hooligan element, which at that time made up a considerable part of

* Joannes Ludovicus Vives, *Opera Omnia* (Valentia, 1783), vol. iv. pp. 23 and 24.

† *Mon. Hist. Soc. Jesu, Mon. Xav.*, vol. I., p. 285.

‡ *Vida de P. Ignatius de Loyola* (French Edition, Paris, 1891), p. 133.

§ Bulaeus, vol. iv. p. 93 (quoted by H. Rashdall).

‖ In 1463 the Faculty of Arts ordered all students who did not board with relatives, or in the house of some responsible member of the university, to live inside the colleges or *pedagogies*. See Bulaeus, vol. v. p. 658. Those who evaded this rule were the martinets—birds of passage. Cf. the *Chamberdekyns* of mediæval Oxford.

university life.   To the inner ring of this group belonged the
galoches.   They trailed their noisy sabots through the
colleges at all seasons, a lazy unkempt crew, never taking
any examinations, grey-haired parasites and loafers.   A few
of them, however, hired themselves out to the wealthier
students as servants.   Such was Miguel the Navarrese,
Francis Xavier's man, " a sad person of low birth and an
evil life."   There was yet another class, the *serviteurs*,
sons of the poorest citizens, and they, in return for washing
and scrubbing the floors and doing the humblest work of the
house, were allowed to attend any of the classes they chose.

Francis, like all students with serious ambitions, elected
to take the Arts course, which led up to the protracted
theological studies.   To gain the degree of Master of Arts,
the student had first an examination in Greek, history,
grammar, and Latin versification.   One or two years,
mostly occupied with logic, followed, and then came the
examination for Bachelorship.   A year later * the student
submitted himself for the licentiateship examination.   This
examination passed, there followed a sort of minor graduation ceremony, a diploma was publicly given, and the
chancellor, in his robes of state, bestowed the Apostolic
blessing.   Towards the end of the same year it was in order
for the student to ask for the " bonnet," and to be officially
and publicly designated Master.   " *Placet ne vobis talem,
licentium biretari ?* " said the professor.   " *Placet*," replied the
other masters.   So the graduation ceremony was called Placet.

Thus the student became a *magister novus*.   He was not a
full Master, or Master Regent, until he had been appointed
as professor in one of the colleges.   These posts were nearly
always occupied by youths on their way to graduate in one
of the higher faculties, and they were only held from year
to year.†

The value of university degrees in those days is very
uncertain.   The registers at Paris show that candidates
were hardly ever rejected.   On the other hand, the students
appear to have been weeded out by various processes before
they took the actual examinations.   Rashdall computes ‡

---

* The intervals between these different examinations appear to have
varied considerably, and by the sixteenth century the whole curriculum,
which had originally occupied $4\frac{1}{2}$ years, was reduced to $3\frac{1}{2}$ years.
  † H. Rashdall, *Universities of Mediæval Europe*, vol. i. p. 457 ff.
  ‡ *Ibid.*, p. 462.

that only half, at the outside, of the students who matriculated in Arts took their Bachelor's examination, and that of these only a small proportion became Masters. If a student was rejected by the examiners, it was generally on moral grounds.*

The college of Ste. Barbe was informally founded in 1460 by Geoffrey Lenormant. Colleges were usually called after their founders, but this man appears to have been graced by an unusual modesty, and gave it the name of a saint. Ste. Barbara, like St. Catherine, is supposed to have confuted the pagan doctors. But we have here as well a characteristic mediæval *double-entendre*, for Barbara is the name of a form of syllogism.

There was no college in Paris at that time with such a high reputation as Ste. Barbe. It had been compared to the wooden horse of Troy, because it had within itself such a number of great men. Francis was very probably advised to go there by his uncle, the scholarly Doctor of Navarre. Between the Doctor and his nephew, as will be seen from later letters, there existed a deep affection. He may simply have gone there because it was a favourite college among Spaniards and Portuguese.

Jacques de Gouvea, the principal, was a Portuguese, and one of the most progressive members of the university; to him, indeed, his college was largely indebted for its high position at this time. He saw, almost before anyone else, the crying need for young men who would go out to the notoriously lawless and demoralised new colonies as priests and missionaries, and he used all his influence with his kings to get them to provide education at Ste. Barbe for that purpose. About a year after Xavier's arrival in Paris, Gouvea succeeded in renting the college in the interests of John III., and fifteen bursaries were given by Portugal for missionary students. Yet, in spite of the large proportion of Iberians,

---

* On this point Rashdall says : " It must be remembered that the degree was not a mere certificate of having passed an examination, but the admission to an official position (*i.e.*, that of regent). Thus at Vienna we find that in 1449 out of 43 candidates for the licence seventeen were rejected, one for having spoken uncivilly to a master, another for irregularities in the matter of academical dress, another for going out to see an execution in the midst of an examination, another for going about disguised, and for the heinous offence of wandering by the Danube, another for gambling, another for taking part in a knife fight with certain tailors, none apparently for failure in the literary part of the examination" (*op. cit.* I. p. 461).

the college was the most cosmopolitan in the university. It had the best of both the Scottish and the French students. And, most portentous fact for Francis, Loyola the Basque was soon to be there, *lucerna ardens et lucens.* Only Germany was ill-represented. For most of her sons Paris had become a dead branch.

During the whole of Xavier's first winter session the king, Francis I., was a prisoner in Spain, and the discipline, both in town and university, was even more lax than usual. Orders were issued and reissued, but the authority of the university could no longer cope with the rising tide of life, nor with its inevitable froth of lawlessness and folly.*

We have but little direct evidence as to the life of Francis during those first college years. His earlier biographers have paid but scant attention to that part of his life. That he worked well is evident. It is evident, too, that he had that usual quality of genius, a power of friendship with widely different types of men. The closest of his friends was probably Peter Faber. With something of the same love and wonder which some of the best men of his time betray when speaking of George Meredith, we find Faber's lovers and friends speaking and writing of him. He and Francis found themselves freshmen together, sharing the same room. And when the young hidalgo from Xavier was not following, albeit with reluctant feet, the dubious ways of his more turbulent companions, he often sat and talked far into the night with the wise and gentle-souled shepherd lad. Faber had been born in the same year as Francis, but in very different circumstances. He grew up to tend his father's sheep on his native heights of Savoy. He was neither the first nor the last shepherd lad to turn saint and scholar. Among his writings is the beautiful *Memorial,* an autobiography of part of his life. In it we find these words :

I went to Paris to the College of Ste. Barbe in the year 1525. I was nineteen. . . . I pray to God that He may ever keep me in grateful remembrance of the good things He gave to me, both bodily and spiritually, by various means, during those three and a half years. I put among the foremost of my mercies that I had such a master, and that I found in the room of his college in which I was installed such good companionship : I

* See Crevier, *Histoire de l'université de Paris,* vol. v. p. 191 ; see also *Journal d'un Bourgeois de Paris,* p. 272.

speak above all of Master Francis Xavier, who is of the Company
of Jesus.*

Many years afterwards, when he was in Cochin, in 1548,
Francis writes of Faber as the dearest of all the departed
souls of the Company.†

Mathurin Cordier, to whom Doumergue, the biographer of
Calvin, gives a place of honour as among the most potent
influences of the great reformer's student days,‡ was almost
certainly one of Xavier's professors. Cordier did not join
the reformers till about 1528, though long before that time
he himself had been, in the deepest sense of the word, a reformer. His orthodoxy probably gave him a greater influence over Francis than he would otherwise have had, and
there are passages in the letters from India curiously akin
to the following passage from the writings of Cordier:

In the schools of this city Christ is so neglected ! There is so
little care for the Word of God ! How many of the masters are
there who lead their pupils, in their rooms or at the lectures, to
the love of God, or the study of things divine ? How many of
them prefer a student who is virtuous and honourable to one
who is learned and clever with his pen ? What teacher is there
who places love above gain ? . . . Why do you force the students ?
Why do you struggle with them ? Why do you torture them ?
Do you wish to teach them easily ? Begin with principles.
Begin with speaking of God and of the things of heaven. Teach
these boys; do not leave them to themselves; but by divine grace,
lead them, I say, to love the Christ, to breathe the Christ, to have
the Christ on their lips.   Pour it, as it were, drop by drop on the
souls of your pupils: make it enter and penetrate into them.
Inculcate them so assiduously with the Word of God that they
shall be at least touched with some spark of the Love Divine.§

Another great man whom Xavier must often have met was
George Buchanan, who had arrived in Paris for the first time
in 1520, and was more or less connected with the university
for many years. It was he who, along with Mathurin
Cordier and Strebée, achieved the classical revival at
Ste. Barbe. There, in 1529, he was regent or professor, and
therefore in the same house with Xavier and Loyola. One

* P. Faber, *Fabri Monumenta, Memoriale*, p. 493.
† *Mon. Xav.*, vol. i. p. 436.
‡ See Calvin's preface to his book on Thessalonians, *Opera* xiii. p. 525.
§ Quoted by Doumergue, *Vie de Jean Calvin*, vol. i. p. 60.

wonders if that most astute fisher of men, the great founder of the Order of the Jesuits, ever set his nets for George Buchanan. Did Loyola know the measure of his power, and shun defeat; did he weigh the Scottish humanist and find him wanting in that which he required, or was he in this instance blind to what lay, perhaps, within his grasp? For Buchanan was in these days of the stuff of which the Counter-Reformers were compact: intellectual, a man steeped in affairs, a seeker of truth, a malcontent, yet no Lutheran.

Erasmus had been in Paris some years earlier, but the study of Greek had then scarcely begun, and the fare and lodging disgusted one whose fastidiousness was in advance of his times. "I carried nothing away from Paris," he says in his *Icthophagia*, "but a body infested with disease, and a plentiful supply of vermin."

Scholars passed and repassed across the Channel. While Erasmus came to Oxford, John Major and Florence Wilson and a host of lesser stars followed in the train of Buchanan to Paris. Some of those Scotsmen most likely saw, if they did not meet, the theologian who has since become almost the special property of their race. Although Quicherat * and Ribadeneira † claim Calvin for Ste. Barbe, the colleges associated with his early university life are la Marche and Montaigu, which latter he left about the same time as Loyola arrived.‡ It is curious to think of Calvin's remaining in this extreme conservative atmosphere for so long, while Loyola only went there for a short period, and then gravitated to the more liberal Ste. Barbe. The college of Montaigu had at that time the most reactionary man in the university as principal. This was Noel Beda; Erasmus said that in one Beda there were three thousand monks. He seems to have combined intellectual mediocrity with a vast conviction of the rightness of his own opinions. Even his friends disapproved of his excess of retrogressive zeal, and Francis I., after making various complaints, finally ordered the university to expel him because he had condemned a book written by Margaret of Navarre. The college itself seems to have been even more disagreeable than the principal. It was

* Quicherat, *Histoire de Ste. Barbe*, vol. i. p. 204.
† *La Vie de S. Ignatius de Loyola, après Ribadeneira*, p. 138.
‡ Doumergue, *Jean Calvin*, vol. i. p. 59, note; T. M Lindsay, *History of the Reformation*, vol. ii. pp. 93–4; and H. Y. Reyburn, *John Calvin*, London, 1914, p. 10.

famous for its exaggerated asceticism, its ceaseless punish-
ments, its indescribable filth, and its unrelenting studies.*
And Erasmus writes of it :

the beds were so hard, the food so meagre, the labours so exacting
that many youths of splendid promise, after the first years of
their sojourn in this college, became mad or blind or leprous, if
they did not die. Some of the bedrooms, because they were
close to the lavatories, were so dirty and infected that none of
those who lodged there came away alive, or without the germ of
some grave disease . . . Oh, how many rotten eggs I ate there,
and how much mouldy wine I drank ! †

There is a letter extant which, as if to make up for the
singularly rare glimpses possible into the youth of Xavier,
gives us a picture both intimate and sad. It shows to us,
too, that the repulsive physical surroundings in the university,
of which Erasmus has given us so vivid a picture, were
matched by the moral atmosphere of the colleges. This
letter is written after Xavier's death by a priest near Meliapor, to whom the Saint had given one of his few personal
confidences :

Talking to me, he told me the story of his life from his earliest
years until that time. He spoke of his native land, of his father
and mother, of the age at which he went to Paris, and of what
happened to him there. And à propos of the students' way of
living, he told me that they—and the professors too—were very
dissipated. Often they went out at night from the college and
led him with them. But Francis was seized with such a dread
of sharing in their physical ruin that he did not dare to behave as
they did. This fear sustained him for one or two years. Then
the Professor died as a result of his excesses, and was succeeded
by a pure and virtuous Master (Juan Pena), whose good example
Francis followed, so that never, from that day onward, had he
such acquaintances as these were.‡

At this time Francis' sympathies lay with the Lutherans,
and he frequented their society. To do so implied either
great bravery or great recklessness, for the martyrs had
already begun to burn. The following extract gives but one
story among many of its kind :

* See Doumergue, *Vie de Jean Calvin*, vol. i. p. 69.
† Quoted by Doumergue, *op. cit.*, vol. i. p. 72.
‡ Delplace, *Sel. Ind. Epist.* (Florence, 1887), p. 180.

In the said year 1526, on Tuesday, August 28th, a young man, a beneficed scholar, not yet in priest's orders, but a Master of Arts . . . native of Théronne in Picardy, because he was a Lutheran, saying that the Virgin Mary had no more power than any other saint, with several other follies, and who persisted, although he was warned, and counselled by the chief confessor of Paris, M. Jean Merlin, Doc.Theo., died in this error. . . . He had, on the previous Christmas Eve, made honourable repentance, a burning torch in his hand, naked but for his shirt, before the Church of Notre-Dame, begging God and the Virgin to have mercy on him, for the many errors and follies which he had held and taught, and which he repented and deplored. Thereupon he was condemned to seven years' imprisonment in the prison of St. Martin des Champs, in Paris, living on bread and water, by order of the court. But having entered the said prison, he returned to his errors and follies. So that, finally, the said court, advised by the prior of St. Martin and others, tried and condemned him, as before, to be burnt.*

And while he read the writings of Luther, and loved the Lutherans, and loved still more the shepherd lad who had vowed perpetual celibacy and had dedicated himself to the priesthood, while he passed all his examinations and associated with the best and the worst men of his college, Xavier still found ample time to devote to his tailor. Old Tursellinus says: " Francis, desirous, as usual, to maintain his nobility and estimation among his equals, fell into extraordinary expense, for which cause his father† began to think of calling him home." And his biographer goes on to relate how his sister Madeline, a nun, wrote: " Do not do this; rather help my brother Francis with his studies, for I am sure that he will become a great servant of God and a pillar of the Church." ‡

When we know that the family of Xavier was now extremely poor, that Francis' mother had exhausted all her resources in the law courts in the attempt to get hold of the sums which had been promised to her, we can understand the desire on the part of his family to see the youngest son at home and making money, and their reluctance to pay for his education and his extravagances. But this advice from

* *Journal d'un Bourgeois de Paris*, p. 292.

† His father, Tursellinus had forgotten, or had not known, was long since dead. He had probably confused him with the eldest son of the family, who bore the same name.

‡ See Tursellinus, Book I., cap. 2 ; also Cros, *Documents Nouveaux*, p. 266.

Madeline the nun appears to have been taken, and Tursellinus says that in his day the prophetic letter was still to be seen among the family treasures at Xavier.

About this time both Francis' brothers married, and in 1529 his mother died, and the old home was broken up.

It was just during those months, which must have been the loneliest of his life, that he found himself beginning to stir beneath the supreme fascinations of Ignatius Loyola.

SIGNATURE OF LOYOLA.

IGNATIUS LOYOLA SETS OUT FOR
MONTSERRAT

E domo & cognatione sua exit, rectaque
ad Virginis templum famulis redire
iussis, in Montem Serratum contendit.

CHAPTER IV

THE FOUNDATION OF THE ORDER

(1528—1534)

ONE February day in 1528 there entered Paris, driving before him an ass laden with books, the radiant knight of the Church in distress who was to win Francis from his earlier dreams.*

On the face of it there was small likelihood that Ignatius Loyola and Francis Xavier would become friends. Eight years ago Miguel and Juan, the brothers of Francis, had gone up against Loyola at the fateful Pampeluna. Since then the God-intoxicated cripple had made of himself a laughing-stock to all but a few, and the whole world of his ambitions was strange to such as Francis was. Yet they had in common a language rarely heard, and high traditions which they had both once dreamed of carrying on, and did still hope to honour, each in his own way. In Loyola the iron endurance of the Basque was blended with the old mediæval Spanish qualities—the quasi-religious mysticism, the fantastic chivalry—which were the web and woof of such romances as his favourite Amadis of Gaul.† His youthful hopes of military and knightly glory were not to be easily broken, and since he could no longer serve his

* Ribadeneira, *Vita*, tom. i. cap. xvi. "Alone, driving an ass loaded with books, he turned into the way from Barcelona that he might take advantage of the studies of Paris."

† There are qualities both in Xavier and in Loyola which can hardly be sympathetically understood, unless one had read one or other of those old romances. Perhaps Southey, the translator of Amadis, was too unmeasured in his criticism when he said: "Amadis of Gaul is among prose what Orlando Furioso is among metrical romances, not the oldest of its kind, but the best." Yet there is no book which gives us a finer picture of the combination of chivalry and mysticism which was so characteristic of Spain at that time. In other countries this mediæval quality had been more or less uprooted by the influences of the Renascence, which had as yet hardly penetrated to Spain. But by a curious evolution of circumstance the enthusiasms which the crusades against the Moors had kindled were fanned into new life at the very moment when they might easily have died. For the final expulsion of the Moors from Spain was coincident with the discovery of America and the opening up of the New World, and once more Spain was to hold up the Cross at the head of her armies. To colonise was to Christianise. This national ideal probably played a larger part in the inspiration of both Loyola and Xavier than we are accustomed to think. And, in their sincere and enthusiastic youth, they must have heard and read with anger of the way in which these sacred traditions were being carried out.

country in the field, nor his " lady more high than duchess or countess," he bethought himself of the great reputations of the saints, and was glad to think that after all he might not find the gates of fame shut upon him. It did not matter how poor or crippled the soldiers were who fought about the walls of Jerusalem or Babylon. The Virgin Mary would be his Oriana; he could already hear her say, like the lady whom Amadis was bidden to serve, that *it pleased her*. Yes, there she stood, with her Child in her arms, and with one long look she rapt his soul from his earth to her Heaven. This vision inspired him to leave his father's castle and go up into the mountains. It was a difficult journey. His wounded leg was still helpless. But he took with him two servants, and the faithful ass upon which his brother had mounted him carried its strange burden carefully up the passes, till, high among the naked rocks, they found the church of Our Lady of Montserrat.

There the cripple hobbled from his beast, and, like Amadis, the Child of the Sea, " he armed himself all save his head and his hands, and made his prayer before the altar, beseeching God to grant him success in arms, and in the love which he bore his Lady."

At dawn on the third day, his prayers and vigils over, the future founder of the great militant order took off his sword and his spurs, exchanged his knightly dress for the coarse garb of a hermit, and descended the rocky path on foot. He was determined to go to Jerusalem, but, afraid that his friends would find him at Barcelona and detain him, he made first for the Dominican convent of Manresa.

From this time he no longer called himself Iñigo Recalde de Loyola, but Ignatius, because of his love for the martyred bishop of Antioch.

At Manresa his soul weathered a storm that has reminded many historians of that storm which had come upon Luther twenty years before in the convent at Erfurt. In both cases there was the same prolonged and anguished struggle, the same despairing resort to all the machinery of the mediæval Church, the same sense of alienation from God through sin, the same hopeless effort to keep a law which unaided human effort cannot keep.

It has, strange to say, surprised many that the same peace came to both alike. But Luther's vindication of the doctrine

Barcinone vt se ad animorum salutem instruat
prima Grammaticæ elementa annos tres, et tri=
ginta natus addiscit; furente ac rumpente se
Daemone, qui importunis rerum cælestium gau=
dijs auocare alio eius animum frustra conatur.

... justification by faith ... and ... necessarily appropr... ... experience for Protestants. Loyola, like L... ... feel in resting on the mercy of God.

It was from these experiences of his own, and from ... eternal perusal there of Garcia de Cisneros and Thom... Kempis, that the formulae of the Jesuits took on the Spir... Exercises. From these experiences, too, came a fresh ... of enthusiasm and prudence. From the hour whe... discovered that his self-chastisements and fasting and ... was vigils had failed to bring him nearer God, he distr... the severer forms of asceticism. He put off his her... dress, and anointed his head and washed his face and trim... his nails. The children in the streets no longer jeer... him. He had yet to renounce worldly poverty. He ... his way to Palestine, but his enthusiasms and his fe... ... alarmed the Christian population in Jerusalem, a... ... persuaded to return. But he had "seen" somethi... ... ..., and he was not to be baffled. He put hims... ... ... amongst ... on the benches ... school at ... ... prepare himself for the university. The boys laugh... him. His brain, long unused to study, was slow to ... But his will was of steel.

Yet he could not keep to himself that which was the ... and flower of all his endeavour. After school hours he ... out into the streets and preached, and taught the chi... their catechism. The Church, seeing him so ... and happy, suspected him of belonging to the heretical g... sect known as the *Alumbrados*.* It was a coarse judg... which placed this most astute of mystics on a plane ... these unbalanced folk, yet one can understand the mi... And a sacerdotal religion has no worse enemy to fear ... the man who claims to be able to commune with hi... without the intervention of a priest. The writings o... great mystics have all a Protestant ring:

> Oh, who can heal me ?
> Give me perfectly Thyself :
> Send me no more a messenger
> Who cannot tell what I seek.†

* The *Alumbrados*, or Spanish Illuminati. See Hanke, *Die Kirchliche...* in den Jahren vor Joh. ..., Bd. I., p. 123 : see also Gothein, *Ignat...* *Loyola und die Gegenreformation*, pp. 91-4.

† St. John of the Cross.

IGNATIUS LOYOLA AT SCHOOL

of justification by faith does not necessarily appropriate that experience for Protestantism. Loyola, like Luther, found rest in resting on the mercy of God.

It was from these experiences at Manresa, and from his ardent perusal there of Garcia de Cisneros and Thomas à Kempis, that the founder of the Jesuits built up the Spiritual Exercises. From these experiences, too, came a fresh rush of enthusiasm and joyfulness. From the hour when he discovered that his self-chastisements and fasting and sleepless vigils had failed to bring him nearer God, he distrusted the severer forms of asceticism. He put off his hermit's dress, and anointed his head and washed his face and trimmed his nails. The children in the streets no longer jeered at him. He had yet to renounce worldly poverty. He begged his way to Palestine, but his enthusiasms and his fearlessness alarmed the Christian population in Jerusalem, and he was persuaded to return. But he had " seen " something at Manresa, and he was not to be baffled. He put himself to school. The man of thirty-three sat on the benches of the school at Barcelona with little boys, to learn Latin and to prepare himself for the university. The boys laughed at him. His brain, long unused to study, was slow to learn. But his will was of steel.

Yet he could not keep to himself that which was the root and flower of all his endeavour. After school hours he went out into the streets and preached, and taught the children their catechism. The Church, seeing him so ecstatically happy, suspected him of belonging to the heretical gnostic sect known as the *Alumbrados*.* It was a coarse judgment which placed this most astute of mystics on a plane with these unbalanced folk, yet one can understand the mistake. And a sacerdotal religion has no worse enemy to fear than the man who claims to be able to commune with his God without the intervention of a priest. The writings of the great mystics have all a Protestant ring :

Oh, who can heal me ?
Give me perfectly Thyself :
Send me no more a messenger
Who cannot tell what I seek.†

* The *Alumbrados*, or Spanish Illuminati. See Ranke, *Die Römischen Papste in den letzten vier Jahrhunderten*, Bd. 1. p. 123 ; see also Gothein, *Ignatius von Loyola und die Gegenreformation*, pp. 61–4.
† *St. John of the Cross.*

Overcarefulness on the part of the Church was therefore pardonable. Ignatius was ordered to study theology for four years before dogmatising again in public.

For most men of his age this would have meant giving up and going down. But Ignatius, after proving his innocence of any taint of heresy, and his entire faithfulness towards the Church, only went on the more doggedly with his studies. He became a prominent figure in Alcalá and in Barcelona, and he did not lack for means or for friends. Some devoted ladies financed him liberally. But he never spent more than a small proportion of these moneys on his own personal needs.

After spending a short time at the college of Montaigu, possibly just before Calvin left there, Loyola entered Ste. Barbe.

Perhaps they [Calvin and Loyola] passed one another in some street of Mont Sainte Geneviève : the young Frenchman of eighteen on horseback, as was his custom, the Spaniard of thirty-six on foot, his purse furnished with gold which he had begged, before him his ass, laden with his books, and in his pocket a manuscript called the *Spiritual Exercises*. These two represented the two opposing worlds which were then separating. Each of them was preparing himself for the formidable contest which was about to shake Christianity to its foundations—Calvin the Reformer, Loyola the counter-Reformer : Calvin the father of the Huguenots, Loyola the father of the Jesuits.*

Faber tells us in his *Memorial* that Francis, Loyola, and himself shared the same room in Ste. Barbe. It is not likely that it held much furniture ; it was unusual for the students even to have beds in those days. In one corner, neatly arranged, we fancy, stood the books which the good ass had borne across the Pyrenees. Among them would be the manuscript Loyola had written and illuminated himself, a quarto volume of three hundred pages, containing a record of the lives of Christ and the saints, the words and acts of our Lord in red and gold, those of Mary in blue, and those of the saints in other colours. Beside it, a Latin Bible surely, and his missal, and a copy, perhaps, of Garcia de Cisneros' *Manual of Devotion*. But the dearest possession of all was a copy of the *Imitation* of Thomas à Kempis, called in the editions of those days *The Ecclesiastical Music*, and supposed to be

* Doumergue, *Vie de Jean Calvin*, vol. i. p. 126.

written by Gerson. Among his school and college books may have been the *Dialogues* of Vives, which were beginning to be very popular, the *Summulæ Logicales* of Peter the Spaniard, the *Sentences* of Peter Lombard, Lebrija's Latin dictionary perhaps, and one of his grammars. Beside them lay the MS. of the *Spiritual Exercises*, which he had been working upon since 1522.

Xavier's library was probably more eclectic. There was some jovial literature in circulation at that time, which we fancy would appeal to the gay and sharp-witted young Navarrese. He probably could not afford to possess many books, but there was an extensive system of lending libraries in the town. *La Celestina*, written by his fellow-country-man, Ferdinand de Rojas, had been published in 1499, and was one of the earliest and most important models of the modern drama. There were popular comedies, too, about, such as those of Torres de Naharro and Gil Vicente; these, for Spaniards, were the literary talk of the hour. On a higher level, and almost certainly among Xavier's treasures, was the *Coplas de Manrique* (published in 1477), a gem of Spanish poetry, and one of the supreme elegies of literature. It is familiar to many of us through Longfellow's translation. The satires of Rabelais, which a few years later were to enjoy such a colossal popularity, were not yet published. Who knows—had they appeared but a little earlier—where this supreme and compelling and destructive humour would have carried the gay Francis? Would it have undermined his devotion to the Church, a devotion that had been faithfully tended at home throughout his childhood, and was about to receive its determining direction from the finger of Loyola? It must have been very difficult ever to feel quite the same again towards the ecclesiastical systems of the day after reading the story of Gargantua and Pantagruel.

But, Rabelais apart, there was food enough for fear on Loyola's part for this disciple-elect of his.

" What is that in the corner there, Master Francis ? "

" That, Sir Pilgrim, is a copy of some most interesting writings by Martin Luther—you have heard of him; they appeared ten years ago, I believe, but have only lately come to my notice."

" Yes, I have indeed heard of him. Tell me, what do you think of him ? How does he appeal to you ? "

Xavier had no affection for Ignatius yet. The " Pilgrim," as they called him, was, in spite of his smouldering beauty, too unconventional, too strange and disconcerting a figure to love without a prelude of fear. But Ignatius, looking on Francis, had loved the laughing boy, so cleanly built and unspoiled, so fluent with his Latin, so keen with his wit. "*I shall win him*," said Ignatius. He did not talk much; his policy was rather to listen and sympathise, to understand his prey, to win trust and affection, and then cast the net. Francis and Peter Faber did most of the talking; talking is always so easy in the presence of those whose very presence is a caress. And Loyola, listening, prepared his big guns.

While within the little room the founder was beginning to learn the amazing power of his personal magnetism, the rank and file of the armies where his battle was to be waged were tuning up in the street below. Down in the rue St. Symphorien the students were shouting:

> Prions tous le roi de gloire
> Qu'il confond ces chiens mauldicts,
> Afin qu'il n'en soit plus mémoire,
> Non plus que de vielz os pourris.
>> Au feu, au feu! c'est leur repère
>> Fais-en justice! Dieu l'a permys;

and their enemies flung back the taunt:

>> La Sorbonne, la bigotte,
>> La Sorbonne se taira!
> Son grand hoste, l'Aristote,
> De la bande s'ostera!
> Et son escot, quoi qu'il coste
> Jamais ne la soulera!
>> La Sorbonne, la bigotte,
>> La Sorbonne se taira!

> La saincte Escriture toute
> Purement se prechera,
> Et toute doctrine sotte
> Des hommes on oublîra!
>> La Sorbonne, la bigotte,
>> La Sorbonne se taira! *

* *Bulletin de la Société de l'histoire de Protestantisme français*, vol. xii. p. 129, quoted by T. M. Lindsay, *History of the Reformation*, vol. ii. p. 536. See also, for another version of these words, Herminjard, *Correspondance des Réformateurs français*, tom. iii. p. 59.

Ignatius apparently entered Ste. Barbe some time before the beginning of the autumn term which was to see Xavier— then only in his twenty-fifth year—established as a lecturer in Greek in the college of Beauvais. There is one curious incident on record of Loyola's college days at Ste. Barbe ; whether it made his conquest of Xavier easier or harder we can only guess. Loyola, who had been talking of heaven and hell on the house-tops as only saints and madmen do, had been allowed to enter Ste. Barbe on the condition that he would leave the consciences of the other students alone. But even the nucleus-ideas of the scheme which was to leave its mark on European history were too much to be contained, if only for a few hours on end, in the mind of their originator. Among the restless group of men and boys sitting and lying on the straw floor of his lecture room, Professor Pena knew none so tiresome as Master Ignatius. Again and again he besought him to leave his fellows alone, and at last he reported him to the Principal, Jacques de Gouvea, who said that this scholar of forty would be punished as he had not been since he was sixteen: He was ordered to submit next day to *La Salle* :

One gave this name to a punishment more infamous than painful, which was administered in the following fashion. After dinner, all the students being present in the refectory, the masters and the scholars, each armed with a whip, ranged themselves in a double row. The delinquent, stripped to the waist, had to pass between them, and got from each of them a lash on his back.*

The masters and pupils were assembled for this affair, but Loyola did not appear. He was in the Principal's room. Presently they came out arm-in-arm, and Gouvea made, not an abject apology, as many of the old biographers love to relate, but a short speech, explaining that he had seen Ignatius to be a man of a holy life, albeit apt to be overcome with too much zeal, that he had promised to be more discreet in future, and that in his, the Principal's, name he renewed this promise before the college and received pardon.

One recalls that among that waiting row of students and masters stood, doubtless, the brooding figure of George Buchanan. " It is certainly odd to think that Buchanan, afterwards the co-churchman of Knox, should so nearly

* Quicherat, *Hist. de Ste. Barbe*, vol. i. p. 193.

E

have missed the privilege of laying his ferule on the bare shoulders of the founder of the Society of Jesus." *

In 1530 Xavier took his Arts degree and was free to teach " Arts, *here and over all the earth.*" As we have seen, he was by no means opulent, and he supported himself during his theological course by obtaining a post as lecturer or regent at the college of Beauvais, where, as Tursellinus says, he " explicated Aristotle publicly and not without praise." Although Le Fèvre d'Etaples, who had taught Greek, as he taught the Gospel, " from the sources," had come and gone, the mediæval Aristotle still held its place in the schools of Paris, and it is not likely that Francis Xavier got behind the treatises of Albertus Magnus and Thomas Aquinas. These scholastics had rendered an unforgettable service to the Church by giving her, for the first time, a version of the master in keeping with her own teaching. For the earliest translations of Aristotle had been taken from the Arabic versions of the exiled Caliphs among the Nestorians, and these versions emphasised the anti-Christian side of the philosopher, the *unitas intellectus*, the indestructibility of matter, the negation of personal immortality. The result was that in 1215 Aristotle had been prohibited by the Sorbonne, and the prohibition was not withdrawn until the labours of the great Dominicans had produced an orthodox philosopher. This, then, was the Aristotle upon which Xavier founded his lectures.

Meanwhile his old dreams of ecclesiastical distinction were not forgotten, and the preparation for the first step towards their fulfilment, the Doctorate in Theology, along with his own lectures, must have kept him hard at work. Although the theological course extended over so many years, the range of works studied was surprisingly small. Beyond the Bible and the *Sentences* of Peter Lombard, no other textbook was used.

How completely the *Sentences* were placed side by side with the Bible as the very source and fountain-head of all theology is illustrated by Albert the Great's disquisition on the knowledge possessed by the Mother of Christ. After demonstrating in detail that the Jewish peasant woman must have been acquainted

* P. Hume Brown, *George Buchanan*, p. 63.

with the *Trivium* and *Quadrivium*,* the Doctor proceeds to discuss the extent of her attainments in the Faculties of Medicine, Civil and Canon Law, and Theology; in the latter he holds that she must have had a summary knowledge of the Bible and *Sentences*. (Beatissima Virgo Bibliam et sententias in summo habuit.)†

Yet, in spite of these crudities of thought and expression, there was then, as always, the possibility of devout and profitable study.   Robert Sorbonne himself, with a greatness which ought to have shamed many who taught in the place which was called by his name, had said that knowledge had no worth if it did not raise the soul toward God. "There are," he said again, " scholars who work ceaselessly in sharpening the sword of the Word of God, and thus put it to use. Others amass thick volumes of argument, and bind them in grand covers painted with red, and go home very proud of their booty, their bags full, their spirits empty."

Xavier's bag was getting full, but his spirit was restless and unsatisfied.   The whole atmosphere of life in the company of Ignatius, during those portentous months, was charged as it were with fire.   The founder had not openly chosen his soldiers, nor formed his constitutions.   Yet, with all his faculties strained to their utmost use, he was in his own mind picking his men and constructing his Order.

Faber and Xavier, his most intimate companions, were alternately repelled and attracted.   Both began to see that their ambitions ran counter to those of Loyola, and both nursed their imperilled hopes with ardent yet flickering zeal.   Francis took clerk's orders.   Then he sent to Navarre for a formal title of his nobility and honourable descent. These things did not count for nothing in the Church.   But even while he dictated his claims to the notary the words that Loyola loved to quote were ringing in his ears: " What shall it profit a man if he gain the whole world and lose his own soul ? "

Faber has recorded his own struggles at this time :

Without being able to fix on anything I wished now to be a doctor, now a lawyer, now a professor.   One day I wished

---

* The two subject-groups of the Arts curriculum.
† Rashdall, *Hist. of the Med. Univ.*, vol. i. p. 465—quoted from Peter Lombard, *Opere* (Lugdino, 1651), tom. xx. p. 80.

to be a doctor of theology, the next a simple clerk.   At one point
I even thought of becoming a monk.*

Meanwhile Xavier's supplies of money from home had entirely
ceased, and he was poor to the point of suffering and actual
privation.   But Ignatius soon saw his wants.   "It was a
door," says Brou, "which God had opened to him, that he
might enter this soul."   So the Pilgrim gave him of the alms
he had received from the Spanish ladies or during his vaca-
tion tours in England and Flanders.   At the same time he
highly praised the young professor's lectures on Aristotle,
and brought numbers of students to his classes.   Master
Francis became very popular.

Xavier began to love this man who knew so well how to
appreciate him, and, encouraged by his success, he would
pour out his plans to him as they sat at night in their little
room in Ste. Barbe.   Ignatius listened with all his immense
natural tact and charm and sympathy, fortified by the real
knowledge and scholarship which had been so hardly acquired.
Yet always, the old biographers tell us, these talks ended with
the words, "What shall it profit a man, Master Francis, if
he gain the whole world and lose his own soul?"

And Francis could not forget those words, and could not
answer them.   Months passed.   Polanco said he had heard
"our great moulder of souls say that the hardest block he
ever had to do with was the young Francis Xavier in those
early days."

He was a young man of a great spirit, with froward and over-
thwart answers; he oftentimes of set purpose carped at Ignatius
and his words; yea, and sometimes, also, in very reproachful
manner scoffed at his excellent piety; but he, on the other side,
used all the sweet means he could to reclaim him from his in-
solency.   And not in vain.   For Patience at last overcame
Pertinacity.   And Xavier, being little by little made tractable
by that so gentle and courteous usage, began to bear some respect
towards him, and at last, touched by God's divine Spirit, let
himself be wholly ruled and guided by him.†

In order to earn the love wherewith to draw him away
from the congenial work at Beauvais College, Loyola
first established there the success and popularity of his

* P. Faber, *Memorial*, p. 13, Fr. ed.
† Tursellinus, *Life*, English edition, p. 8.

disciple-elect. It was a bold game to play, but it answered admirably. Further, he who originally attended the lectures as one of the oldest and most backward scholars soon made it appear that he conferred an honour on Francis by going there, and he discussed the lectures with the kindly condescension of a master towards a brilliant pupil.

Meanwhile the old links which bound Francis to his early surroundings were falling away one by one. With his mother's death his home had been broken up and his youthful ambitions shaken. And now came the news of the death of his sister, the Abbess of Gandia, "a true spirit, who excelled in the practice of humility, love, prayer, gentleness, and silence." * It was this sister who had watched over his career with such affection, and without whose intervention, at the time when he was recalled home, he would have had to return to Navarre and would never have met Loyola.

Once again, perhaps, alone, and in a graver mood than before, he climbed the spiral stairs of Notre-Dame, and looked down upon Paris.

It was more than eight years since he had stood there first, fresh from school, the spurs of undaunted ambition pricking his ardent spirit. And now——? Life had grown very complex. What arid stretches of experience it held, what absurd laughter, what fruitless tears! And the wise doctors of the Sorbonne, amongst whom, in his dreams, he had once seen himself, were mostly fat old men with heavy eyes and stubborn mouths. And the bishops were busy burning students whom he used to think good and wise. It was not worth being a bishop for that. During all these years he had never been home, and now he had no longer a home. The trophies that had once seemed valuable to him because he might lay them at his mother's feet had now a new and a harsher worth. Personal power, riches, authority, had acquired for him an attraction of their own. And in the Church it seemed as if ever since that night in May, 1527, when the Imperialists had burst into Rome it was doubly easy for his fellow-countrymen to attain distinction. It was a fine thing to be a Spaniard. They were gaining the whole world! Ah, "*What shall it profit a man? What shall it profit a man?*" These were the words Ignatius had teased him with night and day, day and night. Did

* Letter from Sor Ana. See *Doc. Nouv.*, p. 311.

that inscrutable gargoyle-face of stone beside him not suggest the same question, as, chin in hand, with gentle brows and mocking mouth, it fixed its great blank eyes on Paris?

Paris had gained the worlds of philosophy and theology—for scholars, once all the roads of Europe had converged there; but where was the soul of that fair city now? Francis knew that the wisest men were turning to other centres of learning, that the Latin texts from which he expounded Aristotle were out of date. Thought was difficult and confused. But he could not blind himself to the fact that in Paris, at least, there was some real bond between the Humanists and the religious reformers, between the new passion for truth from the " sources " of things and the new contempt for the Roman Curia. Luther was shouting that it was the Bible and not the Pope to which they must turn: Pico had lifted his head from his newly found manuscripts to say: "Philosophy seeks truth, theology finds it, religion possesses it," and had turned again to the tales of the gods of Greece. But such men were despicable. This " truth " of the Protestants and the Humanists was a cold thing; men should seek not an idea but a person, serve not Humanity but the Church, the Bride. The most sacred traditions of life could not be held in a printed book, but only in the living hands of the Vicar of Christ. If Pico had put " God " in place of " truth," he would have done better. Religion possesses God—that was what Francis believed. And it was religion that Paris lacked. But where was this religion to be found? Not surely in those burning piles where the Lutherans screamed out their last moments in anguish, nor yet—God grant—in the hands that held the torch to the faggot, nor in those " tomes bound in grand covers and painted with red " that Robert Sorbonne had laughed at, but that the old doctors down there loved so well. What if it *was* religion which was carrying those heretics to their death? Loyola had said that all reform must begin in the individual heart, that the only life that mattered was the life of the soul. Had Luther not said something like that too? And was this zealot from Guipuzcoa, perhaps, after all, just leading them by another road to the same fire? He would leave this fanatical cripple before it was too late. And yet how he loved him! Could he leave him? His father and mother had died, and Loyola had taken him up. Loyola was praying for him continually. How kind he had been, and how generous! How sympathetic he was! Did Francis wonder how he could ever have scorned this knight of Christ, who had sprung from as noble a house as his own, and who had achieved a military glory that he, Francis, had never achieved, who had sacrificed infinitely more than he had sacrificed? He thanked God that He had given him this man for a friend—nay (the subjugation was almost complete), for a Master.

At this time Faber had gone home to Savoy to bid his father and friends farewell. He had offered his whole life to Loyola.

For seven months Francis and the founder were alone. When, at the beginning of 1534, Faber returned from Switzerland, Ignatius had won his second disciple.

Francis wished to fling up all his collegiate duties at once. Ignatius bade him to go on with his teaching, and to take his theological degree. He did not even give him the Spiritual Exercises. That Xavier was the last of the original members to undergo this discipline has been held by some to indicate that Ignatius thought it imprudent to harness the high spirit of the young hidalgo to those stern hours until he was entirely sure of his devotion. But the delay may simply have been caused by the fact that Xavier's time was fully occupied with his work.

Just at this time a curious incident took place, which in its own bizarre way witnesses both to Xavier's devotion to Ignatius and to the devotion, however distorted, which Xavier had inspired towards himself.

Miguel the Navarrese, Xavier's wicked servant and protégé, was made wildly jealous by his master's devotion to Ignatius: the poor fool went to Loyola's window, by night, with a dagger in his hand. The future of the Society hung in the balance. But a voice, the biographers tell us, turned him back from this deed, and he fell down at the bedside, confessing his sin and begging forgiveness.

Ignatius appears at this time to have had, or at least to have expressed, no definite plan of action:

There was no question of the foundation of a new religious order, nor of one definite enterprise. Nothing was defined except certain ascetic principles, the same which formed the foundation of the Exercises : a certain indifference of will towards everything except God : the need of linking oneself to Jesus Christ, winning souls, and working for their salvation, yet working as Christ did, by poverty and the Cross.*

Thus tentatively, slowly, with a curious blending of calculation and fervour, the Company began to take shape. The members of this society were to bridge the gulf between the Crusaders and the modern missionaries. Its earlier dreams were of the Holy Land and the Sepulchre of our Lord : its finest result was the Apostle of the Indies.

Ignatius talked over the future with his disciples individually, and one by one, unknown to the rest, they were asked to go aside alone for some days and seek the guidance of God, and then to return at a stated time to his rooms. One day Francis, Faber, and four others all found themselves there together with Ignatius, and when he, with his magnetic skill, began to question them, they found, with delicious astonishment and wonder, that they were all of one mind and one purpose.

Rodriguez, who was one of them, says that at this point they took the triple vow of poverty, chastity, and pilgrimage to Jerusalem.   But nothing was to be done till the theological studies were ended. A day was fixed (January 25th, 1537) when they should all meet for conference at Venice, and, if possible, proceed from there to the Holy Land. In Jerusalem they would once again ask God to give them special direction. But if anything were to hinder their leaving Italy, they were to present themselves to the Pope and put themselves at his disposal.

A few days after this informal conference Ignatius and his six followers met as a Company for the first time. They had still to obtain the Pope's sanction before they could constitute themselves as an Order. They assembled at the cathedral church of Notre-Dame, and from thence, bannerless, trumpetless, and unnoticed, the little black-robed band, led by Ignatius, made its way to the heights of Montmartre. The citizens of Paris, who loved gay flags and banners, robes of silk and cramoisie and velvet, gaily-trapped horses,

* Brou, *Vie de S. François Xavier*, vol. i. p. 43.

shouting, singing, the noises of drums and tambours, would have jeered if you had told them that this was the most portentous procession that had threaded their streets for many a year. Yet so it was.

In the van limped Loyola, with swift, determined steps, his eyes burning, his brows inscrutably calm. Behind him came those who were, in varying degrees, his devotees, and God's. Faber, with the loose gait and far-focussed eyes of a shepherd, Xavier, of medium height, dark, eager-limbed, his eyes meekly dropped, and a reverent gravity veiling, for this great occasion, the wayward mouth that laughed so lightly and so well. Salmeron and Bobadilla were there, too, both of them restless, energetic, impatient, full of fire, and of desire to go one step farther than their master; Salmeron was to prove a great preacher, and was to discharge the duties of Papal theologian at the Council of Trent. In the same Council Lainez, " a young man with the brain of an ancient sage," the most learned of this strange procession, was destined to be the dominating and fatal influence. And lastly there was Rodriguez, the Portuguese, who was to leave written records of the Company, and to be one of their most outstanding diplomatists.*

The story of how the first Jesuits went to Montmartre has been told again and again, but there is probably no such accurate account of that day as that given in the simple words of Peter Faber in his *Memorial.*

This same year, 1534, on the day of the Assumption of the Holy Virgin, all those of us who at that time shared in the designs of Loyola, and who had undergone the Spiritual Exercises (except Master Xavier, who had not yet received them), rendered ourselves at Notre Dame of Montmartre, and there we made a vow to serve God and to depart on a certain day for Jerusalem, to give up relatives and all the rest, taking with us only the viaticum. Besides, we resolved to go, after our return from the Holy Land, and put ourselves at the disposal of the Pope. Now those who were present at this first re-union at Notre Dame de Montmartre were, Ignatius, Master Francis Xavier, I, Faber, Master Bobadilla, Master Lainez, Master Salmeron, Master Simon Rodriguez. For Le Jay, though in Paris, had not yet resolved to follow us, and neither Master J. Codure nor Master Paul Brouet were yet taken.

* Simon Rodriguez, author of the *Commentarium de origine el progres su Societatis Jesu*, Lisbon, 25 Juli 1577.

The two following years, 1535-36, we returned there on the same day, to the same altar, to confirm the determination we had then taken, and each time we found there great help for our spiritual life.*

Rodriguez adds that Faber, who was the only priest present, celebrated mass. After this consecration before the altar, " the new associates, coming forth from the chapel, sat them down by a spring on the western aspect of the height —a spring, like our white Winefride's Holywell, traditionally stained with the martyr's blood—and there breaking their fast together, spent the residue of the blessed day together in holy and fraternal chat."† " And in the evening, at set of sun," says Rodriguez, " they went homeward, praising and blessing the Lord."

A few days later the term ended, and Francis employed the month of September in taking the Spiritual Exercises. He has left no record of his experiences during those days. But the way in which he henceforth speaks of the Exercises, and his continual recommendation of them to others, shows that he believed they had done much for himself. Possibly he over-estimated how much. It is often difficult to differentiate between the results arising from the state of mind which leads a man to a remedy, and the results of the remedy itself. At the same time it is most probable that the Exercises influenced him enormously. Beside the old sense of individuality, and the desire for personal development, there was awakening at this time a sense of social unity, a desire to live as a worthy part of the whole. This enlightenment came to some through the channels of Humanism : to many devout Catholics it probably came, in part at least, through the military discipline of the Spiritual Exercises, combined with the general influence of Loyola's genius. There Francis Xavier learned that religion and personal culture and social serviceableness could go hand in hand, and with this new programme in his possession he ceased to gaze wistfully toward the more or less forbidden fruits of classicism which had heretofore seemed to him the only food for thoughtful and **progressive** minds.

* Peter Faber, *Memorial*, pp. 14 and 15.
† Francis Thompson, *Ignatius Loyola*, p. 86.

"WHAT SHALL IT PROFIT A MAN, MASTER FRANCIS?"

From an old woodcut of Loyola and Xavier

"The Father Master Francis was a little difficult and obstinate, for though he enjoyed greatly the conversation and friendship of Ignatius, yet he did not dare to change altogether the estate of his life, as he was naturally inclined to the honour and pomp of the world, as some who at this time were very intimate with him afterwards told us" (Teix, *Vita, Mon. Xav.*, vol ii. p 818).

Colla forza di una Maſsima Evangelica
viene da S. Ignazio ridotto
ad una vita perfetta ed Apostolica.

CHAPTER V

No account of the Order of Jesus, nor of the life of Francis Xavier, is complete without some notice of the " Spiritual Exercises." " Most of us," says Lainez, the second general, " received with the Exercises the spirit of vocation, so much so that we might truly say that our Society has been founded and united and developed chiefly by their means." To all who wished to join the Company, Ignatius administered this discipline; it was given, too, to hundreds who found themselves at the cross-roads, and such were almost invariably added to the ranks of the Society. Francis of Sales remarked that the little book had converted more souls than the letters it contained, and it has often been said that the famous meditation of the Two Standards (see p. 79) has peopled monasteries. To this day the Jesuits honour it as a revelation from God, and find in it the apotheosis of the spirit of their Order; Loyola himself had such unbounded faith in this discipline, that if it ever failed to produce the desired effect he blamed only the manner of giving or receiving it.*

To hear such reports of its fame, and then to turn to the book itself, is inevitably to be disappointed. The first thing which strikes you, especially if you expect to find here a work of devotion, is the dryness and reticence of the book. It is like a school text-book, small, precise, divided into portions and headings. Here is no mystical rapture, no poetic beauty. The personality of the author never appears. Dates, hours, subjects of prayer and meditation, physical environment, a confessor or adviser, all are arranged for, and then the soul is to be left alone with God, until the director again demands its confidence. For between the pupil and the director, who represents the Church, there can be no veil drawn. Ignatius did not put this book into the hands of Christians that they might keep it on their shelves and read it now and then, or at stated intervals, as they would their Bibles or their books of devotion. -For the mere reader the book is a door of which he can only see the outside. It is

* Cartas, No. 6.

primarily for the use of priests, and without the help of a priest the layman has nothing to gain from it except a half-satisfied curiosity.

Thus, by always keeping the priest between the soul and God, Ignatius attacked at the same time the sentimental mysticism of certain Catholics, and the independent Protestantism of the reformers, who claimed direct access to God through Jesus Christ. How far, in the case of the Exercises, the director *interfered* between man and his Maker, and how far he was merely a friend and a counsellor is a point on which Romanists and Protestants must be divided. But our study of the Annotations, with which the book opens, may lead us to think that originally the Director was meant to play a humbler part than later he came to do, and the question arises whether, in this usurpation of a right that was not really theirs, the later Jesuits failed to carry out the will of their Founder, and thus brought the Exercises into a disrepute which they do not deserve. *

Let us look first, then, at these " *Twenty Annotations for Obtaining some Knowledge of the Spiritual Exercises which Follow, and for the Help as Well of Him Who is to Give as of Him Who is to Receive Them.*"

These Annotations begin by defining spiritual exercises as

every method of examination of conscience, of meditation, of contemplation, of vocal and mental prayer, and of other spiritual operations, as shall be afterwards declared ; for as to go for a walk or a journey, and to run, are bodily exercises, so is the name of spiritual exercises applied to any method of preparing and disposing the soul to free itself from all inordinate affections, and after it has freed itself from them, to seek and find the will of God concerning the ordering of life for the salvation of one's soul.

The second annotation advises the priest who gives the exercises to keep himself in the background, going through the points briefly and with a short explanation, in order that

---

* Most of the references and extracts which follow are taken from the 1908 English version. (*The Text of the Spiritual Exercises of Ignatius Loyola,* Burns & Oates, 1908.) The Spanish autograph copy was first approved by Pope Paul III. in 1548, and the book was printed in Latin in the same year. The first English version appeared in 1736, but it is far from accurate. In 1847 and in 1870 other editions were published ; that of 1870 was specially arranged for the use of the Anglican communion.

the pupil may " understand and savour the matter interiorly, for that fills and satisfies the soul."

The third declares that there are degrees of reverence required by the pupil, a less degree during intellectual operations than during those " acts of the will," when the soul converses vocally or mentally with God.

The fourth allows that the formal time-limitation of one week for each of the four divisions of the exercises may be lengthened or shortened according to the needs of the pupil, so long as the whole is concluded in about a month.*

The fifth advises " him who is receiving the exercises to enter upon them with a large heart and with liberality towards his Creator and Lord, offering all his desires and liberty to Him, in order that His Divine Majesty may make use of his person and of all he possesses according to His most holy will."

After that come various precepts for the benefit of the administrator of the Exercises. He is especially warned not to allow the pupil to make any rash vows under the impetus given him by the discipline.

he who gives the exercises must not incline him who receives them more to poverty or to a vow than to their contraries, nor to one state or manner of life more than another . . . but keeping as it were in equilibrium, like a balance, allow the Creator to act immediately with the creature, and the creature with its Creator and Lord.

Number XIX. outlines a modified course for those taken up with private affairs and necessary business.

Number XX. runs as follows :—

To him who is less occupied, and who desires in every possible way to profit, let all the Spiritual Exercises be given in the order in which they follow ; and in these generally he will derive all the more profit, in proportion as he separates himself from all friends and relations and from all earthly cares, as for example, by leaving the house he dwells in and choosing another house or room, there to dwell in as great privacy as possible, in such a way that it be in his power to go daily to Mass and to Vespers, without fear that

* Ignatius himself, in his later years, modified the limitations of time and circumstance to such a degree that he recommended lay people, if they desired, to go daily to church for one hour, and in this way go through the Exercises with a confessor ; see Gothein, *Ignatius von Loyola und die Gegenreformation*, p. 242.

his relations will put any obstacle in his way. And, among many other advantages, three principal ones will result from this separation. The first is, that when a person separates himself from numerous friends and acquaintances, and disengages himself from many ill-ordered concerns, in order to serve and praise God our Lord, he gains no little merit in the eyes of His Divine Majesty. The second is, that when a person has thus withdrawn himself, as his understanding is not divided on many subjects, but all his solicitude is placed on one thing only, namely, on the service of his Creator and the profit of his own soul, he enjoys a freer use of his natural powers in seeking diligently what he so much desires. The third is, that the more our soul find itself alone and in solitude, the fitter it renders itself to approach and unite itself to its Creator and Lord; and the nearer it thus unites itself to Him, the more it disposes itself to receive graces and favours from His Divine and Supreme Goodness.

After these annotations come directions for the self-examinations which are to be made thrice daily. The pupil is to keep diagrammatic notes or charts of his sins, in order that his progress or decline may be easily evident from day to day, and week to week. After retiring, if possible, completely from the outer world, closing doors and windows, he is to meditate for a week upon sin and punishment, especially in the morning, at noon, in the evening, and at midnight. At the end of the First Week he is advised to make a general confession, and to receive the Holy Sacrament.

John Calvin's criticism of the Exercise of the First Week is interesting, as coming from so great a contemporary of Loyola's, but some of us will think it unreasonable and over-harsh :

There is no semblance of reason in the absurd procedure of those who, that they may begin with repentance, prescribe to their neophytes certain days during which they are to exercise themselves in repentance, and, after these are elapsed, admit them to communion in Gospel grace . . . such are the fruits which their giddy spirit produces, that repentance, which in every Christian man lasts as long as life, is with them completed in a few short days.*

The Second Week the meditations are taken from selected events in the Life of our Lord, up to the Sabbath before His Passion. Amid these meditations, on the Fourth Day of the

* J. Calvin, *Institutes of Christian Religion*, Book III. cap. ii.

Week, is inserted the Meditation on Two Standards. As the Jesuits have always considered this one of the most efficacious passages in the writings of Loyola, we will quote it in full.

The meditation on Two Standards, the one of Christ, our sovereign Leader and Lord; the other of Lucifer, the mortal enemy of our human race.

The usual preparatory prayer.

The first prelude is the history; it will be here shown how Christ calls and desires all under His banner—Lucifer, on the contrary, under his.

The second prelude is a composition of place, seeing the spot; it will be here to see a vast plain of all the region round Jerusalem, where the Supreme general Leader of all good is Christ our Lord; and to imagine another plain in the country of Babylon, where the chief of the enemy is Lucifer.

The third prelude is to ask for what I want; it will be here to ask for knowledge of the deceits of the wicked chieftain, and for help to guard against them; and for knowledge of the true life which our Sovereign and true Leader points out, and for grace to imitate Him.

The first point is to imagine the chieftain of all the enemy as seated in that great plain of Babylon, as on a lofty throne of fire and smoke, in aspect horrible and fearful.

The second point is to consider how he summons together innumerable devils, how he disperses them some to one city, some to another, and so on throughout the whole world, omitting not any provinces, places, or states of life, or any persons in particular.

The third point is to consider the address which he makes, and how he warns them to lay snares and chains; telling them how they are first to tempt men to covet riches (as he is wont to do in most cases), so that they may more easily come to the vain honour of the world, and then to unbounded pride; so that the first step is riches, the second honour, the third pride; and from these three steps he leads them to all other vices.

In the same way, on the other hand, we are to consider the sovereign and true Leader, Christ our Lord.

The first point is to consider how Christ our Lord, in aspect fair and winning, takes His station in a great plain of the country near Jerusalem on a lowly spot.

The second point is to consider how the Lord of the whole world chooses out so many persons, Apostles, disciples, etc., and sends them throughout the whole world diffusing His sacred doctrine through all states and conditions of persons.

The third point is to consider the address which Christ our Lord makes to all His servants and friends, whom He sends on this expedition, recommending to them that they desire to help all, by guiding them first to the highest degree of poverty of spirit, and even to actual poverty, if it please His Divine Majesty, and He should choose to elect them to it ; leading them, secondly, to a desire of reproaches and contempt, because from these two humility results ; so that there are three steps : the first, poverty, opposed to riches ; the second, reproaches and contempt, opposed to worldly honour ; the third, humility, opposed to pride : and from these three steps let them conduct them to all other virtues.

A colloquy to our Lady to obtain for me grace from her Son and Lord that I may be received under His Standard.   And first, in the highest degree of poverty of spirit, and not less in actual poverty, if it please His Divine Majesty, and He should choose to elect and receive me to it.   Secondly, in bearing reproaches and insults, the better to imitate Him in these, provided only I can endure them without sin on the part of any person, or displeasure to His Divine Majesty ; and after this an *Ave Maria.*

To ask the same from the Son, that He obtain for me this grace from the Father ; and then to say an *Anima Christi.*

To ask the same from the Father, that He grant me this grace ; and to say a *Pater noster.*

This Exercise will be made at midnight, and again early in the morning ; and two repetitions of it will be made at the hours of Mass and Vespers, always finishing with the triple colloquy to our Lady, the Son, and the Father ; and the meditation on the Classes, which follows, will be made during the hour before supper.

There is also included in the Second Week a note on the three degrees of humility.   The first when God's will is man's law, the second when God's will is man's will, the third when God's will is specially pleasing to man when it involves him in the sufferings and poverty of Christ.

This note is followed by a disquisition on the making of choices or decisions in life.   Here are one or two extracts :—

In every good election, as far as regards ourselves, the eye of our intention ought to be single, looking only to the end for which I was created, which is, for the praise of God our Lord, and for the salvation of my soul.   And thus whatever I choose ought to be for this, that it should help me to the end for which I was created ; not ordering and drawing the end to the means, but the means to the end.   As, for example, it happens that many first choose to marry, which is a means, and secondarily to serve our Lord God in the married state, which service of God is the end.   In the same way there are others that first desire to possess benefices and then to serve God in them.   So these do not go straight to

God, but wish God to come straight to their inordinate affections ; thus they make of the end a means, and of the means an end ; so that what they ought to take first they take last. For first we ought to make our object the desire to serve God, which is the end ; and secondarily to receive the benefice, or marry, if it is more profitable to me ; and this is the means to the end. Nothing then ought to move me to take these or other means, or to deprive myself of them, except only the service and praise of God our Lord and the eternal salvation of my soul.

The first rule is that the love, which urges and causes me to choose such or such a thing, descend from on high from the love of God ; so that he who chooses, feel first in himself that the love which he has more or less for the thing he chooses, is solely for the sake of his Creator and Lord.

The second rule is to place before my eyes a man whom I have never seen or known, and to consider what I, desiring all perfection for him, would tell him to do and choose for the greater glory of God our Lord, and the greater perfection of his soul ; and acting so, to keep the rule which I lay down for another.

The third rule is to consider, as if I were at the point of death, what would be the form and measure which I should then desire to have observed in the proceeding of the present election ; and regulating my conduct according to this, I must make my decision in all things.

The fourth rule is, viewing and considering what I shall find myself at the Day of Judgment, to think how I shall then wish to have decided in regard to the present matter ; and the rule which I should then wish to have observed, I will now observe, that I may then find myself full of joy and pleasure.

During the Second Week and thereafter the pupil is advised to read occasionally out of the *Imitation*, the *Gospels*, and the *Lives of the Saints*.

The whole of the Third Week is occupied with the contemplation of the Passion of our Lord. There are added to these meditations some Rules for regulating oneself for the future in the matter of food.

Abstinence is more suitable with regard to drink than with regard to eating bread .... abstinence may be observed in two ways, first, by accustoming oneself to eat coarser food ; secondly, by taking delicacies in smaller quantities . . . while eating let one consider that he sees Christ our Lord eating with His disciples, and how He drinks, and how He looks, and how He speaks, and endeavour to imitate Him. .· . . Let him, above all, guard against his mind being completely engrossed in what

F

he is eating . . . it is very profitable *after* dinner or *after* supper, or at some other time when one does not feel any desire to eat, to determine the amount which it is fitting to eat, and not to exceed this amount. . . .

The attitude of Loyola towards ascetism was clearly defined : he never regarded it as an end *in itself*, and he recognised that there was a point at which it was apt to defeat its own ends. It was his servant, not his master, a servant to be discarded as soon as self-conquest is reached.

The Fourth Week is occupied with the Resurrection and the Contemplation for obtaining Love. In this final contemplation the stern reticence of the Founder begins at last to break. " For after winter followeth summer, after night the day returneth, and after a tempest a great calm." *

The windows, according to the directions, have been opened, the sunlight streams into the cell, the Lord is risen, the disciple is bidden " to rejoice in the exceeding great joy and gladness of Christ our Lord . . . to bring before the memory and think of things that cause pleasure, cheerfulness and joy, as about Heaven . . . to avail himself of light, the beauties of the season, as in Spring and Summer of refreshing coolness, and in winter of the sun or a fire." In this joyous mood the following prayer is to be said, " with great affection, as one who makes an offering " :—

Take, O Lord, and receive all my liberty, my memory, my understanding, and all my will, whatever I have and possess. Thou hast given all these things to me : to Thee, O Lord, I restore them all : all are Thine, dispose of them all according to Thy will. Give me Thy love and Thy grace, for this is enough for me.

There follows a chapter on Three Methods of Prayer. The first method is an examination or testing of conduct in its relation to the ten commandments, the seven deadly sins and their contrary virtues, and the five senses of the body. The second method advises you to pray word by word, pausing at each word and dwelling on its significance so long that, for example, the repetition of the Lord's Prayer will occupy about an hour. The third method is that

at each breath or respiration, prayer be made mentally, saying

---

* *The Imitation of Christ*, cap. viii.

one word of the Lord's Prayer or of any other prayer that is being recited, so that only one word be said between each breath, and in the length of time between each breath let attention be specially paid to the signification of the word, or to the person to whom the prayer is directed, or to one's own lowness, or to the distance between that person's great dignity and such lowness of ours.

Next there comes an annotated summary of the Life of Christ, chiefly in the words of the New Testament, various rules " for the discernment of spirits," by which the disciple may detect what is real and what is false in his spiritual life. There are added Rules for giving alms, Rules on scruples, and the much discussed Rules for thinking with the Church. The knowledge of the inner machinery of the human heart and mind displayed in this book, and specially in these later chapters, is profound. Nowhere else, perhaps, outside William James' *Varieties of Religious Experience*, have we such an attempt at a precise and scientific systemisation of the soul. Yet, like all genuine scientific writing, the book, for youthful spirits, glows with romance. Xavier, we feel sure, found nothing cold or indecent in this searching psychology. That discovery has been left to the modern student and critic.

There must be a deep æsthetic as well as religious delight in shutting oneself within the bare and austere walls of this discipline, and then, after seeing and hearing and feeling the terrors of hell, finding oneself gradually surrounded by all the splendours of this magical architecture; and Francis, with his genius for joyousness, must have benefited to the full by this design of spiritual cunning. But Ignatius never allows the discipline or delights of these Exercises to be an end in themselves; his aim is self-discipline, and the discipline of the regiment of Jesus.

It is this quality which separates the Exercises from most mediæval works of contemplation and meditation. And it is when we come to this point that the question forces itself upon us : Should a man study and contemplate the mysteries of the Christian faith in order to add to the stature of his soul ? " Which of you by being anxious can add one cubit to his stature ? " said Jesus. " If then ye are not able to do that which is least, why are ye anxious concerning the rest ? . . . Seek ye His kingdom and these things shall be added unto you." Loyola's supreme aim was indeed the Kingdom

of God, but he missed, like so many of us, that view of the
Divine economy which shows us that the pursuit of that end
will in itself sufficiently educate and discipline the soul.
When we compare Ignatius with the mediæval mystics we
incline to admire the practicality of his devotions; and the
older mystics we condemn, because they set as their utmost
goal an experience of rapture which was something between
themselves and God and no other, an experience which they
could attain to in the isolation of their own cells. But if
that kind of religion was unpractical, at least it was not
passionless, and sometimes one is inclined to think that the
Spiritual Exercises must tend to expurgate religious passion
from the soul. "This book," says Eberhard Gothein, "is
not a work of passionate reverie, as has often been believed:
rather it is a process of inoculation against that quality."
The same writer goes on to suggest a comparison between the
influence of the Exercises and the influence of tragedy as
defined by Aristotle. Tragedy, Aristotle tells us, is a repre-
sentation (literally an imitation) which produces through pity
and fear the purification or κάθαρσις of emotions of that nature.
" Is this world-drama but a great *tragedy* for Loyola, from
the Creation to the Day of Judgment, with the central tragic
episode of the Redemption ? " *

Perhaps the quality which suggests this comparison to
Professor Gothein is the same quality which is condemned
by most other Protestant critics under the heading of " crass
materialism ":

Materialism of the crudest type mingled with the indulgence
of a reverie in this long spiritual journey. At every step the
neophyte employed his five senses in the effort of intellectual
realisation. Prostrate upon the ground, gazing with closed
eyelids in the twilight of his cell upon the mirror of imagination,
he had to *see* the boundless flames of hell and souls encased in
burning bodies, to *hear* the shrieks and blasphemies, to *smell*
their sulphur and intolerable stench, to *taste* the bitterness of
tears, and *feel* the stings of ineffectual remorse. He had to
localise each object in the camera obscura of the brain.†

* Eberhard Gothein, *Ignatius von Loyola und die Gegenreformation*, p. 235.
† J. A. Symonds, *The Renaissance in Italy*, " The Catholic Reaction,"
Part I. p. 288 ; see also, for an exactly similar criticism, Dr. T. M. Lindsay's
History of the Reformation, vol. ii. p. 548. The passage quoted by Symonds
is, with the addition of comments and italics, taken from the Fifth Exercise of
the First Week ; see p. 27 of English edition (1908).

If this criticism is just, we are forced to ask : What, then, is the orthodox Protestant state of mind and imagination on reading, say, the last few verses of the ninth chapter of St. Mark or the twenty-fifth chapter of St. Matthew ? It would take a most accomplished theologian to read these words of our Lord without the most vivid and, to use Dr. Lindsay's phrase, " crassly material " pictures invading his mind. What is the purpose of the Parables, of all imaginative art and literature, if not just to make us see and hear and feel, and thus to minister to those experiences of the imagination which bridge the life of sense and the life of ultimate reality ? We dwell in a house of shadows and semblances; the things we can touch and handle, and see and hear, are, just because of these physical qualities, the things that we know have no permanent place in a life which is eternal. Knowing this, the ascetic goes on to say that because the material world is not an end in itself, because it is a shadow, a symbol, therefore it is to be despised, to be, as far as possible, ignored. He has seen the supreme value of the life of the imagination, of the soul, but he has forgotten that God *created* the world, and that the " Word was made flesh, and dwelt among us." On this chill ground extreme Protestants and extreme Catholics meet. But it is the unique quality of Christianity that it realises the link between the world of tangible shadows and the world of invisible realities. The Christian has to learn to live in the world and yet separate from it. There is no created thing which cannot help to lift the soul to God. When Paul says, " Henceforth know we Christ no longer after the flesh," he surely does not altogether condemn that earlier knowledge ; when he was a child he thought as a child. Does the history of the Christian disciple not always show a progression from a knowledge of Christ after the flesh onward to a deeper knowledge ? Through the words and actions of our schoolmasters who bring us to Christ, through the Scriptures, through the material images which the Scriptures conjure up in our minds, through Nature, which is the garment of God, through all these " material " ways we enter into the kingdom of heaven and of the things unseen. And the power of the Spiritual Exercises lies in their use of the lower experiences to serve the purposes of the higher. It is the same power which gave distinction to the whole life of Loyola. On the one hand he saw the Church absorbed in material things, in the cleansing and decorating of the outside of the cup and platter, worshipping the customs themselves, forgetful of the reason which lay behind the custom ; and on the other hand he saw the " mystics " and ascetics, despising reason and custom alike, and trying to escape from the senses which God had given them.   Surely Protestants should be the last to condemn this inward eye. In their impatience of outward symbol and ceremony the early Jesuits savoured far more of Scotland or of the English Puritans than of Rome.   George Tyrrell made no ill comparison when he likened Ignatius Loyola to John Bunyan. Bunyan himself says : " It began to be rumoured up and down that I was a witch, a Jesuit, a highwayman, and the like." Both men were making a bee-line for God, and folk who make bee-lines across rough land carry few superfluous goods. The greatest Protestant saints have yet a holy frenzy in their behaviour, the greatest Catholic saints a naked simplicity, and these qualities bring them very close to one another. Ignatius' pages, like John Bunyan's, had been lived before they were written.

And though spiritual exercises were common enough in those days, the confessional quality of this book gives to it an essential originality and an incalculable power.   Loyola lived, like all artists, a double life.   Every crisis of his experience, all times of light and darkness, of joy and sorrow, of ease and difficulty, have, in the full tide of their arrival, been analysed and reduced to a sort of spiritual psychological system.   " After   this,"   says Gonçalvez,   " I asked the Pilgrim about the Exercises and Constitutions, that I might understand how he had written them.   He replied: 'I did not compose them all at once.   As through my own experience a thing appeared to me useful to others, I noted it down.   So, for example, the plan of marking on lines the result of a particular examination, and other things of this kind.'"   This habit he had begun at Manresa in 1522, and the Exercises were not published till 1548.   Apart from his own experiences, the sources of the book are not numerous.   But, as befits the *chef-d'œuvre* of the great cosmopolitan Order, they are representative of many countries.

Spain is represented by Ignatius himself and by Garcia de Cisneros (the author of a book of exercises which Loyola found at Manresa); the Low Countries and Germany by Ludolf of Saxony, Mauburnus, Gerard van Zutphen, and the author of the *Imitation*; France at least by the director of St. Ignatius at Montserrat, D. Chamines; Italy by St. Bonaventura.*

By far the most influential of those books was undoubtedly the *Imitation*, and in the letters and writings of St. Francis Xavier we can see that he, too, was deeply, probably directly, influenced by Thomas à Kempis.

The great motto of the company, *Ad Majorem Dei Gloriam*, was meant to recall the Church to reason, and the mystics and ascetics to a purposeful life. We cannot question the nobility of the phrase. It embodies one of the truisms of Christianity. Ignatius, in taking this for his motto, only echoed the words of St. Paul: " Whether therefore ye eat or drink or whatsoever ye do, do all to the glory of God." He anticipated the first answer of the Shorter Catechism : " Man's chief end is to glorify God and to enjoy Him forever." By this motto, then, the Spiritual Exercises must be judged. In so far as the author's conception of the glory of God is inadequate, they fall short.

But the words *Ad Majorem Dei Gloriam* may have many interpretations; and although the ideals of the greatest saints may be much alike, the little spark of difference is what flashes into flame in the lesser lives of those who follow them. For the passing experience in itself Ignatius never shows anything more than the respect one shows to a good tool. And this supreme emphasis which he puts upon the "end," the lofty disregard of moral or physical damage involved in the struggle, degenerated, because he had never clearly enunciated the spiritual unity of means and end, into the notorious immorality of the later Jesuits.

And although the accusation of materialism may not be convincing, there yet remains, in the way in which Loyola here approaches the sublimest events of history, something which is open to criticism. For while our only approach to spiritual things is through created things, while the Christian religion is the religion of the Incarnate God, yet there is an instinct, at the least, which rebels against the reduction of the highest experiences to a sort of spiritual technique.

* " Etudes religieuses," *Les Origines des Exercises Spirituels*, par P. Watrigant, S J., May, Oct , 1897.

This tendency, however original Ignatius' application of it may have been, is only the expression of something which had taken firm root in the Spanish character. Here we trace the Moorish influence : here we see signs of the highly artificial mysticism of the East. Through Spain, which fathered the Counter-Reformation, this Oriental tendency crept into the Roman Church.

On the whole, it is difficult to approach these pages without prejudice, and to read them without searching for " Jesuitry " between the lines. And the book has that quality of genius, it gives us that for which we seek. But above and beyond every other impression is the impression that the whole composition is *Ad Majorem Dei Gloriam,* and that the glory of God and of the Roman Catholic Church is for Loyola identical.

The only way for Christians outside the Roman Communion to read this book with any degree of sympathy or profit— though, after all, it is not a book to be read, but a set of rules for exercises to be done—is for them to substitute for Loyola's conception of the Church their own conception of a Church Catholic whose glory might be identified with the glory of God, and then to give to that Church, throughout the book, their full allegiance. Thus when the Sacrament is referred to, they may think of the Holy Communion as they receive it ; when confession is recommended, they may, if they choose, understand the Confessor to be Jesus Christ. Hell and Purgatory may be something very real, and yet very different from mediæval conceptions, and there is nothing in the vivid personifications of good and evil spirits which is peculiarly Roman Catholic. When we are here bidden to call upon Mary or Michael, we may fortify ourselves with the recollection and the practice of the Communion of Saints.

Yet though few except Roman Catholics have used, or will use, this discipline, we must not imagine that it has been confined to members of the Order of Jesus :

Among a hundred persons who have undergone, undergo, or will undergo the Spiritual Exercises there are perhaps not five Jesuits . . . the Exercises have built up the characters of doctors and soldiers, artists and priests, mothers of families and workmen. And it is not M. Maurice Barrès who has had the " first inkling that the method of the Exercises is susceptible of adaptation to another end than that of the monastic life."*

* P. Suau, in *Etudes,* 5 March, 1905.

Perhaps the most attractive feature of the Exercises is the revelation in them of Loyola's passionate devotion to the Church. There is something very beautiful about his faithfulness towards her. There was probably no man in Europe in those days who saw her faults more plainly, and yet for the sake of that heavenly ideal of her which was in his heart, and in the hope of happier days to come, this great man was content to lick the dust from off her defiled feet.

" To attain the truth in all things we ought always to hold that we believe what seems to us white to be black, if the Hierarchical Church so defines it ; believing that between Christ our Lord the Bridegroom and the Church His Bride there is one and the same spirit." These words have been so often taken as representing Loyola's attitude to the Church, and so persistently misunderstood, that it is worth while to examine them more closely. What are they, after all, but the quintessence of Roman Catholicism ? There is nothing in them which should be peculiar to the Jesuits. They formulate, for example, the process by which one comes to believe in the doctrine of transubstantiation, or the doctrine of an unchangeable God, Who at the same time became Man. I quote from a luminous article entitled " Philosophy Among the Jesuits," which bears on this point :

St. Ignatius does not take a contradiction of faith with reason as his example, but a contradiction of the senses *versus* faith. He does not say, for instance, that supposing 2 plus 2 equalled 5 were to be decided by a Council, he would have to believe it. Nor is this contradiction of the senses an absolute one. It would be so if he said : You must believe that what *is* black *is* white, if the Church tells you that it is : or you must believe that *what you see to be black you see to be* white, if the Church decrees it.

He does not affirm either of these two contradictions, but only says that what *we see to be* black may *be* white—that is, may not be in itself, what it is subjectively, as preconceived.*

In these Exercises, then, we find nothing which is not consistent with orthodox Roman Catholic belief, but there is no doubt that Loyola emphasised those very points of doctrine with which Protestants have the least sympathy. For example, a Protestant is able to come to ethical conclusions, and to live up to certain ethical standards, without

* *Mind*, vol. xii. p. 234.

the aid of such an elaborate imaginative reconstruction of the material side of the Gospel narrative as the Exercises prescribe : and to a Protestant mind the ethical results are safer if too much time is not spent over such reconstructions. Yet when the Protestant historian comes to illustrate this theory, he finds that he must except the results which the Exercises produced on the early Jesuits, or else say that these men were fired by an inspiration which transcended all the minor practices of faith. For there did unquestionably follow upon the receiving of these Exercises, in the early days of the Order, lives of unparalleled devotion and sanctity. Upon these Exercises were nourished the men who stemmed the tide of the Reformation in Europe, from this discipline there rose up the greatest educationalists of the sixteenth and seventeenth centuries, and the most ardent missionaries of the Roman Catholic Church. "Francis," says Brou,* " emerged from the Exercises changed into another man. From this time onward it is the life of a saint which we write."

But after the death of the founder, Jesuitism became something far less lovely than it was at the beginning, in spite of the fact that the Exercises continued to be given. So we are inclined to believe that it was when the original impetus given by the sanctity and genius of Loyola and his first disciples died out, that the Exercises underwent the real test—and failed. "Before all things," says a Jesuit writer very truly, " the Exercises are a school for the reason and the mind, a school to form self-mastery." If their greatest strength lies here, here also lies their greatest weakness. Loyola may have sighted the Mystic Goal, but surely he set out to reach it by the wrong road. The true mystics have not striven to attain to an ideal, by any mere self-discipline or spiritual technique, or imitation, they have submitted themselves to a Life-force. With the profoundest utterances of St. Paul or St. John, for example, the tone of this marvellous book is hardly in tune.

* Brou, *Vie de S. François Xavier*, vol. i. p. 45.

CHAPTER VI

THE LAST YEARS IN PARIS AND THE JOURNEY TO VENICE

(1534–1537)

THE order of the Jesuits had as yet no formal existence, but during the year which followed the solemn day of consecration on Montmartre, Ignatius and his disciples were constantly together. They supped in one another's rooms, compared their college notes, and discussed plans for the future. Once a week they confessed and communicated. It was during those months that Francis Xavier cemented the strongest and tenderest friendships of his life. The expression of this great affection for the fellow-members of his company, and above all, for Ignatius, runs like a thread of gold through his letters from the East.

But meanwhile the group began to attract the attention of the watch dogs at the Sorbonne.

This frequent intercourse, these meetings, those unusual methods of devotion, this change of life, could not pass unnoticed. Everyone was talking of the heretics (*i.e. the Lutherans*), whose conventicles were multiplying, and the government, provoked by their excesses, felt forced to be severe. The theological faculty allowed nothing to escape them. Naturally the little group of friends was suspected. "They will end by coming under the Inquisition," people said. It seems they had enemies. We do not know who these were, but Ignatius was censured once more. The Inquisitors, who knew him as a converter of heretics, shrugged their shoulders. But bad reports of the Company were abroad and the echoes of these reached as far as Navarre.*

When, in March 1535, Ignatius left Paris for Spain, he carried with him a letter from Francis to his brother, and in this letter we hear something of those troubles. This is the earliest of the Saint's writings in existence.

* Brou, *Vie de S. François Xavier*, vol. i. p. 46.

" Paris,

" 25th March, 1535.

" Señor.

" During the last few days I have written to you by various routes and for many reasons. What chiefly moved me to write you so often is the great debt I owe, since I am your junior and you my Lord, as well as on account of the many favours I have received.

" And that you may not hold me for unthankful and ungrateful for such extreme favours, every time that I find a messenger I shall be sure to write to you ; and if, as the road is so long, you do not get my letters as often as I write them, I beg you to blame the many mischances between Paris and Obanos ; for when I do not get your letters as often as you write to me, in reply to the many I write, I lay the blame on the long road on which many of your letters and mine are lost. So on your part there is no lack of love, but rather the contrary, since you at home where you have in plenty what is needed feel the miseries and hardships of my student-life, no less than I do in Paris where the necessary is always lacking. Yet this lack is only because you do not really know about my hardships, and I suffer them all in the very certain hope that when you know assuredly about them, your great liberality will end my miseries."

We have seen from the accounts of student-life in Paris in those days how real those miseries were.

" Sir, lately the Rev. Father Friar Vear was in this university and he gave me to understand certain complaints which you have made about me, which he related to me at great length ; and if it is as he gave me to understand, your feeling them so much is a sign and very great proof of the love and warm affection you have for me. What I felt so much on hearing this news was the thought of the great pain which you suffered through stories from worthless and bad men whom I desire much to discover in order to give them the pay they deserve. But since everyone here appears very friendly, it is hard for me to know who it is (who has slandered me). God knows the pain I suffer in having to defer punishing them as they deserve. This alone comforts me : *what is divulged is no longer a secret.*" *

The next part of the letter suggests that Francis' wrath was specially roused because Ignatius had been involved in the slanders.

" And so that you may know clearly how the Lord has favoured me in making me acquainted with the Señor Maestro Iñigo, I here give you my word that in my whole life I can never make up all I owe him, both for his having helped me very often with money and with friends, and for his having been the cause of my withdrawal from bad companions, whom I, in my inexperience, did not recognise. And now that these heresies are exposed, I should not wish to have been associated with them for anything in the world. For this alone I do not know when I shall be able to pay Señor Maestro Iñigo, that he brought to an end my conversation and intercourse with persons who outwardly appeared to be good, but within were full of heresies, as has now been shown."

One Jean Calvin, Xavier might have added, was the ringleader of those wicked persons.

" Therefore I beg you to receive him as you would me, myself, since with his good works he has put me under such obligation. And believe that if he were such as they told you, he would not go to your house and put himself in your hands. For no evil-doer puts himself in the power of him whom he has offended, and by this alone you can know that all they told you about Señor Maestro Iñigo is false.

" I beg you very earnestly too not to fail to commune and converse with Señor Iñigo, and to believe what he may say to you, for his counsels and conversations will help you, he is so much a man of God, and so good. . . . give him, to do me a favour, as much credit as you would give to me myself : and from him better than from anyone else in the world you will be able to learn of my needs and hardships. . . .

---

* The earlier collectors of the Letters, who felt it their duty to show a saint flawless from the cradle, have omitted these spirited sentiments. This passage is in Latin in the original, and therefore is printed in italics. This method is adopted throughout the Letters.

" And if you wish to do me the favour of alleviating my great poverty, you will be able to give what you send to Señor Iñigo, the bearer of this, for he has to go to Almazán, and carries certain letters from a student, a great friend of mine—who is studying in this University, and is a native of Almazán, and is very well looked after—by a very safe route. He writes to his father that if Señor Iñigo gives him any money for certain students in Paris, to send it with his own, and in the same coin. And since so safe a way is offered, I beg you to remember me.

" I do not know what more to tell you, except that our dear cousin has fled this university, and that I went after him as far as Notre Dame de Clery, which is thirty-four leagues from Paris (102 miles). I beg you to let me know if he arrived at Navarre, for I much fear me for him, that he will never be any good. Señor Maestro Iñigo will tell you how affairs have turned out about these heresies, as much as I could write by letter.

" So I finish, and kiss the hands of yourself and of the lady (of your wife) a thousand times. May our Lord increase your lives by many years, as for your very noble hearts is desired.

" Your very sure servant and younger brother,

" FRANCIS DE XAVIER."*

It is most likely that Francis over-estimated his brother's financial resources at this time. Political complications had certainly told very severely upon the exchequers of the Navarrese patriots. Whether the Captain of Azpilcueta fulfilled all those requests remains unknown. In the same year, as Rodriguez relates, and almost at the hour of his departure for Venice, Francis got the news that the Chapter of Pampeluna was about to appoint him to a Canonry in the cathedral. This was no greater an honour than a man of his family and attainments might expect as a matter of course, but it must have summed up for him, as it were, the things which he was leaving behind him as he left the gates of Paris for the last time. About this time the certificate of nobility which he had demanded a few years

* *Mon. Xav.*, vol. i. p. 201.

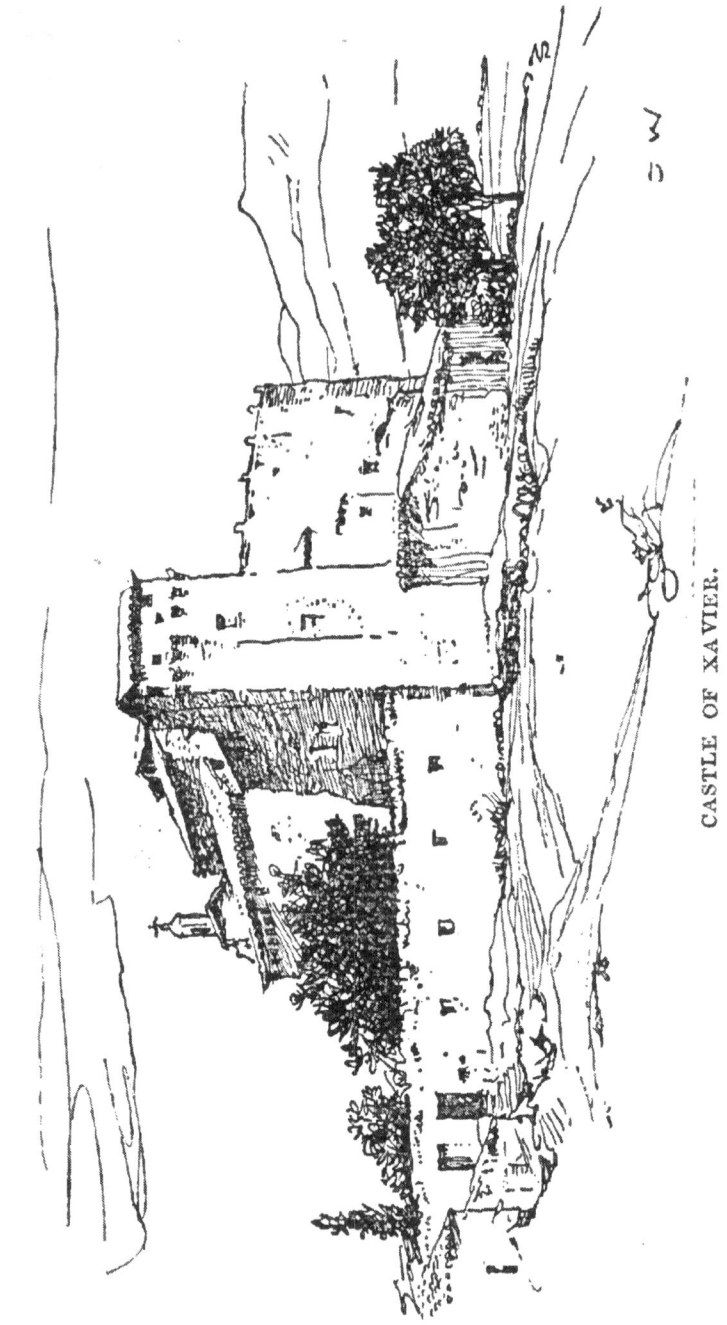

CASTLE OF XAVIER.

earlier was drawn up in Spain, but it is doubtful if Francis ever read it.*

Behind him lay twelve years of college life—of a kind of college life of which Montaigne and Rabelais and Erasmus have left such pitiful and burning records. He had in turn starved, caroused, fasted, frozen. He had studied, talked, quarrelled and made friends in at least five different languages—Latin, French, Spanish, Portuguese, Basque. He was, according to the standards of the Church, a cultured philosopher and an expert theologian. The constant perils of cold and pestilence, of rope and faggot had left him unharmed. But above all, it was here that Ignatius had led him to God. No wonder that those old streets and colleges haunted his imagination throughout the remaining sixteen years of his life. It was for Paris, more than for the high plains of Navarre, that he longed in exile. And it was to Paris that he would fain have returned, and " gone shouting up and down the streets like a madman," telling the students to give up their small ambitions and come eastward to preach the Gospel of Christ.

· Old Tursellinus' chapter on the journey from Paris to Venice is typical and quaint, and gives perhaps as good a picture as exists of that hard journey. I quote from the English version of 1632.†

FRANCIS GOETH TO VENICE WITH EXTREME PAIN OF BODY

He had now almost finished his course of Divinity, when presently he was to depart for Italy. For the Fathers had agreed among themselves that upon a set day, to wit the 24th of January, 1537, they would meet all together at Venice, with

* The certificate runs as follows :
We declare that the said Don Francisco de Jasso y Xavier has duly proved that he was and that he is by ancient origin and descent in direct and legitimate line through parents and ancestors, according to the four branches of his paternal and maternal ancestry, an *hidalgo*, nobleman, and gentleman, legitimate brother of Don Miguel de Xavier to whom belong the estates and *palacios* of Xavier, Ydocin, and Azpilcueta. Therefore We, the Emperor, King and Queen, declare that we hold the said Francisco de Jasso and Xavier for a nobleman, *hidalgo*, and gentleman, and that he and his sons and descendants may and shall use and enjoy all the prerogatives, exemptions, honours, liberties, and privileges which the other gentlemen and *hijosdalgo* use and enjoy in our kingdom of Navarre. (See *Mon. Xav.*, vol. ii. p. 83.)

† The original Latin version of Tursellinus' life was published in Antwerp and in Rome in 1546.

St. Ignatius, who was gone thither before upon certain occasions. In the meantime, before the appointed day of their journey came, France was all up in arms, by reason of Charles V. his war made upon the Frenchmen * : which accident made them hasten their determined journey by setting aside all care of ending their course of studies. Xavier was, indeed, much grieved by this hindrance,† but yet carried it discreetly, esteeming it as good to leave his studies for God's sake, as to follow them.

Therefore upon the thirteenth day of November, a most unseasonable time of the year, having according to their vows given all they had to the poor, except their writings and some little thing to help them on the journey, he, together with his other company, setteth forth on the way. Their manner of travelling was this : they were clothed in coarse and old habits, every one with a staff in his hand, and a short leather mantle upon his shoulder like poor pilgrims : about their necks they hung their beads to be known for Catholics as they travelled among heretics, their writings they carried at their back in a little bag.

They used every day to communicate, being the only comfort of all their labours, thereby both to renew their forces, and to revive their spirits, being wearied with painful travail. When they departed from their lodging, they always commended themselves to God, and when they came into it they gave Him thanks. Being upon the way, they first spent some time upon meditating upon heavenly matters : then they used some pious discourse together, and now and then they lightened the labour and weariness of their journey with singing of hymns, psalms, and spiritual canticles.

In this manner, for the most part taking his way through Lorraine and Germany, to avoid the troubles of the war, he endured the autumn showers of France, and the winter colds of Germany, and though he were not accustomed to travel on foot, yet he cheerfully undertook and performed this long and tedious journey, being loaden with his writings, and this in the dead of winter, and through most foul ways many times encumbered over with snow and frozen up with ice, especially as he passed the Alps. And beside the weight of his bag, and badness of the way, he voluntarily used another mortification which put him to intolerable pains.

Here follows an inaccuracy on Tursellinus' part. In

---

* The war between Francis I. and Charles V. regarding the inheritance of Francis Sforza, Duke of Milan.

† There is a great difference of opinion as to whether Xavier did actually take the final Doc. Theol. examination or not. See note in Brou's *Vie de S. François Xavier*, p. 50.

common with Bartoli and Lucena he tells us that Francis nearly killed himself, on this journey, by tying cords round his legs. But Rodriguez, who was one of the Company at that time, is a more reliable historian, and he dates this indiscretion earlier. It was during the summer vacations of the previous year, while he was taking the Spiritual Exercises, says Rodriguez, that he

macerated his body, carried away with his fervour, with too little prudence. With hard and tightly-bound strings he tied his arms and his legs so that the flesh swelled and broke, and almost entirely covered the cord. It seemed impossible to cut them. His friends, in great sorrow, prayed for him. He endured two days of terrible suffering. We feared that his arms, which were the worst, would have to be amputated. But, by a singular providence of God they healed completely, and I am quite ignorant of how this sudden recovery came about.

Tursellinus' account is exactly similar to this, and unless we are to believe that Francis submitted himself twice to the same ordeal, which is extremely unlikely, we must accept the earlier version of Rodriguez.*

. . . Then they presently set out again to their travel, most joyful for that good success, inciting one another to employ all their labours in the service of so sweet a Lord. And Francis throughout the whole journey (as he was always before wont to do) applied himself with such diligence and alacrity in helping and serving his companions as was wonderful. For as they all strove to the uttermost—this being the one emulation among them—to excel one another in courtesy, he, either out of fervour of spirit, or natural civility, far outwent the rest. And this care and desire of his was no greater to help his companions than to procure the salvation of others. Whensoever occasion was given him of helping his neighbours, either with counsel, advice, or example, he with great zeal made his commodity thereof, and enhanced the same as opportunity served. And herein his labours were not in vain, for many Catholics were thereby reclaimed to a good life, and some heretics also reduced to the wholesome way of truth. Which way soever they passed they left behind them tokens of sanctity, for all to behold, and Catholics to imitate. And so it happened oftentimes that even heretics themselves, taken with admiration at their sanctity, would courteously show them their way, tell them what difficulties

* See Brou, *Vie de St. François Xavier*, p. 45, note.

they were to pass, and, when need was, would themselves freely conduct them on their journey. Thus true and kindly virtue sheweth itself, and putteth even savage people in mind of humanity.

Francis, therefore, by the aid both of Heaven and earth, having waded through all the incommodities and dangers of the way, upon the tenth of January the year following, arrived safe with his companions at Venice. There he found Ignatius Loyola with the greatest desire expecting his dearest sons and companions. Then, according to the custom of the Society, they salute and embrace one another most joyfully, with the greatest demonstration of love that might be imagined. And this joy made them forgetful of all their toilsome past labours.*

* Tursellinus, *Life*, English edition, Book I. chap. iv.

CHAPTER VII

THE ITALIAN YEARS

(January, 1537—March, 1540)

" These first Jesuits were mirrors reflecting holiness, pure doctrine, a singular prudence and a profound humility."
—CERVANTES.

WHEN Francis and his companions sailed into Venice, they found that their leader had arrived almost a year before them. He had passed the time between the study of theology, the care of the sick and destitute and the administration of the Spiritual Exercises. The members of this long-planned Conference found a very different programme awaiting them from that which is put into the hands of the twentieth-century patron of Congresses. Exhausted with the cold and hardships of the journey, they were immediately divided into two groups; one group went with Ignatius to work in the hospital of SS. John and Paul, the other, which included Xavier, went to serve the Incurables. And there, indeed, the bread was bitter and the stairs were steep. Francis was apparently even more sensitive than the others to the physical loathsomeness of his surroundings. The story of how he inured himself to the sights and smells which he could hardly bear reminds us of the account of how Goethe by walking in the Strasburg churchyard at midnight rid himself of fear, and by standing on the pinnacle of the cathedral cured himself of giddiness. And the saint was no less successful than the poet.

It is in Venice that we first hear of Francis preaching the Gospel. His Italian was uncertain, but he talked boldly, catechised, and while he nursed the sick he read and prayed with them. " You would have thought," says Tursellinus, " that he had seen Christ with his eyes in those poor sick persons, and employed all his labours in serving of Him." *

There was no city in Europe more fitted than Venice to be the theatre for the early and heroic enthusiasms of the Jesuits. It was at the same time the city of refuge, and the

* *Life*, p. 22.

hospital, of Northern Italy. Rome was sacked, the patriots of Florence exiled, Milan little else than an army. Venice, insulated, apart, became a spot where men retired; from whence they gained, as it were, a bird's eye view of the turbulent arena of their life. There, serious thought became common, and religious enthusiasm inevitably followed. And there none had to look far in order to see Christ naked and sick and in prison. The story of the foundation of the Somascenes * gives a typical impression of this revival, and shows us that the conduct of Xavier and his companions must have appeared less extravagant to the citizens of sixteenth-century Venice than it would to the citizens of twentieth-century London.†

Xavier's headquarters in Venice, the Incurable hospital, was founded in 1528. Next to the Jesuits themselves, the Theatines were the most important of the non-monastic orders which are so characteristic a feature of this period. The founders of this order, Cardinal Caraffa and Gaetano da Tiene, were members of the Oratory of Divine Love. This was an association of about fifty pious and cultured Italians, who had been united by the earnest desire to bring about a reform in the Church neither by sword nor dogma nor knotted cords, but by personal piety and intellectual earnestness. Gaetano himself, one gathers, was of a timid and sentimental disposition, one of those who believe in being " good to the poor," and living a holy life in order that they may beautify and save their own souls. Added to this was an extreme modesty. It was said of him that he would " like to reform the world without his own existence being known." ‡ Caraffa, after-

---

* " A Venetian senator, Girolamo Miani, gathered together the children who were fugitives in Venice, and received them into his house, seeking them out through the islands and the city. Without paying much heed to the scolding of his sister-in-law, he sold his plate and the handsomest tapestry in his house, to procure for the children lodging, food, raiment, and instruction. By degrees he devoted his whole energy to this vocation. His success was particularly great in Bergamo. The hospital which he founded there was so strenuously supported, that he was encouraged to make similar experiments in other towns. By and by hospitals of the same kind were established at Verona, Brescia, Ferrara, Como, Milan, Pavia, and Genoa. Finally, he entered with some friends of like sentiments into a congregation of regular clergy, modelled on that of the Theatines, designated by the name *Di Somasco*. Their main object was education. Their hospitals received a common constitution " (Ranke, *History of the Popes*, Book II., " New Ecclesiastical Orders "; see also Cocquelines, *Bullarium*, vol. iv. p. 173).

† This passage was written before the European war.

‡ Caracciolus, *Vita S'. Cajetani Thienaei*, cap. ix. p. 101, quoted by Ranke.

wards Pope Paul IV., was of a very different mould—active, violent, business-like, "a builder and a destroyer." But the stormy soul of the future Pope saw as clearly as the contemplative Gaetano that his only peace lay in submission to God and in a life of communion with Him. So these two members of the Oratory of Divine Love united in founding an institution whose members were to cultivate prayer and contemplation, and at the same time to return to the old Apostolic ideals of preaching the Gospel and ministering to the sick and the unhappy.

It was with these men that Loyola associated in Venice, and it was in their convent that he awaited the coming of his disciples. Had either he or Caraffa been less original, or of a less autocratic temper, it is probable that the Jesuits and the Theatines would have merged into one common order. For here Ignatius saw many of his dreams in practice. *Hier bin ich Mensch, hier darf ich's sein*, he might have said with Faust. In so congenial an atmosphere all his charms unfolded, and during the first months of his stay Gaetano found him the gentlest of doves, and Caraffa knew him for the wisest of serpents. But their ideals were not precisely alike; those of Ignatius were larger and more ambitious, and when he tried to impose them upon Caraffa, the almost inevitable rupture came about.

Scarcely had Xavier and his brother pilgrims recovered from the hardships of their fifty days' march across the Alps, when they had again to take to the road. This time Rome was the goal. Ignatius divided them into three bands and sent them southward, to obtain the Papal permission to preach in the Holy Land, and to make arrangements for their ordination. He himself remained in Venice. The accounts of this expedition are, as far as outward circumstances go, lugubrious in the extreme. It was Lent, "a very incommodious time for religious men to travel in," they fasted rigorously, and ate only what the chances of begging put in their satchels. They had neither horse nor ass. Often they spent the night with the cattle, and if they did find other shelter, the beds were such that it took more courage to lie down in them than to share the rush floor with the rats. The rain was continuous and the country so flooded that they had at times to walk in water up to the waist. The best historian of this journey, Rodriguez, who was with them, has an annoying habit of withholding the names of his companions while he tells of their adventures. Brou thinks it is Xavier whom we see in his picture of " one in the market place, bare-footed, his gown kilted up to the knee, asking the merchants for a vegetable, or a little fruit, and taking it with great humility. And then," Rodriguez goes on, " I compared the poverty of this abasement of my companion with his great learning, his talent and deep wisdom, and all those qualities which might have made for him, had he chosen it, earthly fame, and I felt profoundly moved, beyond all expression."

But Francis seems to have shown no signs of self-pity. In the midst of all these privations, we read, his soul overflowed with joy. The spirits of the company were so high that they could take but little sleep.*

At last Francis stood in the Vatican, and found himself by the command of the Pope, and in his presence, arguing with the Papal theologians, in order to prove his ability to preach the Gospel.

> Kings rode from Far, with Splendid Retinues,
> And found their Young Lord Cradled in a Mews:
> Poor Pilgrims came, a naked, sorry Clan;
> They found Christ's Vicar in the Vatican.

Francis and his friends passed the theological test satisfactorily, and the Pope gave them his permission to go abroad. The interview did not last long, and no sooner had the pilgrims quitted the Vatican than they prepared to return to Venice.

In May they were once more with Ignatius, and on June 24th Francis was ordained. Immediately afterwards he retreated, along with Salmeron, to Monselice, a quiet spot at the foot of the Euganean Hills, between Padua and Rovigo. There they found a deserted roofless cottage, which they thatched themselves and made " a little sorry habitation." In this still place they passed forty days in prayer and serious thought. Then, as their leader had not yet recalled them, they went out into the villages, preaching and teaching.

And this was his (Francis') manner of preaching: remembering that Christ was wont to preach in the fields, upon mountains and

* Letter of Father Brandao, Rome, February 1551, *Epistolæ Mixtæ*, vol. ii. p. 515, quoted by Brou, *Vie de S. François Xavier*, vol. i. p. 56.

on the sea-shores, whenever he saw any hope of doing good, there he would put himself among assemblies of people to preach, and especially would he teach such as never used to come to sermons, . . . gathering together people in crossways and streets, and borrowing a stool out of some shop, standing thereon he would speak of virtuous and godly life with more fervour of spirit than flourish of words, to such as either stood there idle, or else were in their plays or pastimes ; insomuch as some who came to his sermon only to get something to laugh at, being moved by the weight of his speech, and the divine force wherewith he spoke, instead of laughing, went away weeping. Nothing caused him to be more admired, or helped on his business better, than refusing to take money, a token of sanctity most pleasing to all men. For when all saw that he neither asked anything of the people about him, nor would take anything which was offered him, they could not but think that he sought the salvation of others more than his own commodity.*

The proposed mission to the Holy Land was still impossible. Venice and Turkey were at war, the Sultan's ships blocked the Adriatic, peaceful transit was out of the question. But wherever the future Apostle of India found himself, he found also souls to be saved.

In the autumn Ignatius recalled Francis and the other members of the Company to Vicenza. They found their leader in a half-ruined and deserted convent, doorless, windowless, unfurnished. There they ate and slept and prayed, and they took their recreation among the poor and sick and ignorant folk in the town.

It was here that Xavier offered his first mass. " To look upon him," they said, " one would have thought, not only that he believed, but that he saw with his eyes that which is hidden in this most holy mystery." †

Nor did he ever lose this fresh ardour. It was " as if coming every day like a new priest to the Altar, he had tasted the first sweetness of those sacred mysteries."

About this time Francis was seized with one of those violent attacks of fever to which he was liable, and to which he probably in some measure owed his early death. Rodriguez writes :

Soon after this, Francis and I both fell ill. They admitted us to the hospital, but we had to share between us one narrow bed,

* Tursellinus, *Life*, p. 31. † *Ibid.*, Book I. cap. vi.

and that was a great occasion of discomfort to us. When, for example, the one was shivering and wishing a dozen blankets, the other was burning with fever and wished none at all; we both profited by this affair in the practice of patience and charity. Further, the room where we lay was open to all the winds of heaven, and we received from the hospitaller hardly any of the attentions which our illness demanded.*

When they had recovered and returned to the ruined convent, where they had the benefit of open-air treatment again during their convalescence, they found hope of an expedition to the Holy Land finally abandoned. Ignatius was about to go to Rome with Lainez and Faber, and the others were told off in couples and sent out on preaching tours to the university towns of Northern Italy. Xavier and Bobadilla were put down for Bologna.

And they began to ask what they should call themselves.

They prayed about this matter, and wondered what name would be best. They remembered that they knew no name but Jesus Christ, and that they served Him alone. And so it appeared to them that they might take the name of their Leader, and that they should call themselves the Company of Jesus.

In October, 1537, Francis and Bobadilla arrived in Bologna. Gonçalvez's and Teixeira's accounts of this visit are probably the most accurate.

Francis' first act was to visit the tomb of St. Dominic, for he had a great admiration for the founder of the Preaching Friars. There, the day after his arrival, he said Mass. There was present that day a holy woman called Isabel Casilini, who, on seeing his devotion before the altar, took him for a great saint. She spoke to him after Mass, and, she records, " this interview inspired me greatly towards a better life."

Isabel had an uncle, Jerome Casilini, a learned and noble canon. . . . At the request of Isabel, Francis visited him, and the canon offered him the hospitality of his house and table. Francis accepted the lodging, but he desired to beg his bread each day. After early Mass and the recitation of the hours, he occupied each day until evening with works of charity towards the prisoners and the afflicted. Besides this, he ran through the streets waving his hat in the air and crying: " Come and hear the Word of

---

* Rodriguez, *Commentarium de origine et progressu Soc. Jesu*, Lisbon, 1577.

God!" The first seat that he came upon served as a pulpit, and he preached in a jargon composed of several languages, because he did not at that time know much Italian. He advised all his hearers to frequent the sacraments of confession and communion, which are of great help against sin. From his time the custom of communion after the manner observed in the Primitive Church was revived in Bologna, and in this town, from that time, there was, among great numbers, a notable change of life. Jerome Casilini said of Francis: "He spoke little, but his words had a marvellous effect. In his sermons, such was his ardour that it quickly communicated itself to his audience. . . . One might well say of him that he was a man of great prayerfulness, and, like Daniel, *a man of desires*."*

In Bologna he was again stricken down with a violent fever, but he hardly allowed himself any rest. Before the ague had left him he was out again in the squares and arcades calling to the students and townsfolk to come and hear the Word of the Lord.

Francis and Bobadilla had this rule between themselves. Each week one obeyed the other. He who obeyed had the duty of calling the people in the streets to the sermon, and when the people had gathered he would get the loan of a bench and put it in the middle of the square, and the one who was superior that week would mount it and preach to the town. The concourse of people who gathered to the sermon on account of this novelty was great, great the fruit which the Lord made by them, and great the alms offered them. . . . If they saw someone moved by the sermons, they spoke to him apart, and instructed him as to what was necessary for salvation.†

In March, 1538, Francis rejoined the rest of the Company in Rome. His friends were horrified by his appearance. "He seemed to me," says Rodriguez, "more like a corpse than a living man, he was so pale and thin and disfigured by his long privations and illnesses. When I saw him so unlike himself, so scarred and sorry and worn-out a figure, I could not help feeling that he would never again regain his old strength, and that his working days were at an end."‡

* Sebastien Gonçalvez, *Historia da Companhia na India*, written in Goa between 1593 and 1619, Lisbon, Ajuda MSS. 26/30. I am indebted to Cros, *Vie de S. François Xavier*, vol. i. p. 144, for this extract.
† Teixeira, *Vita, Mon. Xav.*, vol. ii. p. 824.
‡ Rodriguez, in *op. cit.*

Apparently Francis gave up active work for some little time, for neither Ribadeneira nor Polanco mentions him as being among those who preached in Rome at this period.* But in his weakness there came to him " visions and revelations of the Lord." In remote regions of his soul, he now heard the call from the East.

Even in Bologna, he had spoken of India continually to his friends. And one night in Rome, Rodriguez, who was sleeping in the same room, was awakened by hearing his companion call out in his sleep, More ! More ! More ! Long afterwards, just before he embarked for India, he said to Rodriguez :—

You remember, my brother Simon, how one night in the hospital at Rome I woke you with my repeated cries, More ! More !· More ! You asked me at the time what it was, and I said it was nothing. But I will tell you now that I had seen myself in great labour and peril for the service of God, and at the same time His grace sustained me so marvellously that I could not help calling out for more to do. I hope that the hour will soon come when that which was foreshown me will be realised.†

But now Ignatius and his disciples thought that the time had come for the definite and official formation of the Order. " They unanimously decided," says Polanco, " to give themselves up to prayer, to offer the holy sacrifice of mass and each to devote himself specially to serious thought on the subject, in order the better to know God's will for them." These evening and midnight conferences, in the little room in the Piazza Margana in Rome, lasted for three months.‡ They would use none of their working daytime for this business. Every question, as it came under review, was submitted to three stages, study, discussion, vote. For the first stage each man went apart alone, and prayed and thought over the matter in silence ; secondly, they had an open debate, and lastly the question was put to the vote. The proceedings remind one of a modern study-circle.

The first subject which came under discussion was one which intimately concerned Xavier's future work. Were

* Tursellinus, however, on I know not what authority, affirms that Xavier and Faber were bidden to preach by turns in the Church of St. Lawrence, and that their sermons changed many lives ; see Tursellinus, *Life*, p. 48.
† Cros, *Vie de S. François Xavier*, p. 148.
‡ See Fouqueray, *Histoire de la Companie de Jesus*, vol. i. p. 72.

those of the Company who might be sent to the Far East to be bound by the same discipline as the members at home ? There was a long discussion, for some thought that these men should be more or less free and independent. It was finally decided that if it pleased God and the Pope the bond should be equally close, however far apart the brothers might be.

Secondly, it was debated as to whether the vows of obedience should be added to the vows of poverty and chastity. We have no record of what Francis said, but probably the construction of an outward rule on this matter was of little concern to him. His friendship and devotion for Loyola and the brethren transcended all literal commands or disobediences. He was "theirs in Christ," as he was wont to sign himself in his letters. And one feels that if his life had not so nearly realised his words, his indomitable and naturally autocratic temper would often have made thunder and lightning in the Company. But if he was really theirs in Christ he could transcend all rules and yet break no laws. Here the man of moral genius stands on the same ground as the great artist. And thus, though Francis Xavier was one of the original Jesuits, we can fancy that he looked upon that dread master-word of the Constitutions with something of a child-like innocence. Sometimes, as we think of a certain friend, while we walk through crowded streets, we seem to see him in the distance again and again, and though we are deceived, we do not regard those who deceive us, but go on communing with our friend. So Francis saw Christ in Loyola and his brother Jesuits, and if their orders were not always compatible with the Divine Voice within, he still, with dreamy eyes of love, saw Christ in them, and obeyed that inner Voice.

And as the stranger in the streets may wonder sometimes at the smile which greets him because he has unwittingly fed the memory of a friend, so the friends of Francis may have wondered perhaps at the tender words he wrote to them from the East, at his undying faith in their goodness and in their prayers.

At last a document was drawn up, and on the twenty-fourth of June, 1539, presented to Pope Paul III. (Alexander Farnese). He is said to have exclaimed, on reading the document, *Hic est digitus Dei !* And when we recall the position of the Papacy at this time, his exclamation of joy does not surprise us.

In Germany, heresy was extending with an unheard-of rapidity. In France, Poland, in Spain, in Italy itself, Luther had gained numerous partisans. Scandinavia and England had already quitted the yoke of the Roman Church. The Catholics, even those who were still faithful, were violently hostile to the Papal See and its abuses. The Emperor was energetically demanding a complete reform, and threatening to despoil the Papacy of a great number of its most profitable privileges. From the Papal point of view the situation seemed truly desperate. And just at this point came a troop of men, ardent, belligerent, devout, offering a blind obedience to the Sovereign Pontiff, and ready to fight to the death for his greatness and his authority.*

But the custom of the Papal Court demanded that the document should be read and approved by three Cardinals as well as by the Pope, and although Paul and two of his Cardinals were ready to welcome the new Order with open arms, there remained Cardinal Gia, who would not even look at the papers. There were too many orders already, he said, and he was for suppressing—with one or two exceptions—all those which were then in existence. It was not until Ignatius, with consummate patience, utilised the influence of John of Portugal, of Margaret of Austria, of Carpi and Contarini, that Gia at last consented to the official formation of the Company.

For the student of the life of Francis Xavier, the *Bulla Regimini Militantis Ecclesiæ* has a peculiar interest. For besides giving the authority of the Pope and the Apostolic See to the Jesuits, it contains the nucleus of the famous Constitutions of the Order, and this nucleus is all of these that Xavier ever possessed. They were not completed until many years later, nor were they put into the hands of members of the Society till 1553, a year after Xavier's death.† The revised edition, with large additions and introduction by Lainez, was not published till 1558, after the death of Loyola himself.

Therefore, the Constitutions as they now stand have little

* *La Contre-Révolution réligieuse du 16e siècle.* Martin Philipsson, p. 55.
† See Brou, *Vie de S. François Xavier*, vol. i. p. 67 ; also Philippson, *op. cit.*, p. 104, who quotes from Orlandino, *Hist. Soc. Jesu*, Book III. cap. v., and Book X. cap. 48 *seq.*

to do with Xavier, but the version of them contained in this Bull was the fruit, in part at least, of his own mind and soul. The later edition is a very different and, to many of us, a much less beautiful affair.

I have thought it worth while to reproduce this formula in full. It was the only Rule which the Saint had with him in India. After a preliminary paragraph the document proceeds :

Whosoever in our Society, which we wish to call by the Name of Jesus, wishes to become the soldier of God under the banner of the Cross, and to serve God alone, and His Vicar upon earth, the Roman Pontiff, shall, after a solemn vow of perpetual chastity, agree in his own mind to become a part of this Society. It is instituted for the perfecting of souls in Christian life and doctrine ; the propagation of the Faith by public teaching, by the ministration of the Word of God, by spiritual exercises and works of charity, by the instruction of boys in the Christian doctrine, by giving spiritual comfort to the faithful through the Confession. A member of this Society shall strive to keep God first of all before his eyes, and then the method of this institute which leads to Him. With all his energies he shall aim at this object which is set before him by God, each one according to the grace given him by the Holy Spirit, and the demands of his position, lest he have a zeal which is not according to knowledge. The appointment of each member's special position, and the fixing and complete arrangement of his duties, shall be in the hands of a General or Head, to be chosen by us (i.e., the Society), that a convenient order may be observed, such as is needful in every well regulated community.

This Head, with the advice of his associates, shall have authority to draw up constitutions to help the formation of the object proposed to us, the larger number of votes always having the rights of determination. The Council shall be understood to be the greater part of the whole society which can conveniently be called by the Head, if an important or permanent matter is to be settled. But for lighter or more transient cases, it is enough to call all those who happen to be present in the place where the General shall reside. The whole right of issuing commands shall be in the General.

Let all the association know, not only at their entrance into profession, but so long as they live must they bear it in remembrance, that this entire society and all its members become God's soldiers under the faithful obedience of the most sacred Lord the Pope, and the other Roman Pontiffs his successors. And although we are taught in the Gospel, and in the orthodox faith acknowledge and firmly profess, that all Christ's faithful people are subject to the Roman Pontiff as their Head, and as the Vicar of Jesus Christ, yet, for the greater humility of our Society, and the perfect mortification of every member, and for the denial of our own wills, we have deemed it very good, that each one of us be bound by a special vow, beyond that general obligation, so that whatsoever the present or other Roman Pontiff for the time being shall ordain, pertaining to the advancement of souls, and the propagation of the faith, and to whatever province he shall ordain to send us, we are straightway bound to obey, as far as in us lies without any evasion or excuse—whether he send us among the Turks, or to any other unbelievers in existence, even in those parts called India, or to any heretics or schismatics, or likewise to any believers. So they who wish to join us should, before they begin this work, consider long and carefully whether they are rich enough in spiritual goods to finish their tower, or not, according to the counsel of God—that is, whether the Holy Spirit Who guides them promises to them so much grace that they may hope with His assistance to bear the burden of their calling. And when, by the inspiration of God, they have enrolled their name for this warfare of Jesus Christ, their loins should be girded day and night, and they should be ready for the discharge of their great debt.

And that there may be no seeking or refusing among ourselves of missions or provinces of any kind, let each profess that he will never, directly or indirectly, ask anything of the Pope touching such missions, but put all this care upon God, and the Pontiff as His Vicar, and upon the General of the Society. The General, too, shall profess like the rest, that he will not ask of the Pope touching his own mission into any part, except with the concurrence of the Society.

All shall vow that they will be obedient to the Head of the Society in all things which tend to the keeping of this our Rule.

And the General shall do whatever he thinks good in order to gain the things asked of him by God and by the Society. And in his own high place, he shall always be mindful of the blessedness and gentleness and love of Christ, and of the examples of Peter and Paul, and both he and his council shall diligently regard this rule. They shall, too, be specially advised to teach to boys the Christian doctrines, the ten Commandments, and other like rudiments as they shall deem fit, according to the state of the people, the place, and the time. It is most necessary that the General and his council pay heed to this business, seeing that the building up of faith cannot be done without a foundation. There is here a danger, that we, because of our own learning, may try to avoid this duty, irksome at first sight, but in reality more fruitful than any other towards the edification of our neighbours, and the exercise of charity and humility.

Also, that this all-important humility may be diligently practised, as well as for the advantages of order, inferiors must always obey the Superior in all things that have to do with the Institute of the Society. The inferior must see Christ in the Superior, and, as far as is seemly, worship Him there.

And since we know by experience, that a life far from the contagion of avarice, and as near as possible to evangelical poverty, is the happiest, the purest, and the most helpful to our neighbours, and since we know that our Lord Jesus Christ will give us all we need of food and clothing if we seek first the kingdom of God, so each and all shall vow perpetual poverty, declaring that they cannot acquire, either separately or in common for the maintenance or use of the Society, any civil rights to any real property, or to its proceeds or incomes, but that they shall be content to receive only the use of what is given them to provide things needful.

But they may have in the universities a college or colleges holding revenues, estates, or possessions, to be applied to the wants or necessities of the students, the government or superintendence of the said colleges and the said students as touching the election of rectors and students, their admission, discharge, reception, inclusion, the appointment of statutes for the instruction, erudition, edification, and correction of the students, the manner of supplying their food and clothing, and all other government, regulation and care being always secured to the General of the Society, yet so that the students shall not abuse the aforesaid goods, nor the Society convert them to their private use, but minister to the necessity of the students. And these last also may be admitted into our Society when their progress in the Spirit and in learning has been ascertained, and after sufficient probation.

All associates whatever in this order, though they hold no ecclesiastical benefices, nor incomes therefrom, shall nevertheless be bound each one privately and separately, and not as a body, to say the services according to the ritual of the Church.

These are the matters which, with the allowance of our said Lord Paul, and the Apostolic See, we can in some manner explain of our profession. We have now done so, that by our writing we may briefly inform not only those who question us by touching our manner of life, but our successors also, if by God's favour we shall have followers in this way. And since we have found many and great difficulties in it, we have thought it right to say that no one will be taken into this Society, unless he has been long and carefully tried, and when he shall be found prudent in Christ,

H

learned, or conspicuous in purity of Christian living, then at
length he may be admitted into the army of Jesus Christ, Who
will vouchsafe to favour those humble beginnings of ours to the
Glory of God the Father, to Whom be praise and honour for ever.
Amen.

Then follows the assent of the Pope and the Apostolic See,
and the advice to draw up Constitutions.*

We see in this document the germs of the later Constitutions, the beginnings of that distrust of the free exercise of
personal judgment which is the vitiating element in Roman
Catholicism. The fresh vigour of Francis Xavier was,
however, proof against this comparatively mild edition of
the Constitutions. And the fact that they were partly of his
own devising made the yoke easy to him. The harm only
really began to show when the scheme grew and developed
along its worst lines, while at the same time the enthusiasm
and genius of the originating spirits no longer existed. The
initiators of the Order possessed high gifts of individuality,
independence, and creative imagination, and these qualities
saved their obedience from servility. Ignatius, with all his
astuteness, never perhaps foresaw that the Rules which were
good for those whose whole natures had had free exercise on
the making of them, might not be good for those who had
merely to step into the machine. The founders of the Order
had such a supreme confidence in their own individual
conception of life that they did not see that the worth of that
conception lay, not in the special form which it had taken,
but in the fact that it was original, and had been beaten out
with the hammer of sincere self-expression.

Yet we must not forget that the idea of unswerving
obedience to a superior was not peculiar to the Jesuits,
although the fact that this was, above all things, a military
order† means that it laid a very special emphasis on that
virtue.

St. Basil had told his monks to be in the hands of the
superior as an axe in the hands of the butcher. The monks
of the Chartreuse were to give up their wills as sheep led to

---

* C. Cocquelines, *Bullarium Privilegiorum ac Diplomatum Romanorum,*
Rome 1739; also *Constitutions of the Society of Jesus,* translated from the
Spanish, London, 1839, Appendix.

† "I do not consider myself," says Loyola, "to have quitted military
service, but only to have transferred it to God."

the slaughter. For the Carmelite disobedience was a mortal sin. St. Francis of Assisi and Bonaventura both compare the obedient man to a corpse. Ignatius may have borrowed this figure from them when he wrote, some years later, the often quoted words:

Let everyone be persuaded that those who live under obedience are obliged to allow themselves to be moved and directed by the divine providence working through their superiors as if they were a corpse, which allows itself to be carried about at will, and to be treated it matters not how; or like an old man's staff, which serves him who holds it, in every place and in every way as he will.

The formal proclamation of the Bull did not take place till September 27th, 1540, more than six months after Francis had left Rome.

But on September 3rd, 1539, the Pope gave his oral approbation, and within a few weeks the Jesuits were preaching all over Italy under his orders.

A close correspondence was kept up between Loyola and his followers. He required them to send him full details of all their work, and he on his side sent them constant advice and encouragement. During this autumn of 1539, and until he left Rome in March of the following year, Francis Xavier was kept at Loyola's side as his private secretary.

CHAPTER VIII

THE JOURNEY TO LISBON

(March—April, 1540)

MEANWHILE Gouvea, the old principal of the College of Ste. Barbe, had not lost sight of his former students. The reader will remember that he was a Portuguese, and an ardent advocate of missionary work in India, and that he had under his care a number of Portuguese students, holding special bursaries to enable them to qualify as missionaries. While Ignatius and his disciples were in Rome he wrote to them, asking them if they would accept a mission to India, if it were offered to them by John III. of Portugal. Faber replied in the name of the Company as follows :

A few days ago your messenger arrived here with your letter. And with his own voice, he has given us some news of you. By your letters, we can see in what kindly remembrance you hold us. We see, too, how ardent is your desire to save the souls of your Indian subjects, and to gather in this perishing harvest. Our hearts share your zeal, and we would gladly fulfil your wishes —which are ours too—but there are so many other demands upon us that it is difficult at the moment to reply. But you will pass on the following statement:

All of us who are bound together in this society have made our vows to the Sovereign Pontiff, as to the master of all the harvests of Jesus Christ. In offering ourselves to the Pope, we have declared that we are ready for anything which he may have for us to do in the name of Christ. If then he send us himself to the place where you have called us, *we go rejoicing.* We determined to submit ourselves thus by a vow to the will of the Pope, because he, we know, is better informed than anyone else as to what is most expedient for Christianity as a whole.

Several of us have already besought His Holiness, that he would send us to those other Indies which the Spaniards are from day to day bringing under the Emperor's flag : in their name the proposal has already been made by a Spanish bishop and by the ambassador of the Emperor ; but they understand that the Pope does not wish to send us away from Rome, for the harvest there is great.

The distances which separate us from India and the difficulty of learning their languages would not daunt us. To do anything which will help Jesus Christ, that is our business. Pray to Him then that He may make us His ministers to preach the word of life so that we may not be *self-sufficient as if sufficient of ourselves*, for our Hope is in His abundance and His riches.

As for ourselves and our own affairs, you will be fully informed by letters which we have written to our intimate friend and brother in Jesus Christ, Diego de Caceres, Spaniard. He will show you these letters. You will see there that we have, even up to the present time, suffered many things for Jesus Christ, and how we have won through without harm. There are many people even in Rome who hate the truth, and the enlightenment of the Church. It is for you, then, to watch, and to send out into the world Christian men, who, by the example of a holy life, as well as by the other means which you have put at their disposal for the defence of the faith and of sound doctrine, may instruct Christian people, for how are we to believe that God will keep us in the integrity of the faith if we neglect a holy life ? There is good reason to believe that the chief errors of doctrine proceed from evil lives, and that the former can do no harm if the latter is corrected. But enough of this subject.*

The letter was forwarded by Gouvea to the King, who then wrote to his ambassador at the Papal court, asking him to inquire secretly into the lives and qualifications of these young men, and, if the results were satisfactory, to ask the Pope to allow some of them to go to India.

The ambassador made his investigations, and found that the half of their virtues had not been told him. They said they would willingly go wherever the Pope should send them. The Pope replied that such a long and dangerous voyage ought to be undertaken voluntarily, he would command none of them, but if any of them decided to go, he would give them his blessing.

Then a difficulty arose. Although Ignatius could say that all of the Company were ready to go if called upon, most of them were at the moment engaged elsewhere. King John wished four men, but out of the twenty members who now composed the Society, only two, besides Ignatius, were then in Rome, Francis Xavier and Salmeron. Salmeron was destined for Ireland, and Francis appears at first to have been put on one side ; why, we can only guess. Probably his shattered constitution had not yet recovered ; probably,

* Cros, *Vie de S. François Xavier*, vol. i. p. 150.

also, Loyola was loth to lose his secretary and one of his best-loved disciples. It was impossible to find four men, but Loyola promised that he would send two, and the Pope thereupon gave formal command that two should go. Rodriguez arrived in Rome, and was immediately despatched by boat to Lisbon, as he was not well enough to go by land with the ambassador. With him went a young priest who had volunteered at the eleventh hour, Micer Paulo Camerino, of whom we shall hear later, but he was so young and inexperienced that he hardly counted, and Ignatius still sought his second man. Bobadilla, who was not far away, was ordered to return at once. He came, but he was so ill that for him India was out of the question.

The time passed and no one was found. At last there were only twenty-four hours left before the date fixed for the ambassador's return to Portugal. And Ignatius had promised that one of the Company would go with him, en route for India.

Francis had not hidden his desires from the founder. He could say no more. Loyola must decide.

" All at once," Rodriguez tells us, " Ignatius, who was ill in bed, called Father Francis Xavier, and said to him, ' Master Francis, you know how, by order of His Holiness, two of us must go to India, and that we had chosen Master Bobadilla for this mission, and now because of his illness he cannot go. The ambassador cannot wait till he is better. There now is something for you ! ' And at once the blessed Father Francis, with great joy and promptitude, replied, ' Well, then, forward ! Here I am ! ' " *

There was no time for elaborate preparations or for long-drawn-out farewells. Next morning the traveller must leave Rome. His kit was simple, he rolled up three or four well-worn garments and put them in his little bag, then he put in two books, and that was all. One of these books was his breviary, the other may still be seen in a convent in Madrid, and is largely composed of extracts from the New Testament. You will look in vain for any underlinings or marginal notes, for before he left Europe Francis seems to have learned the rule of the Order that there was to be no marking of books.

* Ribadeneira, *Scripta*, p. 381, quoted by Brou, *Vie de S. François Xavier*, vol. i. p. 78.

On the day of his departure he wrote the three following memoranda, and left them in charge of the brethren in Rome :

Ihus. I Francis declare this. When His Holiness approves of our plans I shall agree to what the Society shall ordain with regard to all the constitutions, rules, and manner of life, by the assembly of those Fathers in Rome who are able at that time to go there : and because His Holiness is sending many of us beyond Italy who will not be able then to be present I now declare and promise that I will agree to whatever is ordained by those who are able to be there, be they two, or be they three, or however many they be. I declare and promise to agree with all that they decide. Written in Rome in the year 1540, on the 15th of March. FRANCISCO.

Also I Francis declare and affirm that, *in no way persuaded by man,* I judge that he who ought to be elected as the Superior in our Company, and to whom we must all show obedïence, seems to me, as I judge by the voice of my conscience, our old and true Father Don Ignatio, who brought us all together with so much labour, and who, still not without labour, knows best how to keep us, rule us, and lead us on to better things, for he knows us all. And *after his death,* according to the counsel of my inmost soul, and as I should declare if I were about to die, I say that the Father, Master Peter Faber, should be chosen ; and here *God is my Witness* that I speak no other than what I think, and to witness this, I sign it with my own hand.
Written in Rome in the year 1540, the 15th of March.
FRANCISCO.

And so also, when the Company shall have met and have chosen a Superior, I Francis promise now for then, perpetual obedience, poverty, and chastity : and so, my Father in Christ, dearest Lainez, I beseech you in the name of God our Lord that in my absence you will offer for me this my will, with my three religious vows to the Superior who will be elected. For from now, as from that day I promise to keep them, in witness whereof I have drawn up this declaration, and now sign it with my own hand.
Written in Rome in the year 1540, on the 15th of March.
FRANCISCO.*

Nothing now remained to do but to go to the Vatican to receive the Papal blessing, and to bid his friends, and above

* *Mon. Xav.,* vol. i. pp. 812–14.

all Loyola, a long farewell. These two were never to meet again. Of that hour we have no record ; but he may well have been thinking of this moment when years afterwards he wrote those words :

" It may be easy to understand the Latin,* and the general meaning of this saying of the Lord, but when dangers arise, where the life about which you wish to decide will probably be lost, and when, in order to prepare yourself to decide to lose your life for God's sake that you may find it in Him, you get down to details, everything else, even this clear Latin, begins to get hazy. And in such a case, however learned you may be, you can understand nothing, unless God, in His infinite mercy, makes your particular case plain." †

He had entered the capital in abject poverty, but now, though against his will, he had to keep state with the ambassador, in whose train he travelled. But even thus he found ample occasion for service.

In his journey he gave no less sign of modesty than of sanctity. For although he were given to the contemplation of heavenly things, yet being not altogether unmindful of human, he showed himself so courteous unto all, that when he came to the Inn he would leave the best chambers and beds to other of his company, contenting himself with the worst things. And when the servants neglected to look unto their master's horses, or discharge other inferior servile offices, he would himself do them all, showing himself therein rather a servant indeed, than a companion. Yet none was more pleasant in conversation than himself, nor more ready in all kinds of courtesies. . . . But, which is hardest of all, he kept such a mean in these things, that, tempering courtesy with gravity, both his actions and words savoured all of sanctity.

Tursellinus goes on to relate how he talked seriously of religious matters with his companions, " and the wholesome bitterness of these discourses he always allayed with the sweet sauce of many courteous offices." ‡

---

* *Whosoever would save his life shall lose it, but whosoever shall lose his life for My sake the same shall save it.*

† *Mon. Xav.*, vol. i. p. 400.   See p. 231.

‡ Tursellinus, *Life*, p. 48 ; see also Teixeira, *Vita, Mon. Xav.*, vol. ii. p. 832. Teixeira adds that he got his details, which are the same as those of Tursellinus, from the secretary of the Ambassador when he afterwards met him in India as Secretary of State.

By way of Loretto they went to Bologna, where Francis had preached two years earlier. From there he wrote to Ignatius. This is the second of his existing letters.

"On Easter Day I got some letters from you with a mail which came for the Lord Ambassador, and with them our Lord knows what joy and consolation. And since *only* by letters I suppose that we shall see each other in this life, and in the other *face to face*,* with many an embrace, then in this little time left us of this life, let us see each other by frequent letters. So I will do as you have commanded me about writing often, keeping the order of the *hijuelas*.†

"I had a long and pleasant talk with the Lord Cardinal Ivrea, according to your instructions. He received me very kindly, making great offerings to favour us all he could. The good old man on my taking leave began to embrace me, and I to kiss his hands, and in the middle of the speech I made him, I knelt, and in the name of all the Company, I kissed his hands. By what he answered me I think he is very pleased with our way of doing things.

"The Lord Ambassador made me so many presents that I could not come to an end of writing them. And I don't know how I could stand them if I did not think and hold almost for certain that *in India* they may have to be paid with no less than life.

"In Our Lady of Loretto on Palm Sunday I confessed and communicated him with many of his household, and in the Chapel of Our Lady I said Mass, and the good Ambassador arranged that all of his household within the Chapel should communicate *along* with him. The chaplain of the Ambassador commends himself much to the prayers of all, and has given me his hand to go with us to the Indies.‡

"Give my greetings to Madona Faustina Ancolina. Tell

---

* "*Videmus . . . per speculum in ænigmate : tunc autem facie ad faciem*" (1 Corinthians xiii. 12). Although the *Mon. Xav.* gives the spelling as *fatie*, it is almost certainly only a copyist's error. The sixteenth-century "t" was very similar to the "c." We may see this in the reproduction of Francis's signature ; see Cros, *Vie de S. François Xavier*, vol. ii. p. xxx, note.

† The word *hijuela* means little daughter, also a patch of cloth joined to another which is too short. Ignatius had given instructions that if members of the Company had anything private to say, apart from the main burden of the letter, it was to be put on a separate sheet ; see *Mon. Xav.*, vol. i. p. 208, note.

‡ He did not keep his promise.

her I have said a Mass for her Vicentio and mine, and that
to-morrow I will say another for her, and that she may be
sure that I shall never forget her *even* when I am in the
Indies.   And in my name, Micer Pedro my very dear brother,
remind her to keep the promise she made me to confess and
communicate, and that she let me know if she has done it,
and how often.   And if she wishes to please Vicentio, hers
and mine, tell her in my name to forgive those who killed
her son, for Vicentio prays much for them in heaven.   Here
in Bologna I am more engaged in hearing confessions than I
was in St. Louis.
"Commend me much to all, for truly it is not through
forgetfulness that I fail to name them.
"From Bologna the last of March 1540.
"*Your brother and servant in Christ.*" *

From Bologna they went on by Modena and Reggio to
Parma.   There Francis had planned to meet his beloved
Peter Faber, with whom he had been so closely associated
throughout his student life, but they missed one another by
a few days, and they never saw one another again.
In Gonçalvez's MS. there is an account given by a fellow
traveller of his conversion by Francis during this journey.

I was an *hidalgo*, young and rich, and I was out to see the
world.   I visited France, Germany, Italy, and finally I reached
Rome in 1540.   I visited Don Pedro Mascarenhas, the ambassador of John III., and he asked me to accompany him on his
return voyage to Portugal.   I had many things on my conscience, as often happens when a rich youth roams at large in
strange countries, free from all surveillance.   On the way, I
made the acquaintance of Master Francis, and he showed great
kindness to me.   He sought out my company, and warmed my
heart by his honest gaiety, as side by side we travelled onwards.
Gradually, he came to speak of general confession, and persuaded
me to make it.   I made it to Francis himself, and with great
satisfaction, in a church which we passed by the way.   From that
time I became, thanks to God, another man.   It is true that
Master Francis had a notable gift for impressing the fear of God
on men's souls : I felt this fear grow within me even as I confessed.   It was then, for the first time in my life, that I understood what it was to be a Christian.†

* *Mon. Xav.*, vol. i. p. 207.
† Quoted by Cros, *Vie de S. François Xavier*, vol. i. p. 161.

During this journey Xavier is said to have saved, on different occasions, the lives of three of his fellow travellers. The following account of one of these incidents is from Tursellinus.

Afterwards they travelled over the Alps where, not being able to take sure footing by reason of the driving of the snow, and the craggy rocks and paths, their horses being tired, with no small danger to their masters, the ambassador's secretary fell by chance from his horse, and was suddenly swallowed up in a huge mass of snow. The place was upon a slippery and steep rock, under which ran a swift torrent. The greatness of the danger stroke all his companions into such a fear that none durst undertake to assist him . . . so they, being all amazed, stood still looking upon one another. As they thus stood, on cometh Xavier, and regarding another's life more than his own, leapt presently from his horse and by main strength drew him up out of the snow and delivered him from manifest danger with no small peril to his own life.*

After crossing the Alps the travellers went through the South of France and thence up one of the northern passes of the Pyrenees.

Some of the old biographers tell an elaborate and pathetic tale of how the company passed close to the castle of Xavier, and the ambassador asked Francis to go and bid farewell to his mother. The Saint refused, and thus provided the historians with a rapturous passage on his other-worldliness, and some readers, at least, with a text for the inhumanity of Roman Catholicism. But Francis' mother had been dead since 1529, and the old home was long since broken up.†

Nevertheless the folk of these parts still show the spot where Francis, they say, paused to look down upon the scenes of his early youth, and to say good-bye to his old home. And they have given to that place the name of the Farewell Rock, *la Peña del Adios*.

Nothing, indeed, can be more likely—though the sensational tale of the biographers is disproved—than that on one

* Tursellinus, *Life*, p. 51.
† Teixeira's account, the oldest of all, is very sober, and makes no mention of his mother. " Passing through to the kingdom of Navarre very near his native place, and his relatives, they could not get him to visit them nor to turn aside a little from the road to see them." *Vita, Mon. Xav.*, vol. ii. p. 833.

of these lonely heights above the ancestral keep, the worn-out youth, clad in a battered cloak, which contrasted quaintly with his handsome mount, drew in the reins, and allowed his eyes to linger for a little while on those walls which had once held all that was most dear and sacred, whispering, as he turned away, tender adieux.

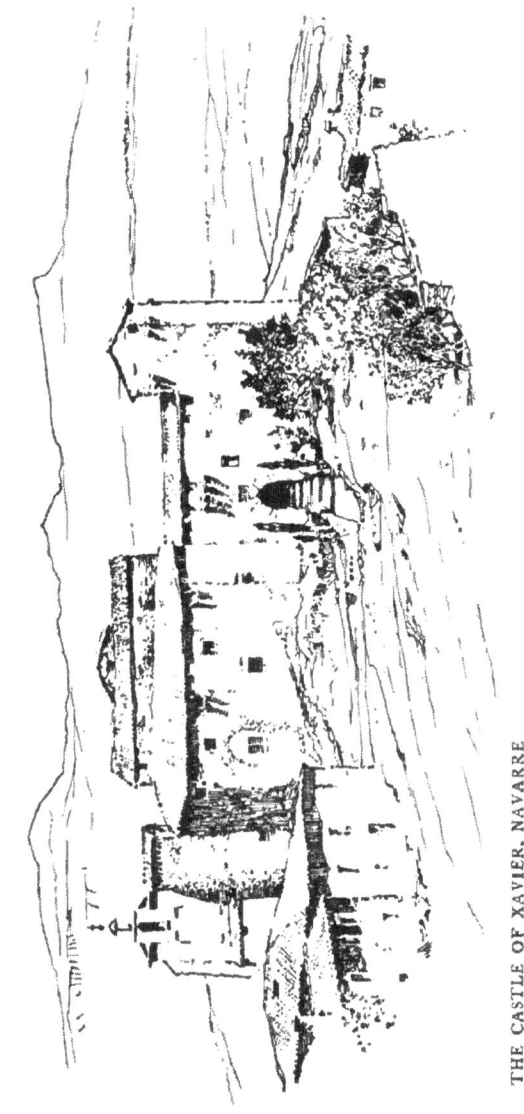

THE CASTLE OF XAVIER, NAVARRE

CHAPTER IX

THE WORK IN LISBON

(June, 1540—April, 1541)

PORTUGAL, when Francis arrived there, was at the height of her brief day. She had drunk of the mysterious and reviving wine of the Renascence, and her renewed vigour had found outlet—shut off as she was by Spain from the rest of Europe—in the only way which was left to her. The sea was her open door. Other lands were giving the world reformers, artists, poets, scholars; her greatest gifts were Bartholomew Diaz and Vasco da Gama and the Navigator Prince. But her glory did not last long. The best of her population was pouring out east and west to the new colonies, and comparatively few ever came back. If the children of the emigrants returned they were often half-caste and of low moral and physical stamina. Then the Inquisition was doing its deadly work, and the fine Jewish population had been sent out of the country. And the best men among those who were left at home devoted themselves rather to the Church than to their country, with a blind devotion which did Portugal small service.

It has often been said that the early thirties are critical years of life. If a sensitive man reaches that age without having chosen his path, he is, indeed, apt to find himself in a mental and spiritual maelstrom. But Francis Xavier came to Lisbon serene and joyful, and the whole town seems to have been astonished and captivated by the spectacle of one whose life not only recalled the meekness and poverty of Jesus, but also reflected something at least of an aspect of Him which was still dearer to the Iberian temperament, His authority and princeliness. And it is not to be wondered at that those who saw him marvelled. For Francis was experiencing in those months the pristine ecstasy of the spiritual marriage; in Paris he had been wooed, and had responded to the call, and made his solemn promises, but now at last all preparations were completed, and the old life left behind, and now he was dead to all save his life in Christ, and the preaching of the Gospel. In all his letters of this time, there is no trace of any regret, no wistful turning toward the glories he had renounced ; though there is a blending, to English eyes most strange, of rapturous love to Jesus and serpentine cunning, of evangelical ardour and suave urbanity, that perhaps none but a Spaniard could in himself contain.

His inward joy must already have been very real, and the new life very satisfying. For in wild spring months on that lovely Portuguese coast, in the dazzling and seductive environment of the Court, where he was soon *persona grata*, there must have been much to lure and disturb a heart not firmly fixed elsewhere. And there, too, he would learn, probably for the first time, from the seafaring folk about the harbour, and the travellers at the Court, of the terrible dangers of a voyage to India. Only a small proportion of the ships ever returned to port. And on every ship, and in every Eastern town, disease took heavy toll of those who escaped shipwreck. But Francis took no account of these things, for his treasure was in heaven, and on earth he had nothing to lose.

From the first moment of his arrival he plunged into work. A smaller man would complacently have viewed the sacrifice he was about to make of himself, and have taken a good holiday before embarking. Not so Francis. He was already on active service, and henceforth always would be, so long as there was within a day's journey of him one soul who did not know Christ Jesus. For he was, above all things, an evangelist. As the architecture of the Church has ever sprung from the minds and hearts of simple laymen, so her inner life has always been fostered, not by an esoteric hierarchy, but by men of a spirit too Catholic to be ecclesiastic. Such were Origen, Augustine, Francis of Assisi, Luther, Xavier. Lisbon was stirred because a living evangelist had come to her.

But although Francis had little care for ecclesiastical concerns, and spent small time on theology, he was, like most great evangelists, an uncompromising dogmatist. His evangelical genius taught him that if a man is to preach at all he must preach passionately—nay, aggressively. We cannot, by any means, always agree with his opinions about the nature of God, but neither can we quench our admiration for the impatience with which he bids his converts repeat the *Credo*, and be baptized, and proceed to more practical business. There is no doubt he left Lisbon a better city than he found it.

Simon Rodriguez, who had gone up with him to Montmartre, was there to welcome him. Old biographers weave a miracle from the story of their meeting, but Francis' own words about it throw light on many miracles. "On the day I got to Lisbon," he says, "I found Master Simon just coming under a fit of ague. My coming was such a joy to him, and seeing him such a joy to me, that the two joys added expelled the fever. That is a month ago, and it has not come back since. He is very well and making much fruit."

The same letter continues :

"There are many good persons here who long to serve our Lord if there were anyone to help them, and to give them some Spiritual Exercises to help them to put into practice the good which from day to day they put off doing. For, however promptly men begin to do the good they know, they will find in fact, if they look well into it, that they are too late in putting it into practice. This full knowledge [given by the Exercises] helps many to awake, and keeps them from finding peace where it is not, chiefly those who, against all reason, try to lead our Lord whither they desire, and do not wish to go whither God our Lord calls them, but allow themselves to be guided by their inordinate affections rather than by the good desires that are in them. Toward such one must have compassion rather than envy, seeing they go so uphill, and by so difficult and dangerous a road and for payment of such labour come to so hard an end.

"Three or four days after our arrival in this city the King sent for us, and received us very kindly. He was alone with the Queen in a room where we were with them more than an hour. He asked many details about our manner of life, about the way in which we came to know each other and unite, what were our first desires, and of our persecutions in Rome.* . . . All here are edified that

* In the summer of 1538 Ignatius and his companions had been accused of being fugitive heretics. In November of the same year the "slander" was publicly and formally declared to be false.

we carried on the affair to a decision, so much so that it seems to them that if it had not been settled as it was, we should never have gained any fruit, and in the opinion of those here we never did a better thing than carry it to a decision and let the truth be seen. The King and Queen were delighted to be so well informed about all our affairs. At the end of all the talk His Highness called his daughter, the Infanta, and his son, the Prince, that we might see them, and told us of the sons and daughters whom our Lord had given him, both of those who were dead and of those who live. And so the King, as well as the Queen, showed us much love.

" That same day on which he talked to us His Highness recommended us strongly to confess the young *gentiles hombres* of his Court, for the King has made a rule in his Court that all these should confess weekly, and he strongly recommended us to look after them. He said to us that if the young men know God and serve Him, then when they are grown they will form sound judgement, and if they turn out as they ought, the humbler people will take example from them, and the laymen of the kingdom will be reformed. For he holds it for certain that if the nobles are reformed the great part of the kingdom will be reformed too. It is a matter for wonder and for thanks to our Lord to see how zealous for the glory of God the King is, and how inclined to all pious and good things ; and all we of the Company owe him much for the good will he has to us, both for those with you, and for us here. The ambassador told me that he had spoken with the King after we had spoken with him, and that the King told him he would be delighted to have all of us here, even though it cost him part of his revenue.

" A number of the people here that we know are trying to keep us back from going to India. It seems to them that we will gain more fruit by confession, private conversations, spiritual exercises, the ministry of the sacraments, exhorting persons to frequent confession and communion and by preaching, than if we went to India. . . . It is marvellous to hear tell of the fruit we may gain in India. Those who have been there many years tell us this, because they have seen the people well prepared to receive the faith of Christ our

Lord. They say that if we maintain out there our present remoteness from any kind of avarice in our way of living, they have no doubt but that in a few years we shall convert two or three kingdoms of idolaters to the faith of Christ, when these idolaters recognise in us that we seek nothing else but the salvation of their souls. . .

"We are trying hard to find here some clerics who for the service of God alone, and for the salvation of souls, will go to India with us. It seems to us at present that we cannot serve the Lord in anything better than in seeking some companions, for if there were even a dozen clerics all of one mind and will, we should gain much fruit. We are finding some; a cleric whom we knew in Paris has promised to come with us, and live and die with us, and to go out with the same aims as we have. We believe that he will be very true, for he has given many securities. There is another in minor orders who will soon be a cleric and who has freely offered, and there is a doctor of medicine, well known to us in Paris, who has promised to come with us, and to use his art only as he sees it will help him to save souls. . . . We always strive to get men to join us who are separate from all avarice, and we are not even content that they should be separate from avarice, but from all appearance of it, to such a degree that none may be able to suspect that we seek the temporal more than the spiritual.

" The King said to his confessor, and to a bishop who is greatly attached to us, that we ought to preach : we put it off for some days, in order to apply ourselves to humble affairs, and showed no desire to preach, though all who know us desire nothing else. His Highness sent for us one day, and after talking for a little said he would be delighted if we preached, and so we offered freely to do it, as well to obey him as for our hope in Christ our Lord that He would favour us and allow us to gain some fruit of souls. We begin the Sunday after next, and we shall surely gain some fruit, as the people here are well-disposed to us. We pray much to our Lord that *He may increase their faith who have any hope or good opinion of us*. And because of the good opinion they have of us we trust much in God that if we do not look to ourselves but to the faith of those who wish to hear us He

I

will give us savour and grace *that we be able also to console them and to say whatever is either necessary or useful to the salvation of souls.*

"Lisbon, 13th July, 1540,
"For all of you most dear *in the Lord.*" *

A few days later, on July 26th, he wrote the following letter :

"To Ignatius Loyola and Peter Codacio, Rome.
"The grace and love of Christ our Lord be always in our help and favour.

"After having written of everything here at great length some things which we had forgotten to write came to mind, among which are the following. If the Brief which concerns all the Company is despatched, send the copy, for the King and those who favour us will be delighted to see it, and the decision which the Governor gave in our favour. The King asked for the Exercises, and wanted to see them. . . . We have got two letters, both very short, one written on the 8th of June, and the other on the 1st May. The Ambassador would be delighted to get a letter from you. Some which you had written and he got on the road coming from Rome to Portugal—just think, he treasures them ! If you are not able to write, arrange that we can show the letters Estrada writes, and speak of him (the Ambassador) in them.

"We are going to give the Exercises to two licentiates in theology, the one a very famous preacher, and the other a tutor of the King's brother, the Infante Don Ennrique, and we are making some other persons of quality desire them, believing that the more they wish to do them, the more they will profit in doing them. . . . To see the numbers who confess and communicate is a matter of praise to God our Lord.

"See what you think about Francisco de Strada's coming to the University of Coimbra, for here what is necessary for their studies will not be lacking for him nor for others. . . . In the course of time we will not fail to speak to the King about a house for students, and for this we will need to know your intention as to its style, and as to who should govern it, and the order they ought to have, *that they may*

* *Mon. Xav.,* vol. i. p. 211 ff.

grow in spirit rather than in learning—so that when we speak to the King we may tell him about the way those who study in our colleges must live. Of all this write us fully. We see no difficulty about building a college here, and the people here would be delighted to put us up houses if there were anyone to live in them.

"The bishop, our friend, has told us that the King is not quite determined about sending us to India, he thinks we should serve our Lord here no less than there. Two bishops urged that we ought not to remain here, but go to India, thinking that we were bound to convert some kings.

" We are always at it to find companions, and I believe that they will not be wanting, as they keep on turning up. If we stay here we shall found some houses, and it will be easier to find men who will stay here than go. And if we go, and God our Lord give us some years of life, we shall, with His help, found some houses among Indians and negroes.

" If the Brief which concerns all the Company is not dispatched arrange that they may give us licence to found houses of our profession among unbelievers. Whether we shall remain here or go to India, for the love and service of God our Lord, write to us the way and order which we ought to pursue in organising our Company, and write *very fully*, for you know well what few talents we have, and if you do not help us the greater service of God our Lord will suffer for want of our knowing how to manage.

" Lisbon, 26th July, 1540.
    " For all of you.   " FRANCISCO." *

It is possible that when Francis suggests in the above letter that it may not be so easy to fill the proposed college as to build it, he betrays some of the disappointment which he already must have felt in the rather rococo piety of the Portuguese Court. While the new Order owed to John III. its missions in India, Africa, South America, as well as colleges at home, and while Francis had, at first, as we have seen, been carried away by this King's full-blown enthusiasms, one could not live long in Lisbon and be ignorant of the gigantic exploitations which were taking place in the new colonies. Xavier soon suspected that a bad conscience was, in part at least, the source of John's devotion, and when

* *Mon. Xav.*, vol. i. p. 219.

this became, in India, quite plain to him, he was at no pains to express what he thought.

Meanwhile the Saint was now, as always, equally at home in palace or pot-house, dining with the King, or binding up some wretched beggar's sores. Although they were offered rooms at the Court, he and Rodriguez lodged in the hospital, where they spent much of their time. They began by begging their food in the streets, although the King offered them supplies from his table. But this begging interfered with their other work, and they soon gave it up—save twice a week to keep them humble—and accepted what the King sent. Of these meals, we are told, they ate but a small portion, and gave the rest to the patients at the hospital.*

At the Court Francis' class for pages and their friends, begun by the special request of the King, did livelier work than perhaps John had intended, for it turned some of the young courtiers into monks, and others into missionaries. Of this work we will hear more from Francis himself in one of his letters.

About this time the Saint's uncle, the Doctor of Navarre, began a correspondence with his nephew. The Doctor was now a professor at the University of Coimbra, and he begged Francis to come and visit him, since they were so near one another. He also wrote to King John, promising to deliver two extra courses of lectures if the Royal approval were given for his nephew to come to see him. Francis' replies to this invitation reveal a singular mingling of deep and simple affection towards his uncle, with priestly admonitions and warnings. These letters show that he really wished and meant to see his relatives before leaving for India, and so contradict all that is implied of his nature in the story of his refusing to go to see his mother, though passing near her home. That story was invented to exhibit his holiness, but has often been read as betraying his heartlessness, and even if we had not had proof that his mother was dead at the time he is said to have passed her by, these letters would have made us doubt the tale. " May it please God . . .," he says,† " that in this life we may see each other before my companions and I depart for India : and then

* Polanco, tom. i. p. 87 ff., quoted by Brou, *Vie de S. François Xavier*, vol. i. p. 91.
† *Mon. Xav.*, vol. i. p. 224.

I shall be able to give you the whole story of what you ask me in your letters."

A little later he writes again to his kinsman :

" My soul received such joy and comfort with your letter of the 25th October that nothing but the sight of you, *longed by me for so many days*, could have given me more rest. . . . I do not pity you as I would if I thought that you did not use that very ample talent which Christ our Lord gave you, as a faithful servant, who holds for certain that the reward of the toil will be greater than the fatigue involved. For then *he will be made ruler over many things who has been faithful over a few things.*" . . .

" I shall write to the Prior of Roncesvalles, as you command . . . as for the rest, I wait till we see each other, which will be when you least think ; for the love which you show me in your letters obliges me to be obedient to you in this " (*i.e.*, in arranging that they should meet). " *I say indeed nothing of the love that links me to you, the Lord, who alone searches out the innermost secrets of both of us, knows how dear you are to me. Farewell, illustrious Doctor, and love me as you are wont.*" *

During the time when Francis was in Lisbon, there was a great fracas going on between the Vatican and the Portuguese Court, as to the conduct of the Inquisition. Our Saint, instead of entering into the dispute, visited the victims who crowded the prisons, and, though he gave them the Spiritual Exercises of the First Week, which, as the reader may remember, are largely occupied with meditations on Heaven and Hell, he seems to have cheered and encouraged them marvellously. We find him writing : " Numbers of them tell us that God has done them great favour in bringing them to the knowledge of many things necessary for the salvation of their souls." †

Amazing spectacle ! If Xavier had been a worldly-minded priest, eager for the promotion which would bring greater opportunities for ease and self-indulgence, one could easily imagine his visiting those cells with complacency, and admonishing the prisoners to think on their sins. But that Francis, the tender-hearted, the sensitive, the pitiful, should go there, day after day, with no word, as far as we know, of

* *Mon Xav.*, vol. 1. p. 234.   † *Ibid.*, vol. 1. p. 232.

protest against the tyrants, how do we account for this ? How did he dare to bid the victims think on *their* sins, and moreover, how did he win their love and gratitude for having done so ? How could he bid them rejoice that they were cast into prison ? He had, indeed, a different sense of proportion from most of us, and did not use his powers along the average lines. One of the first conditions of the development of genius is specialisation, and the genius of Francis had to specialise in its own ways. He had faith in the Church. He was a good Roman Catholic. Therefore, it followed that he believed that there were those who were inspired by God to arrange ecclesiastical affairs, persecutions, and the rest. That was not his affair. His affair was to bring outsiders into the Fold, for that he must answer before his Church and before God, and if the Church called a man a heretic, it was not for him to argue with the Church, but to give the man more light. After all no doubt they were heretics, the Church was right enough there. And the kindest as well as most consistent thing, *according to her lights*, which the Roman Catholic Church can do to heretics is to cleanse them of their heresy, whatever the gruesome cost may be. But we can imagine how Francis would rejoice and sing, when he was brought into contact with those unhappy creatures, that he happened to have been ordained not to hurt but to heal, not to torture their bodies, but to comfort their souls. There is nearly always peace in one's own point of view.

Later on, as we shall see, in India, a very different side of his character appeared. There, emancipated from the immediate authority of the Church, his personal sense of justice and of responsibility for the administration of justice burst forth again and again in fiery splendour. And it was nothing less than his passion for justice which led him, near the end, to make the fatal mistake of asking for the Inquisition in India. But of that more anon.

A few months later, on September 27th, 1540, by the Bull *Regimini Militantis Ecclesiæ*, the full text of which we have already seen,* Pope Paul III. formally established the Society of Jesus as a religious Order. The text of the Bull was not actually published until April, 1541, just after Francis had left for India.

* See p. 111.

On March 18th he wrote two farewell letters to his friends in Rome. The first is addressed to Ignatius Loyola and John Corduri, and we give it almost in full :

" We have your letters, which we were longing for. The joy they gave our souls was as great as our thankfulness for them, for they told us both of the good health of all the Company, and of the holy and pious occupations of you all, in building spiritual as well as material houses, so that the living and those to come, having the needful means *for working in the vineyard of the Lord,* may be able to carry on what is begun in the service of God our Lord. May it please the Lord that to us also, *absent in the body, though never more present in the spirit than now,* He may give His holy grace to imitate you, seeing that you showed to us the way to come to Christ our Lord.

" As to things here, I may tell you that our way of proceeding pleases the King, for he sees the spiritual harvest, and is also hopeful that it would be greater if there were more [workers]. So he is thinking of founding a college and a house for us, that is, for the Company of Jesus. Three men are to stay here to build them, Master Simon [Rodriguez], Master Gonzalo, and another priest learned in canon law. Many others are being discovered who think of entering the Company. The King has taken the making of these houses very much to heart, and sincerely. Always, when we have visited him, he has spoken to us about it without our ever having spoken to him, *neither ourselves nor by third parties,* but he has been moved to wish to build them by his sheer and pure goodwill. He will put up the college this summer in the University of Coimbra, and the houses, I think, in the city of Evora. I believe he is going to write to His Holiness to send him some, or one, of the Company to help Master Simon for these beginnings. The King loves our Company, and desires its increase *like one of ourselves,* and solely for the love and honour of God our Lord. He puts us under an obligation, *for God's sake,* to be his perpetual servants. . . .

" Micer Paulo [Camerino], and another, a Portuguese [Francisco Mansillas], and I leave this week for India. . . .

" The King is sending us away loaded with favours. He has commended us warmly to the Viceroy * who goes to

* Xavier makes a mistake in referring to Sousa as a Viceroy ; there was no Viceroy at this time, and Sousa was only a Governor.

India this year. We go in his ship, and he shows us much love, so much so that he does not wish anybody but himself to be concerned with our embarkation and the things needed at sea, and he has taken charge of providing everything, even to having us at his table.

" I send you these details just that you may understand how much fruit we may gain among those heathen kings through the great credit enjoyed by a Viceroy in these parts.

" The Viceroy who goes this year has been there many years. He is a very fine man. He has a good name in the Court here, and is beloved by all in India. He told me the other day that in an island of India, where there are no Moors or Jews, but only heathen, we are sure to gain a great harvest, and he sees no difficulty in our making the king of that island and all his kingdom Christian.

" . . . By the love and service of God our Lord we pray you to write next March when the ships leave Portugal for India. Tell us what, in your opinion, ought to be our method with the unbelievers. Although experience will teach us partly how we ought to go about it, yet for the rest we hope in God our Lord that it will please His Divine Majesty to make us to know through you the best way in which to serve Him. He has done so until now, but we are afraid of what often happens, and has been the fate of so many. By carelessness, or by not being willing to ask others and take advice from them, they are denied many things by God. . . . *So we pray you, Fathers, and beseech you again and again in the Lord by that friendship which has so united us in Christ Jesus,* write and tell us how you think we ought to proceed. What counsels have you? What means shall we use for the better service of God our Lord? We do wish to have the will of Christ our Lord made clear to us through you. Again we ask you—have us in your prayers *beyond the usual remembrance.* This long voyage, and the new dealing with heathen, and our ignorance, ask for much more favour than usual.

" From India, with the first ships that leave, we shall write fully, and tell you all about everything. The King said to me when I took my leave that I was to write very fully for the love of our Lord about the opportunity there is there for the conversion of those poor souls. He takes their misery hard, and was very anxious that their Creator and Redeemer might not be perpetually shamed by the creatures made in His image and likeness, and bought with such a price. Such is the zeal of His Highness for the honour of Christ our Lord and the salvation of his neighbours ... that I could not believe what I have seen if I were not an eye-witness. ...

"Let me tell you that this court is greatly reformed. So much so that it is more like a religious house than a court. It is a matter for thanks and praise to God that so many make their confession and take communion every week without fail. We are so engaged with confessions, that if our numbers were doubled, there would still be penitents. We are engaged the whole day and part of the night, and this with courtiers alone without others. When we were in Almerin those who came to do business at the Court were astonished to see the multitude who communicated every Sunday and feast day. Seeing the good example of the courtiers they did the same. So that if there were many of us, there would be no one with business who would not search to do business with God before doing it with the King. We have no time for preaching on account of the number of confessions, as we judge it a better service to our Lord to be taken up with confessing than with preaching. There are plenty of preachers in this Court, so we have given it up.

"There is nothing else to tell you but when we are to embark. In concluding, we pray Christ our Lord to give us grace to see each other, and to bring us together in the other life bodily. For in this life I do not know if we shall see each other again, both because of the great distance from Rome to India, and because of the great *harvest*, which is there without going to seek it elsewhere. And let the first (of us) who goes to the other life, and *does not find his brother whom he loves in the Lord*, pray Christ our Lord to join us all there in His glory.

"Lisbon, 18th March, 1541.

"For all of you beloved *in the Lord*,
"FRANCISCO DE XAVIER." *

The next letter to Jay and Lainez, sent along with the previous one, is of a more personal and confidential character, and reflects not a little of Loyola's discretion and careful sagacity.

" ... Don't neglect to write to Don Pedro Mascarenhas,

* *Mon. Xav.*, vol. i. p. 237 *seq.*

for he gets more pleasure and comfort from your letters than I can express. I assure you that he loves you *much in the Lord*, he keeps your letters carefully, and reads them often, and not without great comfort and joy of soul. Seeing how much he is yours, I feel bound to be entirely his all the days of my life. It seems to us here, *unless you have a better plan*, that it would be useful if you wrote to the King, thanking him for the College and House which he means to build for the Company, for here they think a lot of compliments, and I know by what Don Pedro has told him about you, that the King would be pleased with a letter from you. You could say in the letter how we write to you about the College and House which he means to build in the name of the Company. This, too, will be useful in getting on toward putting them up, and I know that a letter will be seen by many here.

" As to Francisco Mansillas, I wish you to know that he has no orders. There is a bishop in India; we hope in God that it will be possible to have him ordained there. The good man has a larger share of zeal and goodness and great simplicity than of learning. If Don Paulo [Camerino], with his wide learning, does not go with him, we shall be in a quandary about ordaining him there in India if God our Lord does not help us. He is very anxious, that if by chance they should not ordain him there, you should send him a dispensation so that *extra tempora* in three feasts* it might be possible to ordain him *ad titulum of voluntary poverty, and most abounding simplicity*, and his great goodness and holy simplicity may make up what he does not reach by learning. . . .

" From India we shall write at great length, when we have had experience of things there. The Viceroy's favour will do much to help us, for he has great credit with those kings who keep the peace with the King of Portugal. . . .

" When you write to us to India, write us by *name* of everyone, since it has to be only once a year. And write at great length, so that we shall have what will take us eight days to read. And we shall do the same." †

Some of those biographers who make his life a peg upon which to hang their ragings against Roman Catholicism talk of the gorgeous state in which Xavier departed for the East,

---

* The sub-diaconate, diaconate, and priesthood are usually conferred on three different days.

† *Mon. Xav.*, vol. i. p. 243.

and contrast his journey with that of good Protestant missionaries to-day. Spleen and ignorance are the parents of this kind of eloquence. The oldest and probably the most authentic account of his send-off is that of Gonçalvez.*

When the time of departure was near John III. commanded Don Antonio de Ataide, the Count of Castanheira, to find out from Master Francis the things which he would need during the voyage, and procure them for him. All that the Count could do was to get the Father to accept, for himself and his companions, a rug of coarse wool, as a protection against the cold weather at the Cape of Good Hope, and several religious books which were not obtainable in India. He would accept no provisions of food. Still less would he accept a servant which Don Antonio offered him. "Your position demands it," the Count said to him, "you can't wash your own linen, nor busy yourself over the stock-pot." To this, with a grave and modest air, Francis made answer, "Sir, this care for an imaginary dignity, this anxiety to fulfil unreal obligations, has put Christianity into the deplorable state in which we now see it. As for me, I mean to wash my own clothes, and watch my own soup-pot, and look after other people's as well, and by doing these things I hope I shall not lose any authority."

The Count remained much struck with these words; often later on he recalled them, and would add, " Entrusted with providing for the passengers on those ships who were in the service of the King, my great trouble was usually with those who asked too much, or even took more than they were given, but the hardest task I ever had was with Father Francis, when I tried to persuade him not to refuse absolutely everything, but to consent to accept some small gift from the King."

The departure of the ships for the East was at that time one of the great events of the year in Lisbon. A small proportion of those who went away ever returned, but those who did often came laden with fabulous wealth, and full of wonderful tales of the new lands. Before the travellers embarked, they used to meet in the Church of Our Lady of Nazareth, where they were publicly commended to the care of God. And all the year round, in the convents near by, they chanted the Mass of the Angels for those at sea. The place of embarkation was known as the Place of Tears.

There is a tradition in Lisbon that Francis, before going on board the ship, preached to the crowds that had come to

* Quoted by Cros, *Vie de S. François Xavier*, vol. i. p. 188.

bid him farewell. A movable pulpit, it is said, was brought from an adjoining monastery, and the Place of Tears rang with the cheerful adieux of the most joyful of saints, the gayest of missionaries.

This man was off to preach the Gospel, because he could not for an hour keep the good news to himself, nor even to Europe, now that the opportunity had come to go farther afield.

Many missionaries have sober faces, and speak often of taking up the Cross, and setting their faces steadfastly to go to Jerusalem. Xavier, because One had gone there already, could see no more darkness in that direction, and to him the Cross which a human back can bear was so small— that other Cross in view—that he did not talk much of it. Yet, like all the gayest souls, he had known well the taste of tears. From his boyhood on he had quitted the easier and more obvious battlefields, and sought the harder. He had left the knightly company of his brothers and cousins, and become a poor student in Paris; after eleven years of hard study and teaching, he had found the Church waiting for him with open doors, and the road to fame free before him; but instead of accepting a canonry, he had gone on foot to Venice—the Swanwick of the first Jesuits—and from that time on to now, and it was to be the same henceforth, his life was one steady crescendo of love and devotion to his neighbour and his God. He was fastidious and sensitive: he spent his spare moments nursing the sick and diseased, and visiting those in prison, and reading to them and praying with them. He was a lover of books and all lovely things, but he had left his *Alma Mater*, and what she might still have given him, far behind. He was a philosopher, and had " explicated Aristotle publicly, and not without praise," but all that he had now put by. All the superb possibilities, social, intellectual, political, ecclesiastical, for which his genius had held the key, he was content to see now, hid with Christ in God: hid there, too, the still dearer and more intimate treasures of family life and love, which few, indeed, dare willingly forgo for the Kingdom of Heaven's sake. For a man so eager, so ardent, so miraculously sympathetic and tender as Francis, this last sacrifice, of which he never spoke or wrote, is perhaps the fullest witness of all to the largeness and simplicity of his faith.

DOORWAY OF XAVIER CASTLE

CHAPTER X

THE sea route to India had been open to Europeans for less than half a century before Francis Xavier sailed for India. Until then only an occasional adventurer from the West had penetrated the lands of the Orient by other ways than the old overland routes from the Red Sea and the Persian Gulf. Pliny speaks of Roman merchants voyaging from Egypt to the coasts of Malabar (Barace) in seventy days, their ships manned with archers as a protection against pirates, and, of course, the Indian Ocean was familiar to the Arab traders from immemorial times, but the first voyage to the East *via* the Cape of Good Hope was made by Vasco da Gama in 1498.* That intrepid adventurer struck a bigger blow at Mohammedan power in the East by that one voyage than did many hundreds of missionaries. It was, indeed, a more effective retaliation against the followers of Islam for their having closed the overland routes to the Christians, than they can possibly have foreseen. Hitherto the aforesaid Arabs, or Moors as the Portuguese called them, had been practically the sole voyagers across the Indian Ocean, and the very names of the cities of their merchandise, such as Bagdad, Venice, Ormuz, Damascus, still breathe an odour of fabulous splendour and wealth. A curious and interesting characteristic of these sea-traders was that they never made any attempts to colonise on the Indian coasts, as the Portuguese immediately did. Political ambition they had none. Commerce was to them an all-absorbing art, loved for her own sake, or for the sake of the voluptuous beauty and luxury with which she could surround them. This may account for the atmosphere of glamour which still hangs over the merchants of the East. Very different are our typical Western merchants, and they get rich for other and much more complicated reasons. But when the

---

* The Cape had first been rounded in 1487 by Bartholomew Diaz.

Muslim wished to establish himself in India these Arab sea-traders did not put themselves at his disposal ; they were too much artists, perhaps, to be warriors, and the Mohammedan armies had to do without their help, and go by land.

Vasco da Gama had landed near Calicut, and had been received by the Emperor of the twelve Rajahs of Malabar, or Zamorin, as he was called, with great courtesy and formality. One piece of information which they brought back to Portugal was that all the Indians, except the Mohammedans, were Christians, only they were in need of teaching. This mistake may have been accounted for by an incident which took place on their landing. They were taken into a temple to be purified, and found it dedicated to a goddess named Mariamma—Mari, for short, the natives called her. This they at once took for the Virgin Mary, and said their prayers to her.

From the first the Portuguese were unhappy colonisers. They did not know the language, took little pains to learn it, and the social and religious customs of the East were a continual occasion of stumbling to them, while their high-handed methods of introducing themselves were certainly an occasion of stumbling to India. Further, they came determined to oust the Mohammedan traders. This purpose the Mohammedans were aware of immediately, and they took full advantage of the impression which the ungracious manners of da Gama and his friends had made on the natives, to maintain their own favour at the cost of that of the new competitors. But the deep-rooted instincts of hospitality were not easily to be overcome, and the first receptions given to the Portuguese were on the whole friendly.

The second expedition left Portugal in 1500, a fleet of thirteen ships, of which only six arrived in India. In spite of fighting both with natives and Arabs, and of innumerable misfortunes, five of these ships returned to Portugal so richly laden that all loss of goods and boats was many times covered. This journey is specially notable because of the discovery of Cochin harbour, which was far superior to Calicut, and opened upon a richer country. Cabral, the commander of this expedition, was able to disillusion the Portuguese at home with regard to the " Christianity " of the natives.

In 1502 da Gama set out again, and by means of brilliant

determination and courage, fortified by the most unscrupulous deeds of injustice and robbery, revolting and often
wholesale acts of cruelty, and artillery far superior to
anything which either the natives or the Mohammedans
possessed, Portuguese power in India soon established
itself all along the western littoral. Impregnable fortresses
were built in place after place, churches and monasteries
were put up inside the forts, and priests and soldiers were
shipped out in the desired proportions.

In 1510 Albuquerque, then Governor of India, and the
real founder of the Portuguese Empire in the East, captured
the island of Goa, and made it the capital of the new colonies.
Under his brilliant administration some sort of solid success
was more nearly achieved than at any other time, but his
policy, although in many ways large and statesmanlike,
had fatal weaknesses.

He was like most men of his age, pitiless and cruel, but he had
a keen love of justice. He kept no doorkeeper, and his door
was never closed save for a short time when he slept after dinner.
It was his maxim that, though the Mohammedans had been
conquered, having once submitted, they should be treated with
more than even justice, to attach them by love. . . . he was
both sagacious and wily, and he was able to foil Orientals with
their own weapons. The value of downright honesty in dealing
with the Eastern peoples had not yet been recognised, and
Albuquerque's successors, imitating his methods, but not posses-
sing his abilities, lost heavily in the game of intrigue. He, too,
had limitations which many of them did not recognise, for though
he certainly acted on standards of truth and honesty which are
not now acknowledged, he saw clearly enough the value of both
of these qualities, and in this very few of his successors followed
him. " I am known all over India," he tells the king, " as a
man of my word. If I send for a Mohammedan from anywhere,
he comes and demands no security. India, sire, in my time, is
governed by truth and justice, though it is true the people of
these parts speak little truth to us, but we must not treat them in
the same way. . . ." He was a man with the true imperial
instinct—the personality the Oriental follows blindly ; clear-
headed, always accessible, he did his work himself ; he might
inadvertently be unjust, but he never allowed subordinates to rob
or oppress, he knew his own mind, and he never let his judgment
be warped by fear or favour.*

* Whiteway, *Rise of Portuguese Power in India*, p. 167 ff.

He was confronted by immense difficulties, and perhaps the considerable measure of his success was due rather to the inevitable influence of a powerful and noble character, working from hour to hour on the events of each day, than to his general policy or statesmanship.

One of his chief weaknesses of judgment was the small respect he showed for the Mohammedans; although he never obeyed the urgent calls of the King to massacre them wholesale, yet he never realised that there was plenty of room for both Mohammedan and Portuguese under just conditions. Again, in the face of the practical insolvency of his government, he had no adequate financial policy to propose. The enormous loss in ships and cargoes, the salaries and extravagances of the officials, the cost of buildings and garrisons, had to be met by plunder, prize-ships, sudden deals of fortune, or by the whole capital of some ambitious and desperate governor.

Nor was Albuquerque's scheme for maintaining and increasing the European population, and manning the navies, practical or wise. He encouraged the colonists to marry native women, and only saw the racial degeneration which that involved when it was too late. He had some scheme in his mind to counteract this error, under which all the children were to be sent to Portugal for education and training, but, of course, this was never carried out.

Albuquerque was followed by a succession of far inferior men, and soon the lurid series of episodes—which never really had enough of unity or dignity to merit the title of government—lost even the brilliance and "dash" that, from the first, had taken the place of more enduring qualities.

The self-deception on the part of the Portuguese about the success of their new conquest was on a vast scale, and was apparently devoid of any conscious insincerity. It has, indeed, a certain bizarre and lurid grandeur of its own. Never were the Cross and the sword more blandly or shamelessly identified than in those days. And if for a moment the clouds of conquest and of battle shifted from the sacred Symbol, the dizenry of ecclesiastical pomp still hid its glory, and put its message to shame.

The Popes, in far-off Rome, had the vaguest notion of what was happening. They poured out indulgences and pardons of every variety to those "who went to India, stayed there, returned from there, those who died in the fighting there *for the spread of the faith.*" *

Colossal raiding expeditions set out again and again with formal and public episcopal blessing, cheered across the harbour bar by the chanting of choristers and the waving of sacred banners. Indian temples were desecrated and despoiled, and their priests slaughtered, in the name of Jesus. Francis Xavier writes enthusiastically of the charm and piety of da Sousa, and we know from other reliable sources that he used regularly to visit the sick in Goa, and that he spent much time and money over charitable and "religious" affairs there. One extract from an equally reliable historian shows us another side of his character, and the two pictures give us a typical impression of Portuguese character in those days:

On this coast between Cochin and Quilon, the Portuguese had been settled for over forty years, and they depended upon the goodwill of the residents for the supply of merchandise which was the bait that drew them to the East. This did not prevent da Sousa from leading an expedition to attack the temple of "Tebelicare," a few miles inland, which local information reported to be full of gold. There were two *jangadas* attached to this temple, but one with almost all the guards had gone to the south when the movements of the Portuguese had first attracted attention. An offer of £12,000 down failed to turn the Governor from his intention, and before nightfall the temple was reached. The building was of the common design, surrounded by a wall, with a few straw huts outside. The Governor and his immediate following went inside the temple and shut the door ; those outside the building passed a miserable night enough, a prey to every imaginable horror—the fall of a shield nearly caused a stampede. Inside the Governor and his friends spent the time in torturing the Brahmins of the temple, and in digging up the floor. It was never known exactly what was found— a gold patten worth £50 was all that was ever shown—but as two barrels of matchlock powder were emptied, and the barrels passed in, and as afterwards they each required eight slaves in relays to carry them, scandalous tongues were busy. When in the morning they started on their return journey, a Nair, dressed with scrupulous care with all his ornaments, followed by ten or

* Rehello da Silvas, *Corpo Diplomatico Port.*, quoted by Brou, *Vie de S. François Xavier*, vol. i. p. 127.

twelve others, flung himself on the Portuguese ranks. It was the remaining *jangada* with the relatives whom he could collect who thus tried to wipe out by their deaths the stain upon their honour. During the retreat the Portuguese were harassed by the country people and suffered a loss of thirty killed and 150 wounded, but on the way they sacked another temple, whence was obtained some small amount in silver coins to distribute among the soldiery.*

Barros, the official Portuguese historian of the period, interprets to the people the teaching of the Church on Eastern affairs in the following words :

It is true that there does exist a common right to all to navigate the seas, and in Europe we acknowledge the rights which others hold against us, but this right does not extend beyond Europe, and, therefore, the Portuguese as lords of the sea, by the strength of their fleets, are justified in compelling all Moors and Gentiles to take out safe conducts under pain of confiscation and death. The Moors and Gentiles are outside the law of Jesus Christ, which is the true law that everyone has to keep under pain of damnation to eternal fire. If, then, the soul be so condemned, what right has the body to the privileges of our laws ? It is true they are reasoning beings, and might, if they lived, be converted to the true faith, but inasmuch as they have not shown any desire as yet to accept this, we Christians have no duties toward them.†

The victims of this alien civilisation were in many respects not far from the kingdom of God, and in Malabar, at least, would quickly have responded to a happier gospel. The Hindoo rulers were gentle and tolerant, and had more advanced ideas of justice than their conquerors. A Persian traveller of the fifteenth century has left us his impressions of Calicut :

Security and justice are so firmly established in this city that the most wealthy merchants bring thither from maritime countries considerable cargoes, which they unload, and unhesitatingly send to the markets and the bazaars, without thinking in the meantime of any necessity of checking the account or keeping a watch upon the goods. The officers of the custom-house take upon themselves the charge of looking after the merchandise,

* Whiteway, *Rise of Portuguese Power in India*, p. 284.
† Quoted by Whiteway, *Rise of Portuguese Power in India*, p. 21. The sentiments here expressed are worthy of most modern daily papers.

over which they keep a watch night and day. When a sale is effected they make on them a charge of one-fortieth part; if they are not sold they make no charge on them whatsoever.*

There is no place in all India says Pyard de Laval, writing of Calicut] where contentment is more universal than here, both on account of the beauty and fertility of the country and of the intercourse with the men of all religions who live there in free exercise of their own religion. . . . It is the busiest and most full of traffic and commerce in the whole of India; it has merchants from all parts of the world, and of all nations and religions, by reason of the liberty and security offered to them there; for the king permits the exercise of every kind of religion.†

Strange and confusing, indeed, is the tapestry which the historians of that period have woven for us. Da Gama embarks from Lisbon, the crowd shouting, " To what mad enterprises covetousness can lead men ! " while King Manuel, with great piety and solemnity, puts a far other interpretation on the " mad enterprise " by placing a banner emblazoned with the Cross in the hands of the great Admiral. And the accusations of the crowd, and the solemn charges of the king, have both a certain relevancy. Da Gama sallies out from the shadows of his gorgeous banner to torture innocent fisher folk; Albuquerque, the best of all the Portuguese governors, cuts off the noses of Arab women; Almeida, another governor, gratuitously tears out the eyes of a Nair in a mood of suspicion. Sousa secretly rolls his barrels of gold out of the temples; sailors fling dead bodies of their captives into the sea, and then watch the shore to extort ransoms from the friends who come to take home the corpses; soldiers kill by torture, or sell into slavery, the prisoners whom they cannot ransom. And again and again those Indians, whom the Portuguese said they were going out to civilise and convert, put their would-be teachers to shame. Malik Aiyaz sought for Don Lourenço's body on the battlefield, that he might give it honourable burial, and wrote to Almeida, the governor, that when the enemy was conquered he should be treated as a brother. A poor native tribe, suddenly disturbed on their rustic green by Portuguese slave-hunters, gave their enemies food and drink, and then went off on parole, such of them as could, to gather

* *India in the Fifteenth Century*, by Abdu-r-razák, p. 13, quoted by Whiteway, *op. cit.*, p. 26.

† Pyard de Laval, vol. i. pp. 366 and 402, quoted by Whiteway, p. 27.

together enough money for their ransoms, and brought it back at the appointed time as they had promised, when they might easily have escaped. But within a few miles of these gentle folk were others who tortured the hours of darkness with their profane and obscene rites, while by daytime their young men hunted for human heads to offer to the maidens they courted, and their womenfolk dressed human bodies for the oven : beyond the next range of hills it was a crime to kill a fly. Upon the edge of this vast and mysterious and chaotic continent the Portuguese colonists had settled with about as much disturbance as a few gnats would make upon an elephant's back.

But Francis Xavier, as he looked upon the fading coasts of Europe for the last time, and turned his face towards the sunrising, saw no clouds there, but only eager hands held out to receive the things he was taking, and dark eyes full of grateful tears.

The ship in which the new governor sailed, with Xavier and his two companions on board, was called the *Santiago*. The immense clumsy vessel, which housed in her dark and unhealthy crevices about a thousand souls, had hardly loosed her moorings before Francis had become the minister of all. There were, indeed, in that motley crowd, many to care for, and few to care. Most of them were poor, not a few desperate. There was no more reckless gamble open to men in those days than a voyage to the Orient. They might return with a fabulous fortune, they might just as likely perish before ever they reached the new lands. Many of the travellers went simply because they were unemployed and hungry, and this voyage, thanks to the self-interested generosity of the Portuguese Government, would provide them with maintenance till they were beyond the help of Portugal, and not likely ever to have either health or courage to return. Contrasting with these were the sharpest-witted merchants of the day, or their representatives, and, lastly, there were the real simple lovers of adventure for her own wild sake, and with these our Saint had probably more in common than with any of the others. For all saints love the spirit of adventure. Are they not themselves the greatest adventurers of all ?

Since Vasco da Gama had embarked in 1497, the conditions of travelling had not much improved, although the expedition had now become an annual one, and consisted always, at the start at least, of a goodly number of ships. This little fleet of five was probably the smallest that had ever set out. The dangers and discomforts of the expedition were legion. Except for the richer travellers, there were no cabins, no sleeping accommodation, no shelters of any kind at all; and the few cabins which did exist had about as much space and ventilation as coffins. The food was scarce, and soon much of it became bad. The water was scarcer still, and was presently so putrid that one historian tells that it could only be drunk in the dark, because of the numbers of distracting creatures in it. Another writer describes how the passengers put a handkerchief across the mouth before drinking, in order to catch the filth. Disease was, of course, rampant, and there was little provision made for its prevention or cure, or even amelioration. There was one official box of medicine, which in a few days was empty. Added to these perils and sufferings within were the terrors of the uncharted seas. Little was known of the times or regions of storms or calms, and the ships were unfitted to combat even with what was known.

The old chronicler Valignano draws a pitiful picture of the gay and ignorant travellers setting out on this journey, bound to be so terrible even at the best, as if they were going for a day's pleasure trip on the Tagus; their only raiment the shirts on their backs, their luggage just what they carried in their hands—a couple of rolls of bread, a cheese, and perhaps a little marmalade.

Of the ships that left Portugal between 1497 and 1579, 90 per cent. returned in safety. A far larger number were lost in the next forty years, when the ships were bigger and less navigable, and never lasted more than two or three voyages at best. The Portuguese had no natural gifts of seamanship, and Couto, the Portuguese historian, who went out to India in 1556, writes :

Both the Dutch and the English, the very first time they went there [i.e., Surat River] found anchorages between shoals and banks where they stay as securely as if they were at home from our fleet, which cannot injure them. Our fleets which go in and out every day know of them (the shoals) what the English have taught us.*

* Couto, *Decadas*, vol. ix. pp. 24 and 25, quoted by Whiteway, p. 42.

On the English ships the taking of the altitudes was a much encouraged and popular diversion; on the Portuguese ships it was done by the pilot only, and he did it in secret.

But it was the conditions on board the ship, more than actual shipwreck, which took the heaviest toll of life. Less than 60 per cent., on the average, of those who left Portugal reached their goal. In 1576 the ship carrying the Viceroy and 1,100 men arrived in India with only 200 men alive.

Xavier, though officially a first-class passenger in the suite of the new Governor, did not keep to his quarters. Remembering, and interpreting in his own matchless way, Loyola's counsel to be all things to all men, remembering it so well, doubtless, because the words echoed the deepest counsel of his own heart, he was immediately ship's doctor, steward, nurse, evangelist, playmate, tutor, cook, in swift and bewildering succession. Of course, it took a man of genius to do this as he did it, but the sincerity and unselfishness, nay, more, the rapture of personal devotion to Jesus with which this *tour de force* was carried through, earned for him on the spot the title of Saint—a title so often only acquired through the gracious or even flattering hand of tradition. A ship's boy who was on board used afterwards in India to tell how this amazing man used to occupy himself in doing all the humblest services possible to the other passengers, how he washed their linen for them, and how he gave up his cabin to one who was sick, and slept himself on the coil of a rope. He appears soon to have become the most popular man on board, and to have had an immense influence on those around him. First and last he was evangelist. "I let things go in at their door, but I take care they come out at mine," he is reported to have said, and as he spoke he may have been recollecting the words of Loyola, "A good hunter of souls ought to pass by many things in silence, as if he did not see them; later, when the will is mastered, he will be able to direct the disciple as he please towards virtue." "Very plain is it," said Francis Thompson, writing of Xavier, in his *Life of Loyola*, "where he learned his divinely unprincipled sleights, his heavenly cunning." He played cards with the young rakes on board, and soon became their boon companions, and, for the time at least, brought them on their knees before the beauty of holiness; their ribald songs died down, and many years later we hear of the hymns still being sung on the Portuguese ships which Francis Xavier had them all singing before they passed Madeira. A curiously modern trait which we discover at this time is his absolute refusal to drink wine. "A priest," he said, "should drink nothing but water; this beverage does not excite evil passions, nor defile speech, nor reveal that which should remain hid."

His place during the journey was at the table of the Governor, but he chose rather to eat with the crowd. His portion was sent to him from the high table; he gave away all but the most meagre remnant to those who were sick. He himself became ill, but, as old Tursellinus puts it, with premonitory hints of a very modern point of view, "The divine virtue which was in him overcame the weakness of his nature, and his noble and constant courage held in the troublesome vomiting of his stomach, and so, when he was not able to help himself, he failed not to help those who were sick." The same writer goes on to give us a vivid description of Xavier's life on board ship, which is carefully founded on contemporary letters and histories.

This tedious and laborious navigation, as commonly it happeneth, had so extremely worn out the marines and other passengers, that now many fell sick in the ships, and their victuals greatly increased the same. For they fed continually on salt meats and oftentimes on musty biscuits, besides, they had, for the most part, no other drink but stinking and corrupted water, which, by reason of the nature of the liquor, and small quantity thereof, did rather increase than allay the extreme thirst which the salt meat caused in them, so that the bad humours of such unwholesome diet being dispersed through their veins engendered in them diseases no less gruesome than deadly. For their gums swelled after a loathsome manner, breaking out into horrible ulcers, and did not only put the sick men to great torment, but also (which was most miserable) made them that they could not eat. And this contagion, by little and little increasing through their grief of mind and want of necessary commodities, began to spread itself over the whole multitude, who were much thronged up in strait places for want of room . . . so the sick, being destitute both of physic and attendance, died not more through the contagious diseases than for hunger, which was a worse plague. Besides the filth of the ship did most extremely annoy those poor wretches, and was far more troublesome and loathsome unto them than unto the others who were in health.

Xavier, therefore, when he saw the ship wherein he sailed full of sick persons, calling to mind what he had accustomed himself unto at the beginning of his conversion, gave an evident proof of his benignity and virtue. That which hastened him on would have made another afraid. He saw the hatches of the ship stowed not only with sick bodies but also with half-dead : he knew the disease to be very infectious, he saw death's grisly look before his eyes. Yet for all this, turning fear into charity, and knowing it was a kind of martyrdom to hazard his life by such contagion for the saving of souls, he resolved to help the said sick as best he could, and so he presently began to hear the confessions of those who lay a-dying, he cleansed the sick men's bodies, he washed their linen, he dressed their meat, minced it small and fed them with his own hand. He ministered physic to the weak, he most lovingly cheered up those who were sad, and put them that were out of heart in hope of recovery both of body and soul.*

Through ignorance and inexperience on the part of the navigators, the ships were becalmed in tropical waters, and the accounts of that part of the voyage are just as frightful as the tale of the Ancient Mariner, if a trifle less artistic. It was many years since there had been such a terrible passage. But every horrible circumstance only served Xavier as a new occasion of devotion. Camerino supported him loyally ; perhaps his other companion hardly rose to the occasion, probably he was too ill to do so ; one does not know. But it is noticeable that Francis in his own letter does not dwell on the terrors of this voyage, and gives but a brief account of his own doings.

At last, after being becalmed for forty days, the wind rose, and soon in storm and tempest they swept round the Cape. Had it struck old Tursellinus he would, no doubt, have drawn a touching picture of the Saint wrapping that one coarse woollen rug of his, which he had accepted with such reluctance, around some poor shivering invalid, while he himself ached with cold. And no doubt the biographer's imagination would still have fallen short of the truth.

From Mozambique, which they reached on September 3rd, Francis writes a letter to Loyola.

" Mozambique.

" From Lisbon I wrote you on my departure of all that happened there. We left on the 7th April, of the year

* *Life*, English edition, p. 71 ff.

1541. I was sea-sick for two months, and suffered much annoyance forty days on the coast of Guinea through great calms. The weather was against us, but God our Lord was pleased to show us great grace and bring us to an island, where we are to the present day.

" . . . Immediately on our arrival here we took charge of the poor sick who came in the armada. My time has been spent in confessing them, communicating them, and helping them to die well. I made use of those plenary indulgences which His Holiness granted me for those parts. Almost all died contentedly when they saw how fully I could absolve them at the hour of death. Micer Paulo [Camerino] and Micer Mansillas occupied themselves with the temporal. All of us did everything for the poor, according to our small and feeble capacity, engaging ourselves with temporal things as well as with spiritual. As for the fruit, God knows about that, for He does it all.

" It is no small comfort to us that at last the Governor and all the nobles who have come out in this armada are quite convinced that all we do is *for God's sake*, and that we do not seek any human favour. For there were such difficulties that in myself I would not have dared to face them a single day for all the world. . . ."

These are very vague complainings, but from our knowledge of what was happening at the time we can be fairly sure of their origins. There was in command of one of the ships of this outgoing fleet a son of Vasco da Gama, Alvaro d'Ataide. It was his brother who was about to be superseded by the new Governor, Sousa, on whose ship Xavier was sailing. Suddenly at Mozambique Sousa suspected, with what foundation it is difficult to say, that Alvaro was sending on word to his brother in advance that his rival was about to appear. He at once deprived Alvaro of his ship, and kept him a prisoner till long after they arrived in India. This was the same Alvaro d'Ataide who afterwards treated Xavier so cruelly and unfairly on the eve of his last voyage, in 1552. It is easy to imagine that his conduct then may have been partly at least inspired by his associating Xavier in his mind with the Governor Sousa, who had dealt him such a hard knock at Mozambique. For we can see by Xavier's letters that he was on close and friendly terms with Sousa. Xavier's overflowing admiration for this man shows us how he was too easily imposed upon by outward professions of piety. For Sousa was in reality a rascal and a scoundrel, and became the most notorious of all the Portuguese Governors in India. We will hear of him again later.

The letter continues :

" We ask you all by the love of our Lord that in your prayers and sacrifices you will specially remember to pray God for us, since you recognise and know of what poor metal we are.

" One of the things which gives us much comfort and a very strong hope that God our Lord will favour us is the full knowledge we have of ourselves. We see how we lack all the things needful for the duty of declaring the faith of Jesus Christ : and since what we do is only to serve God our Lord, our hope and confidence keeps growing that God our Lord will give us, when the time comes, everything that is necessary for His service and glory, in great abundance. . . .

" During the voyage I preached every Sunday, and here in Mozambique as often as I could. . . . I would like much to go on writing, but at present sickness will not allow it. To-day they bled me for the seventh time, and I am middling. Praise God.

" Give my remembrances to all our acquaintances and friends.

" Mozambique, 1st Jan., 1542.

" FRANCISCO." *

The King's ships were that year forced to winter in Mozambique, so late had they been in arriving there. The place was known in these days as the Portuguese cemetery—a title which tells its own tale.

Just after they had arrived, a young man, one of Xavier's fellow passengers, suddenly died. Had he known Jesus Christ ? asked Francis. No, he was told. And those present were astonished at the sight of him completely overcome with sorrow. " But you did not know him," they said. " That is what distresses me," he replied. " If I had known him I would have taught him. To think," he added, " that I should have been in the same ship with him all those months and not have told him of Christ ! "

* *Mon. Xav.*, vol. i. p. 247.

In Mozambique, as on board ship, his devotion to the sick was incessant, and while he nursed and comforted, he taught and prayed. He himself was soon attacked by fever, but one who saw him * tells how when they tried to persuade him to give in he asked for one more night's freedom so that he might pass it with a brother who was very ill and in need of spiritual help. Next morning they found the dying sailor on the Saint's bed, rid of his delirium, and at peace with man and God.

Francis himself was soon at the point of death. A doctor who attended him afterwards related † that he was three days delirious, but that there was interspersed with his ravings, throughout the whole time, a vein of clear and coherent talk about things divine. Be that as it may, his mundane sanity was soon restored to him, and he was hard at work once more.

Toward the end of February he sailed for India with Sousa, leaving his two companions at Mozambique to follow on with the next ships from Lisbon. A letter, written a little later from Goa, gives, in his own breathless, vivid, yet so often inchoate and incoherent style, pretty full accounts of this journey, but, as usual, does not dwell on his own good works. Of this part of the voyage others have put on record that Francis in whatever he did was gentle and full of goodness towards others, but hard and stern with himself, that he gave up his bed to the sick, and found for himself a nest within the hollow of an anchor cable—for pillow, the anchor itself.‡ It was a hard resting-place. Yet we may well believe that the mystic imagination of the Saint soon wove its own dreams and delights about this lovely Christian symbol, and that in these dark starlit hours on the open sea he found the angels of Hope and Faith ministering to him in unforgettable ways.

The journey from Mozambique to Goa took rather over two months. The first pause was at Melinda, then under Portuguese suzerainty. Xavier tells in his letter of a conversation he had with a thoughtful Mohammedan there, who wished to know if Christianity was declining in Europe to the same extent as the faith of Islam was in

---

* " Enquiry at Goa," 1556, in *Mon. Xav.*, vol. ii. p. 212.
† *Ibid.*, vol. ii. p. 188.
‡ Teixeira, *Vita, Mon. Xav.*, vol. ii. p. 840.

Melinda, where out of seventeen mosques only three were now in use, and even these were almost empty. Xavier, instead of giving him an account of the state of the Church in Europe, which at that particular moment would have been rather an undertaking, pointed out to him that the state of affairs in Melinda was only the natural result which must follow on the acceptance of the false teachings of Mahomet. He seems to have regarded this man as typical of the more thoughtful among the inhabitants. He also tells of another who confessed that he had given the Mahdi two more years in which he might come to the rescue, failing which he was going to renounce the Faith. " It is the fate of infidels and of great sinners," Xavier concludes, " to be ill at ease."

From Melinda they proceeded to the island of Socotra. The Saint, as in duty bound, sends home descriptions of the island and the people, but we feel that as a letter-writer he has hardly yet found himself.

" From this city of Melinda, coming on our way for India, we got to a great island of twenty-five leagues, called Socotora (sic), a land shelterless and poor ; and in it is grown neither wheat, rice, nor millet ; no wine nor fruit ; it is very sterile and dry ; there are a lot of dates ; the bread there is made of dates ; there are plenty of cattle, and the people live on milk, dates, and meat. It is a windless place. The people of this island are Christians in their own opinion ; so they regard themselves ; they boast a lot of being Christians ; in their names they show it ; they are a very ignorant folk ; they can neither read nor write ; they have no books nor writings . . . they have churches and crosses and lamps. Each place has its *caciz*, he is like a cleric among us ; these *cacizes* can neither read nor write, and have neither books nor writings. They know numbers of prayers by heart. They go to church at midnight and in the morning, at the hour of vespers, and in the afternoons at the hour of compline—four times a day. They have no bells, they call the people with wooden clappers as we do in Holy Week. Even the *cacizes* do not understand the prayers, for they are not in their own language ; I believe they are in Chaldean. I wrote down three or four of the prayers that they use. I was twice in this island. They are devoted to St. Thomas ; they say they are come from the Christians which he made in those parts. In their prayers these *cacizes* sometimes say Aleluya, aleluya; they pronounce it almost as we do. They do not baptize, nor do they know what baptism is.

" . . . I was at vespers said by a *caciz*; he took an hour to say them, and never did anything but cense and pray. Those *cacizes* are married, great fasters; when they fast they do not eat fish nor milk nor flesh—they would rather die. Although there is plenty of fish on the island, they keep themselves on dates and herbs. They fast two lents, and one is for two months. Those who are not *cacizes* do not enter the church if they are eating meat in these lents, nor do the women go there.

" There was a woman in that place, a Moor, who had two small sons : I wished to baptize them, not knowing they were of Moorish descent. They went fleeing from me to their mother, and told her how I wished to baptize them, and she came weeping to me, not to baptize them, for she was a Moor and did not wish to be a Christian, still less did she wish her children to be so. The native Christians told me certainly not to baptize them, even if their mother did wish. This was because they did not hold Moors worthy of becoming Christians, nor would they consent that they should become so. As a people they are very inimical to the Moors." *

These Christians of Socotra were Assyrian Christians, or Nestorians, as their opponents called them. Nestorius was Patriarch of Constantinople in A.D. 428. The great theological discussion of that hour was as to whether Mary should be called Mother of God or Mother of Man. Nestorius then said she should be called Mother of Christ, and a tremendous controversy followed, culminating in the Council of Ephesus in A.D. 431. The site of the Council was possibly an unfortunate one for Nestorius. It may be that the people there, deprived of the worship of Diana, the virgin of Light and Life, were not content to call her successor in their hearts by any lesser name than that of " Theotokos," the Mother of God. That is mere speculation. The immediate cause of his condemnation was the sharp practice of his enemy, Cyril of Alexandria, who rushed through the business of the Council before the friends of Nestorius appeared. When they did appear they held a rival Council and condemned

* *Mon. Xav.*, vol. i. p. 254 ff.

Cyril. The Emperor impartially deposed both. But Cyril, through his astute diplomacy, got his own sentence removed. Nestorius, condemned and deposed, died in exile. And by the end of the fifth century the persecution against him and his disciples had begun to bear fruit. Dishonoured in their own country, his followers went farther east, and Persia, to which Christ's teaching had already penetrated, received them. Settling there, they spread out eastward and westward with all the missionary zeal of believers whose faith has been bought and held at a high price. By the thirteenth century, before the great persecutions of Tamerlane, they had twenty-five bishops scattered throughout Eastern Europe and Asia. Most of them were then ignorant of their origin, and believed that they were descended from the converts of St. Thomas the Apostle, who was supposed to have penetrated far into Asia. To this day they are often referred to as the Thomists, or Christians of St. Thomas.

It is interesting to notice that Xavier says in the above letter: "They do not baptize, nor do they know what baptism is." It is possible that he may have been mistaken, but his other information about them is so accurate that it is more likely that they had by that time given up the rite of baptism in Socotra. That the sect originally used to baptize is certain, for in 1908 Professor Pelliot discovered a very beautiful Nestorian baptismal hymn at Sha-Chou in China.*

The word *caciz*, which Xavier uses, is a form of the Syrian word for priest, and he is quite right when he says he thinks the prayers are in Chaldean. The form of worship in Socotra must have been very similar, according to this description of Xavier's, to that of the other branches of the Nestorian Church, both then and now. "They call the people with wooden clappers," says Francis. On the Nestorian monument in China, erected in 781 A.D., the following words occur: "(His ministers) carry the Cross with them as a sign. They travel about wherever the sun shines, and try to reunite those that are beyond the pale—*i.e.*, those that are lost. *Striking the wood*, they proclaim the Glad Tidings of Love and Charity."

The little picture which Xavier gives us in the above letter of the Moorish woman and her Nestorian enemies is a

* A translation of this hymn is to be found in *The Nestorian Monument in China*, by Professor P. Y. Saeki, London, 1916, p. 66.

tragic comment on those last words. These Christians had been cruelly persecuted, almost exterminated, by the Moors, and the bitter hatred between persecutors and persecuted had long ago drowned the message of glad tidings, so that now the Striking of the Wood was become nothing more than a meaningless noise. The remembrance of what he had seen in that island made more than a mere sentimental impression on the traveller's mind. He never rested till he had sent them further light. In 1549 he writes to Loyola that they had four missionaries there.

The ships left Socotra at the end of January, and reached Goa on May 6th, 1542. Francis was thirty-six years old, battered and worn with continual hardship and frequent fever, but with ardour undiminished and eagerness unbounded. Between him and the horizon of his days there lay now but ten brief years, but their brevity was to be enriched by a stronger hand than that of time, and this last decade of his life was to burn with an imperishable flame.

CHAPTER XI

IN PORTUGUESE INDIA

(1542)

ALL that Xavier ever saw in perspective in this vivid and complicated maze of life was the vineyard of souls.

> Oft when the word is on me to deliver,
> Lifts the illusion and the truth lies bare :
> Desert or throng, the city or the river,
> Melts in a lucid Paradise of air,—
>
> Only like souls I see the folk thereunder,
> Bound who should conquer, slaves who should be kings,
> Hearing their one hope with an empty wonder,
> Sadly contented in a show of things.*

These lines are as true of Francis Xavier as they are of St. Paul. Take, for example, Xavier's first descriptions of Goa. They are summary, and quite uninforming. He was much too busy, the moment he set foot on the land of his evangelic dreams, baptizing and confessing and teaching, to play the descriptive traveller and historian. We have perhaps a little more leisure than he had—God forgive us—and can pause for a moment to look upon the strange pageant, the grotesque and tragic background of the Saint's earliest labours in India. Although by no means so imposing a city as it became a hundred years later, Goa was already, in the middle of the sixteenth century, beginning to make a fine show. So long as four months after his arrival Francis had not penetrated the sheep's clothing to the ravenous wolf within.

" It is a city wholly of Christians," he writes, " a sight for sore eyes. There is a monastery with a large number of Franciscan monks, and a cathedral, very fine, and with plenty of canons ; and numerous other churches. One has reason to give many thanks to God our Lord that the name

* F. W. H. Myers, *Saint Paul.*

of Christ flourishes so in such distant lands, among so many heathen." *

Descriptive historians of the period call Goa the Venice of the East, but the town can only have had the shallowest pretensions to that title. Exterior brilliance and even splendour were there surely enough, and, as in Venice, the colours and contours of East and West were combined and interspersed. New churches had been built, and the pagan temples had been seized by the Portuguese and their altars redecorated with the symbols of the Christian faith. There were a Governor's palace, gardens, villas ; wide streets, where the richest merchandise of India lay exposed for sale ; market-places, where Portuguese adventurers, drunk with their sudden wealth, bought for themselves silks and jewels and beautiful slave girls. The churches were well attended—for churchgoing was, then as now, a common form of social parade. The favourites of the rich colonists were carried there in litters, surrounded by slaves and admirers ; in one dim corner the priests performed their unobtrusive tasks, while in the centre of the church the riff-raff of Portugal in their silken hose and feathered hats ("*le Cap de Bonne Esperance les avait tous enoblis,*" says one writer) laughed and talked with their latest flames. When the bell rang, and the Host was elevated, there was a moment of pious silence, hands were raised, "Good Lord, have mercy on us!" they cried, and crossed themselves, as they resumed the broken thread of their chatter.

At the moment of Xavier's arrival the titanic famine to which we have already referred was sweeping over the Eastern world. The poorer quarters of Goa were a morass of destitution. But the hideousness of the contrasted social circumstances in so small a space was unnoticed except by a few. Still, men and women alike had an inkling of the desperate brevity of those hours of sensuous splendour. The new colonists demanded a fair exchange of goods. Had they not brought the Cross to India ? And if they gave India a new religion, had they not a right to take from India a new morality ? Climate and custom encouraged them ; there were no Western wives near enough to be jealous, and had not the great Albuquerque encouraged them to mate

* *Mon. Xav.,* vol. i. p. 252.

L

with the native women, and thus loyally provide garrisons for the fortresses and navies of their king? Francis found when he came that the Portuguese harem was a common institution, and he found a large and pitiful population of half-castes, many of them slaves, and all of them ignorant and uncared for. These half-castes fraternised with the lowest native class, the pariahs, who had nothing to lose by coming into contact with strangers. There were not many Brahmins in Goa at this time, and the artisan class was chiefly composed of Hindoos. The Arabs still retained a large part of the trade. This racial and religious confusion, whose only tended growth was the desire for gain, bore in itself from the first the seeds of decay.

The whole scene recalls one of those stagnant pools we sometimes see in summer-time, seething with grotesque and hideous forms, that reek and accumulate, and finally disappear as the water sinks to mud, and the mud cakes into clay.

There were those in the city who foresaw the inevitable doom and called out. In 1552 the judges of Goa sent this real *cri de cœur* to the King of Portugal:

There is no more any justice in India, neither from the viceroy [*i.e.*, Don Alphonse of Noronha] nor from those who are supposed to dispense it. They think of nothing but getting rich, and that by any means. Sire, we remind you of the death of the king of Coulam, and of the king of Pyllor [?], and of cruelties such that the credit of the Portuguese is lost. There is not a single Moor who has any faith in us. The king of Ceylon has been killed, and his treasure seized. The Moors speak of nothing else. Sire, we ask you for pity, pity, pity! Help, sire, help! we are perishing. . . . Destroy this letter. *

Still more striking than the above letter are the words with which Correa, who had come to India in 1512, and had been Albuquerque's secretary, concludes, in 1556, his *Lendas*:

The present evils are caused by cruelty and cupidity; the prosperity of the early days has turned to public calamity. . . . I hoped that my work would have a happy conclusion. It seemed to me that some of the ills which I saw growing up would disap-

* India Office, London, MSS., *Portuguese Records*, vol. ii., quoted by Brou, *Vie de S. François Xavier*, vol. i. p. 150. I have not been able to trace this passage in the numerous Port. Records at the India Office, but that is no doubt only due to the fact that the reference given by Brou is insufficient.

pear in the face of punishment. But . . . here murderers go back to the kingdom without the least fear that justice, either human or divine, will punish their crimes or their robbery of Christians, Moors, natives, and foreigners. How many offences against God and incredible crimes have I seen! The guilty ones would appear before the king, but there was no punishment. . . . The evil is that the governors live with nothing to fear; also captains of fortresses, judges, administrators . . . are reckless and go to great excesses. . . . I have seen those who are deep in guilt and clearly condemned arriving in Portugal and being honoured there because they came back with great wealth. . . . As for the robbers, they give the judges part of the stolen money and keep the rest and triumph and have the favours of the court just like honest men.

Rewards are due to those who conquered India at the beginning. . . . They have never received anything. They have grown old and gone to die in the hospital.

Francis Xavier was by no means the first genuine evangelist to set foot on this continent. Legend has it that it was the doubting Apostle who led the way thither. History does not countenance that tale. It is only known that Nestorian missions flourished as early as the seventh century, and that in the thirteenth century, before the overland routes were closed by the Turks, Franciscan and Dominican friars had penetrated India.

In 1500 eight Franciscans went out with d'Alvarez Cabal, and in 1503 a few Dominicans arrived. Some of these did noble work, but the religious situation was an impossible one. Only a saint—that is to say, only a genius—could make any impression on Portuguese India in the sixteenth century. It is usual to marvel at the meagreness of the results of Xavier's works. For those who know anything of the circumstances the amazing thing is, not how little he did, but how much. There is a phrase in one of his later letters that gives the key to his work: " I must go to open a way." When we discover that he opened many doors, and each at the peril of his life and at the price of untold privation and suffering, we begin to realise that those who say that he was restless and lacking in perseverance and patience have not understood him. There were more men willing to follow him, and to continue the work he inaugurated, than there were men capable of opening up new fields and seeking out the waiting tribes.

He only stayed in Goa for a few months, although the condition of that town, had he been called to work there, would have given his genius ample scope till the end of his days.

One man writes in 1547:

The population here is corrupt, and one would say that people have lost the use of reason. Those who are Christians are so solely because of their temporal aims, and very often bad aims at that. It cannot be otherwise in any place where slavery is the custom. Slaves of Mussulmen or idolaters become Christians in order to get emancipated, or to get protection against their tyrants; others turn Christian for the sake of a new hat, or a shirt, or some trifle, or to save themselves from hanging or to marry a Christian wife.*

But though Francis was soon to leave Goa, he poured out all his strength while he was there, in the tasks he loved. His first step was to report himself to the episcopal palace and present his official papers—the papers announcing his privileges and powers as Papal Nuncio, to the Bishop. " I will use none of these powers without your authority," he said, with a seductive humility which gained for him the affection of his bishop from that time forth.† Immediately afterwards he went to the Portuguese hospital which stood over the harbour, and which was chiefly used to shelter the stream of sick and dying travellers who disembarked from the European ships. There he found a lodging, and began to nurse the patients and minister to their needs. Teixeira tells us that when he was there he used to sleep on the floor at the foot of the beds of those who were dangerously ill, so that he might reach them quickly if they called.‡

The awful contrasts of wealth and poverty provoked him to go from villa to villa, begging for the lepers and the destitute and the prisoners, and Gonçalvez says he gained much help by this means, and that before the end of 1542 the city showed some change for the better, thanks to his zeal. We imagine that this begging from door to door for those

* *Selectæ Indiarum Epistolæ*, quoted by Brou, *Vie de S. François Xavier* vol. i. p. 133.
† See Tursellinus, Book II., cap. 2.
‡ " Such was his charity that it is told of him that commonly he had his bed at the foot of the bed of the sick man who was most needy and dangerously ill, so as to be able to help him at night . . . and this we were told by D. Lewis de Tayde, Ex-Viceroy of India, who was then Mayordomo of the hospital " (Teixeira, *Vita, Mon. Xav.*, vol. ii. p. 842).

in need was not quite the old simple mediæval proceeding, but had already in it something of more modern methods, that Xavier made a reasonable and intellectual appeal to the richest citizens for large sums of money, and laid it out with care and precision on various charities. There is much in that isolated poorly-clad figure, with its meek celestial gestures, of the spirit with which the primitive Italian painters have made us familiar, but there are also tones in his voice and hints in his manner, foreshadowing Arnold Toynbee or Mrs. Sidney Webb.

During his first few weeks in India Francis still wore the old gown which he had had when he left Europe. Then he decided to dress like the native priests, and he begged the major-domo of the hospital to supply him with one of those cheap sleeveless garments which were worn there by the lowest class of native priest. The steward gave him instead a handsome coat of silk, but Francis refused to wear it, and insisted in getting what he wanted.* His shoes soon wore through, and the kindly major-domo, "seeing them to be worn out and broken, and the upper leather and soles clownishly sewn together, brought him a new payre. But he, being everywhere like himself, would by no means be entreated to change his old shoes for new." † The black cotton tunic, too, wore quickly through, for it was not often still, but Francis paid no heed. At last some of his Portuguese friends stole it away by night, and replaced it by a new one. In the morning Francis put on the new one, and wore it all day without noticing the change. Then at night his friends asked him to supper. Dryden, in his translation of Bouhours' *Life*, quaintly tells what happened :

" 'Tis perhaps to do honour to our table," said one among them, " that you are so Spruce to-day in your new habit ! "
Then casting his eyes upon his clothes, he was much surprised to find himself in so strange an Equipage. At length being made sensible of the Prank which they had plaid him, he told them smiling *that it was no great wonder that this rich cassock, looking for a Master in the dark, could not see its way to somebody who deserved it better.‡*

It is now that for the first time we hear of his favourite

* Teixeira, *Vita, Mon. Xav.*, vol. ii. p. 843.
† Tursellinus, Book II., cap. 2.
‡ Bouhours, *Life*, translated by J. Dryden, p. 741.

plan of carrying with him a little bell, to gather his sheep together:

He went up and down the streets, a little bell in his hand, crying, " Faithful Christians, send your boys and girls and slaves to the *Santa doctrina*, for the love of God ! " At this summons, a crowd of people of all sorts would gather round, and he would put them in rows, and lead them to the Church of the Rosary. There all that he did delighted his hearers and the onlookers. As he raised his eyes to heaven, he seemed to raise their souls. Making the sign of the Cross, he spoke to them in a loud voice, with such devotion that the people, and, above all, the children, fell into complete sympathy with him. To these he taught hymns which contained the holy doctrine, and thus he fixed the teaching on their minds. Then, with outstretched arms, he intoned a kind of Litany, of which each verse held very briefly one point of the teaching of the Church, and that was followed by a chanted response, explaining an act of faith. Master Francis finished the service by an explanation of an article of the Creed, or one of the Commandments. In this explanation Master Francis suited his words to the intelligence of the least of his listeners, using a kind of Portuguese patois, the only language which these folk understood.*

On September 20th, 1542, the Saint wrote to Ignatius and the Fathers at Rome some account of the work in Goa:

" Here in Goa I have lodged in the hospital. I confessed and communicated the sick who were there. So many came to be confessed that if I had been in ten places I should have had to confess in them all. After I finished the sick I confessed in the morning the sound folk who came to seek me, and after noon I went to the jail to confess the prisoners. . . . I took a hermitage of Our Lady which was near the hospital, and there I began to teach the prayers, Creed and Commandments to the boys. Well over three hundred often came to the Christian teaching. The Lord Bishop ordered that the same should be done in the other churches, and so it goes on now, and in this way the service which is done to God is greater than many think. . . . On Sundays and feast days after dinner I preached in that hermitage of Our Lady on an article of the faith to the native Christians. So many came that they could not get into the hermitage. After

* Cros, *Vie de S. François Xavier*, vol. i. p. 216, quotes Gonçalvez.

preaching I taught the Paternoster, Ave Maria, Creed and Commandments. On Sundays I went out of the city to say mass to the sick of St. Lazarus evil (leprosy). . . .

" Now the Governor is sending me to a district where everyone says many Christians ought to be made. I am taking three natives with me, two are in deacons' orders. They know Portuguese very well. . . . I believe that much work has got to be done there for God. . . . The district where I am going is called the Cape of Comorin. Please God our Lord that with the favour and help of your devout prayers (God our Lord not looking at my infinite sin), He will give me His most holy grace so that there I may serve Him well."

There follows a page, happy and obscure, almost impossible to translate. Grammar is flung to the winds. He writes in haste, yet his hand lags far behind his thought. He is confident that his friends will understand. He turns back to the time he left Europe and reviews the inner pilgrimage of which the outward journeyings are only a shadow. Faith, indeed, sees the Guiding Hand, yet Loneliness cannot altogether keep silence.

" If the labours of so long a voyage, the care of so many spiritual illnesses, this life in a land so subject to sins of idolatry, and because of the great heat so hard to live in— if all this is undertaken for Whom it ought to be undertaken, it brings great refreshment, and many and great comforts. I believe that for those who delight in the Cross of Christ our Lord such labours are rest, and the ending of them, or the fleeing from them, death. What death is so great as after having known Christ to leave Him, and go on living in the pursuit of one's own opinions and likings! There is no toil like that! But what a rest to live dying every day by going against our own will, *seeking not our own but the things which are Christ's*. By the love and service of God our Lord, I pray you, dearest *brothers*, write at great length about all of the Company, for now I do not hope in this life to see you any more *face to face*, but, *at least, darkly, that is, by letter*. Do not deny me this grace, tho' I am unworthy of it. Remember that God our Lord made you worthy, so that I, through your great merit and refreshment, may hope and attain.

" Write me fully of the methods I ought to use with these heathen and Moors where I am now going, for by your means I hope that the Lord will teach me to understand how I have to do to convert them to His holy faith. . . . Thus by the merits of the Holy Mother Church, in whom I have my hope, whose living members ye are, I trust in Christ our Lord that He will hear me and grant me this grace to use this my useless instrument to plant His faith among the heathen. If His Majesty makes use of me, great confusion will come upon those that are mighty, and increase of strength upon those who are weak.   And seeing that I, being *dust and ashes*, and even more worthless, am fit to be an eye-witness of the need here of workers, I would be perpetual slave to all who may wish to come out here to *labour in the Lord's great vineyard.*

" So I finish, and pray God our Lord that by His mercy He may unite us in His holy glory, since for it we were created.   And may He in this life increase our strength, that in all and for all we may serve Him as He commands, and may fulfil His holy will.

" Your useless brother in Christ,

" Francisco de Xavier."*

On the same day Xavier wrote to Loyola some details about the proposed college at Goa.   It was to be twice the size of the chapel of the Sorbonne, and they had already enough money to keep 100 scholars.   The funds had been mainly supplied by the revenues of the Hindoo temples in the neighbourhood.   (These buildings had, by a royal edict, been forcibly taken over by the Portuguese Government and converted into Christian churches.)   In six years' time, Xavier hopes, there will be 300 scholars of all tongues and nations.   The Governor, the mercurial Da Sousa, is throwing himself into the business and proving of great help, and the Saint asks that he may have the prayers of the Company in Europe.   The line along which he suggested these prayers should run betrays perhaps a deeper insight into Sousa's character than we are apt to give him credit for.   " Pray," he says, " that God may give him grace to govern this great India well, and that he may *so use temporal advantages as not to lose eternal.*"†

* Mon. Xav., vol. i. p. 256.   † Ibid., vol. i. p. 262.

Already a beginning has been made with the teaching, and Diogo de Borba has a class of 60 native scholars. Xavier begs for men of good education and a good preacher to be sent out to train the young priests, and he also begs for a various assortment of indulgences for the Governor and his wife and others. It is singularly disconcerting to hear Francis beg for indulgences. What would he himself have done with such things? He must have felt somewhat like an over-indulgent godparent ordering toys and sweets for the children who " would some day grow out of those childish desires."

There are some pictures of the Saint at this time, during what might be called, for lack of a better name, his leisure hours, that we must not altogether pass by. " Where is this wonderful Xavier? " a Spanish newcomer demanded. He was pointed out, seated on the sea-front at a gaming table, playing cards with a notorious libertine. " *That* a saint? Why, that's just a priest like the rest ! " But a little later Xavier left his companions, and he was followed by the grandee's servant, to see where he would go next. This servant tracked him to a quiet palm grove, and there he was on his knees, his uplifted face lit with a burning ecstasy of adoration, lost in joyful communion with God. And from other tales of the same kind we know that the notorious libertine would leave the gaming-table with some words singing in his ears that were not very easy to forget.

He made many friends among the colonists and was a popular guest in their houses. But there always came a day when the head of the house, thanks to Francis, grew discontented with the social irregularity of his *ménage*, and finally, we are told, the Saint himself would administer the sacrament of marriage to his chastened host and the most worthy female member of his household. So consistently did Francis pursue this course in the many houses which he visited that the moral tone of the city is said to have altered visibly during those summer and autumn months of 1542: this was, of course, not solely due to his own efforts ; his energy and enthusiasm shamed the listless local clergy into some sort of imitation of his ardour, and a genuine revival of morals appears to have taken place. Five years later Juan de Beira writes :

Francis Xavier's methods are followed here. It is a matter

of thankfulness to God to see the children twice a day gather together to hear and repeat the Christian doctrine. And every Saturday the women, and every Sunday the men, spend half an hour in the church in pious exercises.*

But Xavier's duties as Apostolic Nuncio in the largest diocese in the world called him farther afield. He did not even wait for the two companions of the earlier part of his voyage, Camerino and Mansillas, to arrive from Mozambique. In the end of September 1542 he set out for Cape Comorin.

* *Sel. Indic. Epist.,* p. 29, quoted by Brou, *Vie de S. François Xavier,* vol. i. p. 171.

CHAPTER XII

CAPE COMORIN

(September, 1542—December, 1544)

FOR each journey Xavier seems to have allowed himself one
luxury: the last had been a travelling rug; this time, in
addition to some sheets of paper, a few books, and a bit of
leather to mend his shoes with, he is reported to have carried
a parasol. He sailed down the whole length of Malabar, and,
landing somewhere near Cape Comorin, proceeded on foot up
the Piscarian coast. His only companions were three native
Christians from Goa. The Fishery coast to the north of
Comorin is a burning and inhospitable desert. But it was no
random whim which had drawn Francis Xavier thither. He
had heard in Goa how eight years ago they had been " converted," and then forsaken, and pity had brought him to
their succour.

The story of the earlier mission is a curious one. This mild
and harmless race of pearl-fishers had been suffering much at
the hands of extortionate Arab traders, and had at last been
goaded into serious warfare with them. The immediate cause
of the war was the cutting of a Parava's ear by a Moor, a
deadly affront. While this struggle was at its height, a
Malabar prince or nobleman, Juan de la Cruz, who had come
into touch with the Portuguese, and had become a " Christian," volunteered to show the Paravas a way out of all
their troubles. " You must change into Christians," he
said, " and then the Portuguese will come to your help,
and you will see no more of these Mussulmans." So a
deputation was sent up to Cochin, and all turned out as
Juan de la Cruz had prophesied. The deputation was
baptized, and a Portuguese fleet and some Franciscan monks
went off immediately to the rescue. At the first boom of
the cannon the Arabs fled, and the Franciscans came on
shore and celebrated the occasion by baptizing twenty
thousand natives on the spot.

In this way [concludes Teixeira] from a cut ear our Lord drew
the salvation of many souls; for it is His custom and of His
infinite goodness from our small ills to draw for Himself great

goods, and this was the origin and cause of the Christianity and conversion of the Fishery coast and Cape Comorin.*

But the climate and the food were not to the liking of the Franciscans, and very soon they left the neophytes—if they even might merit that title—to their fate and to the coming of Francis Xavier a few years later.   The Government officials were more attentive.   They sent ships at regular intervals to ward off any Arabs who might be threatening to return, and for this protection they took handsome payment in pearls. The episcopal conscience at Goa, however, was not quite at rest about this distant corner of the diocese, and there were several young Paravas, at the time Xavier went to the Fishery coast, in training in Goa and in Lisbon, who were to be sent back later on to tell their fellow countrymen why they had been baptized.   Meanwhile the hamlets and villages along the coast were startled by the visitations of a white man, dressed like their own native priests, and carrying in one hand a little bundle, and in the other a parasol ; young, fearless, gay, singing, as he walked with his three companions, strange songs in a strange tongue.   Soon he was gathering round him all the babies and little children he could find, and sprinkling their faces with water and chanting over them some mysterious incantation, as he made the sign of a cross on their foreheads.   This was what the white men had done eight years ago, and since then the Arabs had never come near, so the people brought their children to Xavier gladly.

No missionaries have spent so much time and pains over the mystic—nay, to them often magical—rite of baptism, as the early Jesuits.   In this they showed their real belief in the teaching of their Church, for according to that teaching a priest who baptized an infant saved it, in the event of its death before it reached maturity, from Limbo.   More than that, he actually, by the rite, switched it on to powerful currents of grace.   Francis Xavier baptized to an immense and unprecedented extent, but he was far more careful to follow up this work, and to keep his converts in touch with the origins of their faith, than has often been supposed.

As far as infant baptism was concerned, his untiring and indiscriminating zeal was of course perfectly orthodox, but the expedition with which he baptized older persons was—and

* *Mon. Xav.,* vol. ii. p. 848.

this is admitted by the Jesuits themselves *—not in keeping with the teaching of the primitive Church. In their disregard for this procedure Francis Xavier and the earlier Jesuit missionaries to India stand almost alone. Their methods are more akin to those first adopted in the reign of Constantine, when heathen converts began to pour swiftly into the fold. It was then that the training which had in earlier days preceded baptism began to be given after the rite. This training was known as discipline, and was regarded in itself almost as a sacrament.†

But there was a certain degree of reasonableness, as well as much of danger, in their method. An adult savage of a low type would probably learn as much doctrine in a fortnight as he would in two years. Was it right, these missionaries said, to hold back from him for so long a time as two years, or even two months, after he had been moved and attracted by the new teaching, the sacramental grace which baptism bestowed? No human teaching, they believed, could advance him so much as could the mysterious ray from heaven which lighted upon everyone who partook of this sacrament.

There were other reasons for hastening on the ceremony. By baptism the native of India became a subject of Portugal. A sudden break was made in his life, which it was very difficult to go back upon. His name was changed, his manner of dress, sometimes, perforce, his occupation. Outwardly, at least, he had become a new creature. Hence the inward change may have been made more easy, the old temptations crippled of some of their power, and, above all, the old fears exposed and defeated. For the brief phrase " perfect love casteth out fear " is a beautiful summary of the effect of Christian teaching upon the heathen mind. In India, and especially among the lower castes, the people have always been under the spell of spiritual terror. The Eastern mind is more sensitive to the Prince of the power of the air and his legions than the Western, and often, while we are ignoring those powers, the Oriental is constructing a fantastic and gruesome system of defences against them. Xavier found those primitive Paravas living in a state of perpetual terror, haunted and harassed by demons, night and day. He gave

* See Brou, *Vie de S. François Xavier*, vol. i. p. 135.
† See A. G. V. Allen, *Christian Institutions*, p. 409.

them a perfunctory enough version of the Gospel of Jesus
Christ, and a version with many defects. Most fatal of all
errors, he did not put into their keeping the Gospel writings
themselves. But one thing he undoubtedly did, he brought
an immense peace and joy to the generation who knew
him personally, he came to them like a friendly voice and a
friendly hand to children lost in a dark night.

Francis Xavier, of course, knew nothing of Comparative
Religion, nor had he studied the psychology of the Oriental.
And for some time, at least, he did not know a word of Tamil.
But his transcendent faith and imaginative sympathy
opened up channels of communication between him and his
fellow creatures that are closed to lesser men. Not that
he had earned his saintship lightly, or kept the fire of his
genius burning without effort. The moral and spiritual
discipline which he had unceasingly imposed upon himself
since first he had come under the influence of Loyola in Paris
was the rightful and exacting homage which genius must
ever pay for its true heritage of saintship.

His letters refer to his linguistic troubles. Xavier appears
to have had a great talent for languages, and to have been a
patient and hard-working student. Many of the old biographers assert that he had a miraculous power which allowed
him to speak in the language of whoever he happened to be
addressing. There is absolutely no historical justification
for this assertion. But before he arrived in India he was
already proficient in at least six or seven languages, and it is
well known that every new tongue acquired makes the next
one easier to learn. From Xavier's letters one gradually
gathers that, like the Portuguese colonists, he used interpreters freely, but that, unlike the colonists, he picked up
a great deal of the native languages as he went along. It is
not at all a miraculous thing for a talented linguist to be
able to converse fairly fluently in a new tongue after living
in the country for a few weeks, and it is easy to believe that
Francis, aided by his Latin versatility and subtlety of
gesture, and by his intense sympathy and splendid imagination and well-trained mind, was able to pursue a course which
accounts for pages both of Roman Catholic credulity and of
Protestant criticism.

On the 28th of October the Saint wrote to Loyola from
Tuticorin :

" On our way here we came through some villages where the people had become Christians eight years ago. There are no Portuguese living there now, as the country is extremely sterile and very poor. As they have no one to teach them our faith, the Christians of these villages know no more of it than to say that they are Christians. They have no one to say Mass, still less to teach them the Creed, *Pater noster, Ave Maria,* or the Commandments. When I arrived in these places I baptized all the children who were not baptized, so that I baptized a great multitude of infants *who could not distinguish between their right hand and their left.* When I came to these places the children would not let me read my office nor eat nor sleep, but made me teach them some prayers. I began to understand then that *of such is the kingdom of heaven.* As I could not refuse such a holy petition, I taught them, beginning with the confession of the Father, Son and Holy Spirit, with the Creed, *Pater noster, Ave Maria.* I recognised great gifts in them, and if there were anyone to teach them the holy faith, I am very sure that they would be good Christians."*

The sentences about the children are delightful : they would neither let him eat nor read his office nor sleep, and so—was there ever a more charming climax penned ?—he began to understand that of such is the kingdom of heaven !

Between this letter of October 1542 and the next existing letter there is an interval of fourteen months, and probably Xavier never accomplished so much as in that time, though it is impossible to follow all the journeys he made from village to village. But when we think of the circumstances under which he worked, and when we remember how largely, humanly speaking, he was his own master, and how easily he might at any moment have made a good excuse for returning to easier fields of labour, we know this at least, that these were months of unlimited heroism. He travelled continually backwards and forwards over a large district, across burning sands, on foot, in tropic sunshine or in tropic rain. He had no provisions against the countless pestiferous creatures that haunted earth and air in those regions. The drinking water was drawn from the same wells in which the natives washed themselves and all their possessions. The food was

* *Mon. Xav.,* vol. i. p. 273.

scarce and monotonous—a little rice, a little fish, or, for a change, a bowl of soup made with rice and peppercorns, and on Sundays a croquette made of rice.   As we know, he was an abstainer on principle, and in those parts he quenched his thirst with sour milk. He took but one meal in the day. During this meal, we read, he was always surrounded by a crowd of the little children whom he loved so well.   Of the details of his missionary work his own letters give the best account. But of his personal habits or circumstances these letters say little.   From other letters, and from native testimony, it would appear that he usually slept no longer than two or three hours each night, and that all the time that was not spent in travelling, or in preaching and teaching and baptising and in works of mercy, was spent in prayer. We may say that it is impossible that he slept so little as these historians say.   But perhaps there is a state—whether in the body or out of the body God knoweth—when the servant of God is caught up into Paradise and given to feast of the heavenly manna to the rest and refreshment of the body as well as to the nourishment of the soul.   Perhaps in these hours of still rapture the unsleeping body may yet mysteriously reap the fruits of sleep.   God knoweth.

We cannot tell how long he prayed by night, but by day he worked both hard and long.   At one of the Enquiries before his canonisation a witness who had known him said that at Cape Comorin Francis worked hard : he drank no wine, nor ate bread ; but when he went to the homes of Portuguese he ate and drank what they gave him.   His common food was this : badly cooked rice and fish badly seasoned, and sometimes some milk with rice, and a rice dumpling.   And however tired the Father came home he always had a lesson with the boys.

Another witness on the same occasion says : " All his life he was very humble and plain, without any show.   And if he went to a house and they gave him food he ate ; and if they jested with him he jested . . . and when he left he always gave some spiritual comfort."†

Those simple Paravas had many amazing tales about this great teacher who had sojourned with them, who had been so like a brother, and yet so like a god.   Their attempts to pass on their impressions of a life which was, in truth, a sustained

* *Mon. Xav.*, vol. ii. p. 372.

miracle, are interesting. A half-blind man describes other men as "trees walking," a half-awakened soul describes a saint at his prayers as "one raised from the ground." A man who is physically dumb conveys his meaning by grotesque gestures, a man who is spiritually dumb by strange figures of speech.

The primitive way of picturing a man in whom God dwells is to paint him in the act of performing in the material world what God does in the spiritual world, to paint him healing the sick and raising the dead. These Paravas described Francis in those terms, and in doing so they were only struggling to express the truth which they so dimly apprehended. The method was not confined to the natives. Wherever Xavier went there were simple souls who used this language in speaking or writing of him.

After he had worked for over a year in the pearl-fisheries, and had established some sort of system of native supervision, Francis left his new converts for a few months and visited Goa and Cochin. He took with him to Goa a number of young Paravas, to be trained in the new college there. He found this college in a flourishing state. Besides a number of other priests and teachers, the two companions of the earlier part of Xavier's voyage out, Francisco Mansillas and Paulo Camerino, were working there. They had arrived in Goa a few days after Xavier had gone south. Camerino was fairly efficient, perhaps; Mansillas appears to have been a lovable but feckless youth. He was no use in the college, and Xavier arranged that he should go back with him to Cape Comorin.

The visit to Goa was a brief one, full of consultations, inspections, reports, and plans for the future. There was a letter waiting from Loyola, written two years before, and announcing that he had been elected General of the Society on April 9th, 1541.

Already in January 1544, a few weeks after leaving the Paravas, we find the Saint on his return voyage, making a halt at Cochin. From here the Portuguese ships were about to sail for Europe, and Francis paused to write several letters for the mail.

He wrote to the King of Portugal: the letter is lost, but it is known to have contained a special appeal for the people on the island of Socotra, that they might have the protection of the royal fleet against the Moors. He wrote to the Queen,

M

and this letter is lost too.   Tursellinus tells us that the Saint
had remembered how that lady received annually the sum of
four hundred crowns to buy slippers with, and bethought him
that some of it might well go to the children of the Fishery
coast.   And while they were saying in Geneva that the boys
there could give a reason for their faith as well as any doctor
in the Sorbonne—thanks to Calvin and his children's
catechism—Francis Xavier was writing to the Queen of
Portugal

so pleasantly and piously, that she could have no better shoes or
pantoffles to climb to heaven than the children of the Piscarian
coast, and their instructors.   Wherefore, he humbly entreated
her to bestow her shoes and pantoffles, as a tribute, unto their
teachers and instructors, thereby to make herself a ladder to
heaven, for she might be glad of such an occasion.*

We know that the Queen agreed to this suggestion, possibly
at the same time making others on her own behalf to the
royal treasury.   For many years the sum was sent out
annually, and after Xavier's death we find Portuguese
officers trying to defraud the native churches of this chief
source of their revenue.

Besides these two lost letters to the King and Queen of
Portugal, there is a very long letter written to the Fathers in
Rome giving a full account of the work in Cape Comorin.

Viewed in the light of modern missionary methods,
this letter is deeply interesting.   We are accustomed to
accept, without questioning, some very severe criticisms of
Xavier's work : this letter is, in some details, antipathetic
to a Protestant reader, but it proves too that the teaching of
the great Jesuit missionary was not so misguided as our
ignorance may have led us to suppose.

A study of the Report of the World Missionary Conference
in Edinburgh shows us what an important place the Apostles'
Creed has occupied, and must occupy, in the work of evan-
gelisation.   Professor MacEwen† says :

In the Conference Reports you will discover an item simple
but grand, repeated by many missionaries—Episcopalian, Baptist,
Wesleyan, Presbyterian—that the statement of faith which they

---

* Tursellinus, Book II. cap. 8.
† *Report of the World Missionary Conference*, vol. ix. p. 205.

find to have most value, and on which they lay most stress, is that same Apostles' Creed. In the seventeen centuries that have passed since it was shaped, the Holy Spirit has taught the Church much. He will teach us more if we listen to His voice, but the foundations of the kingdom stand, although the things that were shaken have been removed. The central beliefs which our missionaries teach were the central beliefs of the men through whose mission Christianity first expanded.

Again we read :

The choice and arrangement of catechetical subjects may, on the whole, follow the example of the ancient Church—Bible History, Old and New Testament lessons on the life of Christ, the Creed, the Lord's Prayer, and the Sacraments.*

The great Apostolic teachers, from whose midst this Creed emerged, were specially fitted, both by outward circumstance and by inward inspiration, to present Christianity in a form which, by its simplicity and its universality, would appeal to East and to West alike.

Outwardly, by their geographical position, they were in touch with the three essential sources of modern civilisation, Judea, Greece, Rome, and they were among these peoples at the very time when they were undergoing a process of fusion.

Inwardly, the makers of the Apostles' Creed had the greatest and, indeed, the only reason for authority. They were convinced that they had *in themselves* no wisdom, that they were entirely taught of God. " God hath spoken unto us." " This is my beloved Son, hear ye Him," " I that speak unto thee am He," " Lo, I am with you alway," " If any man speak, speak as it were oracles of God." These men did not master a faith, a faith mastered them—it was the faith, Paul said, in an amazing phrase, " *to which ye have been delivered.*"

And while Calvin was proving to the Romanists in Europe that, tested by this Creed, they were not such true children of the Church as the Protestants were, Francis Xavier, the greatest missionary of the Roman Church, was teaching this Creed in all simplicity, far away from the noise and clamour of the religious wars. It is but another illustration of the truth which is being emphasised to-day as never before, that

* *Report of the World Missionary Conference*, vol. ii. p. 60.

M2

it is above all in missionary work that the Church must discover the secret of unity.

"... I sought some people who knew both Malabar and our language. Then after many meetings and great travail we drew up a form of worship. First, the Sign of the Cross, acknowledgment of the Three Persons in the Godhead. Then the Creed and the Commandments, Our Father, Ave Maria, Salve Regina and the General Confession from Latin into Malabar. After having translated them into their language and learned them by heart, I went all through the place with a bell in my hand, gathering all the boys and men that I could, and after having gathered them I taught them twice each day; and in the space of a month taught these prayers, arranging so that the boys should teach their fathers and mothers and all the household and neighbours what they had learned in the school.

"On Sundays I gather together all the folk, men and women, old and young, to say the prayers in their language; they seem very happy, and come with great joy. We begin with the Confession of One God, Three in One, with loud voices repeating the Creed in Malabar, I saying it first, and then they all repeating it. When the Creed is said, I by myself go over it again article by article, treating each of the twelve separately. I make them see that to be a Christian is nothing if it is not to believe firmly and without hesitation the Twelve Articles: then, when they confess themselves Christians, I ask them concerning each of the Articles if they firmly believe it. . . . I make them repeat the Creed oftener than the other formulas, because only if he believes the Twelve Articles can a man call himself a Christian.

"I teach them the Commandments . . . the Creed, and the Our Fathers, and the Ave Marias said, we recite the Commandments in the following way :—to begin with, I say the first Commandment, and all repeat it with me, that done we say together, 'Jesus Christ, Son of God, grant us grace to love Thee above all else.' When we have asked this grace, we all recite Our Father. This done, we say 'Holy Mary, Mother of Jesus Christ, obtain for us grace rom Thy Son that we may be able to keep the first Commandment.' . . . In this way we go through the remainder of the Commandments. These are the favours which I teach them to ask in prayer, saying to them that if they obtain these graces from God, in addition He will grant to them all for which they themselves do not know how to ask. . . . Those who are about to be baptized say the General Confession, then the Creed. At each Article I ask them if they believe it firmly, and when they answer yes, and when I have explained to them the law of Christ which must be kept unto salvation, I baptize them. . . .

" I hope in God our Lord that the children will be better than their fathers, for they show much love and desire toward our Law, and toward learning the prayers and teaching them. . . .

" . . . Crowds come to me, asking me to go to their houses to say prayers for their invalids, and the sick have come to me themselves in such numbers, that to read a portion of the Gospel to them, apart from anything else, had fully occupied me, and to teach the children, baptize, translate the prayers, answer questions, bury the dead, respond to the devotion of those who send for me, and those who come to me for help—it is an endless occupation. . . . I could not reject any of these sacred calls upon me, without endangering their faith, yet it became impossible for me to satisfy everyone, little jealousies arose, everyone wanted me first, so I made use of this expedient :—I ordered the children who know the prayers to go to the houses of the sick, to bring together the whole household and the neighbours, to repeat with them the Creed, and tell the sick to believe and they shall be made sound, and then say the other prayers. In this way we get them all visited, and the Creed, the Commandments, and the Prayers, are taught in the houses and in the streets ; and besides, toward the sick, through the faith of their households, their neighbours and themselves, God our Lord has had great pity, giving to them both spiritual and corporal healing. God used much mercy towards those who were ill, in leading and constraining them through their infirmities into the Faith.

" . . . Many are the potential Christians in those parts, they lack only those ready to occupy themselves with devout and holy things. Often I have had a mind to go to your Universities and shout aloud, like a man who has lost his senses—above all to the university of Paris, and tell in Sorbonne those who have more learning than will to make use

of it ; how many souls, through their negligence, fail to go
to glory and are going to hell.   If, while they studied letters,
they would study too the account which God our Lord
will ask of them, and of the talent which He has given them,
many would say :—' *Lord, here I am : what wilt Thou have
me to do ?   Send me where Thou wilt, if even to India.*' . . . I
fear that many University students only want, with the aid
of letters, to gain dignities, benefices, bishoprics, and that
they only conform to rules because it is necessary, to get
those posts.   It is common to hear a student say, ' I only
wish to study in order to get a benefice ; that attained, I
will serve God.'   So their calling in life is determined by
their disordered inclination : they fear God's will may not
be their will, and refuse to leave their calling to Him. . . .
So great is the number of those who have turned to the
Christian faith that often it happens to me to have my arms
tired with baptizing, nor have I any voice left, so often I
have repeated in their language the Creed, the Commandments and Prayers, and have taught—also in their language—
what it is to be a Christian, the meaning of heaven and hell
. . . chiefly I repeat the Creed and the Commandments. . . ."

" . . . Among the heathen here are certain men called
Bragmens.   It is they who maintain all the heathenism.
They have charge of the idol-houses.   They are the most
perverse people in the world.   They make one understand
the Psalm, ' *Deliver me from an ungodly nation and the
deceitful and unjust man.*"*   They never tell the truth ;
they are always thinking how to lie subtilly and deceive the
simple and ignorant poor, saying the idols order them to
bring an offering of various things—the Bragmens are simply
pretending—and these are the things they need for the
upkeep of wives, children and houses.   They make the
simple people believe that the idols eat, and many of these
before they dine or sup make an offering of so much money
for the idol.   They eat twice daily, with a great palaver of
kettledrums, and make the poor creatures think that the
idols are eating.   Rather than want, the Bragmens tell the
people that the idols are very annoyed with them for not
sending what was demanded.   And they warn the people

---

* The Psalm Xavier here quotes (Ps. 43) is the first Psalm of the Ordinary
in the Mass.

that if they don't provide these things the idols will kill them, or cause diseases, or send devils to their houses, and the wretched, credulous people believe it will be so, and out of fear that the idols will harm them, do what the Bragmens wish.

" These Bragmens are men of little learning, and what they lack in virtue they make up in iniquity and evil. The Bragmens of this coast where I am travelling are greatly annoyed because I keep on exposing their wickedness. They confess the truth to me when we are alone, and how they deceive the people. In secret they confess to me that they have no other means of living but those stone idols, on which they live by manufacturing lies. They admit that I know more than all of them put together. They ask me to visit them, and are annoyed that I will not accept the presents they send me. They do all this so that I may not disclose their secrets.

" They say they know very well there is but one God, and that they will pray God for me. In pay of all this I tell them what I on my part think of them, and then I show their miserable deceits and mockeries to the wretched, credulous creatures who from sheer fear are their devotees, till I am weary. As a result of what I say many lose their devotion to the devil and become Christians. If there were no Bragmens all the heathen would become converted to our faith. The houses where the Bragmens and idols are are called pagodas. None of the heathen of these parts have much learning, but they are learned enough in evil. Since I came here only one Bragmen has become a Christian. This young man is a very fine fellow. He has taken up the work of teaching the boys Christian doctrine.

" As I go visiting the Christian villages I pass numerous pagodas. I once passed one where there were more than 200 Bragmens. They came to see me, and among other things we discussed I asked one question, What did their gods and idols whom they adored command them to do in order to go to glory. There was a great to-do among them as to who was to reply. One of the oldest of them was chosen. The old man, who was over eighty, told me to say first what the God of the Christians commanded to be done. I understood his meanness, and would say nothing till he had spoken. So he was forced to exhibit his ignorance. He replied that the gods commanded them to do two things in order to go to where they (the gods) are : the first was not to kill cows, whom they adore; the second was to do alms, giving these to the Bragmens who serve in the pagodas. When I heard this reply it grieved me that the devils could so lord it over our neighbours as to make themselves, instead of God, adored by them. So I rose, and telling the Bragmens to be seated, I said the creed and commandments in a very loud voice in their language, and explained the nature of heaven and hell, and told them who go to the one, and who to the other. When this discourse was ended all the Bragmens rose and embraced me and told me that truly the God of the Christians was the true God, since His commandments were so conformable to natural reason. They asked me if our souls died along with our bodies, like those of the brutes. God our Lord gave me arguments so suitable to their capacities that I clearly explained to them the immortality of the soul, and they seemed to be thoroughly pleased and satisfied. The arguments which you must give to this simple people [*este gente idiota*] must not be so subtle as those written by very scholastic doctors. They asked me whence the soul issued when a man died, and when a man was sleeping and dreamed that he was in a land with his friends and acquaintances (which often happens to me, that I am with you, dearest), if his soul, going there, ceases to inhabit his body. Moreover, they asked me to tell them if God were black or white, according to the diversity of colour seen among men. As all the people here are black and approve of the colour, they say that God is black. Most of the idols are black. They anoint them often with oil and they stink frightfully. They are so ugly that the sight of them frightens you. In the Bragmens' opinion I gave satisfactory answers to all the questions they put. When I wound up by saying that since they knew the truth they should become Christians they answered—like so many among ourselves—what would the world say of us if we made this change in our way of living ? They were also kept back by the thought that they would lack the necessities of life.

"I came across a solitary Bragmen in a village on this coast who had some education, and I was told he had studied in some famous places of learning. I tried to see him, and took advantage of an opportunity of meeting him. He told

me as a great secret that the first thing those who teach in
those places of learning do is to take an oath from the
pupils never to tell certain secrets which they are taught.
Because of some friendship he had for me this Bragmen told
me those secrets as a grand secret.   One was this : never to
tell that there is but one God, creator of heaven and earth,
and that this God should be adored, and not idols, who are
devils.   They have some scriptures, in which they have the
commandments.   The language taught in these places of
learning is like what Latin is among us.   He told me the
commandments very well, each one with a good exposition.
Those who are learned keep the Lord's days—an incredible
thing.   The only prayer they say on the Lord's day is this,
and they say it very often, *Oncerii naraina noma*, which means
I adore Thee, O God, with Thy grace and help for ever.   They
say this prayer very slowly and quietly, so as not to break
their oath. . . .

" This Bragmen . . . wanted me to tell him the principal
tenets of the Christian religion and promised me to make them
known to no one.   I said to him that I should not tell him
if he did not first promise to me not to keep those principal
tenets hidden.   So he promised me to publish them.   Then
I said and expounded, much to my delight, these important
words of our religion, *who believes and is baptized shall be
saved.*   He wrote them in his language with their exposition,
and I told him all the creed.   He told me that one night he
had dreamed with great delight that he had to become a
Christian and be my companion and go with me.   He asked
me to make him a Christian secretly, and moreover with
certain conditions.   As these were not honourable and
permissible, I refused to do it.   I hope in God that he will
have to be a Christian without any of them.   I bade him teach
the simple folk to adore one God. . . . He was not willing to
do it because of his oath, and for fear lest the devil should
kill him.

" I don't know what more to write to you of these parts,
except that such are the consolations which God our Lord
communicates to those who go among the heathen and convert
them to the faith of Christ, that if there be contentment in this
life, it means this.

" I often happen to hear a person who goes among those
Christians say : O Lord, give me not such consolations, and

now that of Thine infinite goodness and mercy Thou dost give them, take me to Thy holy glory, because after Thou dost give such a rich inward communion, it is a pain for Thy creatures to go on living without seeing Thee.*

" O if those who studied learning would only devote as much labour towards the enjoyment of it as they spent toilsome days and nights in acquiring it ! (He means that the true joy of learning is to use it to teach others.) A student seeks contentment in understanding what he studies : O if he sought that contentment in telling his neighbours what they need in order to know and serve God, how much more consoled they would be, and how much more prepared to give an account when Christ said to them, *Render now an account of thy stewardship.*

" . . . So I finish, praying God our Lord that since in His mercy He united us, and in His service separated us so far from one another, He may again unite us in His holy glory.

" And to attain this let us take as intercessors and advocates all those holy souls of these parts where I am, taken by God to His holy glory after they were baptised by my hands and before they lost the state of innocence, the number of which I believe to be more than one thousand."†

This sounds as if Xavier were glad that these children had died and become advocates for the Company, instead of being sorry that human stupidity and carelessness had deprived them of life. The words are indeed the feverish utterance of a fine imagination, hurt and bruised with the sight of over much sorrow. The mystical mind of Francis was normally accustomed to dwell on the borderland regions between the psychical and the physical worlds, and to think comparatively little of physical death ; and in moments of abnormal feeling that death was entirely disregarded.

In February 1544, after an absence of only about two months, we find Francis once more on the Fishery coast. Besides Francisco Mansillas he had with him a few obscure helpers, native and European, of whom the most useful appears to have been Francisco Coelho. But "the early dew

* This passage is probably the origin of the Latin phrase on the portrait in our frontispiece, "*Satis est Domine, satis est.*" The phrase in its Latin form is one of the most often quoted of his sayings.

† *Mon. Xav.*, vol. i. p. 278 ff.

of morning has passed away at noon." Difficulties of all kinds besieged the missionary during this spring of 1544. "It is the morrow of conversions," a French writer has well said, "which is the hardest time both for converts and teachers." And this mission was hopelessly understaffed. The letters of Xavier to Francisco Mansillas, which begin in February and cover a period of several months, show us that, though this missionary should have been the Saint's right hand, he was but a broken reed to lean upon. But, worst of all, Portuguese soldiers and traders, of whom up till now we have heard nothing in this part of the country, began to mingle with the natives on their own errands, which were not those of Francis Xavier.

The situation must have been an intolerable one for the missionary. Hardly had he impressed upon these childish tribes the simplest rudiments of Christian teaching, when his own brothers, professing his own faith, came into the same villages where he was working and perpetrated the vilest acts of cruelty and dishonesty. The natives were incensed, and no wonder, and after a particularly scandalous slave-raid at Punicale, a wild tribe of horsemen from the north, the *Badages*,* fearing probably that the raiding would spread into their own territory, swept down upon the innocent Paravas, and hundreds of them were killed or put to flight because they had accepted the religion of those " Christians." There is a story, probably authentic,† of how a troop of these wild horsemen one day rushed upon a Parava village in which the Saint happened to be working. The villagers fled in terror, but Francis, after kneeling a few moments in prayer, rose, and himself alone confronted them with such an air of gravity and authority that in confusion they turned their horses' heads, and went back the way they came.

In July he went alone on foot to the Cape, throughout this wildly disturbed country, at the imminent risk of his life, in order to organise relief for the hundreds of poor fisher-folk who, in want and sickness, were sheltering in the caves and holes of the earth. In the letters of Xavier to Mansillas, which are given in the next chapter, many of the troubles of this tragic spring and summer are reflected.

* Also known as the *Vadakars*, or *Baddaghars*.
† See Tursellinus, Book II., cap. 11 ; also *Mon. Xav.*, vol. ii. p. 598 ; also Acosta, Lucena, etc.

In the middle of November the Saint set out for Travancore, at the urgent invitation of the Rajah there. He made this long journey, as usual, on foot, attended this time by two or three faithful natives. These, we read, kept guard over him every night while he slept, for the country was still disturbed and full of enemies. They were several times attacked, and once, it is said, he was wounded by an arrow. Another time they set fire to his bed, says one of the fanciful biographers, but he was praying, and noticed nothing until he was surrounded by a little heap of cinders instead of a mattress!

The visit to Travancore was, in the eyes of the Rajah at least, probably largely political. Portugal was a dangerous enemy, but a most helpful ally. In coming here Francis was responding to a series of pressing invitations. The Rajah knew that the Saint was out for souls, and the acute old diplomatist dangled his unconverted subjects before the missionary's eyes, much as a European king might dangle his pretty daughter before some desirable prince. And Francis was only too pleased to pay the price of " favourable recommendations to the Governor," and no doubt thought he had the best of the bargain. For he was publicly proclaimed the Great Priest, and all faithful subjects were told to show him the same obedience which they showed to the Rajah, the Great King.

The Rajah himself, and the Brahmins and Nairs who constituted the upper castes, must have looked on the whole movement with indifference, if not with scorn. Xavier's message was nothing to them. It neither touched them nor moved them. But a change of religion could do the poor outcast Macuas no harm, or even if it did them a little harm the protection of the Portuguese cannon was cheap at the price.

So, for one month, Francis ploughed and sowed, with unprecedented and titanic energy. It was the rainy season, and he went barefoot from village to village, his tunic in tatters and his old black hood a lamentable thing to see. Before the month was ended he had baptized ten thousand persons, and to each one he baptized he gave a new name, written on a piece of paper. This piece of paper came to have a political as well as a spiritual significance. It was a kind of passport, and gave the bearer the rights of protection due to a Portuguese subject. One can believe that the

Rajah scanned these little tickets with a smile of satisfaction, and told himself that the Great Priest was playing a fair game. And the Great Priest smiled, too, as he looked upon the little tickets and remembered the words of Jesus : " Be ye wise as serpents and harmless as doves." Enthusiastic crowds destroyed the idols and the temples. Churches were hastily built, and rude crosses placed there. The Macuas spoke the same language as the Paravas, so Xavier had no difficulty in teaching them the catechism and the creed.

One can hardly explain this tremendous conversion. But the contrast between the outward authority of the representative of Portugal and of Western civilisation, and the personal appearance and bearing of the Saint, must have been a strangely moving one and may account for much. The astonishing result of this mission appears almost to have frightened him. Let us look at his letter of January of the next year to the Fathers in Rome, where he describes what had happened. The letter opens with a passage of heavenly wisdom on the love of friends :

" God our Lord knows how much my soul would be comforted by the sight of you instead of having to write these letters, letters so uncertain because of the great distance from here to Rome. But since it is God our Lord Who has separated us so widely, tho' we were so united in love and spirit, the bodily distance, if I am not deceived, does not occasion any lack of love or care, in those who love one another in the Lord. For we see each other almost always, to my mind, tho' we don't converse familiarly as once we did. But the memory of the past, when it is founded on Christ, has this virtue, that it almost makes what the mind sees a reality."

He goes on to speak of his mission work :

" I have to tell you how God our Lord moved many people in a kingdom where I work [i.e., Travancore] to become Christians. . . . In a month I baptized more than 10,000 persons. . . . Here is how I baptize : I give to each his [Christian] name in writing. Afterwards these men go home and send their wives and families, whom I baptize in the same way as I baptized the men. When the baptisms are finished I command that the houses where they have their idols are to be thrown down, and I arrange that after they are Christians they are to break the images of the idols into the smallest pieces. . . . In each place I leave the prayers written in their language, ordering that each day they shall teach them once in the morning, and again at the hour of vespers.   When this is finished in one place, I go to another, and so I go from place to place making Christians, and this with many comforts, greater than I could write you by letter, or explain to you if you were here."*

The licentiate João Vaz, who returned to Lisbon this same year, has left an interesting account of Francis as he knew him in Travancore.

I lived six months with the Father Master Francis. He went bare-foot, with a poor torn gown, and a kind of hood of black stuff. Every one loved him dearly. He so gained the heart of a king, that this sovereign made a proclamation that the people were to obey his brother, the *Great Father*, as they did himself: he permitted all his subjects to become Christians if they wished to do so, and he gave him large sums for the succour of the poor.

The *Great Father*, that is the name which has been given to Father Master Francis in these lands. He has caused forty-four or forty-five churches to be built along the coast where the new Christians are. . . . He speaks the language of the country very well. Often in that flat countryside, followed by two thousand, three thousand, six thousand people, he would stop, climb up a tree, and from there preach to the people.†

* *Mon. Xav.*, vol. i. p. 306.
† Cros, *Documents Nouveaux*, p. 405.

CHAPTER XIII

THE LETTERS TO FRANCISCO MANSILLAS

(1544)

IN this chapter are gathered together the simplest and in some ways the most interesting of all Xavier's letters, those which he wrote in 1544 to Francisco Mansillas. Only as great a man as Xavier could have given to a creature so evidently insignificant as Mansillas such a wealth of love and care as these letters reveal. It was probably a love which had been born of pity, but it was none the less real for that.

Francisco Mansillas, as we know, was one of the two companions who had left Lisbon along with Xavier. He was a Portuguese, and no scholar. Later, Xavier had to dismiss him for disobedience. There are no records left which bear witness in any way to his worth or charm, if we except the never-despairing commendations of the Saint.* And if Xavier himself at last despaired, he held his own counsel on the subject, and has left us no bitter words about benefits forgot, or man's ingratitude.

Most of these letters explain themselves, and need little comment. Cros has called them a " sort of journal of Apostolic solicitudes," Brou says of them that they are " precious above all the others." Mansillas had at least the grace to treasure them, and leave them to the Company of the Name of Jesus.

These letters belong, of course, chronologically, to the preceding chapter, but we have followed Cros' example, and collected them together by themselves.

" May the grace and love of Christ our Lord help and favour us always.

" Most Dear Brother,

" I am very anxious to know your news. Do by the

---

* One might add that his evidence at the process before the canonisation of Xavier has more sobriety and reality than most of the others (see *Mon. Xav.*, vol. ii. p. 366).

love of Jesus Christ give me very lengthy news of yourself and your companions. When I arrive at Manapar, I will let you know. Remember those things which I gave you in writing, and pray God that He may give you plenty of patience to deal with your people ; and reckon that you are in Purgatory purging your sins, and that God does you a great favour in purging your sins here in this life.

"Tell João d'Artiaga that the Captain has written me that he gave him 10 crowns for me, and that I have written to the Captain that neither you nor João d'Artiaga nor I need money till he comes from Piscaria, and that he must return the money to the Captain, for I have written to the Captain that it would be returned at once. And if the Captain has a money-order for you from the Governor, d'Artiaga could buy an interpreter with the money : but if the money is not sent officially, tell him to return it at once to the Captain.

"Our Lord give you grace to serve Him, and as much as I wish for myself.

From Punicale, 23rd Feb. 1544.

"To João d'Artiaga I don't write, for this letter goes for you and for him.

"Your very dear brother,

"FRANCISCO."

The João d'Artiaga referred to above had formerly been a soldier, but at this time he acted as one of Xavier's assistants in Cape Comorin. His enthusiasms, unfortunately, did not last long.

From the Saint's suggestion that d'Artiaga might buy an interpreter, we see that he was untroubled by the problem of slavery. In another letter he advises the College in Goa to buy a slave to help the lay brothers to keep the garden. Some of his contemporaries had already seen that the system was a disastrous one. See p. 164.

"Very dear Brother in Christ,

"I am very pleased with your letters. I beseech you to behave toward your people as a good father with bad sons. Do not weary on account of the many evils you see. God, though they so greatly offend Him, does not kill them, although He has the power to kill them, nor let them be deprived of all needful for their maintenance, although He has the power to remove the things that maintain them.

"Do not weary. You are gaining more fruit than you think. And if you do not do all you wish, be content with what you do, for the fault is not yours. I am sending you a bailiff who will serve till I come. I will give him a *fanão* for every woman he catches drinking arrack. And more, she may be imprisoned three days. Have this proclaimed all over the place. Tell the village headmen that if I know that more arrack is drunk henceforward in Punicale, they will have to pay dearly for it.

"Tell Matthew [a young native interpreter who accompanied Mansillas and helped with the singing] to be a good boy, and I will do him more good than his own relatives would. Before I come, make these village headmen change their ways. Otherwise I shall have to send them all prisoners to Cochin, and they will not return to Punicale. They are the cause of all the evils done there.

"Be very diligent in baptizing new-born children. Teach the children as I have recommended, and on Sundays teach the prayers to all, with a little preachment. Forbid the pagodas [this word is used for images as well as for temples] to be made. Keep that letter which Alvaro Fogaza sent me till I come. God our Lord give you as much comfort in this life and in the next as I desire for myself.

"Manapar, 14th March, 1544.

"Your very dear Brother in Christ."

"Very dear Brother in Christ,

"I was much comforted that you wrote how comforted you were [text is defective here] . . . . Since God remembers you, remember Him, and do not weary of going on and persevering in what you have begun. Give thanks always to God, because He chose you for so great a task as yours is. I do not wish to burden you with any more than I gave you in that Memorandum. Remember me, for I never forget you. Tell Matthew to be a good boy, and I will be a good father to him. Watch him well. Tell him to speak out on Sundays what you say to him, that all may hear him, loud enough for us to hear him in Manapar ! Let me know the news of the Christians in Tuticurim, if the Portuguese who stayed there did them any injuries, and if there is

N

news of the Governor—if he is coming to regulate things at Cochin.

" Here a great thing for the service of God is coming out. Pray to the Lord God that this may develop. I pray you earnestly to behave very lovingly with these people, I mean with the most eminent people, and then with all the folk. If the folk love you and get on well with you, you will do great service to God. Learn to forgive their weaknesses very patiently. Put it to yourself that if they are not good now, they will be some day. And if you don't accomplish with them all you wish, be content with what you can. I do so.

" The Lord God be always with you, and give us His grace that we may always serve Him.

" March 20th, 1544.

" Your Brother in Christ."

" Very dear Brother in Christ,

" I could never finish writing of my desire to go along your Coast. I assure you that the truth is that if I could find a boat to take me to-day, I should go at once. Just now three heathen came to me, men of the king, with complaints that in Patanão a Portuguese had seized a messenger of the Prince, Iniquitibirim,* carried him a prisoner to Punicale, and said that from there he must take him to Tuticurim. When you know the facts, write to the Captain about it. If the Portuguese is there, whoever he may be, he is to let him go at once. If this heathen owes him anything, let him [the Portuguese] come before the Prince to demand justice. He must not stir up the country more than it is stirred up. It is because of things like this that we are not making more progress. If not [i.e., if the man is not released], in my opinion I cannot go to see the king. The people are angry that they are thus dishonoured and seized in their own land. This was never done in the time of the Pulas [the native princes]. I do not know what to do— except that we should not lose more time in living among

* Iniquitibirim, the Rajah of Travancore. His real name was Udaya-Marthauda-Varna, but Xavier, hearing him called " Ennaku-tamburan," i.e., " our King," thought this his proper name and wrote it out Iniquitibirum (with many variations). The kings of Travancore were at this time among the most powerful of the Indian rulers, and were known as the Grand Rajahs. Their dominion extended over Tinnevelly, from Cape Comorin to Punicale or Tuticorin.

people [that is, the Portuguese] who take no heed. All this is from want of punishment. If those who went to steal that little boat had been punished, the Portuguese would not do what they are doing now. It will not be surprising if the Prince does some harm to the Christians because his servant has been seized.

" Write to the Captain how much I have suffered about the seizure of the Prince's servant. I will not write again, for these people say they h a v e to do ill, and that no one must say an ill word or hinder them. If the man whom the Portuguese seized is in Tuticurim, go at once for the love of God to wherever the Captain is, and get him set free. And let the Portuguese come here to demand justice. For just as it would seem bad if a heathen went to where the Portuguese are, and then seized a Portuguese, though the Captain was there, and brought him to *terra firme* [the Portuguese forts were generally on islands], so it seems bad to them that a Portuguese should seize a man in their district and carry him to the Captain, when they have courts of justice of their own, and we are in a state of peace. If you are not able to go, send Paulo Vaz with your letter to the Captain.

" I assure you that the suffering I have endured has been such as I do not know how to describe. May our Lord give us patience to put up with such unreasonable injustice. You must write me at once what happens about this servant of the Prince, and if it is true that a Portuguese seized him, and why, and if he took him to Tuticurim. And write about the servants and how much this people resent this seizure in their own country ; and what is said about us. For if this be the truth, I have made up my mind not to go to the king Iniquitibirim.

" In order to get out of earshot of such things, and also to go where I desire, to the Land of the Priest [Prester John, *i.e.*, to Abyssinia], where you can serve God our Lord without anyone to persecute you, I have a great mind to get a native boat in Manapar here, and go to India without more delay.

" Our Lord give you His help and grace.

" Manapar, 21st March, 1544.

" Your very dear Brother in Christ."

There are usually just one or two friends at most to whom a man writes in this mood of simple abandon, and the choice is often, as here, arbitrary and inexplicable. Why did Xavier reveal himself to Mansillas in these moods of despondency as to no one else ? We cannot tell. Only we are not surprised that he was disheartened : the knowledge that a man's worst foes are of his own country and his own faith is hard to bear.

" Very dear Brother,

" I am greatly pleased with your news and with your letter, and to see the fruit you are gaining. God give you force always to persevere from good to better.

" I cannot stop feeling within my soul the injuries which heathen and Portuguese alike are doing to the Christians, and no wonder. I am already so accustomed to see the wrongs done to the Christians, and yet not be able to help that it is a bruise, which I have always with me. I have already written to the Vicar of Coulam, and to the Vicar of Cochin about the slaves whom the Portuguese stole at Punicale (see previous chapter, p. 187), that they may learn by means of the great excommunications who the thieves were [*i.e.*, that the vicars might by use or threatening of the greater excommunication come to know who were the thieves]. I sent this message three days ago, as soon as I got the headman's letter.

" Give Matthew everything necessary for his clothing. Be hospitable to him that he may not leave you, now that he is freed. Treat him very lovingly, for so I did when he was with me, that he might not leave me.

" In the Creed, when you say *enquevenum*, instead of *-venum* say *-vichuam*, for *venu* means *I will*, and *vichuam* means *I believe*. It is better to say *I believe in God* than to say *I will in God* [*quero* in Port. means I will, I desire, love, like]. Do not say *vao pinale*, because it means by force, and Christ suffered voluntarily, and not by force.

" When you come from Piscaria visit the sick, making some of the children say the prayers, as in the Memorandum I gave you. And finish up by reading part of a Gospel yourself. Always deal very lovingly with your people, and do your best that they may love you. I should be greatly pleased to know that they do not drink arrack, nor make pagodas [or images], and come every Sunday to the prayers. If at the time they became Christians there had been anyone to teach them, as you now teach them, they would have been better Christians than they are.

"27th March, 1544."

"Very dear Brother,

"I was greatly pleased with your coming to visit the Christian villages, as I told you, and I am more pleased with the great fruit which everybody tells me you gained. I expect to-day or to-morrow a message from the Governor. If it is as I expect, I will not fail to arrive. I will direct myself toward you, for I am most anxious to see you, though I see you always in spirit.

"João d'Artiaga goes, dismissed by me, full of temptations without knowing them. He does not take the road to know them. He says he will go to Combuturé to teach that village, so as to be near you. I believe little in his plans, for, as you know well, he is very fickle. If he comes near you, don't waste much time with him.

"I have written already to the Captain to provide you with what is necessary. I also told Manoel da Cruz to lend you money as often as you have need, and he has promised me to do so, with very good will.

"Take good care of your health, since with it you serve the Lord God so well. Tell Matthew from me to serve you well. If you are content with him, he has in me father and mother. If he is not very obedient to you, I don't wish to see him nor watch over him. Give him what is necessary for his clothing.

"In the villages where you go, make the men meet one day in one place, and the women another day in another place. And make them say the prayers in every house. Baptize those who are not baptized, children and adults alike.*

"Our Lord help and guard you always.

"Manapar, 8th April, 1544."

"Very dear Brother in Christ,

"I am most anxious to see you. Please God that it will be soon. Yet every day I do not fail to see you in spirit, which you do also. So we are continually with each other. By the love of God write me your news of all the Christians,

---

* The rest of the sentence is obscure and untranslatable :—fazendo esta conta : que *se alguma nova for ao moliné, que va ao molinão donde ha esta agoa.* The words in italics seem to be a corruption of a proverb, which some reader may recognise and elucidate. The Editor of the *Mon. Xav.* says this part of the sentence "nullum sensum habet."

how you are. Write very circumstantially. I expect the chief of Travancore this week without fail, for so he has written to me. I hope in God that some service to God will be done. I will let you know all that happens that you may give thanks to the Lord God. I have already written to the headmen about the *ramada*.* It seems that it would be well for the women to go to Church on Saturday mornings, as they go at Manapar, and the men on the Sundays. Do about this as you think best. When you need to write to the Captain, let it be in time that he may provide you.

"Let me know where João d'Artiaga is, and if he serves God, for I fear me much that he will not persevere in serving Him. He is very mutable, as you know. The Father and I are well. Tell Mathew to be a good boy, and to speak loud, and to say in good style what you say. When I come, I will give him something that will greatly please him. Write me if the children come to prayers, and how many know them. Write me at length about everything by the first messenger who comes.

"Livar, 23rd April, 1544."

"Very dear Brother in Christ,

"To-day, the first of May, I got a letter from you, which brought me such comfort—I could never finish writing how much. For let me tell you that I had constant fever for four or five days. I was bled twice. Now I am better. I hope in God to go to see you in Punicale next week. I hope that the chief of Treminancor will come to-day or to-morrow. When I get to you, we shall talk of what is going on here. Please God some service will be done with which He may be pleased.

"Father Francisco Coelho sends you two hats. And since we shall see you soon, I say no more, but that God our Lord give us His holy grace with which we may serve Him."

"Nao, 1st May, 1544."

"Very dear Brother in Christ,

"God knows how much better I should be pleased to be a few days with you than to stay on in Tuticurim. But it is

---

* A church made of *ramos*, *i.e.* branches, a wattle-built church. See *Mon. Xav.*, vol. i. p. 945.

necessary to be here for some days to pacify the people. Since this is so useful to our Lord, I console myself with being where I can best serve God our Lord.

" I beseech you not to fret yourself with those trouble-some people on any account. When you have a lot of engagements, and can't discharge them all, comfort yourself by doing what you can. And give many thanks to the Lord that you are in a place where the many engagements come to you, and all in the service of the Lord God, and keep you from being idle, even if you wished to be.

" I send you Peter. And as soon as Antony is well, which may be in six or eight days, I will send him. I am writing to Manoel da Cruz begging him to build the church soon.

" Send me my little box by the first boat that comes. When I finish affairs here, I will come to see you at once, for I am more anxious to be with you for a few days than you think. Always when you have need of anything, write me by those who come from there. Do always as much as you can to carry on with your people very patiently. When they do not care for good, exercise the work of mercy which says, Punish him who needs punishment. Our Lord help you, as I desire Him to help me.

" Tuticurim, 14th May, 1544."

" Very dear Brother in Christ,

" Yes, with the Lord God's help, I am very well. May it please Him Who gave me my health to give me grace to serve Him with it. Let me know your news and of the Christians constantly, and hasten to build the church, and when it is finished let me know. Those letters which I send to the Captain you must send on by some safe and sure hand. I recommend to you earnestly the teaching of the children. Baptize very diligently the new-born. Since the adults neither for good nor for evil wish to go to Paradise, at least let the babies who die after baptism go. Commend me much to Manoel da Cruz. Let Matthew be a good boy, I mean, a good man. Treat your people always lovingly, both them and the Adigars [agents of the king of Travancore].

" Viranao, Dianpatarnao,
" 22nd June, 1544."*

* This date is almost certainly a mistake for June 11th. See *Mon. Xav.*, vol. i. p. 966, and Brou, *Vie de S. François Xavier*, vol. i. p. 254, note.

" Very dear Brother in Christ,

" I arrived on Saturday afternoon at Manapar. In Combuturé they gave me a lot of bad news about the Cape Comorin Christians. The Badages captured them, and the Christians, to save themselves, made for those rocks which lie out in the sea. There they are dying of hunger and thirst. To-night I leave with twenty boats from Manapar to relieve them. Pray to God for them and us. Make the children especially pray to God for us."

These Badages or men of the north were a wild marauding tribe, noted for their swift raiding expeditions on horseback.

" They promised me at Combuturé to put up a church : Manoel de Lima promised to give 100 *fanoens* to help the cost. Go to Combuturé and give orders how this church is to be built. You can go on Wednesday or Thursday. Next week, God willing, you must visit the Christians of Punicale as far as Alendale. Baptize those who are not baptized. Visit the Christians from house to house. Baptize babies with all diligence. Observe if those who teach the children and those who assemble them do their duty well.

" Charge Manoel da Cruz, who is at Combuturé, to watch carefully over those two villages of Carean Christians, both as to concord between enemies, and that they do not make images. Also that they don't drink arrack, and that on Sundays the men meet in the afternoon and the women in the morning, to say their prayers. If Francisco Coelho is there, tell him that I say he is to come soon. God be your guard.

" Manapar, Monday, 20th June, 1544.*

" I have paid the man who takes this letter of mine what I promised him to go to Vacarapatam."

" Very dear Brother in Christ,

" On Tuesday I arrived at Manapar. God our Lord knows the troubles I had on the voyage. I went with twenty boats to relieve the Christians who had fled from the Badages to

---

* This letter also is wrongly dated. The 20th of June, 1544, fell on a Friday, and the date evidently should be 16th June (see Brou, *Vie de S. François Xavier*, vol. i. p. 254).

the rocks of Cape Comorin. They were dying of hunger and thirst. The wind was so contrary that neither by rowing nor by towing could we reach the Cape. When the wind fell I went back again, and did what was possible to help them. It was the most pitiful thing in the world to see those wretched Christians in such trouble. A lot of them come each day to Manapar. They arrive robbed and needy, and have neither food nor clothing. I wrote to the headmen of Combuturé, Punical, and Tuticurim to send some alms for the unhappy Christians, but not to take anything from the poor. Let the small ship-masters who wish to give of their own will, give. But nobody is to be forced. Do not allow anything to be taken from the poor, for so I write to the headmen. I don't expect any virtue from them. Do not allow any alms to be taken forcibly from anyone, poor or rich. Hope is in God rather than in the headmen.

"Do, I beseech you, write at length, if the church at Combuturé is now made, if Manoel de Lima gave the 100 *fanoens*, and how you got on in your visitation, and if the children are taught in those villages. I paid all, and do not know what is done in my absence. Write me of everything very fully, for I wish to have news of you and of your village. I was eight days at sea, and you know well what it is to be in those small boats with such strong winds as we had.

"Manapar, 30th June, 1544."

With a good wind they should have made the journey in one day. Mansillas said later in the *Cochin Process* that the most wretched of the victims were gathered together at Manapar, and that Francis himself went from village to village begging help for them. During the whole of July he does not seem to have found time even to write to Mansillas. The next letter is dated August 1st.

"Very dear Brother in Christ,
"Our Lord be continually your guard and give you abundant strength to serve Him. I was greatly pleased with your letter which they gave me . . . [words wanting in MS.] . . . your diligence in watching over these people that the Badages may not catch them napping.
"I went the Cape road by land to visit those unhappy Christians who came fugitive and robbed from the Badages,

It was the most pitiful thing in the world to see them. Some had nothing to eat, others, old men, could not walk, numbers of the women were confined on the road, and many other moving sights there were. If you had seen them, as I saw them myself, you would have more pity. I sent those poor people to Manapar, and now there are a lot of needy folk here. Pray the Lord God to move the hearts of the rich that they may have pity on these poor people.

"I hope to go to Punicale on Wednesday. Watch carefully over your people till those Badages go to their own country. Tell Antonio Fernandez the Fat, and the other headmen of Old Cael, that I command them not to rebuild Old Cael ; if they do, they will pay me dear for it. Remember me to Manoel da Cruz and to Matthew.

"Manapar, 1st Aug., 1544."

"Very dear Brother in Christ,

"God always with you [sic]. I was very pleased with part of your letter. I was pleased to see the comfort you had in your visitation. But I was very sorry about your tribulation. I shall be sorry till the Lord God frees you to us [by delivering them from the Badages]. Tribulations are not lacking to us. Praised be God.

"I have sent word to the Father [one of the auxiliary priests] to launch the boats in the sea, all through these villages, and to embark before it is too late. For it seems to me certain that they [the Badages] must surprise you and capture the Christians, as we are told that they will certainly come to the shore. I got this news from a judge who is friendly to the Christians. I sent a man to this judge, who is a favourite of the king Iniquitibirim, with a letter to the king. I wrote that since he was friendly with the Governor he should not allow the Badages to do us harm, for the Governor would be very displeaesd if any harm came to the Christians. The judge, who is my friend, and who loves me because I am so friendly to the Christians of the coast, came to see and help me, as he has a lot of Christian relatives. I wrote to him that he might advise me as to what was happening, and let me know when they come to the shore, that we might have time to withdraw together to the sea.

"I have written already to the Captain to send a small

warship to guard your people and you. Make your people keep a strong watch on the mainland. The Badages come at night, on horseback, and take us before we have time to embark. Look carefully after the people, for they have so little sense that to save two *fanoens* they would give up setting a watch. Make them launch all the ships at once, and put their goods into them. And make the women and children say the prayers, now more than ever, for we have none to help us but God.

" Send me the paper which remains in the box. I have nothing to write on. Send this to me at once by a coolie (culle). Let me know any news; if the boats are launched, and the goods placed in them, and how they get on with this. Tell Antonio Fernandez the Fat from me to watch carefully for the people, if he wishes to be my friend. These people [Badages] do not make the poor wretches prisoners, except those who can be ransomed. Above all, make them keep good watch at night, and have their spies on the mainland. I have great fear that with this moonlight they may come by night to this shore and rob the Christians. Therefore command them to watch carefully at night. Our Lord be your guard.

" Manapar, 3rd Aug., 1544."

" Very dear Brother in Christ,

" This morning I wrote you that you should strengthen your people in that tribulation, and have so much charity as to let me know any certain news from Tuticurim. I'm afraid that some harm may come to those poor Christians from the *cavalerias* from Tuticurim."

This reference to the *cavalerias* from Tuticurim is a dark one. The Portuguese Captain, Cosmo de Pavia, had just come from Tuticurim, officially to protect the Paravas, but really to look after his own interests, which were intimately bound up with the Badages. He was in the habit of buying and selling their fine horses for the increase of his private fortune. These are evidently the *cavalerias* to which Xavier here refers, and to which he refers more explicitly in a later letter (see p. 208).

" This people is more afraid than I can say. It never struck me as a good plan to forsake them, so do not go away with João d'Artiaga till the country is free from those Badages persecutions. Do let me know at once when you have certain news.

" Iniquitibirim sends a Brahmin with the Captain's interpreter to settle [terms of] peace with your people. I do not know what they will do. They are here in Manapar, and leave at once by sea. Please write me very detailed news of the Portuguese of Tuticurim, as soon as you know, to relieve my great anxiety. Tell me if any Portuguese are wounded or killed, and also about the Christians. As for your going, we shall see, or I shall write you after this fury of the Badages is past. Our Lord be always with you. Amen.

" Manapar, 19th Aug., 1544.

" Just now I have got a letter from Guarim, in which your very dear brother lets me know that the Christians have fled into the jungle, and that the Badages have plundered them. They have killed a Christian and a heathen. From all parts we have bad news. Praised be the Lord God for ever."

" Very dear Brother,

" God be with you always, Amen. By the saying of the Lord, *He who is not with me is against me*, you can see how many friends we have in these parts who help us to make this people Christian ! Let us not despair. God gives to each his pay at last. If He please, He can be served by few as by many. For those who are against God I have rather pity than any desire for their punishment, for at the last God punishes His enemies heavily, as we can see by those who are in hell. This Brahmin goes with a dispatch from the Badages to king Betibumal. For the love of God order a boat at once to take him to Tuticurim. Let me have the news of Tuticurim, of the Captain and the Portuguese and the Christians, for I am very anxious. Commend me much to João d'Artiaga and to Manoel da Cruz. Tell Matthew not to weary, that he is not working in vain, that I will do better for him than he thinks. Our Lord be always with you. Amen.

" Manapar, 20th Aug., 1544.

" For the love of God, help this Brahmin with everything for his journey, and say to the Captain, at least to do him honour.

" Your very dear brother in Christ."

" Very dear Brother in Christ,

" God help you always. Amen. Let me know when your district will be safe from the Badages, so that without harm to your people I can send them Francisco Coelho in your stead. Then you could go and do great service to God by baptizing those of the village of Carea, and the Careas of Beadala,* and the Mundaliar [native magistrate]."

At this point in the correspondence we are just beginning to think that things are going to settle down a little at last, when suddenly a new *motif* is heard; the fame of the Saint has been spreading quickly throughout the islands, and he is preparing now to answer a new call from the oppressed subjects of the Rajah of Jafnapatam, in Manar, near Ceylon, who like the Macedonians of old had sent a messenger, saying, " Come over and help us." The letter goes on :

" The Captain of Negapatam has great influence with the Rajah of Jafnapatam to whom the islands of Manar belong. He will have the duty of helping their relations with the Rajah. When your district is safe from the Badages, send the boat to me at once that I may send you at once Francisco Coelho with money and letters and a note of what you have to do in Manar. I commend our Brother João d'Artiaga greatly to you. Write me of all of which he has need that I may provide it, as that is only right. Here I am going alone among this people without interpreter. Antonio remained in Manapar ill; Rodrigo and Antonio are my interpreters. So you can see the life I am leading and the sort of exhortations I can make. They do not understand me. I understand them less. [The gift of tongues with which Xavier has so often been accredited would have been handy here.] Here you can see the discourses I make to these people. [Does this last sentence mean that he gesticulated so much that his preaching was seen rather than heard ?] I baptize the new-born babies, and others whom I find ready for baptism. There is no need of an interpreter for this. The poor make me understand their needs without an interpreter ; and I by seeing them understand without an interpreter. For the chief things I have

* These people are now known as the Kadeyers or Karaiyans, a class of Tamil fishermen or boatmen.

no need of one. The Badages who were in these parts are already gone to Cabrecate. This district is now secure against them. The people of the land are doing what harm they can till things are settled by Iniquitibirim.

"Punical, 31st Aug., 1544.

"I leave to-night for Tale, where there are many poor people."

By the "people of the land" Xavier probably means the Adigars, agents of the king of Travancore, to whom he refers again in the next letter. Mansillas has evidently been complaining of them.

"Very dear Brother in Christ,

"This Prince of Tale, a nephew of Iniquitibirim, is so much our friend that at once, when he heard of the wrongs which the Adigars had inflicted on the Christians, he sent off his servant with a letter which commanded them to allow all the victuals to go from the mainland, and ordering these Adigars to show kindness to the Christians, and that they should tell him the names of the Adigars and give them to me, so that if I went to the king I could tell him the truth of what happened there.

"As this servant of the prince goes for the good of the Christians, see that the headmen do him great honour and pay for his trouble, for that is just. What they spend on women-dancers is wasted money, and would be much better spent on such things, for it is right and supplies all the folk. Give you him something, too, so that with the better will he may tell the Adigars not to do them more harm, but to do them good.

"Let me know if it is true that a Portuguese carried off a servant of the Prince prisoner to Tuticurim, and why. I wrote you before at length about this case. If it be true, it seems to me that it would be better to remain than to go to see the king. The people make the case look very ugly. They resent greatly the taking of the prince's man. He did much honour to Father Francisco Coelho, and did his best for the advantage of these Christians. To do them more honour, he made four men of Manapar headmen, without imposing any tax on the folk, as used to be customary in the time of the Pulas [native princes]. From other villages he made three headmen, without anything. To do honour to the Father, who went to see him, he brought a great procession from those villages.

" For the love of God write to the Captain from me that I pray him earnestly to do me the favour, throughout all this month of September, not to command, nor allow, any harm to be done to the heathen of the Great King's country. They are all very much our friends. As far as the Christians are concerned, it is superfluous to ask them to do no harm. If I have to go to see this king, I should accomplish the going and coming and leaving for Cochin all in this month, and I wish that during this time there should be no complaints to the King about any thing against us.

" Write me by your own hand why you wrote that you could not write without our seeing each other. If there is anything of great importance and service to God, which I could remedy, whether affairs of the Captain and the Portuguese or of the Christians, I would not for anything go to Iniquitibirim, at Cochin, without trying, if possible, to put your troubles right.

" Manapar, 2nd Sept., 1544."

In the above letter the references to the miserable Portuguese Captain are dark and inexplicit, but in the following letter Xavier's wrath is more thinly veiled. " Do not allow those poor people to die for Betibumal and his horses," he says.

The position of the native Christians in these districts had become an almost impossible one. The unconverted heathen looked on them very often with hatred and suspicion, because Christianity was the religion of the Portuguese invaders, and the Portuguese, in whom the converts naturally expected to find friendship and sympathy, were represented by such men as this Captain.

" I am very anxious about the Christians of Tuticurim, as they are destitute of anyone to look after them. For the love of our Lord, let me know at once what happens. If you see that it will serve God, go with a lot of the Combuturé and Punical boats, and take the people from those islands to Combuturé, Punical and Trincantur. At once when you get this, leave with all the Punical boats, ordering those at Combuturé to come after you at once.

" Don't allow those poor people to die of hunger and thirst
for love of Betibumal and his horses.   It would be reckoned
better to the Captain, if he looked after the Christians and not
after Betibumal and his horses.   From here I send a letter to
the headmen of Punical and Combuturé, in which I order
them to make themselves and their boats ready at once to go
with you to fetch the Christians of Tuticurim, who are dying
of hunger and thirst in those islands.

" If you think it will be needful for you to go and send for
those people, give the letter to the headmen, and go to
relieve them.   But if you think it is not necessary, do not
go ; I remit it altogether to your judgment.   If you do go,
see that the boats take water and victuals.

" Our Lord be always with you.   Amen.   Let me know
how Manoel da Cruz and Matthew are, whom I left disconsolate.

" 5th Sept., 1544."

In the following letter we see how Xavier treats his enemy
in distress :

" Sad news they give me of the Captain.   They have
burnt his ship and houses.   He has withdrawn to the islands.
For the love of God, go at once with all your people from
Punical, taking all the water that all the boats can carry.   I
write very strongly to the headmen to go at once with you
to see the Captain, and to take plenty of water, and plenty
of boats to carry the people.

" If I thought that the Captain would like my going, I
would go, and you could remain at Punical.   But he wrote
me a letter in which he told me that he could not write without
making a very great scandal, of the harm I had done him.
God and all the world knows what he could not write without scandal—I don't know how he would be pleased to see
me.   For this and for other reasons I don't go to him.
I write to the headmen of Combuturé and Vunbembar to
go at once with all the boats, and carry water and victuals.
For the love of God do it quickly, for you see the Captain and
all those Christians are in great distress.   For the love of
God do it very very quickly.

" Alendale, 5th Sept., 1544."

" God give us His most holy grace, for in this country we have no other help but His. I was in Tiruchendur on my way to Varivandiao to visit the Christians, as I did in Alendale, Pudicurim, and Trichantur. They have great need of being visited. When on the point of leaving I got news that the country was rising because the Portuguese had carried off a brother-in-law of Betibumal, and so they [the natives] may carry off the Christians of Cape Comorin.

" I am writing to Father Francisco Coelho that I am on the point of leaving for the place where the Cape Comorin Christians are, for if I am not there much harm is likely to come to them. Besides, he has written to me that a prince, nephew of Iniquitibirim, had arrived (to settle) about those miserable people, and would be doing them a lot of harm if I was not there. He wrote further that Iniquitibirim was sending me a letter with three or four of his servants who remained worn out at Manapar. In his letters he asked me to go there to see him. He is very anxious to talk with me about things very important to him. It seems to me that he has great need of the Governor's favour, inasmuch as the native princes are very prosperous and have plenty of money. And it seems to me that it is feared that the native princes do not give so much money to the Governor in order that he may help them.

" Iniquitibirim writes me further: that the Christians are safe in his lands, and that he will show them hospitality. I am leaving at once to-night for Manapar, and from there, for love of the Christians of Tuticurim and Bembar, and that they may be safe in the country of the Great King, I will go to see Iniquitibirim and arrange with him how they may be safe in his country.

" Set the right way about getting those Christians of Tuticurim who are dying on yonder islands to come to Combuturé and Punical. Write me full details of their affairs, and especially how the Captain and the Portuguese are. If you can find time to visit the Christians of Combuturé and the Careas and those of Thomé da Molta village, and those near Patanoa, I should be greatly pleased. I know they are in great need of being visited. I should like much to visit those places.

" Borrow 100 *fanoens* from your friend Manoel da Cruz of

Punical, for teaching the children. Spend it in paying for those who teach the children, inquiring from them what I used to pay them. In this you will do great service to God. A man is coming to you from here—a fine fellow, I think, and anxious to serve God. Show him hospitality, till I return from Iniquitibirim. If you think he will serve God, leave him there. Write fully at once by a barber about your affairs, for I am very anxious about both Portuguese and Christians. Our Lord give us more rest in the other life than we have in this.

" Tiruchendur, 7th Sept., 1544."

" Dearest Brother in Christ,

" I could never end writing how pleased I was with your letter, for I was very anxious about the Captain and all the other people. Our Lord be always with them, as I wish that He may be with me. On Tuesday, two hours before morning, I sent Father Francisco Coelho to speak with the prince at Talla, two leagues from Manapar. The prince, Iniquitibirim's nephew, received him very well. It seemed to me necessary to send him to visit so that this district might be left in peace, as it was almost half in insurrection. He says that Betibumal goes by sea in great haste to the king to fight against Iniquitibirim.

" I sent him also to order the Adigars to allow the fetching of rice and victuals. On Tuesday after midday I got your letters, and at once sent a man with a letter to Father Francisco Coelho, who is with the Prince, bidding him send letters ordering the Adigars of this country to allow victuals to go to Punicale, and that the Christians should show them hospitality."

The unfortunate Parava Christians are no sooner beginning to recover from the Badagar invasion than those tax-gatherers of the Rajah of Travancore, the Adigars, begin to put cruel pressure on them again. Whether they did so with the approval of their master, to whom Xavier refers as the Great King, and who always professed much friendship towards the Saint, or not, is impossible to say. But we can see from these letters how Xavier himself, as the most disinterested representative of justice in the southern districts of Portuguese India, was acquiring a very considerable authority of his own.

As for the next phrases in this letter, we might hardly notice them, but they are very significant, for they record Xavier's forgiveness of the Portuguese Captain, and his desire to be on friendly terms with the man who had caused him so much suffering and bitter disillusionment, and had wrecked the happiness of so many of his hard-won converts. Here we see a great saint very meekly forgiving a great sinner. Later letters show that the Captain had disregarded those approaches. They were pearls flung in a pig-stye.

" I should like to leave this shore in peace somehow or other before quitting it to go to Iniquitibirim, and from there going prudently to oppose the Adigars. I will write to the Captain to-morrow. I cannot just now on account of this man's great haste.

" I expect Francisco Coelho to-night. To-morrow I will write you more fully. Remember me to Paulo Vaz. Tell Matthew that I am writing to Manoel da Cruz to give him twelve *fanoens* which he asked me for his father, and a poor brother he has. When the Father Francisco Coelho comes, I will write you very fully.

" Our Lord unite us in His kingdom.

" Manapar, 10th Sept., 1544."

" Very dear Brother in Christ,

" Antonio is still ill, and cannot serve me. Send me at once Antonio Parava to Manapar, for I need him to do the cooking [obviously this means the cooking for the refugee Christians]. When I arrive at Iniquitibirim's . . . [text defective]. Pray God for me. Tell the children to remember in their prayers to pray God for me.

" I will write Manoel da Cruz a letter to give you a hundred *fanoens* for the instruction of the children.

" Tuticurim, 20th Sep., 1544."

" When I arrived in Manapar, and was just leaving to go to Aleixo de Sousa's, two Nairs arrived [men of the ruling and military caste] with a letter from a Portuguese. He writes me that he is waiting in Bearime and has a letter from a Comptroller of Revenue and certain dispatches for me. So

I am forced to go and see Iniquitibirim. . . . I go the Cape Comorin road by land. I shall visit the Christian villages and baptize the babies.

" On Monday, or when you think best, I should be pleased if you visited Tuticurim Christians . . . [text defective].

" I commend me to your prayers and those of the children. With such help I have no fear of the fears these Christians put into me. They say not to go by land, for all who wish ill to these Christians wish much worse to me. I am so sick of life that I count it more worth while to die in the attempt to help our religion [ley] and faith than see such wrongs as I have seen without being able to help or prevent them. I am sorry for nothing but that I was not in a better position [to deal with] those whom you know, who so cruelly injure God.

" Manapar, 10th Nov., 1544.

" I leave at once for Pudicare and Father Francisco Coelho goes to visit the Christians at Atapanoa."

In November two native priests were sent to Xavier by the Bishop of Goa, and he was able to leave them at the Cape and go on to Travancore, as we have seen in the previous chapter. On the 18th of December he writes to Mansillas :

"On Dec. 16th I arrived in Cochin. Before I arrived I baptized all the Machuas fishermen who live in the kingdom of Travancore. God knows how pleased I should be to go back at once to finish baptizing the rest. But the Vicar-General thinks it is a greater service to God to go to the Governor to deal with the punishment of the Rajah of Jafnapatam (see pp. 216-18).

" I shall leave here for Cambay in two or three days in a very well fitted brigantine. I hope to return very quickly with all the dispatch consistent with the service of the Lord God.

" The Lord Bishop will not go to Cochin this year. The Vicar-General [Miguel Vaz] leaves this year for Portugal. I hope in God that he will return very quickly. Diogo is in St. Paul's [the college]. He was very anxious to go. He and Micer Paulo are well, and all at the College. I got news from Portugal from a number of letters which came to me from there. I see your licence to be ordained a priest, without your having a patrimony or benefice. It seems to me that you have no need of this licence, for the Lord Bishop will ordain you without a licence as he ordained the Fathers Manoel and Gaspar. They are in Cochin so that they may go on to you, to join in the work there. Neither the ships nor two of our companions [text bad] have arrived up to now, I think they will be wintering in Mozambique or have put back to Portugal. One of them is Portuguese and the other Italian. The king writes very highly of these two Portuguese of ours. Please God that they reach you safely. I know neither of them. They were not among those we left. There are more than 60 students of our Company in the University of Coimbra. The many good things they write to me of them is a matter of great thanks to God our Lord. Almost all are Portuguese, which pleases me greatly. Of the Companions of Italy I hear very good news, but as I hope we shall see each other within a month, and I shall show you all the letters, I say no more.

" Whenever you get this letter, for the love and service of God our Lord I pray you earnestly to make yourself ready to go and visit the Christians of the Travancore shore whom I have just baptized. In each place set up a school to teach the boys [bad text] . . . up to 150 *fanoens*. In all these places of the coast leave pay for those who teach the boys up to Pescaria Grande. Ask the Captain for money for your expenses.

" In Manapar take a boat up to the village of Carea. Go to Momchuri, where there are Machuas: they are not baptized : the place is about a good league from Cape Comorin. Baptize them, for they have asked for it repeatedly, and I could not go. Antonio Fernandez, a Malabar Christian, will go in a brigantine and try to find you and remain with you till the baptism of those who remain is finished. He is a very fine man, and zealous for God's honour. He knows the people. He knows well how we ought to deal with them. Do what he tells you, without hindering him in anything. I did so, and I always got on well. I beseech you that you do the same.

" Take Matthew with you, and the bailiff who went with me from Viranoa to Patanoa, and your ' boys ' [servants] and a canacapole, who can write, that the written prayers may be left in each place . . . [text defective]. Pay this canacapole with the king's money, which the Captain will give you for this purpose. *

"Give Father João de Licano the charge of baptizing and teaching.

"Francisco Mendez is in a hurry, so I do not write you more. May our Lord always help you, as I wish that He may help me.

"Cochin, 18th Dec., 1544.

"Your very dear Brother in Christ."†

---

* Teixeira (*Vita, Mon. Xav.*, vol. ii. p. 852) explains who were the canacapoles : "He (Xavier) then and here gave a beginning to the order of the Canacapoles, who are in that coast, and by whom our Lord is so well served, and souls so helped, and who, if it were possible, were a necessity in all new Christianity. . . . Seeing himself alone almost, in that great coast, where there were so many Christian villages, to which he could not go . . . he chose in each village one or two Christians of the most intelligent in matters of the faith, of the best life and conscience, and taught them the form and mode of baptizing, giving them orders to baptize when necessary . . . these are those who now in each village have charge of the church, and are as sacristans of it, and baptize in extreme need, and teach the doctrine twice daily, in the morning to the boys and in the afternoon to the girls, and publish the banns . . . they keep a list of the births, etc., etc."

† The text of these letters is in *Mon. Xav.*, vol. i. p. 310 ff.

CHAPTER XIV

CEYLON, NEGAPATAM AND SAN THOMÉ

(1545)

In December, 1544, Xavier went north to Coulam and Cochin to arrange with the authorities there for the official protection and favour which he had promised to his new converts. He evidently meant to return to the Cape as soon as those arrangements were made, but in Cochin he got news of a great massacre of native Christians in Ceylon. The situation was difficult and complicated, but Xavier tackled it immediately. His first step was to interview the Governor of India, who was at that moment far north in the Gulf of Cambay. The Saint embarked in a *catur*, a swift native boat, and, after a short pause at Goa, in order to arrange for missionaries to carry on his work at the Cape, he reached the Governor, and gave him a *résumé* of the state of affairs in Ceylon. It is difficult, if not impossible, to get a clear idea of the details of the situation, but we can trace abundant material for tragedy, and we know that the tragedy was enacted.

When, in 1518, the Portuguese first landed in Ceylon, they unconsciously invaded a region sacred alike, though for different reasons, to Hindoos, Brahmins and Mussulmans. So from the first they had been particularly unwelcome there. Nor were they the only invaders. Tamils had already crossed from the mainland, the island was divided up into petty kingdoms, and there was a constant competition for these little thrones, and perpetual war between Mussulmans, Cingalese and Tamils. Politically, the moment of their invasion was an opportune one for the Portuguese, for they came upon a country divided against itself. A fort was built at Colombo, and Franciscan monks preached the Gospel of peace. It would take an experienced reader of the detective school of literature to follow the tale of intrigue between the various petty kings and their rivals and the Portuguese government. Commonly, the native bribe was the promise to become a Christian, made by the intriguing king on behalf of himself or the heirs for whom he wished to secure the protection of the white men.

In 1545 the king of Jafnapatam emerges before us, a sinister and hated figure, a man who had succeeded to his crown by murdering his master, and who kept himself in affluence by secret and illegal tradings with the Portuguese commander at Negapatam, over on the mainland. He was especially loathed by his subjects on the island of Manar. This tribe had heard rumours of the coming of the Saint to the Paravas, and of his life among them, and they sent over messengers who came to the new disciples like the Greeks of old, saying : " We would see Jesus." Xavier had sent them a native priest, and he had made six hundred converts. But the king of Jafnapatam feared that open dealings with the Portuguese would spoil his secret dealings with the Portuguese commander, so he gave the six hundred converts their choice between a return to idolatry and martyrdom. They chose the latter. A few months earlier neither they nor their teacher, who died with them, had ever heard of the Christian faith. It is a striking incident.*

In the passion of his righteous anger, Xavier allowed himself to be caught into the whirlpool of local intrigue. The brother of the murderer, who had himself brought the story to Xavier, offered to become a Christian if the Portuguese would place him on the throne. The promise appealed to Francis, who was always anxious to be as wise as the children of this world. But he failed, as the children of light are so apt to do when they tread the debatable ground between religion and politics. He forgot, or was ignorant of, a more reasonable claimant who was already a Christian. Sousa seems also to have been ignorant of this other prince, and he sent Xavier off to Negapatam with full authority to put the offending rajah to death, and establish this new Christian brother in his place. Xavier set out cheerfully on his mission, and in full confidence he wrote that the prayers of the martyrs of Manar would bring their murderer to a sense of his sins, and to true penitence, before he laid his head on the block.†

And the Saint's hopes for this new field, so richly sown with the blood of the martyrs, was immense. With lightning

* See Tursellinus, Book II., cap. 12.
† *Mon. Xav.*, vol. i. p. 369.

speed he returned from Cambay to Cochin, wrote his letters for the home-going mails, and proceeded round the coast to Negapatam.

This batch of letters was to produce a great impression in Europe. The news they carried was sensational enough. At Travancore, in a few weeks, ten thousand converts; in Ceylon, hundreds of native martyrs. The rector of the college at Coimbra wrote: " The letters of Master Francis have just come in. We are all deeply touched. If I could send every man in this college out to India I would do it at once." * King John commanded that twelve new missionaries should be sent out that year. It was after all but a small response on his part to the solemn and prophetic charges which Francis had made to him.

The letter to Loyola is one long appeal for more helpers in the fields that are so heavy with harvest. And Francis is so eager for help of any kind that he too carelessly, as he afterwards realised, discounts high intellectual and religious qualifications.

" Men who have no talent for confessing, preaching, or doing the like for the Company could, after having completed their Exercises and having served some months in humble duties, do much service in these parts, if they had bodily strength as well as spiritual. For in these heathen districts learning is not necessary, except to teach the prayers and visit and baptize the children. . . . I say that they must have bodily strength because this district is very troublesome on account of the great heat and the lack of good water. There is little for bodily sustenance ; indeed, only rice, fish, and fowls. . . . They [the men who come out] must be healthy and not delicate, able to stand the constant labours of baptizing, teaching, walking from place to place . . . but they must go through dangers, remembering they were born to die for their Redeemer and Lord, and therefore they must have spiritual strength. And because I have not, and walk where I have much need of it, I pray you to have special remembrance of me. And those who have talent either for confessing or for giving the Exercises, though they have not the physique to bear other troubles, you

* *Epistolæ Mixtæ*, vol. i. p. 231, quoted by Bron, *Vie de S. François Xavier*, vol. i. p. 296.

should send too, for they can go to Goa or Cochin, where they will do much service to God. . . .

"It is four years since I left Portugal. All this time I have got only a few letters from you from Rome, and two from Master Simon from Portugal. I wish every year to know your news and of all the Company in detail. I know well that you write each year as I do, but I fear me that as I do not get your letters, you may not get mine." *

Meanwhile, the open door in Ceylon which the Manar massacre so abruptly slammed had been locked and bolted. Xavier arrived at Negapatam with dispatches from Sousa, authorising the overthrow of the wicked Rajah of Jafnapatam, to discover that the whole matter was evidently being hushed up as effectively as possible. Instead of finding the Portuguese commander eagerly waiting for him with a fleet prepared and ready to avenge the martyrs, as he had expected, he found himself coldly received, and all his proposals and those of the Governor pushed aside. What had happened? An incident which Thomas Hardy would call one of the ironies of fate. A Portuguese ship, richly laden with cargo, had run ashore on the Ceylon coast, and the Rajah of Jafnapatam had seized it and announced that he would keep it for a surety, in case of any revenge being taken upon him for the murder of the Christians. The Portuguese commander at Negapatam had evidently a good share in this valuable cargo, so he found it convenient to forget the martyrs. Xavier was hopelessly baffled; the arduous work of many weeks had come to nothing, and all chances of establishing the faith in Ceylon blotted out. It must have been one of the most bitter and humiliating moments of his life.

None of his letters evince such strong disgust toward the Portuguese Government as that written at this time to Rodriguez:

"Do not allow any friend of yours to come to India in the employment and service of the king, for it can truly be said of them (i.e., the king's officers):
" Let them be blotted out of the book of life,
" And not be written with the righteous.

* Mon. Xav., vol. i. p. 362.

" . . . . Wrong-doing has become so usual that no one is at all troubled by it. Everyone takes the same road— *rapio, rapis.* And I am terrified to see how many moods and tenses and participles of this wretched verb those who come here can invent." *

It is not likely that he blamed himself for having used the dubious weapons of political diplomacy. He had done so before, and he would do so again. But these weapons were sharpened to other uses than his. It was that which revolted and angered him. He thought it possible to have a political organisation whose sole end would be the coming of the kingdom of heaven. To the last this great Saint was also a man of the world and a diplomatist. These may have been the stains upon his garments, but he never washed them out. Later, from Japan, we find him writing a singular letter to Simon Rodriguez in Lisbon. The Spaniards had been coming from Nueva España to Japan. Apparently he thinks this is not for the greater glory of God. So he wishes them to be told that the voyage is very dangerous on account of reefs in the sea, and that all the Spaniards have been lost. Even if they got there it would do them no good, as the Japanese were very bellicose and covetous, and would take them all. And the country was sterile, and they could not be supplied, and so would die of starvation. And the Japanese would kill them all.

Xavier says all this to Simon in Portugal, who is to tell the King and Queen, and they are to discharge their conscience by telling the Emperor Charles not to send ships to Japan. Besides pleasing his Portuguese friends in the East, he must have known it would please the Court in Portugal to see this letter, and might bring him some helpers and money. Otherwise he could just as well have sent the letter direct to Spain. And, of course, the voyage was dangerous, and the Spanish route may have been especially so. And, of course, it is possible that some of Xavier's commercial friends got him to write this letter for their own interests, and he did it without thinking much about it.†

But let us return to Negapatam. The account he gives of the fiasco is restrained to a degree :

" I was some days in Negapatam. Jafnapatam has not

* *Mon. Xav.,* vol. i. p. 375.   † *Ibid.,* vol. i. p. 730.

been taken, nor was that king who was to become a Christian put into possession : it was not done because the king's ship which came from Pegu went ashore, and the king of Jafnapatam took the cargo, and until they get back what he took, what the Governor commanded is not done. May it please God that it will be done, if it be to His service."*

One might have expected that at this point Xavier would have returned to his new converts in the South : he would probably have done so, but the winds prevented him. These were for him days of perplexity and uncertainty. "I do not know what will become of me," he writes to Mansillas. "May God our Lord grant us at the right time knowledge of His most holy will, and make us always ready to fulfil it whenever it is clearly revealed and made known to us. For to be good we have to be pilgrims in this life, ready to go wherever we can best serve God our Lord."†

He did not forget his new converts, though he did not go back to them.

The same letter proceeds :

"I beseech you not to tire of working with these people. Preach continually in all these places, baptize the babies diligently, arrange that the prayers shall be taught. You will get 2,000 *fanoens* from Juan da Cruz, which have been collected in this Fishery coast for teaching the children . . . do not settle in any one place, but go continually from place to place, visiting all those Christians as I did when I was there, for in that way you will best serve God.

"And also make an account of the expenses incurred in the church at Manapar, for I have remitted 2,000 *fanoens* to Diogo Rebello, which Iniquitibirim gave to make churches in his district. Father Coelho knows what has been spent. Spend what is over in teaching the children. Visit those who become Christians on the coast of Travancore, and distribute these Malabar Fathers all over the country as seems best to you. Be a very careful overseer. . . .

"I commend two things to you specially : the first that you go pilgriming from place to place, baptizing the new-born and seeing that the prayers are very diligently taught :

* *Mon. Xav.*, vol. i. p. 382.   † *Ibid.*, p. 377.

next, that you inspect those Malabar Fathers who are not [words missing] and punish them. . . . Help Cosmo de Paiva [the Captain referred to in the other letters to Mansillas] to clear his conscience of the many robberies he has committed on this coast, and of the evils and homicides his greed wrought in Tuticurim. More, counsel him, as a friend of his honour, to return the money which he took from those who killed the Portuguese, for it is a most ugly thing to sell Portuguese blood for money. I do not write because I have no hope of any improvement [this is what Xavier says, but from the context he would appear to mean : " It is not because I am hopeless of his improvement that I do not write "], and so tell him from me that I must send a written notice to the Governor that he may punish him, and to the Infante Dom Henrique that by means of the Inquisition he may punish those who persecute the converts to our holy law and faith. And so let him amend !

" . . . Welcome Vasco Fernandez who brings my letter, for I hope in God our Lord that he will join our Company. He seems to be a very fine lad and anxious to serve God, and it is right to favour him. Write me fully about yourself and your Christians and about Cosmo de Paiva, as to whether he makes amends and restores what he took from the Christians.

" Our Lord help you always, as I wish Him to help me.

" From Negapatam, 7 April, 1545.

" Your Brother in Christ,

" FRANCIS." *

But the days of darkness and perplexity were not ended. Francis had come to one of the great spiritual crises of his life, and yet the still small voice had not spoken. For the first time since his conversion we see him hesitating, uncertain, tentative. For days he waited, but no light came. Then he felt the need for complete loneliness and silence. " I was obliged," he writes, "to go to St. Thomé."

So the Saint went on furlough for five months. He set out for Meliapor by sea ; but the ship was driven back by tempest, and he had to go on foot. Close by Meliapor, according to the Nestorian traditions, were buried the actual bones of the doubting Apostle. A little heap of ruins marked his legendary tomb, and the Portuguese had built a church upon the spot,

* *Mon. Xav.*, vol. i. p. 377.

where pilgrims might come and pray. And here they were told how St. Thomas had lost his life. One day when he was in his hermitage in the wood, and while he was praying to God, surrounded by a great flock of peacocks, an idolater passed by, and, not seeing the Saint, sent an arrow from his bow towards one of the peacocks. But, instead of hitting the bird, the arrow lodged in the side of St. Thomas, who thereupon very sweetly adored his Creator and gave up the ghost.

Francis lodged in the little clergy house adjoining the church, and the priest in charge has left a written account of the visit. They ate at the same table, he tells us, and often talked together. But St. Francis spoke only of spiritual things. It was not a formal retreat nor a complete holiday. Xavier could not keep himself back, even then, from doing his Master's work. His teaching and his holy life, this priest tells us, made a great change in the town of Meliapor. He turned away many from mortal sin, and married a great number of people. The social life in this Portuguese colony was very much like that in Goa. It was his habit, Coelho goes on to say, to go out of the house every night secretly, cross the little garden and enter the church. Legends of resounding blows with the devil heard in there, and of miraculous illuminations received, suggest that here was Xavier's Penuel, and that the record of the struggle and the victory were somehow visible upon his body, and thus childishly interpreted by the uninitiated, as these things so often are.

But we must turn to his own letter, which is written after his discovery of the will of God.

" In this holy house (of San Thomé) I took it as a duty to occupy myself in praying to God our Lord to grant me to know in my soul His most holy will, and to give me the firm resolution to fulfil it, and the firm hope that *He who has given the will will give the power to fulfil it.* It pleased God to remember me with His accustomed mercy, and with much interior comfort I felt and knew that it was His will that I should go to those parts of Malacca where Christians have lately been made. . . . if Portuguese ships do not go this year to Malacca, I will go in some Moorish or heathen ship. I have such faith in God our Lord, dearest brothers, for Whose love *alone* I make this journey, that though no ship at all left this coast this year, and a *catarmaran* (a small and rudely built native boat) was leaving, I would go in it *confidently*, with all my hope placed in God.   Dearest brothers *in Christ*, I pray you by the love and service of God our Lord, that you remember me a sinner in your sacrifices and continual prayers, commending me to God.

" At the end of August I hope to leave for Malacca, for the ships which have to go are waiting for that monsoon (*monçom*).   I am writing to the Governor to send me a patent for the Captain of Malacca that he may give me a boat and everything necessary for going to the islands of Maquaca. For the love of our Lord see that you get it from his Lordship, and send it on with this *palamar*.*

" Send me with him a small Roman Breviary. . . . From Malacca I will write you at length, giving you accounts of the Christians that are made, and of the opportunities, so that you may provide men who may increase our holy faith. For since your house is called Holy Faith (the college of St. Paul at Goa was also known as the college of the Holy Faith), it is necessary that the deeds and name should correspond. . . . May our Lord unite us in His holy glory, for I do not know if we shall see each other again here.

" Meliapar, 8th May, 1545.

" Your least brother,
" FRANCISCO."†

---

* A native messenger.   † *Mon. Xav.*, vol. i. p. 382.

CHAPTER XV

(1545—1547)

AT the end of September 1545 Xavier arrived in Malacca. His fame had preceded him. " When I was a child," an old man said at the process of 1616, " I saw Father Xavier with my own eyes land for the first time in Malacca. The people ran out from the harbour to receive him. They shouted with joy, ' The Holy Father is here ! ' "

The Portuguese had established themselves in Malacca in 1511. Albuquerque captured the town from the Moors, erected forts and churches, and made it a base for his military operations in the East Indies. But the town was not held without a bitter struggle. It was too valuable a fort to be easily lost or gained. Through Malacca most of the trade from the Far East came westward ; it was the Singapore of the sixteenth century. Before the Western invasion it had been the headquarters of a powerful Malay dynasty which had adopted the faith of Islam.

The harbour was immense, and, when Xavier arrived there, was the rendezvous of many hundreds of trading vessels— Indian, Arabian, Chinese, Levantine, Portuguese. Already the spires of Christian churches rose from among the Eastern mosques and domes. But hitherto Christianity had been little more than a part of the political equipment of Portugal. It was not a religion which the invaders from the West could easily proclaim with any dignity or sincerity as their own. In 1521 the Spaniards, arriving from the East, had annexed the Philippines. Since then it had been difficult to decide where their property ended and that of the Portuguese began. Added to this, there was a constant intrigue going on between the native sultans and one or other of the newcomers.

On November 10th Xavier wrote to the Fathers in Portugal :

" . . . I preach every Sunday in the Cathedral, and I am not so content with my sermons as those who have the patience to hear me. Every day, for an hour or more, I teach the children the prayers. I stay at the hospital, confess the poor sick, say mass and communicate them. I am so importuned with confessions that it is not possible to take them all. My chief occupation is to translate the prayers from Latin into language that can be understood in the Macaçares : not to know the language is very troublesome. . . .

" While waiting in San Thomé for weather to go to Malacca I met a merchant, who had a ship with his merchandise, with whom I talked of the things of God, and God taught him that there is other merchandise, in which he had never dealt, so that he left ship and merchandise, and came with me to the Macaçares, determined to live all his life in poverty, serving God our Lord. He is a man of 35. He was a soldier all his worldly life, and now is a soldier of Christ. He commends himself to your prayers, he is called Juan d'Eyró.

" When I got to Malacca a number of letters from Rome and Portugal were given me, from which I got, and do still get, great comfort. I read them so often that it seems to me that I am there, or that you, most dear brothers, are here, and if not in body *at least in spirit.* . . .

" Above all, most dear brothers, I pray you by the love of God to send out a number of our Company every year, for they are needed, and for going among the heathen scholarship is not necessary, but that they should come very well drilled in the Exercises. So I conclude praying that our Lord may grant us to feel within our soul the power to fulfil and put into practice His will.

" Malacca, 10th Nov., 1545.

" *Your least brother and servant,*

" Francisco." *

" In going among the heathen scholarship is not necessary," Xavier writes in this letter. With regard to this, experience was to teach him a lesson which is still needed.

When in Lisbon he had urged Loyola to send him men even if they had not much *letras,* and he repeats himself continually along these lines till after his return from the Moluccas. The collapse of Francisco Mansillas had probably modified Xavier's views on the subject. For the Saint had commanded him to go out to the Maluccas, and Mansillas had

* *Mon. Xav.,* vol. i. p. 387.

refused. We have seen the wealth of the outpouring of love which Xavier had lavished upon this candidate of " holy simplicity."

When we come to the documents of 1552 we see how he expresses several times the need of more than holy simplicity. For instance, in a letter to Gaspar Barzée* he says : " Beware that you never receive [*i.e.*, take into the Company] persons of little ability, judgment and reason, persons weak and worthless." Again, in the same document, he says : " And don't receive men who have not great parts " [that is the word he uses, just as the Scots talk of a " lad o' pairts "] " and ability for our Company, especially *when they lack learning*." And, again : " Take care that you never make any of them priests ; since our Father Ignatius forbids it so strictly, *unless they have learning* and a life approved many years. Look how many scandals result from the imperfect and *unlearned* who are made priests. Therefore take care not to make anyone a priest *unless he has sufficient learning*. For a man at last shows what he is made of." And to Gaspar also he says the same again ; he tells him to take into the Company few and good, " for we see that they are worth more, and do more, who are few and good, than many who are not." And, again, " Never ordain into the Company persons without knowledge " [sem sciencias].† The Saint's ten years' experience in the East had convinced him that he could not have too good men.

There is another interesting remark in his first letter from Malacca. " My chief occupation," he says, " is to translate the prayers from Latin into a language that can be understood by the Macaçeres ; it is very troublesome not to know the language." Even if there were not other similar passages scattered throughout the letters, which the reader will notice for himself, this sentence would demolish with one stroke the theories of one group of writers who affirm that Xavier possessed the gift of tongues, and the jibes of another group who maintain that he never took the trouble to learn the native languages or to translate anything into them. Some missionaries of the Roman obedience who teach the prayers to their converts in Latin might here with profit take a page out of their great predecessor's book.

* *Mon. Xav.*, vol. i. p. 914, doc. 161, par. 5
† *Ibid.*, doc. 159, p. 907.

A month later, while still in Malacca, Francis writes to his friends in the college at Goa. He has evidently had news of some sort of rebellion on Micer Paulo Camerino's part, and sends him some personal advice.

" Malacca,
" 16th Dec., 1545.

" To the Fathers Paulo Camerino, Juan de Beira and others at Goa,—

" . . . Micer Paulo, I pray you earnestly, for the love of Jesus Christ, to hold your House in much regard, and, above all, I charge you to be obedient to those who govern it; your doing this will give me the greatest pleasure, for if I were there myself I should do nothing against the will of those in charge, but obey them in everything that they might command me. For I hope in God that He has given you to feel within your soul that in nothing can you serve Him more than to deny your own self-will for love of Him."

In this same letter he tells those men who are working in the college at Goa that he is about to set out for the Moluccas, still farther eastward. This journey, like so many of his other journeys, was a tour of exploration. He had learned now, he says, what could be done at Goa and in Cape Comorin, and soon he would be able to see what could be made of the Moluccas.

Xavier's work in Malacca was probably almost altogether, as it had been in Goa, among the Portuguese and the half-castes.

" I did not lack spiritual occupations, both in preaching on Sundays and feast days, and in confessing many—the sick in the hospital where I stayed as well as numbers of sound folk. All this time I taught the Christian doctrine to the children and to those newly converted to the faith. With the help of God our Lord I made peace between many soldiers and citizens, and at night I went through the city with a bell, commending the souls in purgatory, and taking with me a number of the children to whom I was teaching the Christian doctrine."*

One of Xavier's converts here in Malacca was a Jewish

* *Mon. Xav.*, vol. i. p. 398.

doctor. This Jew went often to hear him preach and to mock him, and spent some pains in warning other Jews against the missionary. But Francis got into personal touch with him, talked with him, dined in his house. Soon he was converted, and kept the faith to the end of his days. He had been so clever and so obstinate that his conversion made a great impression.*

Accounts of how the Saint went about in the vicious colonial quarters of Malacca and reformed the morals of those whom he made his friends are very like the accounts of his work in Goa. His manners here, as there, were always joyful, and full of affection and sympathy. When some soldiers put away their cards deferentially at his approach he told them to go on with their game ; soldiers, he said, need not behave like monks. But neither, he said to himself, need they behave like beasts, and he used the popularity he knew so well how to gain for the furtherance of the Gospel. For that end he made himself, as the old historian says, " a soldier to the soldiers and a merchant to the merchants." Du Jarric tells us with what sweet skill he had converted " a man of very loose life " on the way to Malacca :

The pilot of the ship in which he embarked was a man of very loose life, and not one, but many misfortunes had come to him because of this. The Father, seeing the life of this man, set himself to meet him, and went often to the helm of the ship, where he stayed talking with him about the things of his profession, always letting fall, without seeming to do so, some word which touched his heart, and taking care to avoid any subject which might annoy him. The pilot, seeing the great gentleness and meekness of the Father, began to open himself to him, telling him that he was a great sinner and that he wished to make his peace with God by making a good confession, if he would be pleased to hear him as soon as they arrived in port. The Father replied that he was very glad to hear this, and meanwhile entertained him with good and holy talk. Now, when they had landed the pilot did not seem to remember his promise any longer, but put off his confession from day to day, and avoided the presence of the Father as much as possible. But one day as Francis was walking along the sea-shore, his eyes cast up towards heaven as was his custom, they met each other by chance, or rather by divine providence. The pilot,

* *Process*, 1556, Goa (see *Mon. Xav.*, vol. ii. p. 236).

seeing that he could neither hide himself nor fly from the Father, who had already seen him, said to him in jest, "Well, Father, when will you hear my confession?" The Father, smiling, replied thus: "Jesus, my good friend, when will I hear you? Now at once if you wish, and here in this place if you will, walking together on this shore"; and as soon as he had said this he began to make the sign of the Cross, in order to begin the confession. The pilot, making a virtue of necessity, followed, saying the *Confiteor*, although at the beginning he was quite put out, like a man seized suddenly, who does not know what he does; at first he advanced a few steps and then halted, but soon his spirit quite changed, and he took courage, so that what he had begun half perforce, or from shame, he continued with good will and devotion. The Father, seeing this, took him to a little chapel which was quite near by the shore; . . . when they were there alone, the Father, who had heard him say before that he suffered with his knees, brought him a mat to sit upon, not asking anything but that he should have sorrow and repentance for his sins; and the pilot had these in such great measure that he could not continue his confession for the abundance of his tears and sobs, which came from the bottom of his heart. Then, having thrown himself upon his knees and violently beat his breast, he asked forgiveness from God for all the sins he had committed. But desiring to make a general confession of his life he asked the Father for a few days in which to prepare himself. During these he did many acts of penitence and restitution; among others he put away from him his occasions of stumbling, and from that time on gave himself up to virtue and especially to frequenting the sacraments of confession and communion, in such a manner that at the end of his life, full of divine succour, he departed this life in peace, having lived an exemplary life after this change. This he attributed, after God, to the gentleness which Father Francis had had towards him in his weakness.*

Valignano says that Malacca was much reformed by Xavier's visit. But here, as elsewhere, we see him to have been a mighty torrent, ever rushing onward to a further goal. All those conversions and reforms were rather a kind of inevitable accompaniment of his torrential personality than, as those who know him vaguely are apt to think, the first-fruits of harvests which he too soon wearied of reaping. And as Papal Nuncio in the East it was his duty, as his

* P. du Jarric, *Histoire des Choses plus mémorables*, Bordeaux, 1610, vol. i. p. 122.

French biographer says, " to visit, one after the other, all the districts where the faith had already been planted, and to see with his own eyes what ought to be done, what mistakes should be rectified, what activities established, what missionaries sent out." *

On the 1st of January, 1546, he left Malacca for the Moluccas, and on the 14th of February he arrived at Amboina. During the whole of that and the following year he journeyed from island to island, searching out natives who had already been baptized and then forsaken, doing social work among the Portuguese colonists, and preaching and teaching and baptizing wherever he went.

Soon after his arrival in Amboina an armada from New Spain sailed into the port. He writes :

" I was very busy during the three months those eight ships were here in preaching, confessing, visiting the sick, and helping them to a good death, which is very difficult to do with persons who have not lived in great conformity with the law of God, because they lived confidently in continual sins without wishing to break the habit of them. With God's help I reconciled many soldiers, who never live peaceably in this island of Amboina. They [the ships] left for India in May, and my companion Juan d'Eyró and I left for Malucco, 60 leagues from here."

The same letter goes on to tell why he had come to these islands, and describes the voyage eastward from Cape Comorin.

" On the coast of Malucco is a place called Moro, 60 leagues away. In this island many years ago a great lot of people became Christians, but by the death of the clerics who baptized them they have been left abandoned and without teaching. The land of Moro is very dangerous, because its people are very treacherous and put poison in food and drink. So the people who should have looked after the Christians stopped going there. On account of the need of those Christians of Moro for spiritual doctrine, and their need of

* Brou, *Vic de S. François Xavier*, vol. i. p. 371.

somebody to baptize them for the salvation of their souls, and also on account of the need (*necessidad*) I have of losing my temporal life to succour the spiritual life of my neighbour, I determined to go myself to Moro to help the Christians *in spiritual things*. Ready for any danger of death, with all my hope and confidence in God, I wished to be conformed, in my own small and weak way, to the saying of Christ our Redeemer and Lord : *He who would save his soul shall lose it ; but he who has lost his soul for My sake shall find it.* It may be easy to understand the Latin, and the general meaning of this saying of the Lord, but when dangers arise, in which the life about which you wish to decide will probably be lost, and when, in order to prepare yourself to decide to lose your life for God's sake that you may find it in Him, you get down to details, everything else, even this clear Latin, begins to get hazy. And in such a case, however learned you may be, you can understand nothing, it seems to me, unless God our Lord, in His infinite mercy, makes your particular case plain. In such cases we know our flesh, how weak and infirm it is. Many of my devoted friends tried to persuade me against going to such a dangerous land, and, seeing that they could not keep me back, they gave me a number of antidotes against poison. I thanked them for their love and good will. But I omitted to take the antidotes which, with such love and tears, they gave me. I did not wish to load myself with fear which I did not have, and still more, I wished to lose nothing of all my hope which I had placed in God ; so I besought them to remember me in their prayers, which are the surest remedies against poison that can be found.

"In this voyage from Cape Comorin to Malacca I was in many dangers, both from storms at sea and from enemies. I remember one especially. I was in a ship of 400 tons. We sailed more than a league in a strong wind with the rudder scraping the ground all the way. If we had touched any rocks during that time the ship would have gone to pieces. If we had found low water anywhere we would have been stranded. I saw then many tears.* God our Lord wished to prove us by those dangers, and to make us know how little we

* The literature of the sixteenth century makes plain to us that the shedding of tears in those days was by no means regarded as so unmanly a proceeding as it is nowadays.

are worth if we hope in our own strength or trust in created things; and how much we are worth when, getting out of these false hopes and distrusting them, we hope in the Maker of all things, in Whose hand it is to make us strong when dangers are encountered for His love. Those who find themselves in such dangers, and face them for His love alone, believe without any doubt that all creation is in obedience to the Creator, and know clearly that the consolation at such a time is greater than the fear of death, since man must complete his days. And of these experiences, when the work is done and the danger past, a man can neither write nor speak. But an impression of what has been gone through remains on the memory, and forbids us, now or ever, to weary in the service of so good a Lord, and bids us hope in the Lord that He will give strength for His service, for His mercies have no end.*

.   .   .   .   .   .

" I give you this detailed account that you may keep in special sorrow and remembrance this great loss of souls which is due to the lack of spiritual help. Men whose learning and gifts are not enough to be useful to the Company have more than enough knowledge and gifts for those parts, if they have the will to come and live and die with these people. If every year a dozen of them would come, in a short time this evil sect of Mahomet would be destroyed. All would become Christians, and thus God our Lord would not be displeased so much as He is displeased now by there being no one to reprove the vices and sins of infidelity.

" I pray you, my most dear brothers and fathers, by the love of Christ our Lord and of His most holy Mother and of all the saints that are in the glory of Paradise, to have special remembrance of me and to commend me to God continually, for I am in great need of your favour and help. Through this great need of your continual spiritual favour I have come to know by many experiences how God our Lord has aided and favoured me in many works both bodily and spiritual, through your invocations. Let me tell you what I have done, so that I may never forget you. From the letters you wrote me, I have taken [cut out], dearest brothers, as a continual and special remembrance, and for my great comfort, your names, written by your own hands, and these I

* This is the passage quoted on the title-page.

always carry about with me, together with the vow of profession I made,* for the comfort I get from them. To God
our Lord I give thanks first, and then to you, most sweet
Brothers and Fathers. For God made you such that to
carry your names comforts me much. Now, since soon
we shall see each other in the next life more restfully than
in this, I say no more.

"Amboina, 10th May, 1546.

"*Your least brother and son.*"†

To this letter he adds the following vivid postscript, or
hijuela:

" The people of these islands are very barbarous and full of
treachery. They are baser than the black tribes—an utterly
thankless people. There are islands here in which men eat
one another. This is those who are killed in battle when there
is war, and not otherwise. The hands and heels of those
who die naturally are eaten at a great banquet. The people
are such barbarians that in some islands a man who wishes
to have a great feast will ask his neighbour for the loan of his
father, if he is very old, for eating, and promises to give his
own father when he is old and the neighbour wants to have
a banquet. I hope within a month to go to an island where
those killed in war are eaten, and in it also men lend their
fathers when they are old for banquets. The inhabitants
wish to be Christians, and this is why I am going there. There
are abominable fleshly sins among them that you could not
believe, nor do I dare to write.

" The islands are temperate, with great and thick woods
and plenty of rain. They are so mountainous and difficult
to travel that in war the people go up them for defence, so
that they are their forts. There are no horses, nor could
riding be possible. Land and sea often quake. When the
sea quakes those who are sailing think the ship has struck a
rock. To see the earth quake is frightful, and still more the
sea. Many of the islands cast out fire with a greater noise
than any discharge of artillery, however heavy. In the
places where the fire comes out, very large stones are carried

* This was the vow Xavier made, probably in Goa, when in December
1543 he heard from Loyola that he (Loyola) had been appointed General of
the Society.

† *Mon. Xav.*, vol. i. p. 399.

with it by the great impetus with which it comes. For lack of anyone to preach in these islands the torments of hell, God permits hell to open for the confusion of the infidels and their abominable sins.

" Each of these islands has a language of its own, and there is an island where nearly every village has a different language. The Malay language, which is spoken in Malacca, is very general here. When I was in Malacca, I translated with great labour into this language the Creed, with an exposition of the articles, the General Confession, *Paternoster*, *Ave Maria*, *Salve Regina*, and the Commandments, so that they may understand when I speak to them of matters of importance. There is one great lack in all these islands : they have no writings, and very few can write. They write in Malay, and the letters are Arabic, which the Moorish *cacizes* (priests) taught, and teach at present. Before they became Moors [Mohammedan] they could not write. . . .

" I met a Portuguese merchant in Malacca, who was coming from a busy country called China [this is Xavier's first mention of China]. This merchant told me that a very honourable Chinese who came from the King's Court put many questions to him. Among other things, he asked if Christians ate pork. The Portuguese merchant answered ' Yes,' and asked why he wanted to know. The Chinese replied that in his country there are many people who live among mountains, separate from the others, who do not eat pork, and keep many feasts. I do not know what people this is, whether they are Christians who keep the old and new law, like those of Prester John, or if they are the tribes of the Jews of whom nothing is known. They are not Moors, as all say.

" Every year a number of Portuguese ships go from Malacca to Chinese ports. I have charged several to learn about this people, advising them to get information about their ceremonies and customs, so that we may be able to know if they are Christians or Jews. Many say that St. Thomas the Apostle went to China and made many Christians, and that the Greek Church, before the Portuguese mastered India, used to send bishops to teach and baptize the Christians whom St. Thomas said his disciples made in these parts. When the Portuguese gained India, one of these bishops said that, after coming from his country to India, he heard the bishops he met in India say that St. Thomas went to China and made Christians. If I learn anything certain about these parts of China or others, or what I myself may have seen and known by experience, I will write to you."

These speculations of Xavier's about the people who live among the mountains and keep many feasts and do not eat pork are very interesting. It is possible that they may have been Jews; last century there were Jews discovered in China who had been settled there from time immemorial, and who had lost all their Scriptures, and had no Rabbis, and barely a tradition left, but who still "ate not of the sinew that shrank."*

They cannot have been the Nestorian Christians who came to China in A.D. 635, for there were no Nestorians left in China after the great persecutions of Tamerlane in the fourteenth century; but there were—and are still—traces of the Nestorians left among the quasi-Christian secret sects, and especially in the widespread society in Northern China known as the " Religion of the Pill of Immortality." The real name of the great teacher of this society is not disclosed, but his period is that of Jesus Christ, and his symbolical names are " The Warning Bell, which does not trust physical force," " The Quiet Logos," " The King of the Sons of God," " The First Teacher of the True Doctrine of Immortality," " The Teacher from Above."†

Again from Amboina he writes to the recalcitrant Paulo Camerino :

" Amboina, 10 May, 1546.

" Micer Paulo, Brother,

" Many times, both personally and by letters, I have prayed you by the love of God our Lord, and again now once more another time I ask you as strongly as I can, that you try in everything to do the will of those who have the rule in your holy college. For if I were there in your place, in nothing would I take so much trouble as in obeying those who were in charge of my holy house. And believe me, my brother Micer Paulo, it is a very safe rule for hitting the mark in

* See *A Bishop in the Rough* (Diary of the Bishop of Norwich), London 1909, p. 256.
† See P. Y. Saeki, *The Nestorian Monument in China*, pp. 54 ff.

everything to wish always to be commanded by him who commands you, without contradicting him. And on the contrary, it is very dangerous for one to do his own will against orders. And even though you hit the mark when you do the contrary of what is commanded you, believe me, my Brother Micer Paulo, the miss is greater than the hit."

To both Beira and Paulo he adds :

" I beseech you much by the service of God our Lord, that you try to draw into your Company some men of good life who will help us to teach the Christian doctrine throughout these islands. Let each of you try to draw in at least one companion. If he is not a priest, let it be some layman who desires to be avenged on the world, the flesh, and the devil, who have injured him and dishonoured him before God and His saints.

" May our Lord of His infinite mercy unite us in His holy kingdom. More pleasure and rest will be there than we have in this life.

" *Your least brother.*" *

There is yet another letter from Amboina. On May 16th Xavier wrote to John III. of Portugal :

" I have already written to your Highness about the great need India has of preachers. . . . I can say this after the great experience I have had in going through the forts. We have such constant dealings with the infidels and our devotion is so small that men concern themselves about getting rich quickly more than about the mysteries of Christ our Redeemer and Saviour. The native wives of the married, and the half-caste sons and daughters, are content to say that they are Portuguese legally, and not religiously [*portugeses de jeração e nũo da lei.* These native women, this means, acknowledged that they were Portuguese as distinct from subjects of the native princes, but did not consider themselves therefore as Christian. If asked if they were Christians, they would have said, " Yes," because they were subjects of the king, but not otherwise]. The cause is the lack of preachers to teach the religion of Christ.

" The second need which India has in order that those who

* *Mon. Xav.*, vol. i. p. 419 ff.

live in it may be good Christians is that Your Highness should send the Holy Inquisition. For there are many who live by the Mosaic religion and the Moorish sect, without any fear of God or shame of the world. As there are many of them, and they are scattered among all the forts, the Holy Inquisition and many preachers are needed. Let Your Highness provide your loyal and faithful vassals of India with those so needful things." *

Xavier estimated, we see here, that preachers alone could not cope with the Moors and Jews who overran that part of the world. Here he made a fatal mistake, and though the greatness of his life and character overshadowed this mistake, yet we read in it a portentous sign. Here, and elsewhere in this letter, we see that tendency to trust secular and political power and influence which developed after Xavier's death, and made so much of the so-called missionary work in Portuguese India despicable. It is not in its doctrines that the greatest weakness of Roman Catholicism lies, but in its trust in temporal power. If everyone concerned had as single an eye for the glory of God as Francis Xavier, then Church and State and courts of law and Inquisitions and governments and armies and navies would all be but synonyms for the arm of the Lord, and the kingdom of heaven would soon come. But Francis estimated the ideals of those institutions too highly, and so, in time, the vineyard was wasted.

Meanwhile, thanks very largely to the fact that he was separated so much, both by distance and difficult transit, from Goa and all that Goa meant, Xavier appears at this period to be developing a greater air of authority, a new certainty of himself, a more constant serenity. The change can already be felt in some of the letters quoted in this chapter.

Joyfully he went on from island to island, amid almost unparalleled scenes of squalor and savagery. In the little seaport towns there drifted hither and thither the wreckage of humanity, of every race and colour, directed only by avarice and animal desire ; and farther inland the native tribes had hardly yet emerged from the level to which their brothers in the ports, having traversed the long road of

* *Mon. Xav.,* vol. i. p. 421.

civilisation, were now so surely returning. Xavier had entered one of the most stinking backwaters of the world; but here, more than anywhere else even, he comes and goes with laughter and singing, and only weeps when he has to leave his friends, and when he sees them weeping at having to part from him.

Of Ternate, where he arrived in July, 1546, he writes :

" We owe thanks to God for the fruit He has produced through imprinting on the hearts of His creatures chants in His praise and honour among those lately converted to our faith. It was the custom in Malucca for the boys in the streets and the girls and women in the houses, day and night, the farmers in the fields, and the fishers at sea, to sing, instead of vain songs, holy chants, such as the Creed, Paternoster, Ave Maria, Commandments, the Deeds of Mercy and the General Confession, and many other prayers, and all in a language that all could understand, both those lately converted to our faith and those who were not."*

Of these same times Gaspar Lopez, at the Process in Goa in 1556, said :

I saw myself in Malucca how the Malay natives, while carrying goods to the ships, sang the Paternoster and Ave. Formerly, before the coming of the Father, they sang quite other things. And more, in the evenings I could hear those same prayers being sung in all the houses.†

These descriptions remind us of the Bishop of Nola's descriptions of Niceta's missionary work. Niceta wrote the Te Deum, and was " a pioneer spreading abroad the Name of Christ throughout the earth and in the depth of the sea." " O for the wings of a dove," says Nola, " that I might listen to those choirs." And he goes on to describe how Niceta had taught the sailors so that as they rowed they filled the sea-breezes with their godly strains, and the whales heard the loud Amen.‡

* *Mon. Xav.*, vol. i. p. 425.

† There is a hymn beginning " *O God, I love Thee, not because,*" which is popularly ascribed to Xavier. There is no foundation for this supposition, though it is very likely that the Saint had made a copy of the Spanish sonnet on which the hymn is based, and carried it about with him. For an exhaustive study of the question see the *Revue Hispanique*, vol. 1895. See also *Mon. Xav.*, vol. i. pp. 934–940.

‡ A. E. Burn, D.D., *Niceta of Remesiana*, 1905, p. 142, *infra*.

The king of Malucco, Xavier writes, was a Moor, and he gives us a humorous little portrait of him. He was very proud of his vassalage to the king of Portugal, and always spoke of him as " The King of Portugal, my Lord."

" He speaks Portuguese very well. If he does not become a Christian it is not because of his devotion to Mahomet ; the sins of the flesh hold him captive. . . . This poor king shows me such signs of affection that the Moors of his court, important men, are jealous. He wanted me to be his friend, and assured me that in time he would become a Christian. He besought me to love him, though he was a Moor. ' Christians and Moors,' said he, ' we have the same God ; the time will come when we shall be all one.' He took great pleasure in my visits, but I could not persuade him to become a Christian. He promised me to make one of his numerous children a Christian, with an express understanding that he should be the one to succeed him."*

In October of 1546 the Saint passed on to the Islas del Moro. It was the tale which he had heard of the sufferings there which, as we have already seen, had drawn him out to the Moluccas. The Gospel had been preached in these islands, but the inconsistence of the Portuguese manners with the doctrines they preached had made the Gospel of none effect. The story of the career of the Portuguese commander, Don Jorge de Menezes, who went to the Moluccas in 1526 is typical. He landed amiably, bringing with him as a present to the chief a tapestry representing the marriage of the Prince of Wales with Katherine of Aragon. When this was hung up the chief trembled and bade them take it down and put it away, for he believed the figures were enchanted, and would come to life in the night and kill him. Don Jorge, however, took the rebuff smiling, and proceeded to more important business. This was the clearing of the Spaniards out of the Moluccas, which, according to Portuguese interpretation of the Papal division of the New World, did not belong to Spain, and therefore belonged to Portugal. When he had done this successfully he poisoned this native king of Ternate and shut up his heirs in prison. He also imprisoned a near relative of the murdered king's, because he suspected him of having stolen his favourite Chinese pig. The

* *Mon. Xav.*, vol. i. p. 430.

native population revolted, and the King's relative, who was a favourite with the people, had to be released. But naturally the ill-will had not subsided. Natives attacked the colonists; Don Jorge replied by seizing three of them, cutting off the hands of two, and tying up the other alive to be worried to death by savage dogs. Next he captured and beheaded the native regent, and thereupon all the islanders left the island. Don Jorge was then considered to have failed in his office, and was recalled and banished to the Brazils. Missionaries came to Ternate, and some converts were made. In 1536 the imprisoned king was sent to Goa, where he purchased a clean bill at the price of declaring himself a Christian. He died on the return journey, leaving his island by will to the king of Portugal. His late subjects, in disgust, abandoned the religion of their persecutors and reverted to the faith of their fathers.

The sordid tale of Portuguese government in the Moluccas has one bright page, the page which records the administration of Antonio Galvão. Of him Whiteway says: "He broke up the league of the natives against the Portuguese by dint of sheer hard fighting, and then he won over his defeated opponents by his justice." This man spent the last seventeen years of his life in his native land in an almshouse, because he had behaved honestly and generously during his term of office. But it is said that he was never made haughty by his success in the Moluccas, nor soured by his neglect in Portugal. He is called by Jesuit historians the soldier-missionary, for he himself toured about the islands visiting and encouraging the Christians, and establishing missionaries. But even this man could not atone for all that had happened. Shortly before Xavier arrived in the Islas del Moro the missionaries had all been poisoned, and the natives had, for the second time, reverted to their old religion.

These were the islands which Francis, with that remote and mystic humour which is so characteristic of him, called the Islands of Hope in God:

" I never remember having had so great and so continual spiritual comfort as in these islands, nor so little sense of bodily troubles, though I was going constantly across islands surrounded by enemies, and peopled with not very certain friends, and in lands where all remedies for bodily sickness were wanting, as well as all aids of secondary causes, for the preservation of life. Islands of Hope in God, it would be better to call them, than Islas de Moro." *

The material aspect of those equatorial islands is strange and terrifying enough. By day the air is heavy with smoke, and by night the ocean is lit by fire, from the burning volcanoes.

" When they asked me," Xavier says, " where that was, I told them it is the hell to which all those who worship idols go."†

Besides working on the coasts of the islands, Francis made at least one expedition into the wild interior. No journey could have been more perilous or more difficult. He went on foot through forests and jungles where to-day a European only ventures in a palanquin hung from long bamboo poles. The natives were not easy to reach. Partly from choice, and partly out of fear of their Mohammedan enemies, they hid themselves in the very depths of the forests. If a traveller approached, they all fled within doors, and the village became silent and lifeless. Even to-day, a modern traveller says, a visitor to those villages produces the same effect. Xavier passed along the silent rows of huts, singing hymns as he went, till gradually the doors were withdrawn a little, and the natives peered out, and came toward him, like wild birds to a bird-charmer. And then he smiled on them and touched them and caressed them, " as a father does his children," says old Père Jarric.

Of his success among those people Xavier does not say much. Valignano says, " Francis believed that the seed of the word of God then sown in that sterile land was so powerful that it would bring forth fruit and be reaped in abundance by his sons, as it was reaped afterwards."‡ And Xavier, when he went onward, did not leave this difficult field, into which he had cut his perilous way so bravely, without help. Father Beira and others were put in charge, and seven years later we hear of persecutions and martyrdoms at the hands of neighbouring native tribes. In 1569 we read that in the Islas del Moro are the most flourishing missions of all the Moluccas.

In January, 1547, Xavier returned to Ternate, on his way back to India. His plan was to go straight on south to

* *Mon. Xav.*, vol. i. p. 427.   † *Ibid.*, vol. i. p. 428.   ‡ *Ibid.*, vol. i. p. 76.

R

Amboina, and there join the fleet which was shortly going westward *via* Malacca. But his friends in Ternate surrounded the ship on which he was about to embark, and would not let him go. They promised if he would wait with them a little while to send him on to Amboina in a fast boat in time to catch the fleet. So he stayed with them for three months. During those months, besides his usual labours, Valignano tells us that he preached every Wednesday and Friday to the native women belonging to the colonists. He spoke in the patois, half-native, half-Portuguese, which they could most easily understand. After the preaching he questioned them and taught them till they were able to embrace the " law of God."

It was probably at this time that Xavier composed and wrote down in the Malay tongue the following exposition. It was designed, Teixeira says, for the newly converted, for children and for simple folk. He repeated it and taught it to those islanders, and explained one part or other of it to his hearers every day. This document is more characteristic of Xavier than anything else he has left except the Letters, and is very valuable in helping us to gain an idea of his missionary methods.

EXPOSITION WHICH THE BLESSED FATHER FRANCIS MADE OF THE APOSTLES' CREED.

1. Christians, rejoice to hear and know how God in creation made everything for the use of men. First He created heaven and earth, angels, sun, moon and stars, birds and beasts that live in the land and the rivers, and the fish that live in the waters ; and when all things had been created at last He created man in His likeness.

2. The first man whom God created was Adam, the first woman Eve ; and after God created Adam and Eve in the terrestrial Paradise, He blessed and married them, and commanded them to have children and to people the land ; and from Adam and Eve we, all the peoples of the world, come ; and since God did not give Adam more than one wife, clearly it is in opposition to God that Moors and heathen and bad Christians have many wives.

3. And also it is true that fornicators live in opposition to God, since God first married Adam and Eve before He commanded them to increase and multiply having legitimate children [sons of blessing]. And thus those who adore idols as the unbelievers do, and those who believe in witchcraft, in lots and in diviners, sin greatly against God, for they adore and believe in the devil

and take him for their lord, forsaking the God who created them, and gave them soul and life and body and all they have. These miserable creatures by their idolatries lose heaven, which is the place of souls, and the glory of Paradise, for which they were created.

4. But the true Christians and loyal to their God and Lord believe and adore willingly and heartily the one God and Lord, true creator of heaven and of earth. And well they show it when they go to the churches and see the images which are the reminders of the Saints who are with God in the Glory of Paradise.

5. So Christians put their knees on the ground when they are in the churches, and lift their hands to the heavens where is the Lord God, who is all their good and comfort, and confess in the words of St. Peter, " *I believe in God, Father Almighty, Creator of Heaven and earth.*" God created the angels in the heavens before the men in the earth. St. Michael, chief of all, and the greater part of the angels at once adored the Lord God, giving Him thanks and praises that He had created them : Lucifer, on the contrary, and many angels with him, were not willing to adore their Creator, but said with pride, Let us go up and be like God who is in the high heavens ; and for the sin of pride God thrust Lucifer and the angels with him from Heaven to hell.

6. Lucifer, in envy of Adam and Eve, the first human beings who were there created in grace, tempted them with the sin of pride in the terrestrial Paradise, telling them they would be as gods if they ate of the fruit which their Creator had forbidden them. Adam and Eve, desirous of being as gods, consented to the temptation of the enemy, and conquered by the demon they forthwith ate of the forbidden fruit, and so lost the grace in which they were created, and for their sins the Lord God thrust them out of the terrestrial Paradise. Outside it they lived nine hundred years in trouble, doing penance for the sin they had committed ; and so great was their sin that neither Adam nor his sons could satisfy it, nor again gain the glory of Paradise, which they had lost by their pride of wishing to be as God ; so the gates of Heaven were shut upon Adam and his sons because of their sin.

7. Oh, Christians, what will become of us the wretched ? If the demons for a sin of pride were thrust from the heavens to hell, and Adam and Eve for another sin of pride from the terrestrial Paradise, how shall we, miserable sinners, ascend to the heavens with such sins, and we so clearly lost ?

8. The High God, sovereign and powerful, moved with pity and compassion, seeing our great misery, sent the angel St. Gabriel from the heavens to the city of Nazareth, where was

the Virgin Mary, with a message which said: "God hail thee, Mary, full of grace, the Lord be with thee: blessed art thou among women: the Holy Spirit will come over thee, and the virtue of the highest God will lighten thee, and what will be born of thee will be called Jesus, Son of God." The Virgin St. Mary answered the angel St. Gabriel: "Behold the servant of the Lord; be His will done in me." In the same instant that the Virgin St. Mary obeyed the message which St. Gabriel brought her from God, the Holy Spirit formed in the womb of this Virgin a human body of her virgin blood; together He created a soul in the same body, and the second Person of the Most Holy Trinity, God the Son, in that instant was incarnate in the womb of the Virgin Mary, thus uniting and joining that soul and the so holy body; and from the day that the Son of God was incarnate until the day of His birth nine months passed.

9. At the end of this time Jesus Christ, Saviour of all the world, being God and true man, was born of the Virgin Mary, remaining virgin in the birth and after as before it: And St. Andrew confessed it, saying, *I believe in Jesus Christ, Son of God, our only Lord*; and after him at once St. John said, *I believe that Jesus Christ was conceived of the Holy Spirit and born of the Virgin Mary.* In Bethlehem, near to Jerusalem, Christ our Redeemer was born: then the angels and the Virgin His mother, with her spouse Joseph, and the three [Kings inserted in one MS.] and many others, adored Him as Lord.

10. But Herod, who was evil, being king in Jerusalem, with the covetousness of reigning, desired to kill Him. Joseph was advised by an angel to flee from Bethlehem to Egypt, and he took Jesus Christ and the Virgin His mother, because Herod desired to kill Jesus. St. Joseph went to Egypt with Christ and His mother, where he was until Herod died of an evil death; for he was so cruel that in Bethlehem and its neighbouring villages he killed all the men children from two years downwards, thinking that he would kill Jesus Christ among them. After Herod died the Virgin and St. Joseph with the Child Jesus returned to their own country, to the city of Nazareth, by command of the angel.

11. When Christ was twelve years He went up from Nazareth to the Temple of Jerusalem, where were the doctors of the law, and He expounded to them the Scriptures of the Prophets and Patriarchs, who spoke of the coming of the Son of God, and all were astonished when they saw His wisdom. Returning to Nazareth, He was there until the age of nearly thirty years; and then He went to the river Jordan, where St. John Baptist was baptizing many people: and in this river Jordan St. John baptized Jesus Christ; and from there Christ went to the wilder-

ness, where for forty days and forty nights He did not eat. The
demon in the wilderness, without knowing that Jesus Christ
was Son of God, tempted Him with three sins—that is to say,
gluttony, covetousness, and vainglory.

12. And in all the temptations Christ conquered the demon.
And from the wilderness with victory He descended to Galilee
and converted many people, and commanded the demons to
come out of the bodies of the people, and the demons obeyed
the command of Jesus Christ, coming out of the bodies of the
men where they were; and the people who saw this were
astonished and said : " Who is this, whom the demons obey ? "
So the fame of Jesus Christ grew greatly among the people,
because they saw that the demons obeyed Him, and that He did
many miracles. The men who heard the holy preaching of
Jesus Christ and saw the great power which He had over the
demons began to believe in Jesus Christ, and brought Him the
sick : He cured all of whatsoever infirmity they had.

13. And afterwards Christ called the twelve Apostles and the
seventy-two Disciples, and took them in His company around
the districts where He was teaching the mysteries of the Kingdom
of God. Christ preached to the people, and did miracles which
proved the truth of what He preached. In the presence of the
Apostles and Disciples Christ gave sight to the blind, speech to
the dumb, hearing to the deaf, and life to the dead : He healed
the lame and the maimed. The Apostles and Disciples who saw
this each time believed more and more in Jesus Christ. Christ
gave them such wisdom and virtue that they preached to the
people, though they were fishers who had no learning except
what the Son of God taught them. In the name and virtue of
Jesus Christ the Apostles did miracles, healing many infirmities,
casting the demons from the bodies of men in sign that what they
preached of the coming of the Son of God was the truth.

14. Such was the fame of Jesus Christ and His Disciples among
the people that the principal Jews agreed to kill Him, in their
envy of Him and His works, for they saw that all followed and
praised the teaching of Jesus.

15. When the Pharisees recognised that they were losing the
honour and credit which they formerly had among the Jews
before Jesus Christ was manifested to the world, moved with
envy, they took Jesus Christ, insulted Him freely, carrying Him
from one house to another, scorning and making a mock of
Him.

16. And because of the great hate the Pharisees had of Jesus
Christ they carried Him to the house of Pontius Pilate, where the
Pharisees accused Him with false witnesses, and Pilate, to please
the Jews, scourged Jesus Christ so cruelly that from the feet to

the head all His holy body was wounded; and, thus cruelly scourged, Pilate handed Him to the Jews to crucify Him.

17. And before they crucified Him they put on the head of Jesus Christ a cruel crown of thorns, and a reed in His right hand; and the soldiers, to make a mock of Jesus Christ, placed themselves on their knees before Him, saying, "God hail You, King of the Jews," and spitting in His face and buffeting Him; and with a reed He carried they struck Him on the head, and, finally, on Mount Calvary, near Jerusalem, the Jews crucified Jesus Christ, and thus Christ died on the Cross to save sinners; so that the most holy Soul of Jesus Christ was truly separated from His most precious and most holy body when He expired on the Cross, the divinity being always united with the most holy soul of our Redeemer Jesus Christ, the same divinity remaining with the most holy and precious body of Christ on the Cross and in the sepulchre.

18. And at the death of Jesus Christ the sun was darkened, ceasing to give its light; the whole earth trembled, and the rocks divided, striking one another; the monuments of the dead opened, and many of the holy men rose and went to the city of Jerusalem, where they appeared to many; and those who saw these signs in the death of Jesus Christ said, "Truly Jesus Christ was Son of God"; and because this is so the Apostle James said: *I believe that Jesus Christ suffered under the power of Pontius Pilate, was crucified, and dead and buried.*" Jesus Christ was God, since He was the second person of the most Holy Trinity, and also He was true man, since He was son of the Virgin Mary and has a rational soul and human body; and inasmuch as He was man, truly He died on the Cross when He was crucified; for death is nothing else but a separation of the soul, leaving the body to which it gave life, and the most holy soul of Jesus Christ was separated from the body when He expired on the Cross.

19. Then, having expired, the most holy soul of Jesus Christ, being united to the divinity of God the Son, as it had always been from the instant when the Lord God created it, descended to Limbo, which is a place below the ground, where were the Holy Fathers, Prophets, and Patriarchs and many other just men, waiting for the Son of God, Jesus Christ, who was to withdraw them from Limbo and take them to Paradise.

20. In every time, beginning with Adam and Eve until now, were men good and bad; the good, being friends of God, reproved with words of truth the evil for their vices and sins, because they offended God, their Lord and Creator; and the bad, being slaves and captives of the demon, persecuted the good, friends of God, taking them, and exiling them, and wounding them, and

killing them, and doing them many evils : so that when the good died their souls went to Limbo; and the Limbo because it is below the ground is called inferno [hell].

21. Lower than Limbo is a place called Purgatory : to this Purgatory go the souls of those who, when they die, are without mortal sin, and on account of the past sins, which they did in their life, and for which before their death they had not made complete penance, go to Purgatory, where are very great torments of fire, in order to pay the evils and sins done in their life ; and when they have paid the penance of their sins, they issue from Purgatory, and go at once to Paradise.

22. The last place which is below the ground is called the infernal hell [*inferno infernal*], where are great torments of fire and miseries : if men would think on this for an hour daily, and if they knew the troubles of the infernal hell, they would not sin as they do : in this hell is Lucifer, and all the demons who were thrust out of heaven, and all who die in mortal sin.   Those who go to this hell have no remedy of salvation [*nenhum remedio de salvação*], but for ever and ever and without end of ends have to be in it.

23. Oh, brothers ! how is it that we have so little fear of going to hell, since every day we do the greatest sins ?   It is a sign that we have little faith, since we live like men who do not believe in the *inferno infernal*.   The Church and the Saints who are with God in Heaven never pray for those in hell, for these have no remedy to go to Paradise ; but the Church and the Saints pray for the dead who are in Purgatory and for the living.

24. Jesus Christ died on Friday, and the most holy soul of Jesus Christ, always united with the divinity, descended to Limbo, and drew all the souls which were then in Limbo waiting for Him.   Then on the third day, which is the Lord's Day, He rose from among the dead, His most holy soul again taking the same body which it left when He died on the Cross.   After that Jesus Christ rose again in a glorious body, he appeared to the Virgin Mary, His Mother, and to the Apostles and Disciples, and to His friends, who were sad for His death ; and with His Glorious Resurrection He consoled the sad and disconsolate, pardoning sinners their sins ; and many believed in Jesus Christ, after they saw Him rise again from among the dead, who formerly were not willing to believe that He should die and rise again.   And St. Thomas affirmed that this is true when he said : *I believe that Jesus Christ descended to the hells, and on the third day rose again from the dead.*

25. And after Jesus Christ rose again He was forty days in this world, teaching the Disciples what they had to believe and do and teach the world in order to go to Paradise ; and in this time

He showed His Holy Resurrection to be true, and those who doubted in His death, that He would not rise again : and in those forty days He appeared to the Apostles and Disciples, and to many other His friends, who doubted that He would not rise again when they saw Him die on Mount Calvary on the Cross. And in these forty days those who did not believe during the Passion and Death of Jesus Christ that He was to rise again on the third day completely believed without ever doubting that He was true Son of God, Saviour of the whole world, since He rose to life from death.

26. At the end of the forty days Jesus Christ went to the Mount Olivet, whence He was to ascend to the high heavens, and with Him went the Virgin Mary, His Mother, and His Apostles and Disciples, and many others ; and from this Mount Olivet Jesus ascended to the high heavens in body and in soul, and carried in His company to the glory of Paradise all the souls of the Holy Fathers whom He drew from Limbo. The gates of the heavens opened when Jesus Christ ascended to the high heavens ; the angels of Paradise came to accompany Jesus Christ to carry Him with great glory to God the Father, whence to save sinners He descended in the womb of the glorious Virgin Mary, taking human flesh to pay in it our debts ; so that Jesus Christ, Son of God, for sins became man, was born, died, rose again, ascended to the heavens, where He is seated at the right hand of God the Father. And since this is truth, James the Less said : *I believe that Jesus Christ ascended to the heavens, and is seated at the right hand of God the Father Almighty.*

27. And since this world had a beginning, it is bound to have an end, and so it will finish, and thus as Jesus ascended to the heavens so He will descend to give each one what he deserved ; and so it is true that all who believe in Jesus Christ and keep His commandments will be judged that they may go to the glory of Paradise ; and those who would not believe in Jesus Christ, such as the Moors, Jews, and heathen, will go to hell without any redemption. Bad Christians who would not keep the ten commandments will be judged by Jesus Christ to go to hell.

28. At the end of the world all then living will die, for every man is born with this condition that he must die : since Jesus Christ our Redeemer died and rose again for sins, we all must die and rise again. Besides this, the bodies of good men who may be alive at the end of the world will not be holy and glorious, or ready to ascend with them to heaven ; therefore they must die ; and in their resurrection they will take the same bodies, yet not subject to suffering as formerly. So when Jesus Christ descends from heaven on the day of judgment to judge the good and the bad,

all will rise again, beginning from the first to the last who died. And as this is truth, St. Philip said: *I believe that Jesus Christ will come from Heaven to judge the living and the dead.*

29. When we Christians bless ourselves we confess the truth as to the most Holy Trinity, that there are three persons, one God. The first is the person of God the Father, and the second person of God the Son, and the third person of God the Holy Spirit; and all three persons are one only God, threefold and one. God the Father is not made nor created nor begotten. The Son of God the Father is begotten and not made nor created. The Holy Spirit proceeds from the Father and from the Son, not created, nor made, nor begotten. When we make the sign of the Cross we show this order of proceeding, placing the right hand on the head, saying *in Name of the Father*, in sign that God the Father is not made nor created nor begotten; and then placing the hand on the breast, saying *and of the Son*, in sign that the Son was begotten of the Father, and not made nor created; and then placing the hand on the left shoulder, saying *and of the Spirit*; and passing the right hand by the head to the right shoulder, saying *Holy*, in sign that the Holy Spirit proceeds from the Son and from the Father.

30. Every good Christian is obliged to believe firmly, without doubting, in the Holy Spirit and in His holy inspirations, which protect us from doing evil, and move our hearts to keep the ten commandments of God, and the commandments of the holy universal Mother Church, and to fulfil the works of mercy, corporal and spiritual. And as this is truth, the Apostle St. Bartholomew said: *I believe in the Holy Spirit.*

31. All we faithful Christians are obliged to believe, without doubting, what the Apostles and Disciples and Martyrs and all the Saints of Jesus Christ believed of Jesus Christ concerning all that is necessary to believe for our salvation, as to His divinity and humanity, for Jesus Christ was God and true man. Also in general we are obliged to believe firmly, without doubting, in all that those who rule and govern the universal Church of Jesus Christ believe, for they are inspired and ruled by the Holy Spirit in what they have to do as to the government of the universal Church in the matters of our holy faith, in the which they cannot err, because they are ruled by the Holy Spirit. We must also believe Scriptures of our religion [*ley*], and of Jesus Christ; and further we are obliged to believe such of the holy canons and councils as are ordered by the Church, and the ordinances made by the Pope, Cardinals, Patriarchs, Archbishops, and Bishops, and Prelates of the Church, when in all these things, without doubting, we believe all that those who rule and govern the universal Church of Jesus Christ believe. This

is what the Apostle Evangelist St. Matthew charged when he said : *I believe in the holy Catholic Church.*

32. And so we true Christians believe that the good works and merits of Jesus Christ are communicated to and profit all other Christians who are in a state of grace : and as in the natural body the works of one member profit all the body, so it is in the spiritual body (which is the Church).

33. And as chiefly from the head there descends to the members and is communicated to them their sustentation, so from Christ our Lord, only begotten Son of God, who is Head of all the true faithful, there is communicated spiritual sustentation by means of the seven sacraments of the Church—that is to say, by baptism, by confirmation (which we call chrism) by the Most Holy Sacrament of the altar, by the sacrament of penance, by the extreme unction, by the sacrament of the orders, by matrimony. For whoever takes duly any one of these sacraments is granted grace by which his soul lives spiritual life, which Christ our Lord, only begotten Son of God, merited by the most holy works He did in this world, labouring and suffering injuries and the death of the Cross to free sinners from the captivity of the demon, and to turn them to the true knowledge of their God, communicating to them His own merits. And not only are the merits of the Son of God communicated, as from the head to the other members, but further those of the other saints are communicated to all the faithful, who are in grace, as the goods of one member of the body are communicated to the other members of the same body.

34. Christians further confess and believe : that God our Lord has power to pardon the sins by which the sinners separate themselves from Him, and lose the grace which He had before communicated to them : and that this power He gives and communicates to the priests of the Catholic Church, by which communication they now have power to absolve from sins those whom they find worthy to be absolved before God.

35. And accordingly men must so prepare to do what they are obliged for the safety of their soul, so that the priests may judge them (in conformity to what God commands) as worthy to be absolved ; and having done this and having confessed at the obligatory times, and being absolved by the priest, they again gain the grace of God, and are pardoned their sins. And this is what St. Mathias said : *I believe the communion of Saints and the remission of sins.*

36. And because it is a just thing to believe in the goodness of our Lord and His infinite mercy which will not leave without reward those who serve Him in this life, nor without chastisement those who offend and break His precepts : we believe in the

resurrection of the flesh, which is to say, that we all have to rise again in the body, the very same as we are now, after we have passed temporal death, and that it is certain that our Lord, according to His justice, will then give for ever the reward to the bodies which in this world for His love suffered troubles and persecutions, and were afflicted for not consenting in sins ; and since their souls shared in trouble, they also may enjoy glory and rest.

37. And on the contrary (we believe) that the bodies of the bad, who in this life cared to do their own will and fulfil their appetites rather than keep the law of God our Lord, should be eternally chastised in the hells, since they offended the eternal Lord God, their resurrection will be made in the day of final judgment, when all born in this life must rise in body and soul : the bad to be cast into hell for their sins, and the good to enter the glory of Paradise with God our Lord. And this is what St. Thaddeus said : *I believe the resurrection of the flesh.*

38. And as our soul is like God almighty and eternal in so far as it is spiritual, and in the powers which God Himself gave it— that is to say, will, understanding and memory—and the desire of men is to last for ever, it is meet that a creature, so excellent as is man, should fulfil this longing, and so all we Christians believe that it will be fulfilled ; and therefore we believe in the life eternal, which we confess will never have end ; rather after the resurrection of the flesh, wherein the soul, which never dies, has again to take its body, will live together with it, as they are now united, and by a much better mode, eternally with God, and will enjoy in the heavens, together with the angels, the Presence of their Creator and Lord, and of all the celestial benefits, the which are so great that, however much one may in this life think of them and imagine them, it is not possible to reach or understand their grandeur.

39. There the Saints rest, without any opposition ; there nothing is lacking of all they can desire ; there no evil is found, nor can it be found nor exist, nor is there lacking, nor will ever be lacking, all good, which the blessed will enjoy eternally. And this is what St. Matthias said : *I believe in the life eternal.**

Many copies were made of this composition, and it soon became well known throughout the Maluccas. After Xavier's death it used to be read aloud on feast days in places where there were no priests, and those who understood it explained it to the others, while the boys and girls learned it by heart. It was printed in Goa in 1556.

* *Mon. Xav.*, vol. i. pp. 831–44.

At last, in mid-April of 1547, just after Easter, the moment came when Xavier had to leave Malucco. We have his own description of the parting :

"When I left Malucco I embarked about midnight to avoid the weeping and mourning of friends—men and women devoted to me. This was not sufficient, for I could not hide from them. So the night, and the separation from my spiritual sons and daughters, suggested to me that perhaps my absence would make for the salvation of their souls."*

This, in the original, is one of Xavier's most elliptical and obscure sentences, but it seems to mean that as he himself, in the darkness and hour of separation, had felt himself thrown back upon God, so these poor folk, left in the dark without him, might feel the same, and be given what they sought.

" Before I left Malucco I had ordered the Christian doctrine [i.e., teaching] should be continued in a church, and a commentary which I made shortly on the articles of the faith to be learned by the new converts instead of the prayers.
" . . . During this time I was very much occupied in reconciling people to each other, for the Portuguese are very quarrelsome."†

The Saint took back with him twenty young natives to be educated in the college at Goa. During the few days which he spent at Amboina on his westward journey he revisited the seven Christian districts there, and had a little chapel erected in each of them. Not long afterwards many of these Christians suffered martyrdom. From 1558–62 they were constantly persecuted by the Moors. But they had for leader one especially brave soul, a former native guide of Xavier's called Manoel. Gonçalvez tells us that when they threatened him he replied :

I am a poor Amboinese with no learning : I don't know what it is to be a Christian, and I don't know what God is, but I know one thing which Father Francis taught me, that it is good to die for Jesus Christ. Because the Father said this I can't become

* *Mon. Xav.*, vol. i. p. 429.　　† *Ibid.*, vol. i. p. 432.

a Mohammedan. If he had not said it, perhaps I would be fallen like some others, but thanks to that saying, my heart is so fixed that it cannot accept any other faith or any other law but that of our Lord Jesus Christ.

Soon after this some villains got hold of him and were about to shoot him dead. Manoel asked for one instant longer, and pulling out a cross which was planted in the ground, he stretched out his arms upon it, saying, " Father Francis said that a Christian ought to die on a cross. Fire now." But the murderers, abashed before the sacred symbol, lowered their guns.*

A year or two later the persecutions began again, and six hundred converts were tortured to death or burnt alive. One of them whom Francis had baptized is said to have died saying these words : " I love my faith better than life. I am a Christian. If the Moors let me go I will live a Christian, and I will die a Christian if they slay me."

In July, 1547, Xavier was back in Malacca, and he stayed there until December of the same year. In September he was joined by three members of the Company—Beira, Nunez, and Ribeiro,

" During the month we were together," he writes, " I received great consolation in seeing that they were servants of God, very well suited to do good work in the Moluccas . . . helped by the experience I gained there I have been able to instruct them as to how they would have to manage."†

The student of his life begins now to have a growing impression of Francis as a man to whom prayer has become a dominating passion. As we get on intimate terms with him through the study of the Letters, we instinctively weed out many of the old traditions upon which our impression of his character used to be so largely based. But there are some stories which remain, beautiful and stately and, we cannot but see, deeply rooted in truth. Among these are the simple accounts—belonging chiefly to his later period— of his innumerable trysts with God.

* Quoted by Cros, *Vie de S. François Xavier,* vol. i p. 351.
† *Mon. Xav.,* vol. i. p. 431.

During this visit to Malacca he usually slept in the sacristy, and often, by night, he was seen to enter the empty church.

Frequently, while he and his friends were sitting talking together, he would unobtrusively slip away. More than once they followed him at a distance, only to find they had intruded upon a secret and sacred communion.

It was at this time that Francis first heard of Japan. Of the Japanese Yajiro, to whom he refers in the following letter, we will hear more fully later.

" When I was in the city of Malacca some Portuguese merchants gave me great news. They are trustworthy men. Some very large islands were discovered, a little time ago, called the islands of Japon. There, according to the Portuguese, much fruit might be gained for the increase of our holy faith, more than in any other parts of the Indies, for they are a people most extremely desirous of knowledge, which the Indian heathen are not. A Japon, called Yajiro, came with these merchants to look for me, as the Portuguese who went there from Malacca had talked so much about me. . . . He had told the Portuguese of certain sins done in his youth, and had asked them how God might pardon him. The Portuguese advised him to come with them to see me. He did so, coming to Malacca with them. When he came I had left for Malucco. When he found out that I had gone there, he embarked again to go to his own country of Japon. When within sight of the islands of Japon they were surprised by such a storm of wind that they were like to perish. Then the ship returned again to Malacca, where he found me, and was delighted. He came to seek me with a great desire to know about our religion [ley]. He can speak Portuguese pretty well, so he understood all I told him, and I what he said to me.

" If all the Japanese are like this, so eager to learn as Yajiro, I think they are the most inquiring people in all the lands hitherto discovered. This Yajiro wrote down the [teaching on the] articles of faith which I have made, when he came to the class. He went very often to the church to pray. He asked me numerous questions. He is a man who is very anxious to know, and that is the mark of a man who will profit greatly, and will quickly come to a knowledge of the truth.

" . . . I asked Yajiro whether the Japanese would become Christians if I went with him to his land.   He answered that his countrymen would not become Christians straight away. First, they would ask many questions, and would see what I answered and what I knew, and, above all, whether I lived in accordance with what I said.   If I did these two things— spoke well, satisfying their questions, and lived without their finding anything to blame me, then half a year after they knew me the king, the nobility, and all the other people of discretion would become Christians.   He tells me they are a people who rule themselves only by reason.

" . . . I think by what I am feeling within my soul that I or some one of the Company will go to Japon within two years, although it is a very dangerous voyage, both because of great tempests and of Chinese thieves who sail that sea to rob.   Many ships are lost there.   Therefore pray to God, my very dear Fathers and Brothers, for those who may go thither, for it is a voyage on which many are lost.   Meanwhile Yajiro will learn the Portuguese language better, and see India and the Portuguese there, and our style and way of living.   And at the same time we must catechise him.   And seeing that Yajiro can write very well in Japanese, we shall translate all the Christian doctrine into that language with a commentary on the articles of the faith which will treat fully of the coming of Jesus Christ our Lord. . . ." *

In December 1547 the Saint left Malacca for Cochin.

* *Mon. Xav.*, vol. i. p. 433 ff.

CHAPTER XVI

INDIA REVISITED

(January, 1548—April, 1549)

On January 12th, 1548, Francis was once more in India. On reaching Cochin he found the ships almost ready to sail for Europe, so he paused there for some days to get his letters written and sent off. At this time there seems to have surged over him a great wave of depression. There are passages in all the letters from Cochin witnessing to it. And there are words in a letter to Loyola which record that his faith and ardour were flagging beneath the strain.

" I do beg of you, for the Lord Jesus' sake, to look on those children of yours in India, and send out some man pre-eminent in virtue and sanctity whose vigour and ardour may arouse my torpor." *

There is a similar note of profound depression in the following letter to the King of Portugal. The preamble is a curious impressionistic record of a mind that has evidently been in great misery and uncertainty.

" . . . I have been wondering whether it would be well to write to your Highness what I feel within my soul to be the best means for the increase of our holy faith. On the one hand it seemed to me to be a service to God ; and on the other hand I judged that it ought not to come to light, even though I wrote it. Not to write seemed to me a burdening of my conscience. Since God our Lord was revealing it to me for some purpose, I did not imagine it could be for anything else than to write to your Highness, so I write what I am painfully feeling within my soul. What I write of ought not to be done. And now, if your Highness is accused by my letters at the hour of your death before God, the excuse that you did not know of these things cannot be accepted.

* Only a Latin version of this letter has, so far, been discovered (see *Mon. Xav.*, vol. i. p. 448).

" Let your Highness believe that this gives me great pain, since I wish for nothing else but to live and die here, so that I may help to clear your conscience, seeing you have such a great love for the Company. So, Sire, in coming to the conclusion that I ought to write to you, I found myself in great confusion. At last I determined to clear my conscience by writing what it tells me as a result of the experience I have gained out here, in India, Malacca, and the Moluccas.

" Your Highness must know that here, as elsewhere, holy jealousies often prevent much service being done to God our Lord. One says, ' I will do it ' ; another says, ' No, but I will ' ; and others, ' Since I don't do it I'm not pleased that you should'; others, ' I do all the work, and another gets all the thanks and advantage ' ; and in this way the time is passed. . . .

" If there are to be many Christians made here, and if those who are Christians are to be much favoured, and to be free from being harmed or defrauded by anyone, either Portuguese or unbelievers, I know of only one remedy " :—

The remedy which in his misery and disheartenment he proposes, both in this letter and in the next one to Rodriguez, makes rather painful reading. Of course we must remember Xavier was experiencing what nearly all missionaries do, that their greatest hindrance is the godless life of their fellow-countrymen ; he had seen the injustices done by Portuguese to the natives ; he knew the abuses everywhere among Government officials, and he felt the king was responsible for his officers, as, indeed, under such absolute monarchy, he was.

" Let your Highness inform the governor who is here, or whom you send from home, that you entrust him, above all religious persons here, with the increase of our holy faith in India, naming all of us here, and saying that you trust in him alone, after God, for the unburdening of the heavy conscience which you carry, because owing to the fault of the governors so few Christians are being made in India. And direct the Governor to write to your Highness about the Christians made, and the opportunities for making more . . . and if he do not greatly increase our holy faith, assure him that you are determined to punish him, and say with a solemn oath that you will hold all his estates as forfeit

S

for the works of the *Santa Misericordia*, when he comes to
Portugal, and further, that you will keep him in irons for
many years, giving him plainly to understand that no
excuses will be accepted. I cannot here say all I know, it
would hurt your Highness so grievously, and I dare not think
of all I have suffered and suffer, and with no remedy that
I can see.

"If the Governor understand as a certainty that you
mean what you say, and will fulfil your oath, the whole
of Ceylon will be Christian in a year, and many kings in
Malabar and Cape Comorin and many other places. But
so long as the governors have not this fear before them of
being dishonoured and punished, you need not count on any
increase of our holy faith. . . . .

"And because I have no hope that this will be done, I
am almost sorry I have written. . . . I certify that I would
not have written this about the governors if I had thought
that with a good conscience I could satisfy my soul in keeping
silence.

"I, Sire, am not quite determined to go to Japan, but I
am thinking that I will, for I quite despair of any real chance
in India for the increase of our holy faith."

The letter goes on to implore the king to send out more
workers, and then Xavier gives a report of his work in
Malacca, to show, as he says, what room there is for more
missionaries. He signs himself "Your Highness' useless
servant."*

He writes at the same time, and on the same subjects, to
Rodriguez. He literally clamours for more workers.

"It seems to me," he says of the king, "that at the hour
of his death he will find that he has fallen very far short with
regard to India. I am rather afraid that in heaven God and
all His saints will say of him, 'By letters the king shows a
friendly interest about the increase of My honour in India,
since it is only in My Name and for this cause that he possesses
it ; yet, while he apprehends and punishes those in charge
of his temporal profit, if in any way they do not increase his
rents and revenues, he never punishes those who do not

* *Mon. Xav,* vol. i. p. 451 ff.

comply with his letters and commands [about spiritual things].'

" If I were convinced that the king perfectly understood the sincere love I have for him, I would ask him . . . to pray every day for a quarter of an hour to God to give him to understand well and feel better within his soul that saying of Christ's, *What does it profit a man if he gain the whole world, but suffer the loss of his own soul?* . . . . It is time, very dear brother Master Simon, to undeceive the king. The hour is nearer than he thinks when God has to call him to give account, saying to him, *Give an account of thy steward- ship.* Therefore see that he provides India with spiritual fundamentals."

Xavier goes on to say the same things that he had said to the king about forcing the governors to give the Gospel to India. The force, we have in fairness to Xavier to observe, was not to be used towards the converts—he knew well enough that, with those southern tribes of which he was thinking, the Gospel had only to be preached in order to be received—it was the authorities who were to be forced to give opportunities of hearing the Word.

The letter concludes :

" In this way the injustices and robberies towards the poor Christians will cease, and those who are ready to become Christians will get good courage to do so. For in this matter of making Christians you need expect no fruit if the king makes anyone else but the Governor responsible. *I know what I am saying, believe me, and am telling you the truth.*" *

To understand these letters, we must recognise the intense emotion which lies behind them, and the eagerness and earnestness with which every line is surcharged. Not many will think these proposals practicable or wise, but there are few who would care to say so very loudly in the presence of such prophetic passion as this. Portuguese India was in an abominable state, and Xavier was at the same time a man of vision and a man of action. Desperate measures were called for. In the light of calmer days desperate measures often seem more absurd than at the time they really were. We

* *Mon. Xav.*, vol. i. p. 457 ff.

dare hardly judge this scheme. Its aims were after all very simple. Here stood a man with a single eye for the glory of God. And if, from the vast armoury of political and ecclesiastical intrigue in which he stood, he chose a weapon or two, saying, " These will help me in my battles," we condemn his judgment rather than his ideals. These, as outlined in this letter, were three : an end to the persecution of the native Christians by the native heathen, justice and liberty for the native Christians from the Portuguese, and opportunities for every man and woman in India to embrace the " Law of God."

We have no evidence, at this or at any other time, of Francis' inward sorrow telling upon his outward bearing. On the contrary, when, some years later, a pre-canonisation enquiry was held here in Cochin, nearly all the witnesses use the same expression. They say " He was very candid in his conversation, and always with his mouth full of laughter."*

But Xavier did not stay long in Cochin. Towards the end of January he set out to visit the Christians in the south. In the country of the Great King, where he had baptized whole populations three years earlier, he found things going badly. Francisco Enriquez, the missionary in charge, had given up in despair. The Great King had not maintained his former goodwill toward the Christians. Probably he found that his patronage of the Western religion had not brought him all the advantages which he had hoped for. Francisco Enriquez's versions of the persecutions were highly coloured and pitiful, but that may have been partly due to his desire to have a good excuse to quit an uncongenial field. In any case Xavier promptly sent him back to the work he had deserted.

He then proceeded to the Fishery coast, and gathered the workers together at Manapar for review and counsel. Brother Manoel de Moralez wrote from there :

During the fifteen days which he spent with us there he talked with each of us alone, asking us about all those things which were in our minds, from a spiritual point of view, and talking of everything which might help to keep together and increase our converts. When he left us to go to Goa, he gave us some written instructions, that some things which were unsatis-

* *Mon. Xav.,* vol. ii. p. 270 : see also p. 319.

factory might be improved, and that we might know how to proceed in the future.*

These written instructions begin by bidding the missionaries baptize infants whenever possible. After baptism, nothing, he goes on, is more important than the instruction of the children. Each village is to have a teacher of its own. The women are to meet on Saturdays, the men on Sundays, and the great truths are to be preached in simple language. The missionaries are to make a point of reconciling enemies.

When Coelho has finished his translation of the Articles of the Faith into Malabar a copy is to be given to each village.

The people are to be instructed to tell the missionaries when anyone is ill, that he may be visited, taught, and have the Gospel read to him. At funerals they are to address those who are present, reminding them that they too have to die, and that if they wish to go to Paradise they must live a good life.

The missionaries are not to get mixed up in law cases if they can avoid it. And they are most earnestly urged to try to keep on good terms with the Captain, and to live in peace and friendship with all the Portuguese, and return them good for evil, and only speak with them about the things of God, exhorting them to confess and communicate, and to keep the Ten Commandments.

They are to help the native priests in every way, and never to write down an ill report of any. They are to take special care never to run down the native Christians in the presence of the Portuguese, but always to defend them, and speak generously of them. With the natives themselves they are always to deal as lovingly as possible, and punishment is only to be given with the sanction of Father Antonio Criminale, who was the senior missionary. They are to be very slow— even when they think they deserve it—in punishing the children, to beware of offending them, and to " show them much love."

Each man is to keep to his own district, unless with the special permission of Antonio Criminale.

Finally he says :

" Again I charge you earnestly to strive to make yourselves

* Cros, *Vie de S François Xavier*, vol. i. p. 373.

loved wherever you go or are, doing kind deeds to all, and always leaving loving words behind you if possible, for thus you will produce much fruit in their souls. The Lord grant this, and abide with all. Amen."*

After spending about a fortnight on the Fishery coast, Xavier paid a flying visit to Ceylon. Of this visit he says nothing in any of his letters ; he was probably ordered to go by the Bishop, and found the task little to his taste. The King of Kandy appears to have become a " Christian " some time previously, from political motives, and to have been making a disturbance because he had not been given all that he had been promised. In March the Saint was once more in Goa, and had brought back with him an ambassador from the discontented king to treat with the Governor, de Castro. He was on the eve of a journey, and received Xavier and his friend coldly. He could do nothing for Kandy just then, and the other affairs about which Xavier wished to talk to him were pushed aside.

Xavier waited eight days in Goa, and then set out after the Governor, for both the affairs of Kandy and his own business were urgent. By the end of March he was in Bassein, and de Castro was there too. It was Lent, and the Saint, instead of going straight to interview the Governor, began to preach in the town, before resting an hour from his journey. De Castro saw and heard him, and, for Xavier, the rest appears to have been easy.

They met, and the ambassador's requests were granted. Kandy was to become a tributary of Portugal, and in return was to receive Portuguese protection and favour. The foundation of a Jesuit college at Malacca was approved, and the Governor gave his blessing on the proposed voyage to Japan. The old man was dying, and knew it, and would fain have kept Xavier with him till the end came. But Francis was in haste to return to Goa. De Castro made him promise at least not to leave Goa during the next year, so that he might come to him and give him the last rites of the Church. This Xavier promised.

From Goa he wrote to his friend, Diego Pereira :—

" . . . God our Lord knows how pleased I should have been

* *Mon. Xav.,* vol. i. p. 853.

to have seen you before taking the road to China, but the Governor ordered me to winter here in Goa, and I could not do anything but obey, though I wanted to go to Cochin, and from there on to Cape Comorin, where my companions are. And I would have liked so much to have had a talk with you, as with my real soul's friend, about my plans for a voyage and pilgrimage to Japan which I hope to make within a year. For I have got a lot of information about the amount of fruit which may be gained there for the increase of our holy faith.

" . . . I am most anxious to see you before leaving for China in order to recommend a very rich merchandise to you. Those who trade in Malacca and China take little stock of it. This merchandise is called the soul's conscience. It is so little known throughout these parts that all the merchants think themselves lost if they use it much. I hope in God our Lord that my friend Diego Pereira will gain in carrying a good conscience where others are lost for want of it. I continually ask in my poor prayers and sacrifices that God our Lord may take and draw him to a safe haven with greater profit in soul and conscience than in estate." *

The letter goes on to ask help for a certain Ramirez, who wishes to get back to his native country, but has no money to take him there. " I would have helped if I could," Francis writes, " but I am so poor that I do not see how that is possible."

In June the old Governor died, and Francis, as he had promised, was at his bedside. Nothing now detained him any longer in Goa, except the affairs of the college. But these occupied him for some months. The college of St. Paul must have been a unique and curious institution in those days.

Twelve or thirteen different languages were spoken here. Besides Indians from every province, there were Africans, Malays, Chinese, men from the Moluccas, Bonzes from Pegu or Siam, and several young Ethiopians. The preceding year an Abyssinian bishop had died at the college . . . among the catechumens were Cingalese refugees, the ambassador of the king of Kandy, and the three Japanese recently arrived from Malacca.†

The Father of the college sent, about this time, a bright account of the life there to the King of Portugal.

* *Mon. Xav.*, vol. 1. p. 460.
† Brou, *Vie de S. François Xavier*, vol. i. p. 35.

Every day, teachers and scholars, after dinner, go in procession from the refectory to the hermitages at the top of the garden, and there make most special prayers for the Queen our lady, for the Prince, and for the Governors of India. It is a beautiful spectacle to see them thus piously advancing, first the Fathers, then the oldest pupils who are already grammarians, then those who are learning the psalter, then the younger ones. Thus well ordered, two by two, they arrive at the hermitage, and kneel down and respond to the prayers which the Fathers recite, and then go on, in the same order, to the next hermitage. After this they separate into groups in the garden, in times of great heat or of rain under the shelters, at other times on the benches in the *allées*. Each group is formed of boys of one race; they talk in their own language or discuss what they have heard in class, that they may not forget it. There are in the college four very clever lads who preach to the native Christians. One of them, from Tutuan, has remarkable talent; he will become a great preacher. He is only thirteen or fourteen years old and already, in very good Portuguese, he has composed some sermons, in which he quotes the authorities of the Fathers with such *à propos* that they who hear him weep with joy and praise God.*

One smiles a little at this lovely picture when one reads of another letter which went to Rodriguez about the same time as this went to the king, asking him to beg for indulgences for the college. There are other reports, too, from the Fathers of the college which are not so glowing. Most of the boys came to the place too old to have their morals satisfactorily dealt with. Yet this seemed at the time an unavoidable evil, for if they came to the college too young they forgot their native dialect, and were unable to preach to their own people when the time came for them to return. The house was not satisfactorily governed. Xavier knew this, and had already written to Europe begging for a more capable Head. There was a good deal of friction among the various priests and instructors, and Xavier seems to have spent most of his time, from April until September, in trying to get things into better order.

At the beginning of September two new workers arrived from Portugal, Gasper Barzée and Melchior Gonçalez. Before their ships had cast anchor in the harbour, Francis, eager as always for tidings from home, had sent out messengers

* Quoted by Cros, *Vie de S. François Xavier*, vol. i. p. 346.

with refreshments and requests that they might land as soon as possible, for he longed to see them.

Writing of his first meeting with the Saint, Barzée says :

The joy which fills our soul is indescribable. I cannot tell you of the goodness of Father Francis. At first it was, for the Fathers and Brothers, like a whirlwind of love. When he had settled down, after mutual greetings, and a meal which restored us, Father Francis set himself to question us about the state of the Company in Europe. He never could end talking of Father Ignatius, Father Simon [Rodriguez], the other Fathers, the colleges, the number of the Companions, but, above all, of their virtues. It was touching to see how he lovingly praised God, in speaking, or listening to us speak of the fruits of salvation which God, through the Company, had gained in Portugal and elsewhere. As to the other Fathers and Brothers, they are God's elect ; I cannot say any more of them.*

Gaspar was a humble soul and had a sense of humour. He wrote to his friends an account of how he preached before the Saint :

Soon Father Francis told me to be ready to preach at St. Paul's on the Day of our Lady in September, and he warned me well to speak distinctly, because, by what the people in our ship had said, there would be a great crowd. But I spoke so low that they were very displeased, Father Francis among the others. Several of them had hardly heard me. Then he (Francis) went away, leaving me orders to practise speaking during the night in the church. I did this till the brothers were satisfied with me. Since then I have been preaching, and the people are quite pleased.†

Melchior Gonçalez also leaves us an interesting account of his first impressions of the Saint :

He is not old, and his health seems good, although he is ascetic in appearance. I note that he does not drink any kind of wine. Privations are nothing to him, for he is a brave soldier of Jesus Christ, forgetting himself, and thinking of nothing but his King. One can apply to him the words of St. Bernard : " *The faithful soldier does not feel his own wounds when he looks with love on those of his King.*"‡ Truly, dear brothers, there is a living martyr in

* Brou, *Vie de S François Xavier*, vol. ii. p. 48.
† Cros, *Vie de S. François Xavier*, vol. i. p. 384.
‡ Fidelis miles vulnera sua non sentit dum benigne sui Regis vulnera intuetur,

the midst of us, and I am convinced that he will soon die a martyr's
death, for it looks as if he sought no other end. How often
already arrows have been let fly at him! And many a time
they have set fire to the lodging where he passed the night. Three
or four times in the same night the attempt has been made, from
which you can judge what sort of sleep he has had. True soldier
of Jesus Christ is a title which well applies to him.*

On arriving at Goa, numbers of the passengers asked Xavier
to allow them to enter the Company. Gonçalez wrote that
these candidates included the captain of one of the ships,
the governor of one of the forts, several noblemen, a secretary,
a doctor, and a great many humbler folk. Xavier gave them
all the Exercises, and as a result of his observations retained
only one, Luis Mendez. This man died a martyr's death in
South India a few years later.

In September bad news came from Comorin of renewed
invasions by the Badages, and Xavier at once set out for the
south. He was given a royal welcome by his beloved converts
on the Fishery coast. As he disembarked they sang aloud
the hymns which he had taught them, and then carried him
on their shoulders to the church. In spite of, or perhaps
rather strengthened by, persecution and hardship, the
Paravas were increasing in numbers and in faith. The
mission here was better manned, better ordered and dis-
ciplined than any of the other missions in India. Grammars
and dictionaries had been written, and the work of teaching
and translating methodically carried out.†

From the Fishery coast Xavier wrote to Francisco Enriquez.
Enriquez, the reader will remember, was the man who had
run away from his work in Travancore, and had been sent
back again by Xavier. The stern rebuke implied in sending
his subordinate back to the post he had deserted is followed,
in this letter, by a large-hearted trust and affection which
must have fallen like coals of fire on the runaway's head.
The letter assumes that the missionary had given up his work
out of discouragement and disheartenment :

" Do not be discouraged when you see that you are not
gaining as much fruit among your Christians as you wish,
for they are given to idolatry and the king is opposed to their

* Quoted by Cros, *Vie de S. François Xavier*, vol. i. p. 385.
† See Brou, *Vie de S. François Xavier*, vol. ii. p. 52.

becoming Christians. And consider this, you are gaining more fruit than you think, in giving spiritual life to the new-born, when you diligently and carefully baptize them, as you do. For if you consider well, you will find that few go from India to Paradise, whether white or black, except those who die in a state of innocence, as are those who are fourteen years old or under. So you see, my brother Francisco Enriquez, you are gaining more fruit in your kingdom of Travancore than you think. Look how many baptized infants, since you have been there, have died and are now in the glory of Paradise, who would not have enjoyed God if you had not been there. The enemy of human nature has you in great abhorrence and would like to see you out of there, so that no one may go to Paradise from the kingdom of Travancore. It is customary with the devil to hold out to Jesus Christ's servants [the vision] of great services, and he does this with evil intentions, so as to disquiet and to molest a soul who is somewhere doing service to God, in order to draw and cast him out of the district where he is serving God. I fear me that the enemy is combatting you just here and is giving you many troubles and vexations in order to boot you out."*

Three and a half years later Enriquez had established nineteen new churches in Travancore.

In mid-November Francis returned to Goa to plead for the Christians. He had asked Enriquez to bring the affair before God. The Captain of Tuticorin, who, as we saw in the letters to Mansillas, had caused the native Christians such sufferings, had been succeeded by a man as bad as himself, and a long list of his abuses had been drawn up, and was now brought by Xavier before the eyes of the Governor. A letter sent in 1558 by the missionaries on the Fishery coast to John of Portugal shows that these efforts had not much success. This letter complains bitterly of the treatment given by the government officials to the native Christians, and concludes: " Above all more care ought to be taken in the appointments of the captains, and they should be paid a sufficient salary so that they will not be tempted to put pressure on the natives of such a poor country as this."†

January and February of 1549 were spent by Xavier in

* Mon. Xav., vol. i. p. 466.
† Quoted by Brou, Vie de S. François Xavier, vol. ii. p. 58.

Cochin. Besides his usual works he was occupied in the founding of a college or seminary there.

A very revealing letter to Loyola is dated January 12th:

" By the principal letters which all we the least of your sons in India wrote by Master Simon, your holy Charity will be informed of the fruit (gained) and service which, with the help of God our Lord and of your devout and holy sacrifices and prayers, is done in these parts of India, and will be done in future. By this letter I will give you details of some affairs of this land so remote from Rome. First, the native Indians, so far as I have seen, and speaking generally, are barbarians. We of the Company are carrying on a great deal of work with those who are and daily become Christians. It is necessary that your Charity should have special care for all your sons in India in commending them to God our Lord continually, for you know what a great toil it is to have to do with people who through their very habitual evil living neither know God nor obey reason.

" The great heat in summer, and the winds and rains in winter, make life in these lands very troublesome. There is little to maintain the body either in the Moluceas, Socotra or Cape Comorin. The spiritual and bodily toil is marvellously great when one has to deal with such people. Their languages are hard to get hold of. . . . All the Indians whom we have seen up to now, both Mohammedan and heathen, are very ignorant. Those who have to live among these unbelievers and in the work of converting them need many virtues : obedience, humility, perseverance, patience, neighbourly love, and great chastity. For there are many opportunities for sinning. They need too, sound judgment and strong bodies to carry on the work. I give your Charity this account because of the need there is, in my opinion, of testing the spirits of those you are going to send to this country. . . .

" The man whom you, my Father, will have to send to take charge of the College of Santa Fé at Goa, and of the native students and of the Companions, will need, not to speak of all the other things necessary to a man who has to rule and command, these two qualities : first, great obedience, so as to make himself beloved, both by all our greater ecclesiastics and by the laymen who rule the district, so that they may not be conscious of his pride, but rather of his great humility . . . second, to be affable and calm in dealing with others, and not strict, using every means he can to make himself loved, firstly by those whom he has to command, both natives and those of the Company who are here and are to come, so that they may not feel that he wishes to make himself obeyed by strictness or servile fear."

The following passage gives a curious insight into the vigorous discipline of some of the Jesuits. N., the Editor of the *Monumenta* says, was Antonio Gomez. He alleged authority from Simon Rodriguez:—

" I say this, Father of my soul, because the companions here were little edified by a command N. brought to seize and send as prisoners in irons to Portugal those whom he thought did not edify here. Until now I never thought of keeping anyone in the Company by force, if it were not by force of love and charity. . . . Those who seemed to me fit for the Company I treated with love and charity to confirm them the more in it, since they endure such trouble in these parts in the service of God our Lord, and also because it seems to me the Company of Jesus means Company of love and conformity of minds, and not of strictness nor of servile fear. . . .

" I see clearly, my only Father, by my experience here, that no road is opening for the perpetuation of the Company by the natives among the natives. Christianity will last among them only as long as we who are here or those whom you will send from home will last and live. The reason for this is the great persecutions suffered by those who become Christians, of which it would take too long to tell. I refrain from writing them as I do not know into whose hands these letters may come.

" In all the parts of this India where there are Christians there are Fathers of the Company. In Malucco there are four ; in Malacca two ; in Cape Comorin six ; in Colon two ; in Bassein two ; in Socotra four. As these places are very remote from each other, as Malucco more than a thousand leagues from Goa, Malacca five hundred, Cape Comorin two hundred, Colon a hundred and twenty-five, Bassein sixty, Socotra three hundred ; and as in all these places there are Fathers of the Company to whom the others of the same Company who are with them give obedience, since they are persons of good edification ; and where these persons of the Company are to whom those with them give obedience, I am not at all needed.

" The Portuguese here control only the sea and the places on the sea-shore, and so they are not masters on *terra firma*, but in the places where they live. The native Indians are of this kind : through their great sins they are not at all inclined to the things of our holy faith, but rather abhor them greatly. It bores them mortally when we speak to them and ask them to become Christians. . . . With all this, if the unbelievers here were favoured by the Portuguese, many would become Christians. But the heathen see that those who are Christians are in disfavour and persecuted, and so they are unwilling to become Christians.

" For these and many other causes, too long to relate, and because of a great deal of information received about Japan, which is an island near China, and because all in Japan are heathen, and there are no Mohammedans or Jews, and they are curious and eager to know new things, alike of God as of natural things, I determined, with much inward satisfaction, to go to this land. It seemed to me that among such a people it would be possible that they themselves might perpetuate the fruit which we of the Company might gain in our lifetime.

" There are three Japanese youths at the College of Santa Fé. They came back with me in 1548 from Malacca. They told me a lot about Japan. They are men of good customs and great gifts, especially Paul. . . . Paul learnt to read, write and speak Portuguese in eight months. He is now taking the Exercises, and is sure to profit much. He is far advanced in matters of the faith.

" I have great hope, and that all in God our Lord, that many will become Christians in Japan. I am determined to go first to the king's court and afterwards to the universities where they have their studies, with great hope in Jesus Christ our Lord that He will help me. Paul says their religion was brought from a country called Chengico, which is beyond China, and after Tartary. . . .

" When I see the Japanese writings [*or scriptures*] and deal with the men of their universities, I will write fully of everything, and I will not fail to write to the university of Paris, and through it all the other universities of Europe will get word. I am taking a priest with me, a Valencian, Cosmo

Ex lr̃is B.Xauerij.ad Ignatium ex India scriptis
GRATIA ET CARITAS X.D.Ñt.Mi pater in X̃ visceribᵛunce
Te ego pater animæ meæ,sũmeq̃ mihi venerande positis hum ge
nibus (sic.n.hanc tibi ep̃tam scribo) suppliciter oro,vt mihi a
Deo impetres,vt dum viuam sanctissimæ voluntatis suæ mihi det
et plane agnoscendæ,et omnino exequendæ facultatem.Vale
Tuus minimus filius.longissimeq̃ exulans. FRANC.XAVERIVS 59

a n ir anni
m so much

the long sat
... So I
ther of my a
s, an if I hac
rd to your h
y as real Hi
    grace to f
pound to sh
Dublin, 18

... King, vol
On Irishman ha

ST. FRANCIS XAVIER WRITING TO LOYOLA
FROM INDIA

de Torres . . . and also the three Japanese youths. We leave, with God's help, this month of April, 1549.

" . . . In making this voyage I could never finish writing of the inward comfort I feel, though there are many and great dangers of death, of great tempests, winds, reefs, and many pirates. When two out of four ships are saved it is a great success. I would not give up going to Japan though it were certain that I should be in greater danger than ever, so strongly have I felt within my soul, and so very great hope I have in God our Lord that our holy faith will be greatly increased. By the report that Paul gave us you will see the opportunities there are of serving God our Lord there. I enclose it.

" . . . Your Charity would do a great service to God our Lord if you would write to us, your least sons of India, a letter of doctrine and spiritual advice, as a will in which you would divide with these, your exiled sons, so far from the bodily sight, the riches which God our Lord has given to you. For the love and service of God our Lord, write us, if it is possible.

" A priest of the Company is at Cape Comorin, who came from Portugal, Enrico Enriquez by name, a very virtuous man, and of great edification. He can speak and write Malabar, and gains more fruit than any other two, as he knows the language. The native Christians love him frightfully, and he has a great name with them for the sermons and talks he gives them in their own language. For the love of God our Lord write and comfort him, for he is so good and gains so much fruit."

The long letter concludes thus :

" . . . So I stop, praying your Holy Charity, *tenderest* Father of my soul, my knees placed on the ground as I write this, as if I had you here, to commend me much to God our Lord in your holy and devout sacrifices and prayers, that He may reveal His holy Will to me in this present life, and give me grace to fulfil it perfectly. Amen. And the same I commend to all those of the Company.

" Cochin, 12th Jan., 1549.

" Your least and most useless son,

" FRANCISCO." *

* *Mon. Xav.*, vol. i. p. 473 ff. There is an old MS. copy of this letter in the British Museum, but not, of course, an original.

A few days later he writes to Rodriguez :

" The Chinese ports have all risen against the Portuguese. But not for that will I give up going to Japan, as I have written you. Since there is no greater rest in this laborious life than to live in great danger of death when it is all undertaken without any other motive than the love and service of God our Lord, and the increase of our holy faith." *

And in another letter to Rodriguez he writes :

" All my devotees and friends are frightened at my taking such a long and dangerous voyage. It puzzles me to see how little faith they have. For God our Lord has command and power over the tempests of the Chinese and Japanese seas—which are the greatest known—and has control over all the sea robbers. . . . I have no fear of any but of God, lest He give me some chastisement for being negligent in His service, unfit and useless for the increase of the Name of Jesus Christ among men who do not know Him."†

Before leaving India for Malacca *en route* for Japan, Xavier sent one more letter to the King of Portugal. Much of it is a repetition of what he had said before, put even more strongly :

" It is almost a kind of martyrdom to look with patience on the destruction of what one has gained with so much labour."

And again :

" At last experience has taught me that your Highness is not powerful in India for the increase of Christ's faith, and is powerful for carrying off and keeping all the temporal riches of India."

And again :

" I, Sire, because I know what goes on here, have no hope that commands or prescripts sent in favour of Christianity will be fulfilled in India ; and therefore I am almost fleeing to Japan, not to waste any more time."

* *Mon. Xav.,* vol. i. p. 508. † *Ibid.,* vol. i. p. 513.

And finally :

" Be prepared, for kingdoms and lordships finish and have end. A new thing it will be, and something that never happened to your Highness before, to find yourself dis-possessed at the hour of your death of your kingdoms and lordships, and to have to enter into others, where this new thing must happen to you, to be sent, may God forbid it ! out of Paradise." *

One of Xavier's chief anxieties in leaving India was the college at Goa. The new Rector, Antonio Gomez, who had just arrived with great *éclat* from Coimbra, was proving himself a thorn in the flesh to all concerned. Before leaving for Japan Xavier tried to get him to go, but without success. He then arranged that the more popular Camerino should be superior over all the missionaries who were not actually living in the college, and Gomez was to have no authority over Camerino. There are some pages of instructions to Camerino, written out at this time by Xavier. Their chief burden is that peace should be kept with Gomez.

" Above everything else live with much prudence, humility, and sense, in love and charity with Antonio Gomez and all the Fathers . . . do not order him in anything by obedience, but as by love and advice . . . let there be between you and Antonio Gomez neither discords nor quarrels, but much love and charity. . . . Write me fully of your news, and of all the house, and of the love and charity between you and Antonio Gomez."†

In April Xavier left Goa for Malacca and Japan. With him were Cosmo de Torres and Fernandez, the three Japanese youths, and three missionaries who were going to the Moluccas.

On Easter Day they came to Cochin, and there made a short halt. They preached in the town, and were lodged by the Franciscans there. By the end of May they were in Malacca, where they were very joyfully welcomed by their friends. From there Xavier wrote a large budget of letters.

From his friends in the college he begs and begs again for

---

* *Mon. Xav.*, vol. i. p. 510 ff.   † *Ibid.*, vol. i. p. 881, 882, 883.

T

long and full letters; he wants to know all about them, and especially about the fruit which they are gaining.

To the troublesome Antonio Gomez he writes:

"Antonio Gomez, I commend you much to charity, friendship, and love with all the blessed friars of the Order of St. Francis, and of St. Dominic. Be very devoted to them all. Beware of having any disedifying thing with them. I hope you will always fulfil this, great humility dwelling in you. Now and then you will visit them, so that they may recognise in you that you love them, and the people, lovers of discord, may see the charity which is among you towards all." *

In the same letter he begs that they may pray for his companions and himself:

"Let all of the house have special care to commend us to God, Father Cosmo de Torres, Juan Fernandez, and Paul Japan with his companions, and Manoel China, and Amador, and me, since we have such need in this dangerous and difficult voyage in which we go." †

In another letter he reports on the school work in Malacca:

"Roque de Oliveira teaches the children to read and write, and he makes no less progress here, as the trouble he takes in teaching them is great. He has a great number of youths; to some he teaches reading and writing, and to others grammar. A few have now gone, as they are more advanced, and have learnt all they wished. They read by primers and prayer books. They behave (as well) as if they were friars: it is a thing to give thanks to God our Lord when one sees their modesty. Never an oath, however little, is heard in their mouth." ‡

Writing to Loyola about the Japanese youths who were with him, he says:

"I asked them often in which prayers they found most

* *Mon. Xav.*, vol. i. p. 522.   † *Ibid.*, vol. i. p. 525.
‡ *Ibid.*, vol. i. p. 559.

delight and spiritual comfort, and they told me in the Exercises on the Passion, to which they are very devoted.

"During these Exercises they experienced great grief, comforts, and tears. For several months before the Exercises we occupied them in explaining to them the articles of the faith and the mysteries of the life of Christ, and the cause of the incarnation of the Son of God in the womb of the Virgin Mary, and of the redemption of all the human kind made by Christ. I asked them often what in their opinion was the best in our religion [*ley*]. They always answered me that it was confession and Communion, and that no reasonable man, it seemed to them, could fail to be a Christian after our holy faith had been explained to him. I heard one of them, Paul de Santa Fé by name, say with many sighs, 'O people of Japan, how wretched are you who adore as gods the creatures which God made for the service of men.' I asked him why he was saying this. He answered me that he was saying it on account of the people of his country who were adoring the sun and the moon, while the sun and the moon were like ministers and servants of those who know Jesus Christ, and are only of use to lighten the day and night that men by their brightness may serve God, and glorify His Son Jesus Christ in the land." *

He goes on to speak of the work which lies before them :

"We are not afraid of meeting the learned of those parts, for what can he know who does not know God nor Jesus Christ? And those who desire nothing but the glory of God and the manifestation of Jesus Christ with the salvation of souls, what can they be afraid of or fear? Not only going among unbelievers, but, moreover, where there is a multitude of demons, why should we fear, since the barbarous people and the winds and the demons can do us no more evil or annoyance save so far as God gives permission and licence?

"Only one dread and terror we bear, which is fear to offend God our Lord. For we have certain victory against our enemies, if we keep us from offending God our Lord. And since God gives to all grace sufficient to serve Him and to keep them from sinning, we thus hope in His Divine

* *Mon. Xav.*, vol. i. p. 544.

Majesty that He will give it to us.   And since all our good or
evil is in the good or bad use of His grace, we trust greatly
in the merits of the holy mother Church, the Spouse of
Christ our Lord, and particularly in the merits of the Companions of the name of Jesus, and of all their devotees, male
and female, that their merits will extend even to us, and we
shall come to use well the grace of the Lord God.

"It has often struck me that our very learned companions
who may come out here will have to put up with no small
hardships in those dangerous voyages, and they may think
that to face such obvious peril, in which so many ships are
lost, will be tempting God.   But then I have come to the
conclusion that there is nothing in that.   For I feel sure in
God our Lord that the learning of our companions must
be dominated by the Spirit of God, Who abides in them.
For otherwise they will have trouble, and not a little.   Nearly
always I carry before my eyes and mind what I often heard
our blessed Father Ignatius say, that those who were of
our Company ought to strive hard to vanquish themselves,
and, by taking the proper means, to cast out all those fears
which hindered their faith, hope, and confidence in God. . . .
And although all faith, hope, and confidence are the gift of
God, and the Lord gives this to whom He pleases, He gives
commonly to those who force and conquer themselves by
taking the proper means. . . ."*

Xavier then proceeds to less abstract topics :

"The Japanese, our brothers and companions who go
with us to Japan, tell me that the Japanese Priests [Padres]
will be scandalised if they see us eating flesh and fish.   So
we go determined to be vegetarians [*comer continuamente
dieta*] always [evidently Paul's friends were Buddhists]
rather than give scandal to anyone."†

On June 23rd, 1549, he writes a very characteristic letter,
evidently in even more of a hurry than usual, to Rodriguez.

"The grace and eternal love of Christ our Lord be
always in our aid and favour.   Amen.

* *Mon. Xav.*, vol. i. p. 548.   † *Ibid.*, vol. i. p. 549.

" This January of 1549 I wrote you a long letter from Cochin, both I and all the Brothers of the Company. By this letter I let you know that it would be a great service of God our Lord if you would send some man who had served in the College of Coimbra as Rector, or who was fit for it, and a man to whom neither the duty would cause qualms in his conscience [he puts in "neither," meaning, no doubt, to come in with a " nor " farther on, but he jumps away in the idea of the dangers of commanding, and never gets on the grammatical rail again] as the office of command is very dangerous for those who are not perfect, and of great perfection, as you know very well, and who was a man who'knew how to watch for all the Brothers in India with great prudence and discretion, knowing how to have compassion, to lead, and deal with the Brothers of the Company. You must therefore send a man whom you have seen tried in such positions. Antonio Gomez has a great gift for preaching, and produces fine results in his preachings, but he has not such qualities as I desire for him who has to take charge of the Brothers in India, and of the College. Antonio Gomez would do great service to God by going about and preaching in the forts of India.

" For the love of our Lord send me some Fathers preachers, for the forts of India have great need of instruction. We are greatly in debt to the king and to the Portuguese of these parts, and we cannot pay our great debt with anything but by watching over their consciences, and by watching over the many obligations of the king, and unburdening his conscience in these parts. For the love of our Lord let the men you send here, whether preachers or not, be men well proven in their life and virtues, for occasions and opportunities for evil are many here. Though the preachers you will send here may not have much learning, for the love of our Lord let them be men of great life (*de grande vida*), for here they look little to learning and much to life."*

In the letter that follows we have a delicious exhibition of our Saint as a match-maker. It is addressed to Paul Camerino and Antonio Gomez at Goa :

* *Mon. Xav.*, vol. i. p 563.

" Malacca, 23 June, 1549.

" After having written you a very long letter about everything, it seems well to me to send you these lines to tell you how I met here in Malacca a great friend of mine, Christopher Carvalho.

"He is a bachelor, far advanced in virtue, rich, honourable, and of very good parts. I asked him in the zeal I have for the salvation of all, and for the great friendship there was between us, to try for the love of our Lord to take and choose some method of living in the service of God, and for repose, since he knew well in what dangers men walk who do not have method in their living. He told me that he now greatly desired to repose in some good state of life, which might be service to God our Lord, and to enjoy the favours and alms which our Lord God of His mercy had done him.

" And thus going on from one subject to another, I began to remember the many kind deeds which we have all received from our ' Mother.'*   I spoke to him about marrying some girl.   I told him all about her customs and virtue, and he was very pleased with the veracious story of her virtue. He became quite seized and gave me his word.   I believe he will fulfil it as my sincere friend, and because it is a matter of so much honour, advantage and repose to him.   I have written about this to our ' Mother.'

" And as I think your help will be very necessary, I beg and pray you to remember the hospitality and kindness which all of us have always received from our ' Mother.'   You and the Comptroller of Revenue put your heads together, and arrange so that this honoured widow may be relieved, and her daughter get shelter and protection.

"My friend Christopher Carvalho is going there (to Goa). You will make his acquaintance, and you will know his wish and the word given me.   You will speak to the Comptroller of Revenue and place before him the great service to God our Lord to be done in this matter, and the great honour and repose which will result to him from it, by protecting the orphan and comforting the widow.   And I trust in God our Lord that it will be done, for he is a good and honourable man.

* Ed. of *Mon. Xav.* gives a note from Filipucci : " In India the old women are called Mây [*i.e.*, Mother]. This one so called by the Saint was a Benefactress of ours."

"And you are aware that the King our Lord by letter-patent gifted to our 'Mother' the office vacated by Diogo Froes, who is now in glory, for whoever should marry her daughter. Now Christopher Carvalho is honourable and rich and in easy circumstances, and does not need to serve offices. So I recommend and beseech you earnestly for the love of God our Lord, and for the great and many obligations of us all to our 'Mother,' that you two with the Comptroller of Revenue get licence from the Lord Governor that Christopher Carvalho may be able to sell the said office, since, as I have said, he is in easy circumstances through the favour of the Lord God. I make no more recommendations or charges about this, for I know the special care which you will take of it, as every day you will see reasons obliging you to it. And I pray you to arrange that the marriage may come off, for I shall be most glad and contented when I see this orphan, such a good girl, protected, and our 'Mother' relieved. For I know and am sure that my friend Christopher Carvalho is a man who will stay and be very kind to our 'Mother.'

"And therefore I am so pressing. For I have already his word, and he promised me to do it and recognised that it was a great favour which the Lord was doing him in my thinking of such a good plan. And thus I have written to our 'Mother.' And yet it seems to me that it will not take place if there is nobody to hasten it, and take special care of it. And therefore I pray you to have great care of it.

"Our Lord unite us in His holy glory, for in this life I do not know when we shall see each other.

"Malacca, Eve of St. John, 1549.

"Your Brother in Christ."*

One wonders what the *mây* said ! And the *tão boa filha*, did she shut her eyes and open her mouth and take what Xavier sent her ?

There is another very interesting document written at this time—the Instructions to Preachers in the Forts.

These Instructions are full of very self-revealing passages, and valuable on that account to the student of Xavier. And twentieth-century preachers will find here much good advice that is by no means out of date. We give a few extracts :

* *Mon. Xav.*, vol. i. p. 566.

3. Visit the poor in the Hospital and from time to time preach to them to discharge their conscience, and exhort them to confess and communicate, for diseases generally rise from sins, and you yourself will confess it when you can.

6. Let all your conversation be spiritual. And yet in this take care to deal with the greatest friends as if they might come to be your enemies. Avail yourself of this reflection : on your part to edify them in all your deeds and talk, and on their part when they give up your friendship, that they may be blamed, and confound themselves.

8 and 9. Preach constantly and as often as possible, for this is a universal good of great service to God and advantage to souls. You will beware of preaching doubtful matters and Doctors' [scholars'] difficulties. Let your teaching be clear, acceptable, and moral. Reprove vice ; grieve over the offences against God ; be compassionate about the eternal condemnation of sinners to the pains of hell ; treat of sudden death which takes men unprepared, and touch at the same time on some point of the passion, by way of a colloquy or talk of a sinner with God, or of God's wrath against the sinner : move your hearers with all your power to contrition, grief, and tears for their fault, exhorting to confess and receive the most holy Sacrament.

10. And beware particularly of blaming from the pulpit the person or persons who have command in the same district. For men of that kind when publicly reprimanded become worse more quickly rather than amend. If it is necessary, preach to them in their own houses. Take them apart, and speak with a pleasant countenance. Do not use harsh words, but loving and mild. Embrace some, humble yourself before others, according to their nature. If they come to be friendly, then you can blame them with more confidence, and more or less as the friendship is greater or less. In short, harshness is taken badly by the rich and powerful. They easily lose patience and respect and think it does not matter at all to them to have us as enemies.

11. When men of affairs confess, and those who live in hate or sensuality, you will try two things : first, they should take some days to think carefully of their past, and put down exactly all their sins ; and it would be better to have them in writing. Secondly, to do before you absolve them what they are obliged to do afterwards, making restitution, withdrawing from the occasions of vice, and being reconciled with neighbours. For, generally, to get absolution they make great promises in confession, and when absolved do nothing. That they may put up with the delay in absolving them, and fulfil their duties, give them during some days while they are waiting some of the meditations we call " of the first week," that they may understand

the end for which God made them, and how they have erred from it by so innumerable sins, by the heinousness and ugliness of these same sins; how much God resents them, and how He punishes them; the certainty and uncertainty of death, the account which must be made, the greatness and eternity of the pains of hell.

12. The devil embarrasses many with a false shame of their base and ugly faults so that they never completely disclose them, as is proper, to the confessor. He disheartens and fills with want of confidence others by the same means.

13. With all these it is proper to use great sweetness until they have completely confessed, not putting on them fear of the divine justice, but making everything easy for them with the divine mercy. It will often help to overcome this temptation that they should understand from you that those things are not news to you, nor other greater sins.

15. When you confess Captains, Factors, or any other officials of the King, and persons who act as Factors in the affairs of others, take the greatest care to get complete information of the way in which they gain their living. You will ask them if they pay *partes* [taxes ?], if they make monopolies, if they help themselves with the King's money for their own business, and the like details. Do not be satisfied with asking them in general if they are holding what is of others. They will answer you that they owe nothing to anybody, for they easily take no notice of such things, as they are now well established, and they are so little affected by the many injustices involved. Really they are under obligation to restore much to many, as you will understand and make plain to them, if you proceed in your questioning in the manner I indicate.

16. Be extremely obedient to the Vicar of the city, to whom you will go at once on arrival to kiss his hands, with both knees on the ground. You will preach and confess and exercise spiritual functions by his licence. Never break with him in any case. Rather strive to make him your friend, with a view to give him the spiritual exercises, at the least, when you cannot manage more, those of the first week. Deal with the priests of the district in the same way, endeavouring to keep friendly with all, having and showing great respect to them and leading them to make a retreat for some days and to take these same meditations.

17. I charge you to have no less obedience, humility, and respect to the Captain. Do not break with him, however badly you see him doing. But when you have got him to be friends, and hope that you may be able to be of use, then with a pleasant face, with mildness and humility and love, so that he may understand that

you do it because you are pained at seeing his soul and honour tainted, represent to him what is said of him in the district.

18. But as many are sure to come to you with complaints and importune you to speak to him, be very cautious about this. It is best to excuse yourself, and say that you are engaged in spiritual affairs, and that if he does not make account of God, and of his own conscience, still less will he with you.

20. And remember, always go, you or your companion, about the streets with a bell, calling the people to the holy doctrine an hour before you begin teaching.

24. In conversation be pleasant and merry that fear may not keep people from profiting by you. Let your words be affable and mild, and even when it may be necessary to reprove some one in private, let it be with love and good grace, so that it may be seen that you abhor not the person but the fault.

27. If any come to you with desires to be received into our Company, and you think him fit, take charge of him. Be cautious that the works of abstinence are not beyond his capacity and spiritual power, and instead of feeding and strengthening the spirit make him lose courage. Do not use novelties in this, for these make laymen mock rather than be edified.

35. If you wish to gain much fruit, alike in your own soul and in those of the neighbours, and to live in spiritual comfort, converse with sinners so that they may come to trust you, and disclose their conscience to you. These are the living books which teach more than the dead. You must study them not only for your sermons, but for your own private comfort. Here you will find the points on which you ought chiefly to preach. I do not mean that you are not to read written books, rather you ought to do that, and to seek places of the Holy Scriptures and examples from the Fathers, with which you will give authority to the remedies against vice and sin which you see and read in the living books.

36. Advises not to take gifts—*i.e.*, big things—but the small, such as a little fruit, ought to be taken. Yet even these should be sent to the hospitals or prisons. People take it as an insult not to accept what is sent you when the things are small. The Portuguese of India are offended if you take nothing at all from them. And this is enough for the present. The Lord go with you, and remain with us. Amen.

Goa, Jan., 1549.*

* *Mon. Xav.*, vol. i. p. 870 ff. There are two versions of this document. The above is a translation of the second, except the last paragraph.

CHAPTER XVII

JAPAN

(August, 1549—November, 1551)

WE have seen from Xavier's letter from Cochin of January, 1548, how the earliest intimations of his mission to Japan came to him. A year and five months later, on June 24th, 1549, he left Malacca, and on August 15th arrived at Kagoshima.

Francis Xavier's letters from Japan were the earliest first-hand reports of that country to come to Europe. A Portuguese captain had sent home some descriptions of it in 1547 * gleaned from one of his passengers, the Japanese Yajiro, who a few months later was to meet Xavier in Malacca, be converted by him, and accompany him on this voyage. Marco Polo had brought rumours of *Zipango*, as he called it, to Italy, but he had not been there. Mendez Pinto, in his *Travels*, claims to have witnessed many of the scenes that Xavier describes, but his claims are unauthenticated. The first Europeans actually to touch Japanese soil were probably some Portuguese sailors who were driven ashore in a storm in 1542. Since then, before the arrival of Xavier, Europeans had called at the ports occasionally, but no one appears to have landed, or at least gone beyond the harbours. That adventure was reserved for Francis and his friends.

The little party numbered nine in all. Besides Xavier there were three other Jesuits—Cosmo Torres, Juan Fernandez, and Dominic Diaz. There was also the Japanese Yajiro, or, as he was now called, Paul of the Holy Faith, two other Japanese, and two " boys," one a native of Malabar, and the other a Chinese.

Of the Portuguese Dominic Diaz we know little. Cosmo Torres was a Spanish priest from Valencia. For ten years he had been an adventurer and a wanderer, but the sight of Xavier at work in the Moluccas had rekindled the ardours

---

* The text of these letters is in C. Manoel, *Missoas dos Jesuitas no Oriente*, p. 112.

of his youth, and in Goa, after due probation, he had been admitted to the Society. Juan Fernandez had come out in 1548 from Córdova, where he had been a wealthy silk-merchant. He had been "hardened" for missionary life by the bizarre methods at that time in usage at the College of Coimbra, and his earnestness and sincerity tested in a way thought to be very searching to an elegant young *mondain*: he was bidden to ride upon a donkey with his face towards the tail, dressed in fantastic silks, through the chief streets of Lisbon. Nine months later he was sent to India. Xavier wished to ordain him, but he preferred to remain a lay brother.

Of Yajiro we already know something from Xavier's letter on p. 254. He was the first Japanese convert to Christianity.*

The voyage was not without adventure, and in a letter written from Kagoshima on November 5th Xavier gives a very full account of it.

"... On the afternoon of St. John's Day, 1549, we embarked [from Malacca] in a heathen Chinese merchant ship.... When we left, God did us great favour, giving us very good weather and wind. Then the captain began to change his mind, as the heathen are very inconstant, and not to wish to go on to Japan, and to stop unnecessarily in the islands he found.

"What irritated us most in this voyage were two things— first, to see that we were not taking advantage of the good weather and wind which God our Lord was giving us, and that the monsoon taking us to Japan was ending, and we were thus being forced to wait a year and to winter in China till the next monsoon; and, second, the great and continual idolatries and sacrifices made, without our being able to hinder it, by the captain and the heathen to the idol which they carried in the ship. They often cast lots, and made inquiries if we could go to Japan or no, and if the favourable winds would last. Sometimes the lots fell out well, and sometimes badly....

"On the way to China, 100 leagues from Malacca we

---

* Less than a year after his conversion he wrote a very remarkable letter to the Society in Europe, the full text of which may be found in Cary's *History of Christianity in Japan.*

touched at an island and provided ourselves with rudders and the wood necessary for the great tempests and seas of China. After this was done, they cast lots, first making numerous sacrifices and feasts to the idol. . . . The lot fell that we were to have good weather, and should not wait longer. So we weighed anchor and set sail with much pleasure, the heathen trusting in the idol which, with great veneration and lighted candles, and perfumings and odours of eagles' wood [a kind of incense], they carried in the ship's poop ; and we trusting in God, Creator of heaven and earth, and in Jesus Christ His Son. . . . As we came along the heathen began to cast lots and make inquiries of the idol whether the ship would return again from Japan to Malacca. The lot fell out that she would go to Japan, but not return to Malacca. As a result . . . they resolved to winter in China and wait till next year. You see what we had to put up with on this voyage—our getting to Japan was at the discretion of the demon and his servants. . . .

" Coming slowly along, before reaching China and while close to Cochin-China, near China, we had two disasters in one day, the Eve of the Magdalen. Heavy seas were running, and there was a high wind, and we were full of water. The well of the ship happened to be open through carelessness ; Manuel China, our companion, was passing it, and not having a good hold, owing to the heavy rolling of the ship, fell down the well. We all thought he was dead from the great fall, and because there was so much water in the bottom : God our Lord willed that he did not die. His head and more than half his body were below water for some time, and he suffered for a good many days from a wound in his head. . . . With great trouble we drew him from the well, and he was unconscious a good while. . . . When he had recovered the storm continued, and with the tossing of the ship a daughter of the captain happened to fall into the sea: We could do nothing to help her owing to the heavy seas, and so, in the presence of her father and close to the ship, she was drowned. The cries and lamentations that day and night were very pitiable, and the sight of so much misery in the souls of the heathen. . . . All that day and night, without rest, they made great sacrifices and feasts to their idol, killing many birds, and giving it food and drink. Then they cast lots, and asked it why the captain's daughter had died.* The lot fell out that she would not have died or fallen into the sea if our Manuel, who fell into the well, had died.

"You see the peril our lives were put in by the demon's lots and the power of his servants and ministers. What would become of us if God allowed the demon to do us the harm he wanted to do us ? . . .

"The day these disasters happened, and all that night, it pleased God our Lord to do me much grace. He was pleased to cause me to feel and experience many things anent those fierce and frightful fears imposed by the enemy when God permits him, and he finds a chance of causing them ; and also anent the remedies against the temptations of the enemy which a man ought to use when he finds himself in such trouble . . . The sum of all these remedies is to show very great courage against the enemy ; for a man must distrust himself totally, and trust in God grandly, placing in Him all the force and hope he possesses, and then, having so great a Defender and Protector, he must show no cowardice, and not doubt but that he will be victor. Many a time I thought that it was as if God our Lord had increased the demon's sufferings to a greater pitch than before, and that he was out that day and night to revenge himself, for he seemed to be keeping on saying to me that we were in his time of vengeance."

Xavier, we gather, had prayed that God would come down on the devil every time the devil moved the captain to cast lots, as it was the lots which made the captain hesitate about going on to Japan. And now Xavier believed that God had answered his prayers, and that the devil, having a bad time of it, naturally wanted to get back a bit of his own. So often, in that day and night of the two disasters, he had before his mind that the devil was taking his revenge. The letter goes on :

"And in such times want of confidence in God is more to be dreaded than fear of the enemy, for the demon cannot do any more harm than God allows. God allows the demon to discomfort and vex those creatures who through pusillanimity stop trusting in their Creator, and do not force themselves to hope in Him. Many who began by serving

* Compare Jonah i. 7.

God have comfortless lives . . . because they do not keep on carrying the sweet Cross of Christ with perseverance. . . . These do not know their own weaknesses, and put them down to the Cross of Christ, and say it is troublesome to keep on carrying it. O Brothers, what will become of us at the hour of death, if in life we do not prepare and set ourselves to learn to hope and trust in God ? For in that hour we shall find ourselves in greater temptations and troubles and dangers than ever we have seen, both spiritual and bodily. Therefore let those who live with the desire to serve God strive to be humble in small things, always distrusting themselves, and establishing themselves entirely on God. . . .

"If men would only regard it as certain that to fail in duty to God must bring them more harm than could happen to them from the demon's side, what consolation they would experience! How much they would profit when they knew their own little worth from their own experience, and yet saw clearly their great worth when they closed entirely with God! And how confounded and weak the demon would be on finding himself conquered by those whose conqueror he once had been!

"To return now to our voyage. The seas went down, we weighed anchor and set sail with much sadness [because the captain had decided not to make direct for Japan]. . . . In a few days we arrived in China at the port of Canton. All thought it well to winter at that port, the sailors as well as the captain; we were the only ones to oppose this plan, which we did with petitions and with some threats [to report the shipmaster to the Captain in Malacca] . . . God our Lord was pleased to make them unwilling to remain in the isles of Canton, so we weighed anchor . . . and in a few days, with a good wind, which God was giving us continually, we reached Chimceo [Tchintcheo], another Chinese port. We were just entering it with the intention of wintering there, as the monsoon to take us to Japan was coming to an end, when a sail came to us. They gave us the news that the port was full of pirates, and that if we entered we were lost. . . . It was a head wind to go back to Canton. and a stern wind to come to Japan. Thus, against the will of the captain of the ship and the sailors, they were forced to come to Japan. So neither the demon nor his ministers were able to prevent our coming, and so God brought us to this so-longed-for land.

"I arrived on the Feast of the Assumption, August, 1549. Without being able to touch any other Japanese port, we came to Kagoshima,* which is the home of Paul of the Holy Faith. There all, both his relatives and those who were not, received us with much love." †

Kagoshima, the port at which Francis and his companions landed, was the native town of Paul of the Holy Faith, and his return was the occasion of a great welcome, both to himself and those whom he brought with him. They were not at all scandalised that he had become a Christian ; the fact that he had embraced a new religion only added to the interest aroused by his reappearance. He introduced Xavier to the Governor of the town, who received the missionary with much kindness. This kindness was doubtless reinforced by commercial instincts, for the merchants of Japan were just awaking to the fact that it was desirable that the Portuguese ships should visit them, and the different ports were ready to vie with one another in hospitality toward strangers from the West.

As an interpreter, Paul was indispensable, and he took great pains to teach his Western friends the language. Already, during the voyage, Juan Fernandez had made good progress.

After six weeks the *daimio* of the province invited them to appear before him. He received them kindly. Francis expressed his desire to go on to Kioto,‡ the capital, but the *daimio* dissuaded him, telling him the weather and the wars would make his passage quite impossible until later on. At the same time he put a house at the disposal of the missionaries. There Francis occupied his leisure moments in composing, with the help of Paul, a document similar to that which he had composed at Ternate (see p. 242).

The first converts in Kagoshima were the relatives of Paul of the Holy Faith. Another of the earliest converts was one who received the Christian name of Bernard. This man became one of Francis' most faithful helpers, accompanied him in all his journeys through Japan, followed him to

* Spelt throughout by Xavier Cangoxima.   † *Mon. Xav.* vol. i. p. 572 ff.
‡ Then known as Miaco.

India, and after the Saint's death went to Europe, visited the Jesuits in Spain and Italy, and finally died in the college at Coimbra.

But Francis, in Japan, made no attempts to repeat the methods which he had used in Southern India. There, as an old chronicler has said, he had fished with a drag-net, but here he had to fish with a line. The first three months were chiefly spent in preparation. Fernandez, evidently a brilliant linguist, Cosmo de Torres and Francis became the industrious pupils of Paul of the Holy Faith. Besides studying the language, Francis studied the people, with whole-hearted gusto.

In the letter written on November 5th, of which we have already quoted a part, he goes on to give his first impressions of the Japanese, or rather of the Japanese of the province of Satsuma:

" The people with whom we have conversed so far are the best yet discovered. In my opinion no people superior to the Japanese will be found among unbelievers. They are of good behaviour, and good generally, and not malicious, marvellously honourable. They esteem honour more than anything. They are mostly poor, and neither the nobles nor those who are not esteem poverty as a reproach. They have one quality which I do not think is to be found among any Christians, and it is this—the nobles, however poor they may be, and those who are not nobles, however rich, honour a very poor noble as much as if he were rich; and not for any price would a very poor noble marry into another caste if it were not noble. . . . So they esteem honour more than riches. They are very courteous among themselves. They prize arms greatly and trust much in them. They always carry swords and daggers—all the people, high and low alike, from the age of 14 years, they carry sword and dagger.

" They will stand no insults nor slighting words. The people who are not noble have great reverence for the nobles, and all the nobles are very proud to serve the lord of the land, and are very obedient to him. This I think they do because they hold that if they did the contrary they should lose their honour. . . .

" They are abstemious in eating, though they drink a

U

good deal. They drink rice wine, as there are no vines in these parts. They never gamble, because in their opinion it is very dishonourable, for gamblers desire what is not their own, and thence may come to be thieves. They swear little, and when they do it is by the sun. A great part of the people can read and write, which is a great help for learning the prayers and things of God quickly.

" They have not more than one wife. It is a land of few thieves, because severe justice is meted out to those who are found to be thieves, and none of their lives spared. They are kindly, very conversable, and eager for knowledge. They rejoice much to hear of God . . . most of them believe in men of ancient times, who, as I have managed to understand, were men who lived as philosophers. Many of them adore the sun, others the moon. They rejoice to hear things conformable to reason, and though there are vices and sins among them, yet when they are given reasons, and shown that what they do is ill done, then what reason defends seems good to them.

" Among the secular I find less sin, and see more obedience to reason, than among those whom they regard as Fathers. They call them *bonzes* [bonjos]. They are inclined to sins which Nature abhors. They confess and do not deny it. . . . Among these *bonzes* are some who live like friars. They go clothed in grey gowns. They are clean-shaven, head as well as beard. . . . They are very licentious, and have nuns of the same order living together with them. The populace have a very evil opinion of them. . . .

" I can tell you one thing for which you may give thanks to God our Lord : this island of Japan is very ready for the great increase of our holy faith in it. If we could speak the language I have no hesitation whatever in believing that many would become Christians. May it please God our Lord that we shall learn it in a short time, for already we begin to have a smattering of it, and we have expounded the Ten Commandments in forty days which we gave to learn them. I give you this so detailed account that you may all give thanks to God our Lord for the discovery of this country in which your holy desires can be employed and fulfilled ; and also that you may apparel yourselves with great virtue and with the desire to suffer greatly in the service of Christ our Redeemer and Lord. And remember that God sets more value on the offering of a good will full of humility presented for His sole love and glory than He prizes and esteems the actual services done Him, however many they may be.

" Be prepared, for likely in less than two years I may write to you that a number of you should come to Japan. So strive after great humility, persecuting your own selves in the things for which you feel repugnance. Strive with all the power God gives you to know yourselves as you are. Thus you will grow in faith and hope, and confidence and love toward God, and charity with your neighbours. From distrust of oneself is born the trust in God that is real. . . . Take care not to plume yourselves upon the good opinion others may have of you, or you will be confounded. For some by their carelessness in this come to lose inward humility, and grow in pride. . . . In all your affairs establish yourselves altogether in God, without trusting in your own powers or knowledge, or in human opinion, and so I reckon you will be prepared for all the great adversities, whether bodily or spiritual, that may come upon you, for God lifts up and strengthens the humble, and chiefly those who in small and lowly things have seen, as in a clear mirror, their own weaknesses, and have conquered themselves. Neither the devil and his ministers, nor the great sea tempests nor the evil barbarians, nor any other creature can harm such as these. For their confidence is all in God, and they know for certain, even when facing tribulations greater than ever they saw, that without His leave all these can do nothing . . .

" I know a person to whom God did great favour, who occupied himself often, both in peril and out of it, in placing all his hope and confidence in Him, and the advantage that came to him from this would take too long to write. And because all these troubles which you have hitherto had to endure are small compared to those which you will have to put up with when you come to Japan, I pray and beseech you as much as I can by the love and service of God our Lord, to make yourselves ready for much, overthrowing your own affections since they are a hindrance to good. And look well to yourselves, my brothers in Jesus Christ, for many are in hell who when they were in this life were the cause and instrument through which others, by their words, were saved and went to glory. . . .

" Remember that saying of the Lord, *What does it profit a*

man if he gain the whole world, and suffer the loss of his own soul? Let none of you build on its seeming to you that you have been a long time in the Company, and that you are older than others, and that therefore you are more worth than those that have not been so long. . . . I do not tell you these things to make you think the service of God troublesome, and the yoke of the Lord not light and sweet [*suave*]. For if men set themselves to seek God, and take and embrace the means to do it, they will find sweetness and comfort enough in His service, to make it easy to overcome all the repugnance they feel to conquering themselves. What delight and contentment of spirit men lose, because they do not master themselves in those temptations which are wont to keep back the weak from good and from the knowledge of the infinite (*suma*) goodness of God, and from rest in this troubled life ! For to live here without enjoying God is not life, but one continued death."*

" . . . And be well assured that you will undergo many kinds of temptations ; when you go alone, or two by two, placed in many trials, in countries of the unbelievers, or in storms at sea. You had not such things when you were in College. If you are not well exercised [*i.e.*, drilled in the Spiritual Exercises of Loyola], and experienced in knowing how to conquer your own inordinate affections and in great knowledge of the deceits of the enemy, judge, brothers, the dangers you will run when you are exposed to the world, which is founded on wickedness, and how you will resist it if you are not very humble. . . .†

" May it please God our Lord to give us language, so that we may be able to speak of the things of God, for then with His aid, grace, and favour we shall gain much fruit. Now we are among them like statues. They speak and talk a lot, and we, as we don't understand the *lingoa*, are silent. And now we must be as infants, in learning the language. God grant that we may imitate them, too, in simplicity and pureness of mind. . . .‡

" I think that we shall this winter be busy in making an explanation of the articles of the faith somewhat fully, in Japanese, for printing. All the principal people here can read and write, and so this will be a way of spreading our

* *Mon. Xav.*, vol. i. p. 579 ff.   † *Ibid.*, vol. i. p. 587.   ‡ *Ibid.*, vol. i. p. 591.

holy faith, as we can't go everywhere. Paul, our very dear brother, is going to translate faithfully into their language all that is needful for the salvation of their souls. . . .*

" I pray you earnestly [he concludes] that there may be true love among you ; and do not bear any bitterness of mind. Convert part of your fervours into love one towards another, and part of your desires to suffer for Christ's sake into suffering [one another] and conquering all the aversions which do not allow this love to grow. You know what Christ said, that in this He would know His own if they loved one another. God our Lord grant us to know within our souls His most holy will, and grace to fulfil it perfectly.

" Kagoshima, 5th Nov., 1549.

" Your Brother in Christ."

In another letter written on the same day he says to the heads of the college at Goa :

" Work hard at teaching and instructing in your college, especially Chinese and Japanese youths. Be careful for them spiritually. See that they can read, write, and speak Portuguese, so that they may act as interpreters for the fathers who, please God our Lord, will come before many years are out to Japan and China. For in my opinion there is a finer harvest to be reaped in Japan and China than in any of the other newly discovered countries. Therefore I charge you earnestly to care for the Chinese and Japanese. . . . If the two bonzes who are going to Malacca this year get to Goa do your best to make them welcome among the Portuguese. Show them much love, as I did to Paul when he was there. For they are a people who will be attracted only by love. Don't be at all hard on them."†

On the same day Xavier despatched a letter to three of the Fathers at Goa, bidding them come out to Japan. He hopes to meet them at Kioto. To Gomez, the Superior of the College, he writes :

" When the Fathers come, arrange with the Governor to send out some objects as presents for the King of Japan, with a letter. For I trust in God that if he were converted

* *Mon. Xav.*, vol. i. p. 600.   † *Ibid.*, vol. i. pp. 644 and 646.

to our holy Faith great temporal advantage would result
to the King of Portugal by making a factory in Sakay.*
This is a very large port, and is a city where there are numbers
of rich merchants, and plenty of silver and gold, more than
in any other part of Japan.   Judging by my experience of
India, I am not so sure that they would send a ship [here]
with the Fathers, if they had nothing else to look to but
the mere love of God.   It may be that I am wrong, and if
so I should be glad.   So in forwarding the Fathers, go about
it in this way.   Let the Lord Governor, if he wishes to do a
great favour to some relative or friend, and secure him
considerable profit, give him a licence to send a ship to Japan
with the Fathers.   For this I am writing a list of the things
most valuable at the port of Sakay.   It is two days' journey
by land from Kioto [*i.e.*, Kioto is two days' journey inland].

" Whoever conveys the Fathers will gain plenty of silver
and gold, if he brings the merchandise entered in this list.
In this way the Fathers will be able to come very comfort-
ably and safely, for this ship will come well armed, and provided with everything needful.

" Give a warning that the Fathers come very soon to Japan.
The ship that comes from Goa must leave Goa with all its
cargo in April, and has to leave Malacca in June.   It must
take all needful provisions, and must not touch at China at
all, however much they may hope to do business there.
Nor must it take in provisions, save water, from any of the
islands, but must make a straight course for Japan.   For
if it touch at China to do business there, you must understand
that it will spend seventeen months between Goa and Japan,
but, not touching at China, it will be in Japan in four and a
half months.

" It is necessary that the ship should not bring much
pepper, but at the most eighty *bares*.   For, bringing little,
they are sure to sell it very well in Japan, and they will gain
plenty of money, as I have said, if they come to the port of
Sakay.

" And see that you are cautious about the licence which
the Governor gives to the man who has to bring the Fathers.
It must stipulate that he does not touch at China to do
business . . . if they don't leave China for Japan on August
1st there is no monsoon for a year.   The priests who come

* Near the modern port of Osaka.

should be well provided with Portuguese clothing and with boots, for here we are dying of cold."*

Xavier was very full of this project, for sent off at the same time as the above letter is one to his friend Pedro da Silva da Gama, son of the great Vasco da Gama, and at this time Captain or Commandant of Malacca.

" In Sakay, which is the principal port of Japan, two days' journey by land from Kioto, a factory will be erected, which, please God, should pay very well. . . . If you would trust me, and make me your factor in these parts of all the merchandise you send, I assure you of one thing, you will by a sure way make more than 10,000 per cent. profit, which no Captain in Malacca has done hitherto. Here is the way : Give all to the poor who become Christians. The gain will be most secure, and there will be no risks, for it is certain that for him who gives one for Christ's sake a hundred is kept in the other life. I'm much afraid that you don't approve of so much profit. The Captains of Malacca have this fault, that they are not disposed towards the largest merchandise."

We know that Pedro da Silva liked to do things in great style. He had wished to send Xavier and his party off to Japan much more magnificently than they chose to go. Later on Xavier sighed for him, when he was finding difficulty in getting a ship to take him to China. The two *hidalgos* had always got on well together. But here Xavier seems to be " taking off " his friend's way of talking about things, and of calculating the profits and losses of mercantile enterprises.

The letter goes on to report the death of the man who had shipped them to Japan, the most famous Eastern pirate of these days :—

" The Pirate died here in Kagoshima. He was kind to us all the voyage, and we could not be kind to him, for he died in his unbelief. Nor could we be kind to him after death, for his soul is in hell."†

Xavier was very sure of God, but here, as so often elsewhere, we see how very sure of hell he was too.

* *Mon. Xav.*, vol. 1. p. 648   † *Ibid*, vol. i p. 654.

A little later the Saint writes:

" We are engaged in teaching the Christians and learning
the language of Japan, and in translating some articles of
our holy faith, beginning from the creation of the world
to the final judgment, and the life of Christ our Lord, and
His Sacred Passion. From all this we have made a book
in Japanese, and we read from it to those who wish to become
Christians, that they may know what they have to believe
and do. They are glad to hear these things, for they begin
to see they are all truth. This shows that the Japanese
have good brains. This year about six hundred have
become Christians. Many more gave up, not because
they did not understand that our faith was true, but because
they were afraid of the Duke [the daimio]." *

Among the bonzes with whom Xavier used to talk in
Kagoshima was one old man called Ninjit, the superior of
the chief monastery of the place. One day Xavier, seeing a
number of them engaged in meditation, asked Ninjit what
was the subject of their thoughts. The old man, smiling,
replied, " Some of them are calculating how much they
have got out of their parishioners during the last month,
others are planning how to dress themselves and feed themselves, others how they are going to amuse themselves.
None of them are dreaming about anything important."

Another time Francis asked Ninjit which period of life
he preferred, and Ninjit answered " Youth." And then
Francis said, " When sailors leave one port for another,
which hour is the happier for them, the hour when they are
in mid-ocean, or the hour when they are almost in haven ? "
" All that is not for me," said Ninjit, " for I do not know to
what port my ship is going."

Other bonzes were less ready to talk with the strangers,
especially when they saw that some of the townspeople
were becoming Christians. They knew that if all the town
were converted their living would be gone. So they began
a kind of underhand persecution. They circulated gruesome
tales about the missionaries, saying that they lived on human
flesh, and to confirm this they strewed blood-stained garments
about the place where they lodged. At the same time the

* *Mon. Xav.*, vol. i, p. 659.

daimio heard that a Portuguese ship which he had been hoping would visit Kagoshima had passed them by, and he suddenly wearied of his calculated friendship for the " barbarians of the south." He published an edict, saying that whoever in the future became a Christian would be killed, but that those who had already been baptized would not be harmed. Xavier thought it time to seek out a more hopeful soil. "When we saw," he writes, " that we could not in the meantime gain any more fruit we went to another district. We took leave of the Christians, and they took leave of us, with many tears and much sorrow."*

This was in September, 1550, after a sojourn of thirteen months in Kagoshima.

Paul of the Holy Faith was left in charge of the little Christian community, and for five months he was faithful to them. Then, harassed and persecuted beyond the limits of his patience, he retired from all spiritual conflicts, bought himself a ship, and spent the rest of his days as a *bafan*, or pirate, on the Chinese coast.

Juan Fernandez and Cosmo de Torres went with Xavier. As they left the outskirts of Kagoshima they came to the fort of Ycicu, where they had already made a number of converts. These they visited, and before they left, taught how to baptize, and gave away some of the literature which they had been so much occupied in composing—some prayers, a Calendar, the Seven Psalms of Penitence, and the Story of the Passion, all in the Japanese language. Ten years later a Jesuit brother visited these people. They had not seen a European since Xavier left them, but they still kept the faith.

By the beginning of ·October the missionaries found themselves in Hirado. There were Portuguese ships in the harbour, and thanks to that fact, probably, Xavier was able to record that the daimio had received them with great affection. But this was not their goal. Xavier had made up his mind to go on to the capital, " to plant there the law of God." " Such an attempt," says Valignano, " needed a truly great and confident spirit. To penetrate a country thus, dressed in so new and strange a manner, and thus attired having to meet all the heathendom of Japan, with no other guide and no other hope but in God, was a proceeding which those who

* *Mon. Xav.*, vol. i. p. 659.

know what Japan was then would call one of supernatural and heroic faith." *

The old chronicler Frois had a first-hand account of this journey from Juan Fernandez.

Neither the cold, nor the snow, nor the fear of unknown peoples hindered the Father Master Francis in carrying out his plans for the service of God. On the sea the pirates were everywhere, and we had often to remain hidden at the bottom of the hold, so as to escape them. Going by land, our troubles increased. We carried all our luggage in two wallets, like those of the mendicant brothers. It consisted of a surplice, three or four shirts, and an old blanket which we both used at night. For there are no beds in the Japanese inns. We did very well if they lent us a straw mat, or a wooden pillow. Sometimes when we arrived in the evenings, frozen with cold and famished, there was no kind of shelter for us. At other times, owing to the deep snow, our legs swelled, and we fell in these bitter mountain paths. Poor, badly clad, strangers, and recognised as such, we were very badly received in certain places, jeered at by the children, and even stoned.

We arrived thus at Facata, a populous trading city in the kingdom of Chicugen. The Father went to visit a large monastery of bonzes of the sect of the Jenxus, who believe only in the present life. These people were notorious for their evil living. . . . The bonzes imagined that the Father came from Siam, from where they believe their gods to have come; they received him with great demonstrations of joy, and took him to their superior, who was like a bishop. He received us with pleasure and had some fruit served to us.

The Father at once raised his voice, and speaking very distinctly reproached the superior and the others with great severity for the abominable vice which reigned among them. He also rebuked them for letting the people believe that there is nothing after this life, and, again, for deceiving them by exhorting them to make offerings to the dead by which they (the bonzes) alone profited. As they listened to him the bonzes were stupefied to think that a man whom they had never seen should reprove them with such energy. Some of them, it is true, laughed at him; the others were amazed. Without further formality the Father left them and we continued on our road.

The five or six days which followed our departure from Facata were very rough. Yet all the way the Father added to the troubles of the road a continual voluntary mortification. One

* *Mon. Xav.,* vol. i. p. 123.

would have to have seen him as I did, with my own eyes, to get
an idea of the details of this mortification. Even his way of
saying prayers on the road had this mark of penitence. Meditation and contemplation were so familiar to him that the snow-
covered mountains and valleys all around could not distract
him ; all the time of prayer Father Francis did not raise his eyes
or turn his head ; his arms and hands were motionless, only his
feet moved, and that with difficulty. Truly he showed by this
humility and reverence of bearing that he walked in the presence
of God.

Also at the inns, which were hardly more than stables, he was
so temperate at table that, fatigued by the journey as he was,
he appeared more like a slave whom his lord has condescended
to invite to eat with him, and who cannot forget how unworthy
he is to receive food from the hand of his master.*

Of Yamaguchi, the next town which they came to, Xavier
writes :

" It is a city of more than a thousand heads of families.
The houses are of wood. There were many gentlemen and
others anxious to know about the religion we were preaching.
So we stayed some time and preached twice daily in the
streets. We read from the book we carried, making short
discourses on what we read. Crowds came to the sermons.
We were also invited to the houses of the principal gentlemen,
they asking us to explain that religion which we were
preaching. They told us that if it were better than their own
they would adopt it. Some of them showed great satisfaction
in hearing the law of God. Others made game of it. Others
were bored by it. When we went into the streets the children
and others followed, making game of us. . : ."

The daimio then sent for them and commanded them to
declare the " law of God."

" So we read a great part of the book. He was very
attentive all the time we were reading, which would be
more than an hour. Then he sent us away. We persevered
in this city many days, and preached in the streets and houses,
and many were glad to hear the life of Christ our Lord,
and wept when they heard some passages from the Passion." †

* *Primera parte da Historia de Japam* (1549–1578), MSS , by P Louis Frois,
quoted by Cros, *Vie de S François Xavier*, vol. ii p 99 ff.
† *Mon. Xav.*, vol. i p. 660 f.

The Annalist of Macao* gives more details of this visit than Francis does.

He tells us that when the Saint and his companions arrived in the town they looked so poor and wretched that no one would give them a lodging. They at once began to preach in the open streets. Crowds gathered, and they were rudely treated, but they would take no rebuff and went on preaching. Besides preaching Francis would read aloud to them from the little book which he had made. Some continued to laugh at his pronunciation and at the expressions he used, but others showed interest in what he said. So he went on, never showing any impatience, but declaring the truth and condemning their sins, till the Japanese, who, the old Annalist says, are experts in judging men, saw that they were irreproachable, and began to venerate them. But this veneration did not come to much. There were very few conversions. The interviews with the *fidalgos* of the town, as Fernandez calls them, were for him, if not for Francis, full of trepidating anxiety. Francis frankly and fearlessly denounced their vices, and warned them of judgments to come. And when their hosts upon this *thee-and-thou*'d them, or used other such impolite forms of speech, the Saint said to Fernandez, "Thee-and-thou them too," till the poor Brother expected each moment to see one of those long swords their hosts were wearing flash in front of his own neck. But Francis cheered him on with the words, "There is nothing in you you so much need to mortify as this fear of death. Despise death and these men will respect you, and know our teaching is from God."

"With all this," Xavier writes, "very few became Christians. Seeing the small amount of fruit gained we determined to go on to Meaco [Kioto], the principal city of all Japan. We spent two months on the road, and underwent many dangers and travails."†

Neither Francis nor his companions knew the roads, and the country was at war and overrun with soldiers. The cold for them was very trying. Often in the inns there was

---

* This title is given by Cros to the author of an old contemporary MS. See Cros, *Vie de S. François Xavier*, vol. ii. p. 37.

† *Mon. Xav.*, vol. i. p. 661.

nothing to eat, and they had to fall back upon the little wallet of rice which they had brought for emergencies. Francis and Fernandez carried on their backs the silver for the celebration of Mass, and a blanket for night. Several times they met travellers going towards the capital on horse-back, and they used to run after them on foot as long as they could so as not to lose the way. Soon their appearance became so disreputable that the innkeepers would not give them any other shelter than that of a shed in the garden. In spite of their woes, Fernandez tells us that Francis was joyful all the time, and would tramp along with his eyes turned heavenwards, and his bare feet among the sharp stones, feeling nothing. Then later on he would see the blood on his feet and say with surprise, " Whatever is this ? How did this happen ? "

At last they came to Sakay, the town where Xavier had hoped to help his Portuguese friends to get a factory put up. No one would take them in, and the whole town seemed to have turned out to mock them : they tried to preach, but it was hopeless. Then they went just beyond the town, into a pine-wood, and there they made themselves a little cabin of fir-branches. But even there they could not rest, for bands of children came running out to see them, and flung stones at them. " Here one thing alone mars my delight," said Francis ; " it is that I cannot preach."

The Saint had brought with him an introduction to a citizen of Sakay : at first he had not been able to find this man, but he discovered him later and was hospitably received by him, and given an introduction to a Japanese nobleman who was travelling to Kioto. Without this it would have been impossible for the travellers to enter the capital, as all the surrounding country was in a state of war. The nobleman and his pages were carried in litters, and the servants ran behind on foot. With these ran Francis and his companions. " Never," says Fernandez, " have I seen Francis so gay as on this occasion. He wore a Siamese hat. And thus, à galope, we covered the eighteen leagues which separate Sakay and Kioto." *

Xavier's reception in the capital of Japan must have been one of the most disappointing experiences of his life. In his dreams he had seen Kioto as the Paris of the East, and

* See Cros, *Vie de S. François Xavier*, vol. ii. p. 117.

had thought to discover there another Sorbonne, ready to open its doors to his sweet and reasonable appeal. But it was not to be in the capital that the first foundations of the great Roman Catholic missions in Japan were to be laid. His own account is brief, for he never spent his eloquence over his disappointments :

" On our arrival at Kioto we tried for some days to get speech with the king [the Mikado], so as to ask him for leave to preach in his kingdom the law of God. But we could not get speech with him. After we had been told that even his own people did not obey him, we gave up trying to get leave. We looked to see if there was any inclination among that people (to listen) to the manifestation of the law of God our Lord. We found none, on account of war being expected. This city of Kioto was once very great ; now it is much ruined with wars. They say that in old days there were more than 180,000 houses, and I think that there would be from the site. At present, though it is greatly ruined and burnt, yet I think there will be more than 100,000 houses.
" When we saw that the land was not peaceful enough to allow the manifestation of the law of God in 'it, we returned again to Yamaguchi." *

" As the boat sailed down the river," says Fernandez, " the blessed Father could not take his eyes from off the city, but looked towards it, repeating with great emotion *In exitu Israel de Egypto* . . . and several verses from the same Psalm."
The great emotion with which Fernandez says he repeated this Psalm was far from a feeling of anger or despair. Even in this bitter moment we hear the same undaunted faith ringing in his voice, and see the same mysterious smile lighting his lips and eyes, that we have heard and seen at every crisis since his conversion. And he goes down the river singing like a troubadour :

When Israel went forth out of Egypt,
The house of Jacob from a people of strange language,
Judah became his sanctuary,
Israel his dominion.

* *Mon. Xav.*, vol. i. p. 661.

The sea saw it and fled ;
Jordan was driven back.
The mountains skipped like rams,
The little hills like young sheep.
What aileth thee, O thou sea, that thou fleest ?
Thou Jordan, that thou turnest back ?
Ye mountains, that ye skip like rams,
Ye little hills, like young sheep ?
Tremble, thou earth, at the presence of the Lord,
At the presence of the God of Jacob ;
Which turned the rock into a pool of water,
The flint into a fountain of waters !

Xavier never returned to Kioto, but in 1577, the first Christian Church was built there. It was called the Church of the Assumption of Our Lady, because on that feast-day* Xavier had first landed on Japanese soil.

An account of how they came back from Sakay to Hirado has been left us by Fernández:

The hardships were greatest on our return journey. It was February, the time of the greatest cold, snow, frost, and wind, and for us there was neither shelter nor succour.

The Father used to buy dried fruits at the inns and carry them in his breast or in his sleeves, and then when, by the roadside or in the villages, we came across little children, he gave them some of the fruits and his blessing.†

This little fragment is surely very touching. On the outward journey Francis had constantly been hooted and jeered at by the children. We fancy he had found that harder to bear than anything else—for he was a very great lover of children—and so he had thus tenderly provided against the same thing happening on his returning way.

By the end of February, 1551, they were once more in Hirado. They had been away four or five months, and had been walking almost all that time, very often with bare feet, and they had brought back no bright tale of success.

Cosmo de Torres was able to give a cheering report of his work in Hirado ; the household with whom he lodged were converted, and many of their relatives and friends. But Xavier did not stay there more than a few days. He

* August 15th, *The Day of Our Lady in Summer*, it used to be called.
† Cros, *Vie de S. François Xavier*, vol. ii. p. 122.

had come to the conclusion that in Yamaguchi the soil was better prepared to receive the Gospel than in any other part of Japan. Before he set out on this new journey he procured for himself some richer garments than hitherto, as a missionary, he had worn. He had learned by experience that in Japan people would not listen to his message with much respect if he were poorly and strangely clad. So the Siamese hat and the ragged cotton cassock were laid aside, and he donned instead a handsome Japanese gown, and set out for Yamaguchi.

The change of dress was significant of a complete change of policy. For in his pocket he put letters from the Governor and from the Bishop of Goa, which he had not hitherto used, offering the King of Portugal's friendship to Japan, and asking protection for the missionaries.

Besides these he carried with him several European books, some spectacles, a musical instrument with a range of 70 notes, called a *manicordia*, a piece of brocade, a Portuguese dress, an arquebuse, three beautiful crystal vases, some mirrors, a richly decorated striking clock, and various other attractive articles.

The daimio of Yamaguchi was delighted with the presents, gave them formal permission to preach, and put an empty monastery at their disposal.

" While we stayed in this monastery many came to hear the sermons. Generally there was preaching twice daily. At the end of the sermon there were discussions, which lasted a long time. We were continually taken up with answering questions and preaching. Numbers of bonzes, nuns, gentlemen, and crowds of other people came to the sermon, so that the house was almost always as full as it could hold. The questions they put to us were such that by our replies they knew that their laws and the saints in which they believed were false, and the law of God true. They kept up the discussions for many days, and then they began to become Christians. Many of them were gentlemen. After having become Christians, they grew more friendly than can be told.

" Those who became Christians showed us very faithfully all the things the heathen have in their religions . . . After getting correct information about their religions, we began to seek reasons for proving them false. So every day we smashed up some points of their laws, and put before them arguments which neither the bonzes nor monks nor wizards nor any of the people who abhorred the law of God could answer.

" When the Christians saw that the bonzes could not answer, they were greatly delighted, and became confirmed more every day in the faith of God our Lord. The heathen present at the discussions lost belief in their former sects and errors. . . .

" The Japanese are full of curious questions, with a keen desire for knowledge. So much is this the case that they never stop discussing with others about the questions they put to us, and the answers we give them. They are very inquisitive, especially about religions. They say that before we came here they were always discussing which of their religions was the best. . . . It is a wonderful thing to see, in a city so large as this, people speaking of the law of God in every street and house. . . .

" The Japanese regard the Chinese as very wise, both about religions and the other world, and about the government of the commonwealth. So one of the questions they put to us . . . was, How did the Chinese not know, if these things were so ? . . . . In the space of two months more than 500 Christians have been made, and so it goes on every day. . . . It is wonderful how truly friendly the Christians are. They are always coming to visit us, and to see if we want anything. The whole nation in general is much given to compliments and courtesies, and the Christians seem to give all the greater care and attention to this, especially with us, for the great love they have to us." *

After the fiasco in Kioto all this is very cheering. Among the converts was a man to whom the name of Laurence was given in baptism. Frois gives a vivid little sketch of him :

In the streets of Yamaguchi there was a blind man who earned his living, as many do in Japan, by singing and playing the violin. He was quite blind in one eye and nearly so in the other. He used to go often from house to house among the rich folk, to tell old stories and entertain them by his wit, and he

* *Mon. Xav.*, vol. i. p. 662.

was well received.   Besides the qualities which he would naturally acquire by such a life this blind man had also a quick and penetrating intelligence and an excellent memory.   Having heard, then, quite soon of the arrival of strangers who were preaching a new religion, he presented himself to Father Master Francis, and asked him many questions.   Satisfied with the replies, he came back and asked others, and every day he learnt something and became more capable of better teaching.   In this way he was soon well informed on the things of the faith, and the Father baptized him and gave him the name of Laurence.   The charity of Father Francis delighted him, and he was struck with the greatness of his plans for converting souls to the true God.   He admired the way in which the strangers had come over thousands of leagues, through many dangers, and without seeking any temporal gain, for this beautiful and unique end.   So he left his songs, his violin, his stories, and the vain amusements of men, and begged for the favour of being allowed to work, according to his gifts, for the glory of God and the salvation of souls ; and God, who is pleased to choose the weak things for his great works, chose this man who was blind, and whose face was of a ridiculous appearance, to be the first lay brother of the Company of Jesus in Japan and the first preacher and missionary of the Holy Gospel in the town of Miaco and the seigneuries round about ; there he worked with such abundant and special grace that he has a noted place among all the eminent preachers of the Faith in these lands.   His words have converted many thousands of souls ; he used to argue in public with the most learned of the bonzes, and with the most cultured of the nobility, and he was never worsted.   Indeed, the power of his teaching was so great that the proud men of letters humbled themselves at his feet, and many of them were won over by him and embraced the Gospel.

While he was an unconquerable preacher of the truth, Laurence was no less exemplary in fulfilling all the duties of a religious and holy life ; in this he came behind none of those who had grown up in Europe at the heart of light and Christianity.   All those of the Company who have lived beside him have admired his virtues, and even now, although he is more than sixty-five years old, very infirm, and weakened by forty years of hard toil, he still preaches in the kingdom of Nixo on the territory of D. Bartolomeo. Two or three times a day, when it is necessary, Brother Laurence preaches to the Christians and to the heathen.*

The Annalist of Macao gives some other interesting details of the sojourn at Yamaguchi.   The bills which were put up

* Cros, *Vie de S. François Xavier*, vol. ii. p. 148.

in the town authorising the preaching of the Gospel ran, he says, as follows :

I (the Daimio) am pleased to allow that the Law of God may be taught and preached throughout my territories and that those who wish to embrace it may do so freely. My vassals are all forbidden under grave penalties to hinder or molest any of the Fathers who preach the Law of *Deos.*

At first, the Annalist says, they had no converts. But one day, when Fernandez was preaching, surrounded by a great crowd, a rough fellow came up and began to mock him, and then spat on his face. Fernandez, showing no resentment, quietly went on with what he had to say. This behaviour so impressed the people that from that hour they began to ask for baptism. Two months later there were a hundred Christians in the town, many of them belonging to the nobility.

Xavier worked on in Yamaguchi for six months, and then he summoned Cosmo de Torres from Hirado, and put him and Fernandez in charge of the new community, and set out for the province of Bungo, where he had heard that there was a Portuguese ship ready to sail for India. "I leave you good guardians in Father Torres and Brother Fernandez," he is reported by a Japanese chronicler to have said, " but remember to put all your trust in God alone."

He then knelt down and all the Christians with him, and they all prayed with tears and groans, and Father Francis commended them to God. When the prayers were finished Father Francis tenderly kissed Father Cosmo de Torres and Brother Juan Fernandez, holding them in his embrace, while the tears ran down his cheeks. Then, raising his eyes to Heaven, he said, " Now, more than ever before, I commend you to God from the bottom of my heart. It is He who will give you all the spiritual strength that you need, it is He who can protect you." *

Earlier in his life the Saint would have bid them call on other names as well ; since then experience had taught him a simpler and grander faith.

In November, 1551, Xavier left Japan. He took with him to India an ambassador from the daimio of Bungo, two samurai who had followed him from Yamaguchi, and who were to go to the college at Goa, and two of his Japanese converts.

* Cros, *Vie de S. François Xavier,* vol. ii. p. 153.

It was a fortunate thing for the Roman Catholic missions that Xavier left behind him so capable a man as Fernandez. Cary, in his *History of Christianity in Japan,* estimates that he did more for Japan than Xavier did, and in many ways this is true. Xavier, here as elsewhere, opened up the way, and searched out the fruitful soil, and then left others to plant and water, while he again prepared to go forward into the unknown.

From Cochin the Saint despatched a letter to Ignatius, which is full of references to his work in Japan :

" Those who come out will be much harassed, for they will have to oppose all the Japanese sects, and will have to expose to the world the deceitful way by which the bonzes get money from the laymen. And in this our people must not be too patient, specially in affirming that they cannot get souls out of hell . . .   They will be much more put to it than many think. They will be very bothered with visits and questions at all hours of the day, and even of the night. . . . They will not have time for prayer, meditation, or contemplation, nor for any spiritual recollection. They will not be able to say mass, at least at first. . . . They will not have time to say their office, or even to eat or to sleep. The Japanese are very importunate, especially with foreigners. Of these they make little account, and are always making game of them. . . .   Learned men are needed to reply to their questions, chiefly those who have done well in Arts, and those who were sophists, and who can catch them at once in obvious contradictions. . . .*

" I hope this year of '52 to go to China ; our God might be greatly served thereby, both in China and Japan. For when the Japanese learn that the Chinese are adopting the law of God, they will lose faith in their own sects more quickly†. . . . We made a book in Japanese, treating of the creation of the world and of all the mysteries of Christ's life. Afterwards we wrote this same book in Chinese letters, to be ready when I go to China, that it may be understood till I can speak Chinese." Xavier concludes by signing himself Your least and most exiled son (*menor hijo y en destierro mayor*).‡

* *Mon. Xav.*, vol. i. p. 669 f.   † *Ibid.*, vol. i. p. 672.
‡ *Ibid.*, vol. i. p. 674.

SPECIMEN OF ST. FRANCIS XAVIER'S
HANDWRITING

(*Part of this is translated on page 308*)

la chyna es una tyerra muy grandissyma, paryssima y pobladas tā grandes

de todos ay un solo rey y es en grande manera obedescydo es [...]ygullysymo

reyno y abundantissymo de todos los mantenimientos no ay sino una pequ[eña]

ma tadessa de chyna a[...]on estos duros por muy Ingeniosos y duros a[...]

[...]pelymente este reyes y [...]manos [...] la goyerna[...]on de la republyca

es muy descuydos de saber es [...]enta [...]omo [...]ba los ojos muy pequeños

y gente lyberal [...]er todo muy parysysyma no ay guerra entre ellos

y aguy en la yndya no [...]ye[...]e alga[...]os Impedymientos q me estorbar la y[...]

yda este a[...]o de 52 empero de y[...] ala chyna por el grande serujcyo

de dios mo que se puede seguyr assy en la chyna como en Jupo por q

abyendo los Japones y aley de dyos sea [...]yesen los chynas ande perder muy

At the same time he wrote to the Companions in Europe :

" The Japanese are strongly of opinion that there is none to match them in arms and chivalry. They despise all foreigners. They are proud of nothing so much as having good arms, well garnished with gold and silver. Constantly they wear sword and dagger at home and abroad, and sleep with them at their pillow. . . . They are very good bowmen. They fight on foot, though they use horses on the land. They are a people of great courtesy between themselves, but they do not use courtesies to foreigners, because they despise them. They spend all they have on clothes, arms, and servants, and save nothing. . . .*

" I arrived from Japan with plenty of bodily and no spiritual strength. Nevertheless I hope in the mercy of God our Lord, and in the infinite merits of the death and Passion of our Lord Jesus, that He will give me grace to make this troublesome voyage to China. I am now white-haired. But it seems to me that I was never so strong bodily as now. Work among an intelligent people, who are eager to know in what religion they can find salvation, carries with it a grand contentment. . . .

" Would to God that, as I write here these joyful and happy details, I might actually send to the universities of Europe the pleasures and comforts given to us by the sole mercy of God. I well believe that many and learned persons would fundamentally change their way of life then, and use their great talents for the conversion of the heathen. If they only felt the spiritual delight and comfort which follow such labours, and knew the great opportunity here in Japan for the increase of our faith, I think that many of the learned men would give up their studies, many canons and other prelates would leave their dignities and their revenues for another and a richer life, and come and seek the Japanese.

" . . . I have so much to write about Japan that I could go on for ever. I fear lest what I have written may be a nuisance as there is so much to read. I console myself with this, that those who are annoyed can throw it away and stop reading. With this I finish, though I can't finish

* *Mon. Xav.*, vol. i. p. 676.

when I am writing to my Fathers and Brothers so dear and beloved, and of friends so dear as the Christians of Japan.

"May God our Lord unite us in the glory of His Paradise.

"Entirely yours *in Christ,*

"FRANCISCO."*

* *Mon. Xav.,* vol. i. p. 695 ff.

CHAPTER XVIII

(January—April, 1552)

XAVIER left Japan in November, 1551, and by January 24 he was once more in India. He paused at Cochin to despatch his letters to Europe, and to visit the new Governor-General of India, Noroñha. He told Noroñha he wanted to go to China as soon as possible, to open up a way there for the Gospel. He then laid before him his proposed method of getting into that closed country, where the only Europeans were those who had been taken captive in attempting to land there. The first visit, Xavier maintained, must be made on a magnificent scale. An ambassador must be sent from the King of Portugal to the King of China, bearing rich presents. He had already found a man willing to act as ambassador. This man was his friend Diego Pereira, a Portuguese merchant, on whose ship he had made part of the homeward voyage from Japan. This merchant had given Xavier letters of credit on his agent in Goa for thirty thousand ducats, to expend on presents and other expenses of the voyage. Yet even that would not be enough. He begged for more from the royal treasuries : money spent in opening up so rich a land as China would be well spent ; Portugal would profit immensely in the end. The Governor smiled upon these proposals, and promised that the expedition should have every possible assistance, and that Diego Pereira should be allowed to go as ambassador of the king.

From Cochin Xavier went on to Goa to visit the college and set his affairs in order before leaving for China. It was there that Teixeira, his oldest biographer, saw the Saint for the first and last time. Teixeira had been ill, and was in the hospital of the college. He writes :

He had a very particular care for the sick, toward whom he had great charity, as he showed as soon as he arrived. When he had embraced the brothers he asked at once if any were sick.

Being told there were, at once before entering his own room he went to visit them. We had at the time a brother very near the end, and given up by the doctors. They watched him at night and had prepared everything for the burial. But the brother nevertheless had such faith and trust in God, and devotion to Father Master Francisco, whom we were expecting every day, that he thought that if the Father Master Francisco found him living, he would not die of that illness. And so it was, for, finding him alive and going at once to visit and comfort him, he (Francisco) said a Gospel, and placed his hands on his head. And it pleased the Lord that from thenceforward he went on getting better, and is still alive.*

Then Teixeira goes on to give us the most authentic description of Xavier's appearance which we possess :

The Father Master Francisco was tall rather than small in stature, his face well proportioned, white and ruddy, happy and very attractive (*alegre y de muy buena gracia*), the eyes black, the brow high, the hair and beard black. He wore poor and clean clothes, the gown loose without a cloak nor any other garment, for this was the mode of the dress of the poor priests in India, and when he walked he lifted it up a little with both hands. He went almost always with his eyes placed on the sky, with the sight of which they say he found particular comfort and joy, as of the Fatherland to which he thought to go. And thus he walked with his face so happy and ardent (*alegre y inflamado*) that it caused much happiness to all who saw him. And sometimes it happened that if any of the brothers were sad the way they took to become happy was to go and look at him. He was very affable with outside people, happy and familiar with those of the house, especially with those whom he knew to be humble and simple, and with little opinion or thought of themselves. But, on the contrary, he showed himself severe, grave, and at times rough with the proud and those who had a great conceit and opinion of themselves, until they knew and humbled themselves. He was a man of small appetite,

* Teixeira says in his preface to the *Vita* (*Mon. Xav.*, vol. ii. p. 815) that he, when he wrote, was the only one of the Company left of those who had known Xavier in India. This proves that it was he whom Xavier visited and revived on this occasion.

although to avoid singularity, he ate of all they put before him when he was with others.*

One of the new missionaries who had just arrived at Goa wrote home his impressions of the Saint at this time :

Imagine, my brothers, what it is to see, coming and going in this earth, one whose conversation is in heaven. . . . His smiling face is so joyful and peaceful ! He is always smiling; yet no, he does not smile, it is a spiritual joy that is on his face.†

It was either at this time or just before he left Japan that Francis got the letter announcing his appointment as Provincial in India. This position gave him complete authority over all the affairs of the college at Goa, as well as over all the missions throughout the East. During his absence in Japan the affairs of the Society, both in Cochin and in Goa, had got pretty thoroughly out of hand. Antonio Gomez, the Superior at Goa, appears to have been original rather than discreet, ardent rather than wise, and persistently obstinate and autocratic. Xavier did not hesitate to use his new powers. Various novices, too hastily accepted, were dismissed. Gomez himself was directed to go off immediately to Diu, some hundreds of miles away, and found a House there.

Besides Xavier himself there were in the East at this time three Jesuits of especially outstanding character and capacity ; to wit, Fernandez in Japan, Enrico Enriquez in Cape Comorin, and Gaspar Barzée, who had just returned from Ormuz in order to go to Japan. Xavier chose the last of these three to be the new Superior of the college at Goa. The position had become an important one. The college had an income of 2,500 ducats, a chapel, a hospital, a large garden, accommodation for at least thirty Europeans, besides a considerable number of native boys.

Gaspar Barzée, the Fleming, chosen by Xavier to look after this work, had been in Ormuz for over two years.‡ Xavier had no disciple who followed his methods more closely.

* Teixeira, *Vita, Mon. Xav.*, vol. ii. p. 882.
† Melchior Nunez, *Sel. Ind. Epist*, pp. 161-2, quoted by Brou, *Vie de S. François Xavier*, vol ii. p. 277.
‡ In a letter to Loyola, giving an account of himself, he says : " I am Flemish, of the islands of Zeeland ; I took the arts course in the university of Louvain " (*Mon. Xav.*, vol. i p. 486, note).

In Ormuz he had lived and worked in the hospital. On Fridays he preached to the Mohammedans, on Saturdays to the Jews, on Sundays to the Christians, on Mondays to the idolaters, and on the remaining days to those in prison. He had a most outstanding gift of eloquence, and soon crowds came to the confessional. Of what he heard there he says, " It is enough to keep one in tears day and night." His boldness in preaching amazed the colonists, who compared his sermons to thunderstorms. He is said to have rid the town of public prostitution, and to have given a course of Saturday lectures on the immorality of usury and founded an orphanage with the conscience-money which the lectures brought in. His encounters with the Mohammedans were perhaps more humorous than practical. One morning they woke up to find an immense cross crowning the minaret of one of their mosques.

Besides reorganising the college at Goa Xavier made a number of changes in the various mission stations. Two missionaries took up Barzée's work in Ormuz, Gonzalvez Rodriguez and Alvaro Mendez. Melchior Nunez went to Bassein, in the Gulf of Cambay, where there was a flourishing house with an income of a thousand ducats. Lancilotti remained at Coulam, where he had been for some time, instructing fifty children whose parents had been converted, and preaching to natives and to the Portuguese. Antonio de Eredia was sent to Cochin, Francisco Enriquez to Tana. There were two missionaries in Malacca, and about seven in the Moluccas. Perhaps the most prosperous of all the missions was in Cape Comorin, to which Xavier now sent the Brothers Madeira and Antonio Fernandez, to take the place of Mendez, who had just been killed. Polanco says there were in 1552 60,000 Christians in the Cape, and thirty churches.* The success of this mission was largely due to the work of the Father Enrico Enriquez. He was a

---

* We recollect, of course, that South India was then, as it still is, a country of " mass conversions." On Tuticorin and other places on the coast of Cape Comorin, where this flourishing mission existed in the sixteenth century, there was little trace left, says Sharrock (*South Indian Missions*), in 1771. In 1785 a church was opened for about forty Christians in Tinnyvelly. Then the " mass conversions " of Xavier's time began again. " In one short tour in 1803 Gerické baptized no less than 1,300 people, and Sattianâthan shortly afterwards baptized 2,700 more. When they visited a village they would find as many as 500 people waiting for baptism. The missionary would be engaged till near midnight in preaching and baptizing " (p. 48).

man of Jewish origin, and brought good brains, as well as a good heart, to his work. He was the first of the missionaries to make a serious study of the Tamil language, and he composed a Tamil grammar and dictionary.

In San Thomé, the only other mission in India besides those mentioned above, no change was made, but Father Cyprian, who was in charge there, seems narrowly to have escaped being dismissed with some of the others. We feel rather grateful to Cyprian for having quarrelled with the Vicar at San Thomé, since it has left us the following gem of admonishment.

" To Father Alfonso Cyprian, Meliapor, from Goa (about) April 14th, 1552.

"You have badly understood the note of instruction I gave you as to what to do at San Thomé. It is plain how little remains to you of the conversation of our blessed Father Ignatius. In my opinion your demands on the Vicar show small respect to the Articles. You always bring your harsh temperament to bear on things. All you do on one side, on another you undo. I tell you I am disgusted with the dissensions you bring about there. If the Vicar does what he ought not, he is not to be corrected by your reprimands, especially when they are made with as little prudence as you make them. You have so got into the habit of doing your own will that, wherever you are, you scandalise everybody with your ways, and you give others to understand that it is your temperament that is harsh. Please God that you may do penance one day for these imprudences.

" By the love of our Lord I pray you to put your will under restraint, and in the future correct the past. For to be so passionate is not a matter of temperament, but comes from a great carelessness you have of God, and of your conscience and of love to your neighbours. I assure you that at the hour of death you will certainly find that what I tell you is true. I do pray you in the name of our blessed Father Ignatius that in these few days remaining to you, you may correct yourself and be tolerant, meek, patient, humble. And you may be sure that humility achieves everything. If you are not able to do as much as you would like, do willingly what you can. Nothing is achieved by violence in these parts of India, and the good which would be done by humility ends when you try to do things with shoutings and impatience. . . .

" Gonzalo Fernandez also, it seems to me, has your temperament, intolerant and impatient. And you cover your impatiences with the pretext of serving God our Lord. You say that what moves you to do what you do is the zeal of God and for souls. What you can't achieve with the Vicar through humility, you will not achieve by dissensions.

" By the love and obedience you owe to Father Ignatius, I pray you when you see this letter to go to the Vicar and place both your knees on the ground and seek his pardon for all the past and kiss his hand—I should be more comforted if you kissed his feet—and promise him, all the time you are to be there, not to go against his will in anything. And believe me, at the hour of your death you will be glad that you did this. And trust in God our Lord, and do not doubt but that, when your humility is seen and becomes manifest, all you ask for the service of God and the salvation of souls will be granted you.

" You and others clearly err in this—that without having much humility, or giving great signs of it to those with whom you deal, you wish the people to do what you ask, just because you are brothers of the Company. And you do not remember to imitate the virtues of our Father Ignatius, to whom God gave such great authority with the people, because he laid a good foundation. So you wish to make use of authority over the people and to neglect the virtues which are needful before the people will obey you.

" I am very sure that if we were together you would tell me that there was no fault in what you had done, but that you did it for the love of God and the salvation of souls. You may be sure, and do not doubt it, that I should take no such excuse from you. Nothing would make me so disconsolate as your justifying yourself. But I also confess that you could not comfort me so much by anything as by your accusing yourself.

" Above all, I pray you to have no more dissensions with the Vicar, Fathers, Captains, or authorities, in the country, though you may see things done badly. What you can put right in a kindly way, do so, and do not risk losing with quarrels what you can achieve kindly through humility and meekness.

[What follows is in Francis' own handwriting.]

" O Cyprian, if you knew the love with which I write you these things, you would remember me day and night, and perhaps you would weep when you remembered the great love I have to you.   And if the hearts of men could be seen in this life, I believe, my brother Cyprian, that you would see clearly into my soul.

" Entirely yours, without my ever being able to forget you,
                                        " FRANCISCO." *

The ending formula is an unusual one for Xavier.   But perhaps we understand why he used it.   The words are almost the same as those with which Loyola had ended his last letter to Francis, and we remember how deeply the phrase had moved the Saint.

Almost the whole of the two months which Xavier now spent in Goa before setting out on his last journey must have been spent in rearranging the college and missions, and in writing out instructions and letters of counsel to those under his charge.

His position was now one which is more common to women than to men.   For he had two great spheres of work, either of which could easily have occupied his whole attention.   As domestic cares he had all his duties as Provincial ; as outside work, the mysterious Farther East, where he was going to " open up a way " for the " Law of God," and to obtain release for the European captives who were there.   And while he was planning with Diego Pereira and the Governor for the imposing embassage to China, he was also spending infinite time and care and thought on the setting in order of his own house in India.

At mealtimes in the college the brothers, Frois tells us, gave him, each in turn, the story of his past life.   Francis then asked them about the difficulties they had met with, and the mistakes they had made, and would talk to them in a way that humbled them to the dust, and then he would begin " to speak and to dwell upon the hope of the eternal glory."

From his many letters and notes of advice written during those weeks, the following extracts are taken.   To Father Gonzalvez Rodriguez, at Ormuz, he wrote :

* *Mon. Xav.*, vol. i. p. 745.

" Preserve yourself from trying to impress the world by your singularity. Abhor all vain opinion. . . . Beware in your preaching of scandalising anyone. Don't try to preach subtle matters of learning, but morals. Reprove the sins of the people with great modesty and piety. Fraternally reprove in secret those who are public sinners. And know well that I should be better pleased by your reaping as much fruit as might be contained in this space of line —— without scandal, than I should be delighted if you reaped as much fruit as would be contained in a full line with some scandal or scandals." *

And to Barreto, at the College of Bassein, he writes :

" . . . Look well to it that you are very watchful over yourself, and then over others. And be careful to dismiss at once from the Company those whom you find caught in public sin or in grave scandal. I will regard as dismissed any whom you dismiss from the Company. . . . As for the rents of the college, arrange to spend them in spiritual temples rather than in material. . . . I command you to take the native children when they are small, and teach them, so that when they are big they may bear fruit." †

To Antonio de Eredia, in Cochin, he wrote :

" In dealing with your people do not show yourself as a solemn person who desires to have authority over them, or as if they were beneath you. . . . Be affable in your visits and talks. And in preaching to religious and to the general public, undeceive them about two errors in which they live, speak of the justice of God towards those who do not wish to amend, and of the mercy of God towards those who give up running after sin. Thus be rigorous against those who persevere in sin, but that they may not say that you put them to desperation, speak of mercy, as I said before. In conversing with the people, which you must do constantly, let it be in all humility, taking account of all, both ecclesiastic and lay. And if some good is done, attribute it to them, and then you will form them into supporters of good works.
" . . . Do not do what many do. They seek artificial

* *Mon. Xav.*, vol. i. pp. 707 and 709.   † *Ibid.*, vol. i. p. 717.

means of making themselves acceptable to the people, and think and hope that they will succeed. All such are more concerned to be in the good books of the people than they are with God's honour or zeal for souls. This way is very dangerous, for it is inevitably accompanied by pride in having a good name among the people, and of being believed in by them. . . .

"What the saints wrote comes infinitely short of the pleasure and the experience which they had when they wrote; and men who do not have this inward contentment find little profit in the saints' descriptions. So I advise you to write down, and keep in the greatest esteem, your spiritual experiences and to humble and abase yourself more and more while the Lord increases you."

Xavier recommends him to keep a record of his spiritual experiences, because the record may make them permanent and help the inward spiritual life. It is not things that matter, but the inward experiences they occasion; and one cannot understand the things, still less the description of them by the godly, unless one ponders them in the heart, like Mary. And the written word is cold, unless one has the inward spiritual feeling. It is a recommendation of spiritual biography like Bunyan's *Grace Abounding*, to name but one of many.

The letter goes on :

"In confessions, if there is any impediment, before you absolve, see that promises—such as of reconciliations, restitutions, or weaknesses, of sensuality and the like—are fulfilled before you absolve. For the men of these parts are generous in promises, but slow in fulfilments." *

To Father Gaspar Barzée, the new Rector of the College, he left some Rules for Humility. The copy, which is reproduced by the Editors of the *Monumenta*, has evidently, they say, been a copy made by Barzée, and modified for his own personal use. This accounts for the confusion of mood and person in the grammar.

Xavier, it is clear, has had a lively fear that Barzée's grand reputation as a preacher might be his undoing.

* *Mon. Xav.*, vol. i. p. 897 ff.

RULES FOR HUMILITY WHICH FRANCIS LEFT FOR FATHER GASPAR
WHEN HE WENT TO CHINA IN THE YEAR '52.

1. Seek great humility as to preaching, first attributing everything to God very perfectly.

2. Have before my eyes the people, that God may give devotion
to the people to hear His Word, and in respect of this devotion
give me grace to preach, and to the people devotion to hear.

3. Labour to love the people much, considering the obligation
I owe them, since God by their intercession gives me grace to
preach.

4. Also I shall consider that I possess this virtue because of
the prayers and merits of those of the Company, who with great
charity, love, and humility, seek grace and gifts from God for the
Companions, and this for the greater glory of God and the salvation
of souls.

5. Take care continually that I have plenty of humility, since
what I preach is not mine at all, but liberally given by God.   And
seek with love and fear this grace, of which strict account has
to be given to God our Lord, guarding myself from attributing
anything to myself if it be not many faults, and sins, and much
pride, and negligence, and ingratitude, as well against God as
against the people and the Company, for whose sake God gives me
this grace.

6. Entreat God to reveal to me the hindrances caused by me
which keep Him from doing me greater favours, and making use
of me in great things.

No. 7 is a warning to beware of causing any kind of scandal,
in preaching, speaking, or acting.

8. What, above all, you have to do . . . is to note very
carefully the things which God our Lord reveals to your soul,
writing them in a little book, printing them on your soul, for this
is fruitful. . . .

9. Do not ever forget to reflect that many preachers are in hell.
They had more grace for preaching than you, and in their sermons
they reaped more fruit than you.   And—most frightful of all !—
they were the instruments which sent many to glory while they,
the miserable, went to hell.   They attributed to themselves
that which was of God : they laid hold of the world : they
delighted to be praised by it : they grew in vain opinion of themselves and in great pride.   So they were lost.   Therefore, let
each one watch over himself, for if we watch well we have
nothing to boast about but our evils, which are all we do by
ourselves. . . .

10. Mind not to despise the brothers of the Company, when
it seems to you that you are doing more than they are, and
that they do nothing.   Be very sure that it is for the sake of the

brothers who are serving in lowly and humble duties that God chiefly favours you and gives you grace to work well. So you are more indebted to them than they to you. This inward knowledge will help you never to despise them, but rather love them, and always keep yourself humble.*

To Gaspar he also leaves some directions on the "way to converse with the world so as to avoid scandals."

In what he says about women we have to remember that the wives referred to were the native women, generally of a low caste, belonging to the Portuguese colonists. These were very apt to be badly affected by the freedom which they had gained from Hindoo restrictions. We have also to remember that the etiquette in Spain and Portugal between men and women was, as it still is, very different from that in England.

. . . These visits (to women in their houses) you will make as seldom as possible, for much is risked, little gained, for the increase of the service of God, and women are generally inconstant, and unpersevering, and take up a lot of time. Behave with them as follows :

If they are married do your best that their husbands draw near to God. Spend more time over the husbands than over the wives, for more fruit may be reaped, since men are more constant and the government of the house depends on them. . . .

When there are discords between a wife and a husband which are leading to separation, be always for bringing them together. Have more converse with the husband than with the wife, strive to get them to make a General Confession, and give them some meditations of the First Week before absolving them. . . .

Do not trust the devotion of wives when they say that they will serve God better separate from their husbands than with them. That is a kind of devotion which does not last long, and is seldom without scandal.

Guard against putting the blame on the husband in public, though he be in the wrong. Counsel him in secret to make general confession, and in confession blame him with much modesty. Do not allow him to feel that you favour his wife more than him, even though he be guilty. Rather provoke him to accuse himself, and by his own accusation condemn him with much love, charity, and meekness. With these men of India much is accomplished by asking, but nothing by force.

Watch, I repeat, that you never lay the blame on the husband

* *Mon. Xav.*, vol. i. p. 908 ff.

in public. Women are so untamable* that they seek occasions to slight their husbands, alleging to religious persons [*i.e.*, priests, etc.] that their husbands are the culprits and not they. Even though the wives are not the culprits, do not excuse them, for they excuse themselves : rather show them the obligation they are under to bear with their husbands. Often they deserve [punishment] because they have behaved unmannerly to them. Show them that they should take their present troubles patiently, and provoke them to patience and humility and obedience to their husbands. Do not believe all they tell you, whether the husband or the wife. Hear both of them before you lay the blame on either. Don't show yourself to side more with one than with the other. . . .

And watch that you use great prudence with this evil world, keeping your eye on what may happen, for the devil never sleeps. . . .

And be watchful never to rebuke anyone in anger . . . Always humble and abase yourself to friars and Fathers, giving place to anger and passion. I mean this not only when you are the culprit, but much rather when you are blameless and they are the culprits. You will not wish a greater vengeance than to be silent with reason, when reason is not heard nor valued. Have pity on them when they do what they ought not, for late or early the punishment has to come to them from God, much greater than you or they think. So keep praying to God for them, out of pity for them. Seek no other vengeance, either of thought or speech or deed. These are dangerous and harmful, as is all else of flesh and blood.†

In a letter to Rodriguez in Portugal we have a document which might be useful as a model to anyone who wished to effect a dismission gracefully.

" By the present I shall be brief, as I have to be lengthy in a lot of other letters. . . . It seems to me well to send André Carvalho, the bearer of this, to Portugal. He is ailing in these parts, and in his native air might become better. He is a man of importance in your kingdom, according to what everyone tells me, and one of whom much is expected, because of the many virtues with which God our Lord has endowed him—and which by His mercy will increase.

---

* The text in *Mon. Xav.* is : *molheres são tão yndomabeles.* But Cros (*Vie de S. François Xavier*, vol. ii. p. 292) has used a different text, which gives *endemonaveis*, translated by Cros *endiablées.*

† *Mon. Xav.*, vol. i. p. 924 ff.

I cannot write anything but good about him.   I hope in God our Lord that after he has increased in learning and virtue he will gain much fruit in the Company.   I pray you by the love of God our Lord, my brother Master Simon, to receive him with that love and charity with which both himself and I hope he will be received and comforted." *

Ten years later, Cros tells us, Carvalho died a captive in the hands of the Moors in Africa.   His ransom money had been sent to him from Portugal, but he had given it up to another Christian captive, who was his friend._

* *Mon. Xav* , vol. i. p. 714.

CHAPTER XIX

THE FINAL VOYAGE

(April—November, 1552)

ON Maundy Thursday, the day of the institution of the Lord's Supper, Francis and his friends sang together the *Gloria in Excelsis*, before the white-decked altar of the college chapel in Goa, and there received the Blessed Sacrament.

From the choir of the chapel the Saint then spoke with so much grace and power to those whom he was about to leave that Frois says they felt themselves like new men.

A few of the brothers accompanied him as far as the harbour. The others waited in the chapel, kneeling before the altar of the Sepulchre to adore the Presence of Jesus, and to pray for those about to put to sea.

The companions chosen by Francis for this journey were three—Brother Alvaro Fereira, a Portuguese ; a Chinese youth called Antonio, who had been trained at the college ; and Christopher, a Malabar coolie. The appointed ambassador, Diego Pereira, and his rich cargoes, awaited the missionaries at Malacca. To add to the splendours of the embassage, Francis carried with him some brocades and tapestries and pictures which Gaspar Barzée had brought back from Ormuz.

Bad news, involving a complete rearrangement of the missionary staff at Cape Comorin, awaited the Saint at Cochin, and the halt there was fully occupied by the letter-writing which these rearrangements demanded.

The ship reached Malacca at the end of May, and there Xavier's battle to enter China began in earnest.

Pedro da Silva da Gama, Xavier's friend, was in the act of resigning his post as Captain of the Fort to his brother Alvaro. This was that Alvaro d'Ataide who had come out to India in the same fleet as Xavier. A letter from Mozambique gave us hints of some kind of storm there (see p. 153). Some men can treasure a grudge for many years. Perhaps Alvaro d'Ataide was one of these. Perhaps his heart had found a new occasion of mischief. Valignano and Teixeira put down his behaviour to greed and self-interest. The Embassy would probably have interfered with his own private smuggling affairs. In any case he ruined all Xavier's fine plans for entering China with Diego Pereira. He is said to have been jealous of the honour shown to that merchant, and to have thought that he himself should have been appointed the ambassador to China. He took advantage of his position as Captain-General of the Sea to forbid Diego Pereira to sail, and there was a great uproar. The Captain of the Sea got hold of the rudder of the ambassador's ship, hung it up over his door, and set a guard before it. Diego Pereira had his men too, and they prepared to fight. But at this point Francis intervened. They must not, he said, shed blood in such a cause. In place of their swords, he drew forth his pen, and wrote to Alvaro, through the episcopal vicar, reminding him that he was exposing himself to excommunication by thus hindering the apostolic mission of the Papal Nuncio. He also reminded him that Diego Pereira was the officially appointed ambassador to China, and that he, Alvaro, had no right to interfere with him. Xavier thought that the very word excommunication would have frightened the Captain into amiability, but it had no such effect. Alvaro accused the Saint (who had left his Papal briefs in Goa) of having forged his claims, and worked himself and all his household into a great state of rage against "that perverter and hypocrite." The affair spread over the town, and for days the great adventurer had not the heart to stir beyond his own lodgings, except after dark. We read of him spending long nights in the church of Our Lady, and in the early morning being seen there saying a Mass for Don Alvaro. Valignano says that against the demon who had taken the Captain Alvaro for his medium, Francis armed himself with the Love of God.

Nevertheless Alvaro carried his point. He forced Diego Pereira to stay in Malacca, and allowed Francis to go on if he liked in his friend's ship, and make his way alone into China as best he might. Valignano says that the Saint's heart "remained entire and victorious"; but this letter to Diego Pereira is not very cheerful :

" Since your sins and mine are so great that on this account God our Lord was not willing to make use of us, there is nobody we can blame but them. And mine were so huge that they sufficed for my perdition and your ruin. You may well accuse me, Sir, of having ruined you and all who came in our company. I've ruined you, Sir, to the extent of four or five thousand *pardoas*, which at my request you spent in presents for the King of China. . . I beseech you, Sir, to remember that my intention was always to serve you, as you and God our Lord know. If this were not so, I should die of pain. I beseech you, Sir, not to come here, it would only make my pain worse, for it would be renewed and intensified to greater sorrow through seeing you, when I remembered that I had ruined you. I am going out to the ship, that the men may not come to my lodging and tell me with tears in their eyes that I have ruined them [*i.e.*, the men who were to have shared in the mercantile side of Diego Pereira's enterprise]. . . . I have already taken leave of Senhor Don Alvaro, since he was pleased to think it well to prevent our going."

Xavier goes on to say that he is writing to the King of Portugal to explain the catastrophe, and to point out to him that he ought to recoup Diego Pereira for all he has lost, as the expedition was to have been for his honour and the increase of his state. He concludes :

" It grieves me for the punishment from our Lord which must come on him (Alvaro), greater than he thinks."

And he signs himself, " Your sad and disconsolate friend, FRANCISCO." *

About July 15th, accompanied by Alvaro Fereira and Antonio the Chinese, and the Malabar coolie, Xavier left Malacca. As he bade his friends farewell he is reported to have said, " Take care that we meet each other in heaven,

* *Mon. Xav.*, p. 757 f. There are two copies of this letter with very little difference. The second copy has this docket : " Copy of a letter of S. Francis Xavier all written in his own hand : Malacca : to Diego Pereira : also in Malacca, January 25th, 1551. Addressed to my special Senhor and friend the Senhor D. Pereira." Teixeira says that the Captain Alvaro afterwards became a leper, and was taken from Malacca to India, and thence to Portugal, where he died (see Teixeira, *Vita, Mon. Xav.*, vol. ii. p. 893, and Valignano's *Vita, Mon. Xav.*, vol. i. pp. 149 and 151).

for here we shall meet no more. Live in peace: you will see me next in the valley of Jehoshaphat." *

Some of the old historians say that the vicar of the town came to him and asked him to salute Alvaro d'Ataide before he left, and that Francis replied, "Don Alvaro will never see me again. I will wait for him at the judgment-bar of God, where he will have to render an account of that which he has done." He stood still and lifted up his arms and prayed for his persecutor, but sobs choked his voice and so he knelt down in silence. When he rose he took off his shoes and shook the dust from them. Then, without another word, he boarded the ship.

He had planned that this should be a triumphal voyage. It was, indeed. But the triumph was quite hidden from men's eyes, for it now consisted in his going on in spite of a complete outward collapse of his plans. "As for me," he writes, "unmoored from any human help, I am going to the islands of Canton." †

From Singapore he despatched several letters. The only reference to the débâcle at Malacca is found in these words to Gaspar Barzée: "You could not believe, Master Gaspar, how I was persecuted in Malacca. I will write you no details. Francis Perez will do that."‡ The letter then speaks of more practical matters. The following is a fac-simile of his signature at the end of this letter:

Next day he writes again to Barzée:

"The alms which you have to send to the Brothers in Japan, let it be only in gold, and this gold the best you can get, like the Venetian. For the Japanese like the best gold for working and gilding their arms, and gold is put to no other use in Japan. If anyone comes out in '52 for Japan, nothing is needed so much as to come prepared for many troubles,

* "Let the nations bestir themselves, and come up to the valley of Jehosha-phat (that is, for the Lord judgeth), for there will I sit to judge all the nations round about" (Joel iii. 12).
† Mon. Xav., vol. i. p. 767.   ‡ Ibid., vol. i. p. 765.

both at sea before getting there, and then on landing. He must be well equipped against the cold, and take Portuguese cloth for himself, as well as for those already there."*

In another letter Xavier advises Flemings or Germans to be chosen for Japan, as they would be better hardened against the cold than men from Southern Europe.

In August the *Santa Croce* arrived at Sanchian. In those days, when foreign ships were not allowed to touch at Chinese ports, this barren little island was used by the Portuguese and Chinese traders as a rendezvous. It lies a little west of Hong Kong. Even here the Portuguese were not allowed to build themselves stores or houses. Very daring, they used to erect huts of wood or branches, where they ate and drank and gambled in the intervals of doing business. But these they always burned before they left, to show that they made no claim to the island. They had good reason to beware of offending the Chinese. There were horrible tales of how those who had ventured too far were kept imprisoned in dungeons. We read of one de Britto, a gentleman, hung about with chains, and a log tied round his chest, who about 1555 was seen by a Portuguese captain and a priest, greatly disfigured, and in deep misery.

In 1556 the Dominican Gaspard da Cruz visited the same prison; he describes for us the long galleries where in the evening hundreds of prisoners filed in to sleep. A thick iron chain which went through rings fixed in the ground and over their chests prevented them from moving, all through the night. A heavy wooden herse weighed them down and made any movement almost impossible. These were a small part of the tortures which awaited unfortunate strangers who were bold enough to violate the frontier: this hell was accepted by Saint Francis Xavier as he went to carry to the captives the comfort, if not the liberty, of the faith.†

On October 22nd Francis wrote to Father Perez at Malacca:

" By the mercy and pity of God our Lord Diego Pereira's ship and all we who came in it arrived safely at this port of San Chan, where we found a lot of other merchant ships. This port is thirty leagues from Canton. Numbers of merchants

* *Mon. Xav.*, vol. i. p. 774.
† Brou, *Vie de S. François Xavier*, vol. ii. p. 341.

from Canton come here to trade with the Portuguese. The Portuguese have done their best to see if some Cantonese merchants would convey me. All decline. They said they would put their lives and estate in great danger if the Governor of Canton knew that they had taken me. So they would not take me at any price.

"It pleased God our Lord that an honourable man, an inhabitant of Canton, offered for 200 cruzados to take me in a small boat in which there would be no sailors but his sons and servants, that the Governor might not come to know from the sailors what merchant took me. And more than that, he has offered to put me in his house, and hide me for three or four days, and from there to place me some day before daylight, with my books and little bundle, at the gate of the city. From there I would go at once to the house of the Governor. I would tell him that we came in order to go to the king of China and I would show him the letter which we bear from the bishop, telling him that we are sent from His Highness to explain the Law of God.

"The dangers we run are two, according to what the Chinese say. The first is that the man who takes us, after having received the 200 cruzados, may leave us on some desert island, or throw us into the sea, that he may not risk being discovered by the Governor of Canton. The second danger is that if we are taken to Canton, and get before the Governor, he will order us to be tortured or make us prisoners. (This may well be) because this (our attempt) is such an innovation, and because there are in China such prohibitions that no one goes there without the king's safe-conduct and the king strictly forbids foreigners to enter his country without his safe-conduct.

". . . Besides these two dangers, there are many others, and greater, which do not concern the Chinese. To count them would be tedious, nevertheless I will mention some.

"The first is the loss of hope and trust in the mercy of God. By His love and for His service we go to declare His Law and Jesus Christ His Son, our Redeemer and Lord. This, indeed, He knows, since by His holy mercy He gave us these desires. Now, to distrust His mercy and power on account of the danger in which we may possibly find ourselves in His service is a much greater danger than all the ill that the enemies of God could do us. For, without the licence and permission of God, the devil and his ministers can do us no harm at all.

"And also we confirm ourselves with the saying of the Lord, 'Who loves his life in this world will lose it, and he who loses his life for God's sake will gain it.' Which agrees with what also Christ our Lord said, 'He who puts his hand to the plough and looks back is not fit for the kingdom of God.'

"Considering these dangers of the soul, which are much greater than those of the body, we find that it is safer and surer to pass through the bodily dangers than that we should be convicted before God of spiritual dangers [i.e., defeats]. So, by whatever way, we are determined to go to China. I hope in God our Lord that the issue of our voyage will be for the increase of our holy faith, however much the enemies and their ministers persecute us, for 'If God be for us, who will have victory against us?'" *

We do not wonder at the fighting tone of this letter, of all the letters of this time. We feel with Francis that the Devil is determined to hinder him if he can; in a Spanish version of the above letter, Xavier mentions at the beginning that he had been ill for fifteen days. His companions, he adds, are recovered from their fever; but Antonio, from whom he had hoped for so much as an interpreter, had had all the Chinese knocked out of his head by his education in Goa. He had, indeed, got someone else instead, a certain Peter Lopez, of what race we are not told, but he could read and write Portuguese, and "read well, and write a little Chinese," but a little later this man lost courage, and deserted his master.

Barzée, Xavier's *locum tenem* in India, continues to receive numerous letters of careful advice and help. "I greatly commend you to take very special care of yourself, for if you do the contrary, I hope for nothing from you. Do not neglect to read and fulfil the memoranda which I left you, especially that in which I recommended you to exercise yourself every day." He goes on to say that the three new missionaries have left Malacca for Japan, and in another letter, written a few days later, he advises the complete withdrawal of the mission from Malacca. The city, he writes, no longer deserves them, because of her opposition to his going to

* *Mon. Xav.*, vol. i. p. 783 ff.

China. And he hopes that the Bishop will be persuaded to
excommunicate Alvaro for his interference with the Nuncio
and legate of the Pope. There was something of the haughty
Spanish *hidalgo* left in Francis still.*

On November 12th he writes to Father Perez in Malacca
that he has at last arranged with a Chinese merchant to take
him to Canton eight days hence. He (the merchant) is sure
to go, Xavier says, for he is giving him enough pepper
to allow him to make a profit of 350 cruzados. The letter
goes on :

" Pray much to God for us, for we run the very greatest
risk of being made captives. Nevertheless, we comfort
ourselves by thinking that it is much better to be a captive
simply for the love of God than to be free by fleeing the
labours of the Cross. And if it happens that he who is to
take us changes his mind, because of the great risk he runs
. . . in that case I will go to Siam, so as to go from there to
Canton in the ships which the king of Siam sends. Please
God we shall get to Canton this year." †

Meanwhile this little company of Christ's adventurers is
thinning down. " I have dismissed Fereira from the Company," Francis now writes, " because he is not fit for it."‡
Valignano says his health had failed him. Christopher, the
Malabar boy, was of little use. But Antonio the Chinese was
a very faithful servant.

On November 13th Francis dictated his last letter, and
we seem to hear the beating of the demons' wings around
him as he writes. It is addressed to Father Perez, who is
to send it on to Gaspar Barzée at Goa.

" . . . Since this voyage to go from this port to China is
difficult and dangerous, I do not know what will fall out, yet
I hope that it will fall out well. If by chance I do not enter
Canton this year, I will go, as I have already said, to Siam.
And if I do not go from Siam to China within the year, I will
go to India. Yet I have much hope of getting to China.

" Know assuredly one thing, and don't doubt it. The

* *Mon. Xav.*, pp. 793 and 803.   † *Ibid*, vol. i. p. 800.
‡ *Ibid*, vol. i. p. 799.

devil will be tremendously sorry that those of the Company of the Name of Jesus should enter China. I give you this certain news from the port of Sanchian. Be in no doubt of this. For the hindrances which he put in my way, and puts every day—I could never tell you all of them. Be sure of one thing. With aid, favour, and grace of God our Lord I will confound the devil on this point. What great glory to God, to confound by a thing so vile as I am such a grand reputation as the devil's ! "

" Master Gaspar, remember the counsels I left you on my departure, and those which I have written to you. Do not neglect to keep them, if presently you think, as others have done, that I am dead. For, if God will, I shall not die, though it is a long time since I felt so little inclined to live as I do now. . . . Notice that I charge you to receive very few men into the Company. Pass those that are already received through many proofs. I fear that it would be better to dismiss some who are received already, as I did Alvaro Ferreira. Do not receive him into the college, if he go (to Goa). Speak to him in the lodge, or in the church. If he wishes to be a friar, help him. . . .

" Sanchian, 13th Nov., 1552.

" FRANCISCO."*

The end had almost come, and the gates of China were still closed. We find the history of the last days in a letter written a few years later by his companion Antonio to Teixeira,† and also in a report which Antonio made to Valignano.‡

Antonio says that one of the Portuguese merchants had given his companions shelter in his cabin. The Saint had asked the merchants to erect a little chapel of wood and straw where he might say mass and teach the native children so long as he had to wait on the island. He had talked very often with the Chinese merchants, either in Portuguese, which some of them knew, or by means of an interpreter.

---

* *Mon. Xav.*, vol. i. p. 808 f.

† *Vita, Mon. Xav.*, vol. ii. p. 894, and vol. i. p. 190.

‡ These accounts are simple and convincing, and can, in the main, be easily believed. Antonio was not illiterate. He had been in the college at Goa for seven or eight years. Frois says he was one of the ablest of all the boys they had at that time. When they went to Sanchian he was about twenty years old.

He had not spoken about Christianity, but of ordinary affairs, so as to get into friendly terms with them. They had questioned him much about the origin of the soul and the meaning of life, and were pleased with his answers, saying among themselves that he was a good and a wise man.

All the time that he was there, his one anxiety had been as to how he was to get on to the mainland, and he discussed his hopes with all the merchants, and made great efforts to get one of them to take him. At last, as we have seen from his own letter, the matter had been arranged, but the expedition was put off till all the ships had left Sanchian, so that, if the Chinese were over-annoyed by his visit, they could not wreak their vengeance on the merchants.

At last all the ships except the *Santa Croce* had left the harbour. Francis' host, who had given him shelter, was gone with the rest. There was no one left, says Antonio, to give the Father Master Francis food or shelter. Often, being hungry, he sent the Chinese lad out to the ship to ask them for the love of God to give them a little bread.

The nineteenth of December, the day appointed for the entry into China, came and went, and the junk which was to have taken them did not appear. Day after day passed, but it never came.

It was then that Francis began to feel ill. He was determined to get to China, with a determination that even he had never before known. But the body, as well as the heart, was sick with uncertainty and with the postponement of his desperate hope. There was no food such as he could enjoy, and no decent shelter. He and Antonio resolved to go out to the ship. On the evening of the 22nd they rowed out. For Francis a night of great misery followed. He was in a high fever, the ship was cold, and the waves were high. In the morning he said he must go back to land. So the two returned, Francis carrying with him a pair of cloth boots and a few almonds, the gift of some kindly sailor. When they reached the shore he sat down, almost overcome with weakness and cold.

Presently a friendly Portuguese came along and, seeing him in this plight, rowed him across the bay to his little cabin. This Portuguese advised Francis to allow himself to be bled. So they bled him, and he fainted, for it had been badly done ; but when they threw some water on his face he came to himself again.

He could eat nothing. Next day they bled him again, and again he fainted. He was tormented with the fever and sickness ; but all the time, Antonio says, he was so patient and enduring that not a word escaped his lips.

That evening, Thursday the 24th, he became delirious. His face was then very joyful and beautiful, and he talked aloud in a high voice as if he were preaching.

Toward the end he spoke in a language that Antonio did not understand. It was not Latin nor Spanish nor Portuguese, for he knew all these. It often happens that at the hour of death, the mind returns to its native haunts, and the last words and recollections are those of far-off days of childhood. "My language," Xavier had written in 1544, "is Basque." * Had the rude walls of that little hut on the desolate beach of Sanchian been transformed in the eyes of the dying saint into the tapestried hangings of his old nursery in Xavier, and the rich murmur of the waves hard by re-awakened in his fevered mind the tones of his mother's voice, telling him, ere she bade him a final good-night, some old Basque fairy tale ?

On the 25th, two days before he died, Antonio heard him repeating some of the Psalms to himself, and remembered one line :

Tu autem meorum peccatorum et delictorum miserere !

These words seem already to fall upon our ears from beyond the veil. They are the first utterances of the Supreme Encounter. Thus it is that man always speaks when he looks upon God.

" Woe is me," cried Isaiah the prophet, " for I am undone ; because I am a man of unclean lips, and I dwell in the midst of a people of unclean lips ; for mine eyes have seen the King, the Lord of hosts ! "

And Peter, when he knew that he looked upon the Son of God, said, " Depart from me, for I am a sinful man, O Lord ! "

" A broken and a contrite heart, O God, Thou wilt not despise," murmurs Santa Teresa with her latest breath, and we know that she is at last face to face with her Love.

* *Mon. Xav.*, vol. i. p. 279.

And now the Very Hand of Love has touched Francis' quivering flesh, and we hear once more this old cry of human anguish at the revelation of the Purity of God.

Tu autem meorum peccatorum et delictorum miserere!

And then there is silence, while the heavenly Father wipes away the first and the last tears that His child ever sheds in Heaven, and while with His own lips he sets upon the brow of His saint the everlasting seal of His Love.

FINIS

APPENDIX I

THE MIRACLE-STORIES

WHEN the student of the life of Xavier comes to examine the miracle-stories he makes a pleasing discovery. He finds that his poetic sense and his historic sense are always satisfied or outraged at the same points. Both history and poetry protest if they are asked to see heaven in a grain of sand, or a world in a wild flower.

The common affront is felt most keenly in the later biographies, from the seventeenth century onward; and of these Bouhours' *Life* (1682) is the most notorious example. Here we have numerous instances of every conventional and fashionable type of miracle, told with every possible flourish and accompanied by every conceivable platitude of piety. None of these tales are succinct enough to excuse quotation, but the picture facing p. 342, of a crab bringing back a crucifix which the Saint had some time before thrown into the sea to quiet a tempest, is a typical example.* It sometimes happens that as time goes on reliable material for a biography becomes increasingly available, and the later life is therefore more authoritative than the earlier. In Bouhours' time that point had not yet been reached with regard to Xavier. He had access to no information that was not at the disposal of the earlier writers, so his work is simply an example of "how stories grow." With nothing fresh to help him but his own and other people's fanciful imaginings, he relates tale after tale, neither lovely nor true. Going back still farther, we come to Tursellinus (1594), who, though a much less muddy source than Bouhours, is nevertheless infected with the germs of inaccuracy, which, when transferred to Bouhours' pages, multiplied so abundantly. Where Tursellinus makes the Saint raise four people from the dead, Bouhours adds other ten.† Tursellinus says Xavier was transfigured twice; Bouhours says four times. And Bouhours throws in a miraculous draught of fishes and two extra miraculous supplies of fresh water. Yes, here History and Poetry have withdrawn together, and Sanctimoniousness and Credulity have met and kissed. And with regard to the gift of tongues, let us take one example from Bouhours, and then see what Tursellinus says on the same matter. "He preached in the afternoon to the Japanese in their language, but so naturally and with so much

* The earliest versions simply say Xavier lost the crucifix and was very upset about it.
† See the *Life of Francis Xavier*, by P. Dominic Bouhours, translated by J. Dryden.

ease that he could not be taken for a foreigner." *   Thus Bouhours. But Tursellinus says: "Nothing was a greater impediment to him than his ignorance of the Japanese tongues; for ever and anon, when some uncouth expression offended their fastidious and delicate ears, the awkward speech of Francis was a cause of laughter."

On the whole, Tursellinus (1594) is much more beautiful than Bouhours; a mediæval *naïveté* and glamour still lingers on his pages, and there is a child-like fervour about his adoration of the Saint for the sake of which we can forgive him much.   Moreover, quite a number of his miracle-stories can be traced back to a real incident, and many of these stories are quite accurately founded on the Letters.   For example, we saw how the Badages had suddenly retired from one of their marauding expeditions. Tursellinus says that as they came riding up " they could not endure the majesty of his countenance, and the splendour and rays which issued from his eyes, and out of reverence for him they spared the others."   And when Francis arrived at Lisbon on his way to India he writes (p. 127) that though Rodriguez was ill when he (Francis) got there, their united joy at meeting quite chased the fever away.†   But Tursellinus when he tells us about this says the cure was either brought about by joy " or *much more* through the virtue of Xavier, which drove away all sickness." ‡

In addition to this comparatively quiet and unextravagant vein, Tursellinus has times when he must needs give a fuller scope to his fancy.   He too, like Bouhours, records how the Saint stilled a raging tempest, raised the dead, cast out devils, and prophesied; and yet, as we have said, there is a certain artistic decency about the *way* he tells those stories that does not offend us as the later writers offend.   And when we keep in view that the conventional attitude of that time toward the miraculous was different from what it is to-day, and that for Tursellinus to have written a life of Xavier with no mention of miracles in it would in itself have been a miracle, we find ourselves able frankly to appreciate a really beautiful biography.

It may surprise to find that the miracle-stories, which so far

* The belief in this so-called gift of tongues (a gift evidently far removed from that gift of tongues which St. Paul gives directions about) is firmly rooted in the minds of most of Xavier's biographers right up to the present time, though his own Letters, as we have seen, say enough to make very small change of the whole thing.   Father Coleridge, in his *Life* (1872), says of Xavier in Japan: " He spoke freely, flowingly, elegantly, as if he had lived in Japan all his life."

† His words remind us of the story of how once, when Melanchthon was very ill, and thought to be dying, a long-delayed visit of Martin Luther completely restored him.

‡ *Vita*, Book I. cap. 10, par. 1.

z

have diminished as we have pursued them toward the earlier sources, should suddenly increase when we come to the various Enquiries or pre-canonisation processes (1556–1616). Here we find the artistic coherence and dignity of Tursellinus entirely absent: here we literally wallow in the miraculous. There are several clear enough reasons for this. First, these witnesses were expected to relate miracles; that was chiefly what they were there for: the psychological effect of such a necessity is, of course, considerable. Second, many of them, though not all, were old men and women, come to a time of life at which reminiscence is apt to be fanciful; and few of them were real "witnesses" at all. They had "heard it said," or So-and-so "had told them." Third, most of these people had very elementary ideas of miracles, and none of science, as it presents itself to our minds, and they clutched at the crude and figurative language which seemed most quickly to convey to their hearers their conviction that God was working in and through the Saint. They knew that *they* could not work miracles, and they knew rightly enough that they were not good enough to work them. Here was a man really better than they were, and he must have done them. Such minds represent a stage: they would like to see God everywhere, and they felt He was everywhere. The definitions of miracles given by the witnesses at the Enquiry at Pampeluna* amount to no more than that they were astonishing and unexpected events: the word "miraculous" was, then as now, used in a loose and popular sense. The witnesses were not trying to prove that miracles "happened"—for them there was no "problem of miracles"; they only wanted to say they were sure that Francis had been a great saint and had lived very near to God. They, or their friends who had told them of him, would never have had these crude little stories if they had not had Francis, though the crudeness was their own. And it is, after all, to the credit of these men that saintship was a condition of the miracles, not the miracles a condition of saintship.

And even here among those crude records we find gleams of light and notes of questioning. The tales about the raising of the dead are not always so convincing as the occasion demanded. A witness at Goa says that the Father Master Diego told him that he had asked Father Master Francis about the story of his having raised a boy from the dead, going up to him and saying, "O Father Master Francis, for the glory and praise of God, what happened about that youth you raised from the dead at Cape Comorin?" To this he replied, very shamefaced and smiling, embracing him, "Jesus! Senhor Padre Maestro Diego, I raise from the dead! *Ho peccador de mim!* A sinner like me! They brought the boy so, and he came living, and I told him to

* *Mon. Xav.*, vol. ii. pp. 667, 673, 678.

rise in the name of God, and he rose, and the people made a story of it." (*A gente fary ad'eso admiracão,* the people wondered.) The witness adds that Diego said to him: " Doubt not that the Father, by the grace of our Lord, raised that dead youth." *

At Cochin one witness said that he knew nothing about Xavier's miracles, but he had heard of a youth who was dead, and Xavier came to him and knelt down and prayed to our Lord and the child came to himself and rose well. All then began to shout " A miracle ! A miracle ! " and Francis said to them : " Be silent you, and do not speak ; the child was not dead, and it was our Lord's will to give him health." † Mansillas tells the same story, of which he had knowledge only by hearsay, and he adds : " The Father Maestro Francis, with great humility, said the youth was not dead." ‡

About the same tale Juan de Cruz, a native Christian of the Fishery Coast, and " one of the principal men of that land," has nothing to say, and nothing to say of any other miracle except this, " that he did indeed much and very miraculously (*e de grande mylagre*) in separating the Christians from their sins and vices, so that after becoming Christians they might not go the way to hell, for few and good is better than many and bad." §

This creditable testimony sounds like an echo of Xavier's own judgment ‖ and unconsciously rebukes his interlocutors : Francis had given to this Parava convert a fair grip of the " Law of God our Lord."

But, finally, let us turn to the earliest *Lives* of all, Valignano's and Teixeira's, and to Xavier's own Letters.

From the Saint's contemporary, Teixeira,¶ we have stories recording the impression made on a sober and educated mind in an age and of a faith which expected a holy personality to express itself by deeds transcending those of common men. Teixeira's intellectual attitude is fundamentally much the same as that of the less educated witnesses at the Enquiries. To him miracles were quite simple and possible, yet—and this is important—those he relates (and he relates far fewer than Tursellinus does) have, we recognise, come to us through a mind which already has certain standards of criticism with regard to the miraculous. He has rejected numerous grotesque stories which, as we see from the Enquiries, were already drifting about; he is very cautious in his accounts of a tale of raising from the dead; and all the other incidents have, we are made to feel, received the sanction of his

---

* *Mon. Xav.*, vol. ii. p. 185.   † *Ibid.*, vol. ii. p. 303.
‡ *Ibid.*, vol. ii. p. 319.   § *Ibid.*, vol. ii. p. 311.
‖ " We see that a few good people are worth more, and do more, than many people who are not good " (Xavier. See *Mon. Xav.*, vol. i. p. 906).
¶ Teixeira had been sent to Goa towards the end of 1551 or beginning of 1552. When he wrote he was the only survivor of the Jesuits who had known Xavier. He died in 1590.

own belief—an advanced one for his times—in the limitation of miraculous powers to healing the sick, and to the gifts of prophecy, second-sight, and " exorcism." There is a remarkable reticence about all his pages. For example, where later writers give an elaborate miracle-story, Teixeira tells of a ship almost [" *casi* "] wrecked, and saved almost miraculously ["*casi milagrosamente* "]. His account of how the brother at Goa (which it is pretty certain was Teixeira himself; see p. 312) was cured, is simply and naturally told. When Francis returned to Goa, and when he got to the house and had embraced the brothers, he asked if there were any sick in the house. Hearing that there was one, he went to visit him before entering his room. This brother was far through and had been given up by the doctors, and everything had been prepared for his burial. But he had such faith and confidence in God our Lord, and devotion to Father Master Francis, " whom we were expecting every day," that he thought that he would not die if Father Master Francis found him living. " And so it was, for, finding him alive and at once going to visit him, he said a Gospel, putting his hands on his head, and it pleased the Lord that from then he went on improving, and he is still alive."[*]

Again, Teixeira tells of a young man who " had a devil." Diseases of the mind were not then recognised as physical. The relatives of this boy sent for Francis, and when he came into the room the boy began to make strange gesticulations like one possessed, and Francis lowered his eyes and read in a prayer book, and then exorcised the demon and the boy was quieted.[†]

Along with these stories of healing, so simple, so natural, we should look at Xavier's own account of the cures at Cape Comorin, which he believed to have followed on the preaching of the Gospel there.[‡] The barometer of life and vitality rose when this great Saint and his great Gospel came near.

Teixeira also gives a number of instances of second-sight, and some of these are confirmed by the Letters themselves. For example, Francis foretold a miserable ending to d'Alvaro d'Ataide, and afterwards the man died a leper in Portugal. There are various other pretty well authenticated instances—instances very similar to the stories of second-sight which are often heard, for example, in the Highlands of Scotland at the present day.[§]

---

[*] *Mon. Xav.*, vol. ii. p. 882.   [†] *Ibid.*, vol. ii. p. 862.
[‡] See p. 181. The incident which Xavier records in another letter (see *Mon. Xav.*, vol. i. p. 274) is the only other reference he himself makes to anything which might possibly come under the definition of miracle, and it certainly need not be interpreted in that way, though there are many devout minds which would accept it as such, and fortify their position by quoting present-day instances of the same kind.
[§] A typical tale is that recounted by R. L. S. in his ballad *Ticonderoga*.

This gift, or, as some might call it, affliction, has, of course, no particular relation to saintship, but the likelihood that Francis possessed it, added to the fact that he was a saint, probably gave the start to many of the wilder tales.

On the whole, then, if we compare the records of the Enquiries with Teixeira's accounts, the upshot is this: that whereas Teixeira's quiet little stories have a considerable artistic and spiritual coherence with the impression given by the Letters and by authenticated facts, the stories told at the Enquiries picture a figure too abnormal to be real and too conventionally marvellous to be interesting; and anyone who wishes to study this side of Xavier's history more closely must go back to Teixeira (and Valignano is nearly as good) and examine their accounts for himself. We cannot get any farther back, for Xavier himself was far too true a mystic to have been interested in miracles, even if he had performed them, and his experience of religion was too real to need any such support. Some parts of his Letters are written in a language in which the very word *miracle*—at least as applied to his own doings—would appear strange and out of place, for each day brought to him a revelation of the special Providence of God through deeper channels than that little word can plumb.

Doubtless most of us are happier to believe it so. Nowadays even biographers prefer to record greatness of character in terms of psychology rather than in terms of miracle. And Bouhours and his fellows have done a great injustice to Xavier in this matter. A list of miracles to his name robs a saint of character and individuality just as paint and powder rob a woman of her most distinctive charms.

The earliest authorities were the first to criticise the acceptance of these deviations from history and poetry. Already in 1583 Valignano, at the close of his *Vita*, draws the attention of his readers to the fact that many miracles have been related at the Enquiries which he does not mention, and he goes on to warn them to imitate Father Francis rather in their labours and works and sufferings than in prophesying and miracle-mongering, for " in this we can and should imitate them (*i.e.*, the saints), and not in prophesying or in miracles, in the which holiness does not essentially consist, since they are graces, given for the good of the community, which God communicates when and to whom He thinks fitting."*

Still more interesting are some notes on Ribadeneira's *Life* of Loyola sent to Rome by Valignano and Teixeira, with corrections of some references to Xavier. At one point Valignano says: " Item: page 202 and over—lines 10 to 14 are a very great

* *Mon. Xav.*, vol. i. p. 198.

exaggeration, and in my opinion should be altogether cut out. Indeed, however true many of the facts related may be, there is nothing to be certain about regarding the miracles in India and Japan except what is told in the first part of the *Historia Indica*" [*i.e.*, in Valignano's *Vita*].*

Teixeira's comments are even more pointed. He says : " What is said in the same chapter [of Ribadeneira's book] that the Lord raised the dead by Father Master Francis—although his virtue and sanctity were such that our Lord of His infinite goodness and power could have done it by him—yet, on enquiry, no certainty of this is found, but it is commonly said that our Lord did it by him. The most that is said on this matter was that in Cape Comorin our Lord raised one from the dead by him. But when it was wished to settle this, no one could be found who had seen it. The Brother Amrique of the Company, who was in the Pescaria for forty years and more, told me that he had purposely and by order of obedience inquired, and that he did not find anything that could with certainty be affirmed. This is not said because there was no virtue and sanctity in the Blessed Father that the Lord might do all that is said, but because to assert a thing of such importance certainty seems necessary, or, at the least, evident probability ; since, as your Reverence well says in the Preface of your book of the life of our Father Ignatius, ' If all lying in anything whatever is unworthy of a Christian man, much more in the lives of the Saints. *Non indiget Deus nostris mendaciis.*' " †

With this wise and trenchant conclusion of old Teixeira, and with the following distich, which is inscribed on the documents of canonisation at Rome, we may leave the subject :

" Sunt plurima, et sunt maxima
Xaverii miracula :
Ignatii miraculum
Est maximum : Xaverius."

---

* The following is evidently the passage referred to : " Such things were said of the miracles he did on that coast as quite exceeded the truth : and it is commonly said all over India, that among other things he did, he had raised one from the dead, of which case, although the certainty cannot be known, this was public rumour then and still current " (*Mon. Xav.*, vol. i. p. 53). These remarks are especially interesting when we know that Valignano had no objection to miracles *a priori* ; he relates ridiculous ones about St. Thomas and his grave.

† *Mon. Xav.*, vol. ii. p. 805. The Editor of the *Monumenta* blames Teixeira for saying that there is no certainty about the raising from the dead, and he (the Editor) prefers the testimony of a Cardinal at the canonisation, and the evidence of the Jesuit General, the 6th from Ignatius, who " asserted in the presence of 18 Cardinals that among Francis's miracles was the raising of 23 or 24 from the dead : and of 17 the evidence was so clear and irrefutable that there could not be the least shadow of doubt." And that settles it.

THE LEGEND OF THE CRAB AND
THE CRUCIFIX

exaggeration, and in my opinion should be altogether [...] Indeed, however true many of the facts related may [...] nothing to be certain about regarding the miracles in Japan except what is told in the first part of the *Histor*[...] [i.e. in Valignano's *Vita*]."

Teixeira's comments are even more guarded. He says it said in the same chapter [of Ribadeneyra's *Vida*] tha[...] raised the dead by Father Master Xavier, although [...] and sanctity were such that our Lord by his miracles and power would have done it if it were necessary, n[...] of this is found, nor is it even probable that it was d[...] him. The most that can be said with truth is that the [...]

THE LEGEND OF THE CRAB AND
THE CRUCIFIX

Sedata una tempesta coll'attuffare il suo
Crocifisso in mare, lo perde, e lo ricupera
miracolosamente da un Granchio, che glie lo reca al lido.

APPENDIX II

NOTE ON XAVIER'S RÚBRICA

THE Dictionary of the Royal Spanish Academy defines *rúbrica* as a stroke or combination of strokes of a fixed form which as part of the signature anyone puts after his name or style. It may take the place of a signature. It is, therefore, important. It may be intricate; often it is neat; now and then it achieves beauty. It is very different from the hasty scrawl or careless flourish with which some of us disguise our signature. Xavier's *rúbrica* (see cover of book) is characteristic It has one peculiarity: it is double, being placed before as well as after his signature. In his time this was not so uncommon as it is now.

It is a simple affair. It consists of three strokes sloping from right to left parallel with his writing. In the earlier forms each stroke is separate, but later he formed them more hastily, without lifting his pen from the paper. After making these strokes, he wrote the " F," and then drew his pen horizontally across the strokes to form the cross of the " F," and went on without lifting his pen to write the "r," etc. He then drew two other horizontal strokes, and repeated the operation at the end of his signature. Sometimes he added a hasty stroke beneath. The whole is simple, it is done hastily, and is quite individual. One cannot mistake it, but it is done without any thought of form or of pride in it, or even of pleasure. It has only one object—to be his *rúbrica* The haste is not carelessness; it is eagerness, the desire to get on to something further.

The *rúbrica* characterises the Letters. They are hasty, simple, formless, and unmistakable. Each has a purpose and achieves it. Here is an example of his hasty writing from a letter to the King of Portugal: " Your Highness ought to give him many thanks for the many labours which in these parts of India he has taken for the service of God and discharge of your Highness' conscience; for the bodily labours which the Father Friar John has endured in these parts of India, although they are many and great and continual, in comparison with the labours of the spirit in seeing the bad treatment which the captains and factors do to the newly converted, they who ought to help them, are intolerable and almost a kind of martyrdom to have patience and see being destroyed what with such labour he has gained.". The meaning is unmistakable, but the form—— His incorrect quotations of Scripture exhibit the same qualities.

Yet he was careful of his letters, because they were to his beloved brothers from whom he wanted letters. He is constantly asking for news. He gives frequent instructions about sending letters, and makes careful plans both as to their being written and forwarded. He wants to know everything about everyone. It is the personal spiritual news, never literature, that is always in his mind. There is only one limitation—" Things which are not edifying, beware that you do not write them." * And this warning is given when he is instructing the Companions in Molucca to write to Loyola. He observed this limitation himself. Reading between the lines of his letters to Rome or Coimbra as to the kind of man he wants, we can see the character of the " unedifying things " and how they tried him. As to everything else, he wrote, as the lark sings, because he must. And so these letters are marked by the intense affection they express and desire. There are no letters less literary than Xavier's, yet their intensity, with their eager, simple individuality, achieves that reality which, after all, is the aim of literature.

D. M.

* *Mon. Xav.,* vol. i. p. 516.

BIBLIOGRAPHY

IN giving this list of the books which have been consulted we must record our especially outstanding indebtedness to the Editors of the *Monumenta Xaveriana*, to J. M. Cros for his *Vie et Lettres* and his *Documents Nouveaux*, and to A. Brou for his *Vie*. Without Cros and the *Monumenta* the present work could never have been accomplished. The translations from the Letters are all based on the documents printed in the *Monumenta*, and we are much indebted to the Editors for their kind permission to translate from their pages.

ACOSTA. *De rebus Indicis.* . . . 1573.

ACTA SANCTORUM. Vol. VII. of July. *Ignatius.* Paris: Palmé. 1868.

AMADIS DE GAULA. Caragoça. 1508.

ANALECTA BOLLANDIANA. Vol. XVI. Article on *Xavier's Miracles.*

ANNALES INDIQUES. 1590.

BACKER, A. DE. *Bibliothèque de la Compagnie de Jésus.* Toulouse. 1890.

BARBER, W. T. H. *Raymond Lull.* London. 1903.

BARTOLI, D. *Dell' Istoria della Compagnia di Gesu. L'Asia.* Rome. 1653.

BARTOLI, D. *Les Miracles de S. F. Xavier. Traduit de l'Italien.* 1673.

BARTOLI, D., AND MAFFEI, J. P. *Life of St. Francis Xavier.* London. 1858.

BELLESORT, A. Articles on Xavier in the *Revue des Deux Mondes.* 1916.

BOUHOURS, D. *La Vie de S. François Xavier.* Paris. 1682.

BOUHOURS, D. *Life of St. Francis of Xavier.* Translated by John Dryden. London. 1688.

BROU, A. *Saint François Xavier.* Paris. 1911.

BROWN, P. HUME. *George Buchanan, Humanist and Reformer.* Edinburgh. 1890.

CAMBRIDGE MODERN HISTORY. Vol. I. London. 1902.

CARY, O. *A History of Christianity in Japan.* New York. 1909.

CARYON, A. *Bibliographie Historique de la Compagnie de Jésus.* Poitiers. 1863.

CATALOGUS PATRUM SOC. JESU. Paris. 1683.

CATHOLIC ENCYCLOPÆDIA. Articles on *Xavier, Counter-Reformation, Loyola, Ximenes,* etc.

COCQUELINES, C. *Bullarium Privilegiorum ac Diplomatum Romanorum.* Rome. 1739.

COLERIDGE, H. J. *Life and Letters of S. F. Xavier.* London. 1872.

CONSTITUTIONES SOCIETATIS JESU. Translated from the Spanish by J. Polancus (Rome, 1559). London. 1838.

CREIGHTON. *A History of the Papacy during the Period of the Reformation.* 5 volumes. London. 1882-94.

CRÉTINAU-JOLY, J. *Histoire réligieuse politique et littéraire de la Compagnie de Jésus.* Paris. 1844.

CROS, J. M. *Saint François de Xavier : sa Vie et ses Lettres.* Paris. 1900.

CROS, J. M. *S. François de Xavier : son Pays, sa Famille, sa Vie. Documents Nouveaux.* Toulouse. 1894.

DOUMERGUE, E. *Jean Calvin.* Paris. 1899.

ERASMUS. *The Epistles of Erasmus.* London. 1901–4.

ETUDES. Articles in October 20th, 1908 ; June 5th, 1901 ; August 5th and 20th, 1902 ; and December 5th, 1903.

FABER, P. *Mémorial.* Paris. 1873. (See also *Mon Hist. Soc. Jesu*)

FAIRA Y SOUSA. *Asia Portugeza.* Lisbon. 1674.

FELIBIEN. *Histoire de la ville de Paris.* Vol. II. Paris. 1725.

FOUQUERAY, H. *Histoire de la Comp. de Jésus en France.* Vol. I. Paris. 1910.

GENELLI. *The Life of St. Ignatius Loyola.* London. 1871.

GOTHEIN, E. *Ignatius von Loyola und die Gegenreformation.* Halle. 1895.

GRAF, C. H. *Jacques Le Fèvre d'Etaples.* Strasburg. 1842.

GREFF. *Das Leben des Heiligen Franz Xavier.* Einsiedeln. 1885.

HAAS, H. *Geschichte des Christentums in Japan.* 1902.

HELFFERICH, A. *Raymond Lull und die Anfange der Catalonischen Literatur.* Berlin. 1858.

HERKLESS, J. *Francis and Dominic and the Mendicant Orders.* 1901.

HERMINJARD, A. L. *Correspondance des Réformateurs.* Geneva. 1866-97.

HERZOG. *Real-encyclopädie fur Protestantische Theologie.* Leipzig. 1896-1913. Vols. IV., VI., IX., XVI., XIX.

HISTOIRE DE L'EXPÉDITION CHRÉTIENNE EN LA CHINE. Rome. 1605. French translation by T. C. D. A. Paris. 1618.

HOME AND FOREIGN REVIEW. Article *Francis Xavier,* in Vol. II. January, 1863.

JAPON. *Lettres nouvelles du Japon.* Paris. 1584.

JARRIC, P. DU. *Histoire des choses plus mémorables, etc.* Bordeaux. 1610.

JOURNAL D'UN BOURGEOIS DE PARIS. Société de l'Histoire de France. 1854. Written between 1522-30.

KIDD, I. *Documents of the Continental Reformation.* Oxford. 1911.

LEA, H. C. *Chapters from the Religious History of Spain.* Philadelphia. 1890.

LEA, H. C. *History of the Inquisition in Spain.* 1906.

LETTERS. For a study of the sources of the Letters see Cros's *Life,* the prefaces to Vols. I. and II. Also the *Monumenta Xaveriana.*

LINDSAY, T. M. *History of the Reformation.* Vol. II. Edinburgh. 1907.

LOYOLA. See *Monumenta Ignatiana* in *Mon. Hist. Soc. Jesu.*

LOYOLA. *A Series of Engraved Plates relating to Loyola.* 1609-22.

LOYOLA. The text of the *Spiritual Exercises of St. Ignatius Loyola.* London. 1908.

LUCENA. *Historia da vida do P. Francisco de Xavier, etc.* Lisbon. 1600.

MACLEAN, M. H. *Francis Xavier, the Story of His Life.* London. 1895.

MALSAC, M. *Ignace de Loyola.* Paris. 1898.

MONTAIGNE. *Essays.*

MONUMENTA HISTORICA SOCIETATIS JESU. *Chronicon societatis Jesu, par Polanco. Epistolae Mixtae. Monumenta Xaveriana. Monumenta Ignatiana.* Madrid. 1894-1914.

MURRAY. *Dictionary of Christian Biography.* London. 1911.

PHILIPPSON, M. *La Contre-Révolution religieuse de 16e siècle.* Brussels. 1884.

PIALE, S. *Fatti pui rimarchevoli della vita di S. Francesco.* Rome. 1793.

PLUMMER, A. *The Continental Reformation.* London. 1912.

POLANCO. See MONUMENTA HISTORICA. *Historia Societatis Jesu.* Vol. I.

CONTEMPORARY CHRONOLOGY

1506 Francis Xavier born.
1506 Death of Christopher Columbus.
1506 Bramante began building St. Peter's, Rome.
1509 Henry VIII. became King of England.
1509 John Calvin born.
1510 Erasmus teaches Greek at Cambridge.
1511 Machiavelli Secretary of State at Florence.
1513 Battle of Flodden.
1513 Leo X. first Medici Pope.
1515 Santa Teresa born.
1515 Francis I. became King of France.
1517 Reformation in Germany.
1517 Luther nailed his Theses to church door at Wittenberg.
1519 Leonardo da Vinci died.
1519 Charles V. became Emperor of Holy Roman Empire.
1520 Raphael died.
1520 Field of Cloth of Gold.
1520 Straits of Magellan discovered.
1521 Diet of Worms.
1522 Adrian VI. Pope.
1522 Michael Angelo *floruit* (1475–1564).
1523 Clement VII., Pope.
1527 Constable Bourbon at Rome.
1528 Death of Albrecht Dürer.
1529 Birth of Palestrina.
1529 Diet of Spires.
1529 Reformation in England.
1530 Confession of Augsburg.
1533 Titian *floruit* (1477–1576).
1534 Copernicus studies true system of Universe.
1535 Cromwell Vicar-General.
1538 Suppression of monasteries in England.
1540 Execution of Cromwell.
1540 Calvin at Geneva.
1541 Death of Paracelsus.
1543 Mary Stuart crowned (*æt.* 1 year).
1545 Council of Trent began.
1546 Burning of Wishart.
1546 Murder of Cardinal Beaton.
1546 Death of Luther.
1547 Succession of Edward VI.
1547 Birth of Cervantes.
1547 Henri II. King of France.
1548 Benvenuto Cellini *floruit* (1500–1571).
1550 Vasari published his *Lives of the Italian Painters*.
1552 Metz taken by France.
1552 Francis Xavier died.

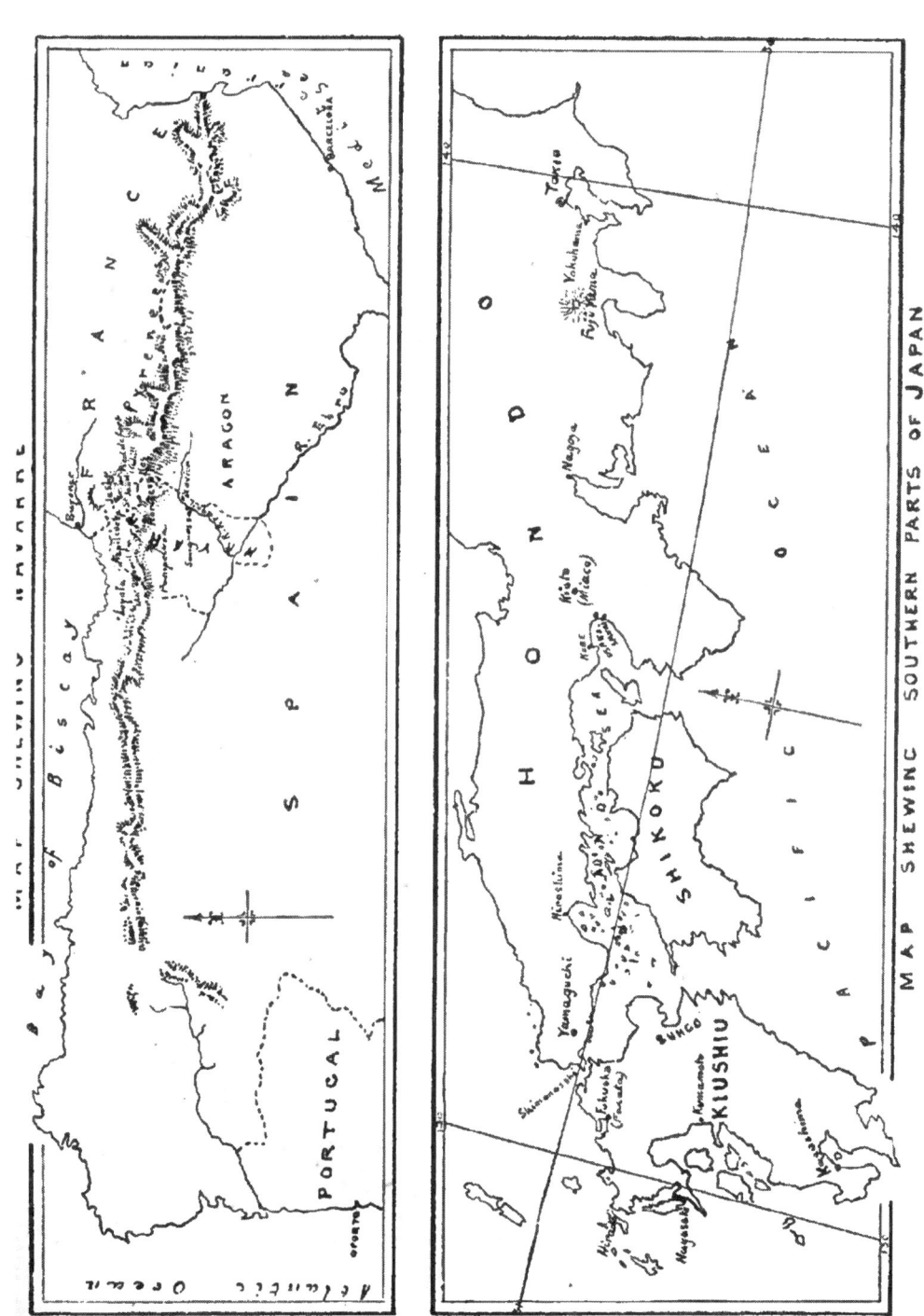

MAP SHEWING SOUTHERN PARTS OF JAPAN

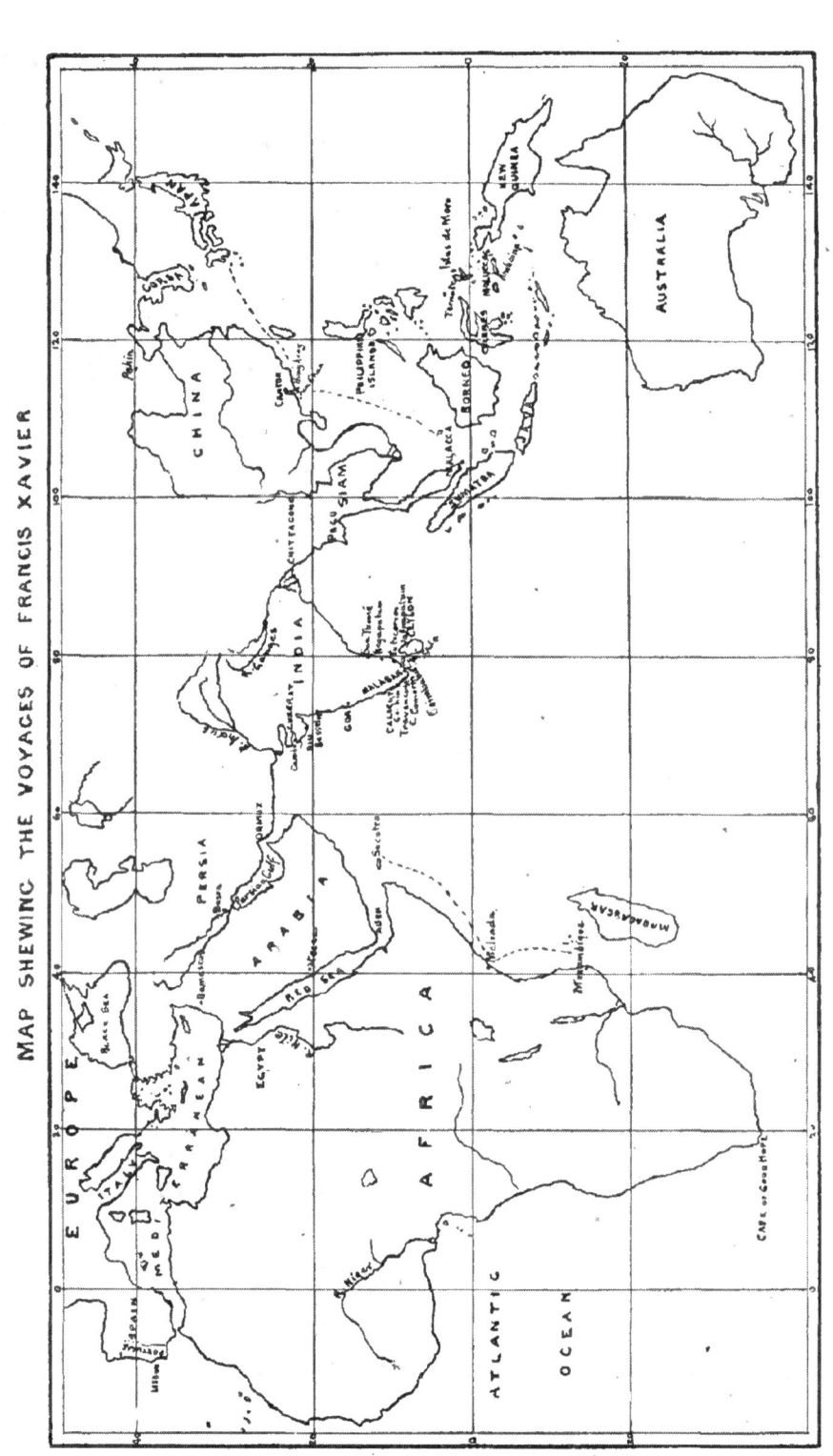

MAP SHEWING THE VOYAGES OF FRANCIS XAVIER

INDEX

W. H. SMITH & SON, The Arden Press, Stamford Street, London, S.E.

CPSIA information can be obtained at www.ICGtesting.com
Printed in the USA
LVOW02s0229120315

430240LV00010BA/90/P